Fast Tracks

THE HISTORY OF DISTANCE RUNNING

Since 884 B.C.

RAYMOND KRISE
and BILL SQUIRES

THE STEPHEN GREENE PRESS
Brattleboro, Vermont
Lexington, Massachusetts

To Julie Cahill, who started me running and helped keep me going.

RK

To my family, athletes, peers, and all others whom I've tried to touch in my life. I hope an understanding of their history will inspire all runners on their hardest days and give them a sense of humility on their greatest ones.

BS

First Edition

Text and illustrations copyright © 1982 by The Stephen Greene Press

This book is manufactured in the United States of America. It is
designed by Irving Perkins Associates and published by The Stephen
Greene Press, Fessenden Road, Brattleboro, Vermont 05301.

Library of Congress Cataloging in Publication Data

Krise, Raymond.
  Fast tracks.

  Bibliography: p. 270
  Includes index.
  1. Running—History. I. Squires, Bill. II. Title.
GV1062.K74 1982   796.4′26   82–12095
ISBN 0–8289–0482–0

Contents

Preface

This book grew out of the authors' mutual desire to help modern runners better understand the nature of their sport and, by extension, better understand themselves. As an Olympic coach and former All-American miler, Bill Squires recognized a significant gap in running literature: there was nowhere an athlete could read, from one source, the full history of his or her sport. As Communications Director of the Greater Boston Track Club and a competitive runner, Raymond Krise noticed that the wild popularity of road running in the U.S. and elsewhere had destroyed the formerly adequate channels of athletic socialization, whereby a new racer was introduced to the mores and norms of the roads. There was an obvious need for a book to help teach the *culture* of running to enthusiastic newcomers. We decided to team up in an effort to bring history alive and make it relevant for athletes. We believe running a unique sport, one that is, as Bill Rodgers put it, more "a way of life" than other sports. We have therefore strived to produce a unique book by combining Coach's encyclopedic knowledge and running library with Ray's writing skills and personal observations of athletics informed by his love of psychology and religion. We have trained together as coach and athlete as well as worked together as co-authors; each of us stands at least partly responsible for the thinking of the other.

No work can be perfectly comprehensive, and a groundbreaking effort such as this one must needs be imperfect in its first edition. We therefore invite readers to contribute comments and materials concerning any important aspect of distance running they may see missing in the following pages. Later editions will, we hope, fill in the inevitable current gaps in the history. We also hope the reader will derive more pleasure from what we have uncovered than he or she will take displeasure from any oversights in the 3,000-year period discussed herein.

Two notes on our selection of subjects seem appropriate. First, we decided to cover all facets of women's running history, sprinting as well as distance running, because women were long forbidden to run middle and long distances. It seemed cruel to ignore women runners until the year 1928, when they were permitted to run middle-distance races. Women deserve a knowledge of their running "roots" every bit as much as do men, and we hope we have provided it. Second, and related, we have not rigidly confined our scope to distance runners alone. Whenever a supremely important athlete, such as Jim Thorpe or Babe Didrickson, passes across history's stage, we acknowledge him or her. There is more to athletics and humanity than distance running.

Regarding the symbols used in the text, K stands for *kilometer*; M means *mile*; m stands for *meter*; y equals *yard*. Times normally are given in the order: hours, minutes, seconds, fractions of seconds. Thus, 2:33:15.6 means a time of 2 hours, 33 minutes, 15.6 seconds. This would probably be a time for running a marathon or other very long distance race. Occasionally, however, results are abbreviated. The same time might be rendered 2:33, meaning a 2-hour and 33-minute marathon. A small problem arises in that 2:33 could also mean a 2-minute, 33-second half-mile run (which, in track "longhand" would probably read something like 2:33.07). In sum, occasionally the first figure given refers not to hours, but to minutes. If we are discussing middle distances, the first number is in minutes (one hopes!); for the long distances—including all road races—the figure probably indicates hours. If there is no colon dividing the numerals (such as 10.6), the figure given refers strictly to seconds and fractions thereof.

Last, but perhaps most important, we wish to thank the following for their special contributions to the current volume: Doris Brown Heritage, Amby Burfoot, Ron Daws, Don Facey, Roberta Gibb, Nancy Gregorio, Joe Henderson, John A. Kelley, Tommy Leonard, Arthur Miller, Walt Murphy, Larry Newman, Raymond J. Plante, Bill Rodgers, Craig Virgin, and Arthur Webber. Without their suggestions, contributions, patience, and friendship, there would be no *Fast Tracks*.

Raymond Krise
Coach Bill Squires
Boston, Massachusetts

I

Running for Glory and Money

884 B.C.–1890 A.D.

The runner barely feels the sand shifting under his pounding feet. Instead he concentrates, parceling his remaining strength and breath for the sprint to the finish. There is only one athlete between him and victory; two of his fellows toil behind the battling leaders in this, the longest Olympic race. He runs well because he is elated, and he is elated because he runs so well.

His lungs, trained by ten hard months of exercise in the gymnasion, breathe easily. He closes on his rival and listens for labored breathing, the sure sign of his own impending victory. There is none. Like he, the rival has also completed ten tough months in the gymnasion. Like he, this athlete has prepared for this moment for a lifetime.

One more stade! Fifty thousand men roar their approval from the spectators' verdant slopes. Now the athlete feels his breath come hard, feels his lower tendons ache from running through the soft sand that flows as gracefully as he moves. He swings his arms harder and in a burst is past the other runner. He looks eagerly to his right as he sweeps past the finish line and, yes!, the judges wave their banners at HIM. The musicians play for HIM. Ladas of Sparta has won the "dolichos," the longest race in the Olympics, 2.618 miles as a test of human endurance. The judges wave and the music plays and, exhausted by his feat, Ladas dies on the spot!

1

The first Olympics began in Greece sometime before 776 B.C. Up until the fourteenth recorded meeting, the Games consisted of preliminary religious festivals and of the *dromos*, a sprint the length of the Olympic stadium, a distance of about 192 yards called a *stade*. Coroebus of Elis was the first recorded Olympic champion and the Elis city-state had already established a tradition of winning the Games by the time records were kept. Elis gave a permanent home to the Olympics. In return for that generosity, the other city-states accorded Elis permanently neutral political status, which probably gave the Eleian *hemerodromi*—the trained long-distance runners who served each city as couriers—time to train to become Olympians instead of running messages through risky battle lines.

There was no marathon race in the Hellenic Olympics. It seems likely that poet Robert Browning exercised artistic license in combining Ladas's story with the tale of the one he called Pheidippides, who allegedly ran from the plains of Marathon to Athens (a distance of 22 miles) to deliver news of the strategic Greek victory over the invading Persians with the cry, "Nike!" In the classic Olympics, the *dolichos*, which comprised 24 lengths of the Olympic stadium, was the longest footrace in the Games.

The Games' expansion started in either the fourteenth or fifteenth recorded Olympics, when a 2-stade event called the *diaulos* appeared. Other events gradually sprouted on the program: increasingly longer distance running events and races for boys; discus and javelin throws; standing and running broad jumps (sometimes with handicapping weights affixed to athletes); boxing, wrestling, and a vicious combination of these called the *pankration*; horse racing and chariot racing; the pentathlon; and eventually even nonathletic contests in such disciplines as poetry, music, and eloquence. The Games' card became so crowded that, by the seventy-seventh recorded Olympics, Callias, an Athenian boxer, complained about the lengthy chariot racing forcing the boxers to fight by moonlight.

Running contests were the Greeks' most honored form of athletics. Xenophanes wrote that "swiftness of foot . . . is the most esteemed of all contests." Running was the first Olympic event. Each Olympiad was named for the champion in the Games' footrace, although whose name was used when there were multiple running championships added is not known. Running was the game in which Olympians were first handicapped. From the very first Games, the stadium track consisted of soft, shifting sand designed to hinder the runners' efforts and make graceful form all the more difficult.

Women were banned from attending or competing in the Olympics. The maiden priestesses of Demeter were the exceptions; they could go to the Games as spectators. They probably also took an active part in the religious festivities surrounding the contests. The priestesses could not compete, however, and no other woman could even watch the Games. The penalty for violating this taboo was death, inflicted by throwing the offending woman off a large rock near the Olympic site. Women could enter their horses in the Olympic chariot race and could celebrate the animals' victory by erecting a statue to them, but they could not drive their own teams nor watch them compete.

The Greeks celebrated a quadrennial women's athletic festival, the Heraea, at Olympia. Like the earliest Games, the Heraea consisted of only one event, a 500-foot run. Women competed in age-group categories, and they ran with free-flowing tresses while wearing a short tunic.

Women were eventually admitted to the Olympics, perhaps partly as a result of pressure from Sparta which, unlike Athens, urged its women to train and compete as athletes equally with men. Another factor leading to the revision of the anti-women rule was its violation. At least two stories survive to the present day: In one, Pherenice, mother of a boxer unnamed by Pausanias the historian, attended in disguise and forgot herself in joy at his victory and was found out by officials. She was forgiven because not only her son but also her father and brothers had been Olympic champions. In another, similar story, the mother of Pisidorus, the runner, also lost her disguise while celebrating her son's win; she was also forgiven by the Games' officials. Her story is more significant than Pherenice's in terms of liberating female ath-

The ruins at Olympia, site of the classic Olympic Games. (Photograph courtesy of the Greek National Tourist Organization.)

letes, for she was not only Pisidorus's mother but also his coach! The father had died while Pisidorus was training for the Games, so the mother took charge of his regimen. That a woman could coach an Olympic champion must have startled the Greeks.

At some undetermined point, the barriers against women attending and competing in the Games were lowered. By the 128th recorded festival, the champion in the race for chariots powered by a pair of colts was Belisiche of Macedonia—a woman.

Training for the Olympics in Hellas was arguably even more rigorous than training for the modern Olympics, for virtually every Greek freeman trained as an athlete and was, of course, coached by other men, not by women. Not to train as an athlete meant to be less than a whole man. Some few intellectuals, such as Euripides in his *Autolycus* and the orator Isocrates in some of his speeches, complained about the pervasive celebration of the physical instead of the cognitive man.

The Greek believed athletic training was for everyone, not just for the aspiring Olympian. The Hellenes valued truth and beauty above all else. By the same token, they valued the poised, graceful athlete far more than the record-setting but oafish runner. Spectators would hiss at an ungainly athlete regardless of his position in the race. The Greek ideal was not as much to win as to finish the race with excellent form.

Olympic champions were considered celebrities in their native city-states. Plato, for instance, referred to "that life full of bliss led by Olympian victors." When a winner returned to his home city, he would not enter through the usual fortified gates. Preceded by a grand parade, he would be led to a point at the city's surrounding wall where he entered through a hole which had been punched especially for the occasion. A city with such a champion did not fear harm from enemies, and having such a champion made a strong protective wall unnecessary.

An Olympic champion's rewards went far beyond the building of his ego. Pindar and other accomplished poets composed odes to his glory. If he were thrice victorious, his city-state could erect a statue of him in action. Musicians sang his praises. He received valuable gifts, often domestic animals, but sometimes something even more substantial. In the *Iliad*, Homer enumerated the prizes given the winners of the chariot race:

> A magnificent prize, a captive girl to take with them and who knows how to work impeccably. This will be the lot of the winner. The one who comes in second will get a six year old mare, not yet tame, and carrying a mule.

This desire to honor Olympic champions with gifts eventually led to the ultimate decline of the Games.

According to legend, the classic Olympics began for political reasons. King Iphitus of Elis was troubled by the turmoil afflicting the city-states. In 884

B.C., Iphitus sent a messenger to the Delphic oracle to seek counsel. The oracle advised

> that the Olympic festival should be restored; for its neglect had brought upon the Greeks the wrath of Zeus, to whom it had been dedicated, and of Heracles, by whom it had been initiated; and that a cessation of arms must therefore be proclaimed for all cities desirous of partaking in it.

The truce that prevailed during the Olympics was so vital to Greek political integrity that it was respected even by combative Sparta, which was once heavily fined for breaking the truce and apparently learned its lesson.

How unfortunate, then, that the Olympics finally took a turn directly away from the goals of democracy and political harmony. The very importance of the Games sowed the seeds of Olympic destruction, as city-states vied for Olympic championships. Some cities eventually hired top athletes to compete for them. Every city began a stringent selection process for potential Olympians. No longer could any freeman who had trained the requisite ten months enter the festival; training for the Olympics became a fulltime profession. Although the Games had begun as a means of honoring personal merit instead of fortunate circumstances of birth, they ultimately created their own aristocratic system. Only those athletes who were independently wealthy or who could support themselves from their athletic winnings could afford to train for the Games.

The Delphic oracle again provided guidance. She suggested that champions receive nothing more materially rewarding than a crown of wild olive leaves. This was the origin of the symbol of amateurism that continues to the present.

Unfortunately, the oracle's advice did not preserve the Olympics, although it perhaps prolonged them. The age of the all-around athlete had passed. Men and women now trained for specific events. They were no longer runners; they were either sprinters or distance runners. Although the only direct reward to champions was a leafy crown, the athletes—as they have done consistently throughout history—found ways to translate their wins into more substantial incomes. The cities offered stipends to champions, and wealthy patrons took them under their protection. The Greeks found it impossible to prevent the spread of athletic professionalism, hence, the spread of athletic elitism. The Olympics no longer served the practical purposes for which they had been created, and in 393 A.D. the Emperor Theodosius halted the contests. The Hellenic Games were finished, but the flame of the Olympic ideal was not extinguished. It was only dormant.

Robert Dover attempted to revive the Olympics in England in 1603. Called "Mr Robert Dover's Olimpick Games upon the Costwald Hills," these meetings lasted for forty years, presumably at four-year intervals. The Greeks themselves tried to reinstate the Games, holding four rather makeshift Olympics in Athens from 1859 to 1888.

Neither did the flame of professionalism die out. A professional track circuit offering hefty purses developed in England and the U.S. during the 1840s, lasting through the 1920s. The term *pedestrianism* also marked the history of distance running. A pedestrian was a professional runner in the mid-1800s in England and America, or, strictly speaking, an athlete who covered huge distances on foot for money. Peds, as they were called, almost always followed a "go as you please" racing policy. They could walk, skip, run, or crawl. They could rest and eat whenever they wanted. It was much like ultramarathoning in the late twentieth century. When Foster Powell tallied 100 miles in 22 hours in 1788, the feat did not fit the normal conception of walking. A 13:12 average for the mile isn't fleet by normal running standards, but this was not normal running—this was money sport.

In 1806, Captain Barclay of England pushed the 100-mile pace up to 11:24 per mile when he covered the distance in 19 hours flat. Three years later Barclay would win what was described as "a huge wager" by doing 1 mile for 1,000 consecutive hours.

Money was the objective, with chauvinism a distant motivational second. The average American's salary circa 1850 was a little less than $500 a year. In 1867, the great American pedestrian Edward Weston traveled the 1,326 miles from Portland, Maine, to Chicago in 25 days (it actually took him from October 29 to November 25, but the pious ped never worked on Sundays) and, incidentally, scooped up $10,000 for his persistence. Weston was hardly the first pro American ped, but he was the preeminent distance man of his era.

A money sport depends on the whim of the spectators: no interest, no money, hence, no sport. The English were much more interested in professional pedestrianism than were the Americans. Some of the difference in interest undoubtedly stemmed from England's deeper tradition of schoolboy athletics. Long-distance racing on both sides of the Atlantic—except for that practiced in schools—grew out of a desire to make book, not out of a selfless desire to make sport. In England, pedestrian races were usually sponsored by public houses, which often built running tracks (with strategically high fences to force spectators to pay for the privilege of watching and wagering) immediately adjacent. In America, footraces were originally sponsored by horse-racing tracks, which used humans as the attraction on days when the ponies were out to pasture. Because pubs were not considered fit places for the English gentry circa 1850, the crowds at the races were of the lower classes, with the occasional sporting toff tossed in. The large working class population provided plenty of potential spectators for distance running. In America the runners, who were (not surprisingly) usually poorer than the spectators, were very often blacks and American Indians.

Promoters found that about the only time most Americans wanted to pay to watch a black man run was when he was racing against one of the hated English. Enter chauvinism. Races drew only a small crowd by having contests between minority-group athletes, but drew a large crowd by featuring an "England vs. America" event. That's why the first notable pro—or any other sort of—distance race in the U.S. happened in 1844 at the Beacon Raceway outside Hoboken, New Jersey, where four English runners went off against thirty-two other peds in a 10-mile go that promised the victor $1,000. Between 25,000 and 30,000 folk turned out to watch unheralded New Yorker John Gildersleeve, an American Indian, trounce the field to the delight of the partisan patrons and the horror of the bookies, who'd figured the English (most likely star ped John Barlow) would take it.

The English *weren't* going to take it. They did not protest. Instead, they called for a rematch to be held later that same year.

The rematch produced three new records. One for the size of the purse: $1,400. One for running 10 miles: 54:21. One for the magnitude of the crowd: reckoned to be at least 40,000 strong; a local newspaper gave up trying to make an accurate estimate, pointed out it was by far the largest racing-track crowd to watch either humans or equines, and described the throng as "an army three times larger than that with which Napoleon made his Italian campaign."

The English took this one, Barlow (spurred both by his pride and, even more undoubtedly, by his financial backers) grabbed the lead at the start and slogged it out all on his own thereafter. Indian John Steeprock claimed second spot, while Gildersleeve came home fourth, although with a faster time than in the first edition of the event.

This 10-miler soured the Yanks on such stuff. They'd lost pride and, vastly more important, a whole lot of money to these *English*. They accused Barlow of sandbagging in the first race just to raise the stakes. (The accusation was plausible, because the results of one of Barlow's races in England in 1843 had been voided due to a probable "fix" on the contest.) The accusations, never proved, may or may not have been valid but, as international diplomats and press agents know, appearance is often more important than reality. The American public perceived big-league running as crooked because it would be so easy for it to *be* crooked, and public esteem for and interest in the sport declined. By the end of the 1850s no race track in America featured pedestrian contests.

Ironically, around 1850 interest in amateur distance running in England took off. Eton introduced formal athletics for students in 1837. In the 1830s the Exeter undergrads at Oxford initiated the Oxford "Grind," which consisted of footraces at 100 yards, 440 yards, 1 mile; a 120-yard hurdling event with 10 hurdles; the high jump and long jump; putting the stone; and throwing the cricket ball. The schools in Cambridge quickly embraced the Oxford program, and by 1850 university athletics were commonplace.

British schools also developed a strong cross-country running tradition, which began sometime before 1830, probably at the Royal Shrewsbury School. Scholastic cross-country running was not originally racing per se, but a running game called "hares and hounds" or a "paper chase" (a term coined by author Charles Dickens). Students were divided into two groups according to ability, fast and not-so-fast, and one group would be given a head start, after which their peers were sent off in hot (or at least lukewarm) pursuit. The slow group wasn't always sent off first. Frequently, the plodders *were* granted a huge lead over the trotters, who would follow the trail of torn paper scattered by the pursued. Sometimes the hotshoes would be sent off ahead of the softshoes to trail the paper bits over a physically challenging course, to the athletic improvement of both groups.

Paper chasing transformed into formal, competitive, cross-country racing as the schoolchildren grew to adulthood and wanted to continue frolicking in groups over rolling landscape, but felt silly trailing (or chasing) tiny bits of torn paper. Agricultural development also put a damper on the merry sport, as farmers understandably protested schoolchildren running through the rutabagas.

Although the form of running cross-country changed, the training benefits of running freely and happily over rolling, grassy terrain remained. Further, because the sport was taught to thousands of schoolchildren, many of whom continued to run cross-country far into their mature years, a base of popular support for distance running in England developed that was simply lacking in America. England had the training methods, the runners, and the tradition. Small wonder Barlow made off with all that Yank gelt—but what a big wonder that it would take a native American to show the British how to *race* the distances.

His given name was Louis Bennet, but history remembers him as Deerfoot, although he sometimes used the name Red Jacket. The following announcement that appeared in a popular British periodical, *Bell's Life*, on August 11, 1861, tells us a lot—and implies even more—about both Deerfoot and the sport of professional pedestrianism:

> An Indian of Catterangus, North America, known by the names of Deerfoot and Red Jacket, has visited England for the purposes of testing the fleet powers of our pedestrians and aims at nothing lower than the 10 miles Champion's Cup and 6 miles Champion's Belt. Ready to make a match at each distance, he has left £10 with us, and the acceptor has only to cover this sum, and meet the Indian (or his representative) at Mr Wilson's 'Spotted Dog', on Friday next, and the match will go on.

The money, the intrigue, and the bravado were all typical of professional running in Victorian England and would also become typical of American pro track. After all, pro track is as much show business as it is sport.

Deerfoot excelled at both the sport *and* show biz sides of pro running. He had been brought to England by running impresario George Martin, who noticed Deerfoot while on a trip to Buffalo, New York, with some star British peds. Imagine the sensation this athlete must have caused in the British throng arrayed at the running track adjacent to the White Lion pub on the Metropolitan Ground at Hackney Wick on September 9, 1861, when he strode out to meet his opponent, Edward Mills (nicknamed "Young England") in a 6-mile footrace: Deerfoot was in full Seneca regalia! He stood nearly six feet tall and weighed about 160 pounds. His steady gaze and commanding figure belied his advanced age—he was 35 at the time of his first English race. In a trim red headband on his smooth brow stood a single, very erect, eagle feather, symbolizing the Eagle tribe of the Senecas. He wore a short loincloth festooned with tinkling brass bells. In later meets he would parade about in a heavily furred Seneca costume before the race.

Colorful, indeed, Deerfoot was also blazingly fast. More important, he introduced a radical change in distance-running strategy.

Consistent pacing, touted as the key to success, had worked for the British peds until Deerfoot came along and beat them with his shifty speed. Deerfoot changed the face of distance running singlefootedly. The world-class athletes of the Victorian era competed as if they were the serious amateur runners of today: The first mile would be moderately brisk (about 5:00 pace); the following miles would be around 10–20 seconds slower-paced; and then everyone would sprint like mad at the finish. The pack would run together the entire way. When the finish loomed, the kickers would inevitably win.

Louis Bennet, popularly known as Deerfoot, America's first great long-distance runner. (Illustration by George Guzzi.)

Deerfoot, from an 1835 lithograph

This approach to distance racing not only made for boring spectating, it also left the English top-notchers vulnerable to an athlete who knew how to pepper his pace with surges and to burn the speed out of the kickers' legs long before the crucial last lap. There was a practical basis to the pacing tedium: It was not uncommon for distance runners, trained by the inadequate methods of the period, to "pull a Ladas," i.e., drop dead, at the end of a race. One Woolley Morris clocked a 10-mile time of 54:30 in 1753, only to die of a burst blood vessel in about the same time after the race. Enter Deerfoot . . . only to lose to "Young England" by 12 yards in their first encounter, Mills stopping the ticker at 32:20. However, Deerfoot eschewed his pace-pushing ploy in this event, hanging on Mills's shoulder from start to finish. Possibly the American was too tired from his transoceanic crossing to go hard, or possibly he was delighted to lose his English debut and so up the odds on him at the next race.

Deerfoot won the next race, a 4-miler, by 9 yards; however, he'd been given a 50-yard handicap start, a common practice in professional racing. He'd won, but the win was hardly staggering. The English running crowd would wait until the American Indian's next race to make up its mind about him.

In that next race, a mere two days after, Deerfoot burned off the cream of England's peds, becoming Champion of England. Deerfoot squared off against Mills, John Brighton, and Jack White. White, known as the swiftest 6-mile runner of the day (for which he earned the soubriquet, "The Gateshead Clipper"), had beaten Deerfoot in a 10-miler in the States some years earlier. Because White was apparently as surprised as anyone else by the American's tactics during the English championship race, one infers that Deerfoot had only recently developed them. The 1861 Champion's Cup race may have inaugurated the strategy of shifting speed to stupefy the competition.

Possibly Deerfoot had no predetermined plan in mind when the pistol shot rang out, immediately following the call of "Are you ready?" Possibly what happened was divine inspiration, not crafty calculation. "Young England" took the field out at a muscle-tearing tempo, and he and Deerfoot quickly left Brighton and White to ponder their dust. Deerfoot hung on Mills's shoulder, as he had in their first competition, until the 6-mile mark, where the American burst past "Young England." What followed presaged the 1936 Boston Marathon clash between "Tarzan" Brown (a Narragansett Indian, ironically) and Old John Kelley: Mills struggled to regain contact with this crazy man. Every time the huffing "Young England" almost pulled even, the chugging leader would sprint off into the middle distance. Ten laps from the end "Young England" smooched the sawdust, and Deerfoot loped the last mile-and-a-half (it was a 776′ track) to finish in 54:21, claiming the two-foot–tall solid silver trophy that was the Champ's lot—and a whole lot of loot.

Deerfoot's victory meant a complete revolution not only in terms of tactics, but also in terms of training schedules and, more profoundly, in terms of mental attitude. Long-distance racing was no longer a matter of jogging X miles with the real race starting one lap from the finish. Distance racing now meant precisely that—*racing* the entire distance. Merely to finish would no longer ensure a respectable placing, hence, a respectable remuneration.

Deerfoot's flamboyance enhanced the sport financially as well as artistically. An overwhelming, if culturally perverse, curiosity of the English public for the American Indian resulted in an unhappy point in Deerfoot's English sojourn, when he joined a troupe that put on running "exhibitions," or fixed races, in the British hinterlands. However, all the swells wanted to see the red Indian run. They were, of course, willing to pay for that privilege, especially since race promoters were practically obliged to provide sturdy enclosed areas for the upper classes so they wouldn't be jostled by the hoi-poloi. Deerfoot's celebrity status was confirmed on December 4, 1861, when the Prince of Wales watched Deerfoot win a 6-miler at Fenner's Ground in Cambridge. The Prince (who would later become Edward VII) was so impressed he tossed another £10 into the winner's stakes. The Sunday after the contest Deerfoot had dinner with the Prince at Trinity College Hall, where another of his companions was Prince Edward of Germany.

Princes as dinner companions and luxurious surroundings were not Deerfoot's normal milieu while in England. Like every other professional runner of the day, Deerfoot frequented pubs when he wasn't training or racing. Practical as well as playful reasons account for this phenomenon. The bars were where the races were set up and where the financial "angels" who would put up a runner's share of the proposed stakes were found (the alcohol almost undoubtedly had a salutary effect on the optimism of a potential backer). They were where runners found out about the condition of their competitors. (Although whether this was from word of mouth or from assessing how much beer they could hold is unclear from the era's records.) In short, Deerfoot patronized bars because every other runner did, and every other runner did because that's where all the runners were.

On January 12, 1863, Deerfoot established a new standard for the 1-hour run: 11 miles, 790 yards. Four months later on April 3, he extended the record slightly to 11 miles, 970 yards, where it stayed for thirty-four years. Deerfoot's earlier record may actually be the more impressive: It was run during a downpour that demolished the soft, slushy surface of the Hackney Wick track. Furthermore, Deerfoot always ran in moccasins, while the other professional peds used spiked shoes. Clearly, spikes would have been an advantage in the muck at Hackney Wick that day.

Although Deerfoot set another world mark of 12 miles in 1:02:00.5 that 1863 April, his golden age was about over. After several sub-par races against his various English opponents, he left for America in May, 1863. His departure sounded the funeral bell of pro track in England, although various stirrings of revival occurred in the succeeding decades. English athletes followed

Deerfoot to America, where they managed to regain some of their lost fame and fortune on the pro circuit there, largely as a result of what they'd learned from Deerfoot (specifically: force the pace early and often, and don't be afraid to take big strides, à la Deerfoot's 7-footers!).

Most experts feel that Deerfoot's example was also responsible for the increased interest in, and quality of, amateur distance running in England, too. Amateur track took off in England in 1864, taking up the slack left in the sporting world by the fall of professional pedestrianism. Amateur track would rise in the U.S. as well, but not until 1875 with the founding of the Intercollegiate Association of Amateur Athletes of America.

The end of the Civil War in the U.S.A. marked a revival in interest in running for dollars. The revived green-paper chases took two distinct forms, each of them quite different from the track meets conducted on horse tracks 20 years earlier. Sprints for cash were professional races and were conducted as such. However, distance runs began as amateur events, as part of the "good clean fun" of the American county fair circuit.

The "good clean fun" was actually fun that was good and fixed, though a slight element of chance did exist. In races composed strictly of professional runners, such as the two "England vs. America" contests of 1844, fixing was accomplished by the pros getting together before the event and determining who among them would win. The "take" would be divided more equitably after the race, and everybody would profit because everybody (on the track, if not in the stands!) would be in on the "fix." When distance-for-dollars moved from private stadia to the county fairs and community picnics, not every athlete in the race participated in the fix. This was because not every runner in the race was a professional; indeed, *none* of the runners was *supposed* to be a pro (a phrase with a familiar ring in the age of the International Amateur Athletic Federation). After all, what pro would compete in a race that offered nothing but a trophy as a prize?

The distance races on the county fair circuit were ostensibly amateur affairs, but were in fact professional races. The money came from gambling, not from pre-established purses. Three small groups of professional runners, located in Boston, New York, and Philadelphia, supported themselves primarily by running these "amateur" races. These athletes, usually foreigners from England and Ireland, used assumed names when entering the fair races, none of which was more than 1.5 miles long—a distance short enough to permit a rematch or two the same day. The pros would sandbag the first race, allowing the local hero to tear off into the distance and grab the alluring laurel crown. The peds would then ask for a rematch (almost invariably at stakes vastly more favorable than wagered on the first go), and, almost as invariably, race away with the victory, the money, and, if they were truly speedy, their lives intact. Thus only one fellow in the race wasn't in on the fix, and that was the local champ who'd been unilaterally designated the loser!

Women competed in their own races on the county fair circuit in the late 1800s, but their events were always sprints, never middle- or long-distance races. Sprinting must not have been easy for women compelled to compete in long dresses. (Illustration by George Guzzi.)

The distance-running pros made most of their lucre on the county fair circuit, and it appears they did not make a lot of it, if the manner in which they lived was an accurate reflection of their finances. The group of pros based in Boston lived in a shanty they built themselves on the esplanade along the Charles River in Boston's Back Bay neighborhood. (The shanty was in the same spot as the modern concert shell where the Boston Pops give the annual July 4th holiday concert.) In front of the shanty these men laid out a small practice track. Used for time trials and testing racing strategy, the track was either dirt or grass (probably the grass track was little more than limestoned markings on the lawn). The pros got in their conditioning road-work on the paths along the Charles, the same ones used over a century later by an estimated 160,000 Boston joggers.

The life of a fair-circuit pro clearly posed cash-flow problems. Not surprisingly, many decided to give up the life to enter a similar profession, coaching college track teams. The collegiate athletic departments reckoned that if these fellows were good enough runners to eke out a living on the hustling pro circuit, they must know enough about pickin' 'em up and puttin' 'em down to give the alma mater's athletes an edge over rival schools.

A runner who typified the transition from pro running to coaching collegiate runners was Jack Moakley, a great miler and half-miler who went on to coach the Cornell University track team for forty-eight years. Moakley also served as head U.S.A. Olympic Coach in 1920. Depending on one's personal sense of humor, the irony of a former pro track man worrying over the amateur status of his athletes is either delicious or bitter.

Other pros accepted positions as high school track coaches, such as Doc McCarthy at Arlington High in Massachusetts, who eventually coached both John Kelley the Elder and Billy Squires.

For those whose livelihood was based on running, the real money wasn't made on the fair circuit; it was made openly on the pedestrian circuit. If it was a more honest way to make a dollar, it was also a more brutal existence. In a 6-day race run from April 28 to May 3, 1884, the coaches of leader Patrick Fitzgerald cut incisions in their athlete's thigh muscles to limber up his legs and allow him to stay ahead of fast-closing challenger Charles Rowell. In 1888, the *New York Times* gave a detailed description of the agonies endured by champion ped George Littlewood (affectionately nicknamed "the Sheffield Blond" in honor of his hirsute, reddish-blond features) in a 6-day indoor race. The *Times* observed that "It was pluck alone that enabled Littlewood, the Englishman, to win the six-day go-as-you-please contest which ended Saturday night. . . . He must have been in excruciating pain during the greater part of the contest."

It was on the second day of the race that the first blister appeared. It was smack on the ball of Littlewood's right foot, the one that hit the ground hardest on his 100-mile-a-day pace. He altered his stride. There were four more days to go in the race.

The second blister grew the next day. It was on the ball of his left foot. The blister on the right foot was getting raw.

On the third day his right hip swelled up with rheumatism.

The fifth and sixth days were the worst. The blisters burst. Blood gushed against raw flesh as Littlewood ran. The skin of his little toes on both feet had swollen and burst away from the skeleton beneath. The flesh flapped in pools of blood, and the bones chafed against Littlewood's shoes.

He ran on, ignoring his handlers' pleas that he cease. He had the lead. He meant to hold it. He ran on.

Then the six days were up, and George Littlewood could stop running. He had won, and his prize was nearly four thousand dollars.

"The Sheffield Blond" received $3,974.12 for his heroic efforts. The prize money was determined both by finishing position and number of paid spectators over the 6-day period, hence the odd sum. Six days of torture snared Littlewood nearly eight years' wages by the standards of the day. Later that same year, on November 27 to December 2, Littlewood established the all-time 6-day record: 623.75 miles. Littlewood can at the very least be acknowledged as a persistent chap, especially considering the uninspiring conditions that invariably prevailed in the indoor racing arenas. As the *New York Times* described the scene at a typical 6-day event:

> The hours from midnight until daylight are always gloomy, damp, and uncomfortable in Madison Square Garden. There generally is an overpowering smell of stale tobacco smoke. There are very few spectators, and half of these

are asleep, or would like to be. A good proportion of the pedestrians are generally in their tents, and the whole place is sleepy.

The tedium of the arena didn't dull Littlewood's wits. Experts believe he could easily have broken 650 miles on that November 27–December 2 march. The savvy "Sheffield Blond" pulled up far short of that mark, so he would find it easy to break his new record and claim a great bonus prize in another 6-day race. (He never did it, though.) Littlewood took home a total of $5,400 for his 623-mile effort: $4,400 as his share of the gate receipts and $1,000 as a grand bonus.

The indoor pedestrian races were apparently far less civilized than outdoor pedestrian exhibitions, which usually consisted of one person attempting to cover a certain distance in a given time, as Edward Weston did in his jaunt from Portland to Chicago. The preeminent distance man of his day, Weston dressed in a manner suggestive of the more genteel nature of open-air pedestrianism, as opposed to the grueling 6-day indoor go-as-you-please contests. A typical Weston costume consisted of white ruffled shirt, black velvet knee-breeches with black leather leggings, and leather shoes with very low heels.

Weston could easily afford dandy dress. Although he never again won so huge a purse as for his Portland-Chicago trek, he made a rather comfortable living during his competitive years (although he encountered poverty when he retired). On December 14–19, 1874, "Payse" (derived from Payson, Wes-

The athletes and spectators alike are fresh and enthusiastic at the start of a typical six-day indoor pedestrian race circa 1880. Athletes and onlookers alike were normally exhausted by the end of the competition. (Illustration by George Guzzi.)

ton's middle name) hotfooted 500 miles in less than 26 days (26 minutes less, to be exact) and was rewarded with a solid gold watch and $1,000 cash. As further proof of Payse's solvency, he and a rival pedestrian, Irish immigrant Daniel O'Leary, each put up $5,000 of his own money in a winner-take-all "world championship" of pedestrianism in November, 1875. Weston lost, logging 450 miles to O'Leary's 6-day total of 501.25.

Weston worked hard for his money and eminence. He finally cracked the 6-day, 500 mile barrier in four tries. He survived 47 trials before finally hoofing 100 miles in under 24 hours, which he finally did in 22:19:10 at White Plains, New York, in 1868.

British runners learned from watching Weston, as they had from Deerfoot years before. When Payse was encouraged by the wealthy Sir John Astley to tour England in 1876, he was again defeated by O'Leary and other British peds in a best-of-five series (O'Leary tallied 519.9 miles versus Weston's 510 miles in the final race), on which Sir John dropped £20,000 in his sponsorship of the American walker.

Weston's defeat failed to dampen Sir John's sporting spirit. The next year he established the most lucrative 6-day pedestrian series of all time, the Astley Belt contests to determine the "Long Distance Championship of the World." Weston appeared in only one of the Astley Belt duels, but the peds who met in most of them constituted the "Who's Who" of distance athletes of the era: Daniel O'Leary, Charles Rowell, John Ennis, Charles Harriman. There were five Astley Belt contests held from January, 1878, to September, 1879, each one for the "world championship," as symbolized by the belt itself, which was worth £100.

Daniel O'Leary won the belt and $4,000 in the first Astley contest, covering 520.24 miles from March 18 to 24, 1878. O'Leary was again victorious in the Second Astley Belt race, which took place in Madison Square Garden toward the end of 1878. This time, however, he logged an unpressed and unimpressive 403 miles. His closest competitor was 93 miles behind him.

The Astley Belt races emerged from the doldrums with the third contest, a race that typified all that was exciting and terrible about 6-day pedestrian races. It was won by an unheralded ped, Charles Rowell, whom Sir John had encouraged to enter so that an Englishman might finally win the belt and the title. Prior to winning the Third Astley Belt go, Rowell's main claim to celebrity was a 1-hour run of 9.5 miles—speedy by pedestrian standards, but not extraordinary. In claiming the belt, Rowell triumphed over two Irish-Americans, O'Leary and John Ennis. This fact did not please a sizable portion of the Madison Square Garden crowd, who were Irish-Americans themselves. This faction grew testy on the third day when O'Leary quit, exhausted. They grew even more restive when it was clear Rowell was going to beat Ennis. One drunk leaped onto the track with the obvious intent of going upside the Englishman's head, but was carted off by the rented constabulary before doing any damage. At this point, Ennis sportingly took Rowell by the hand and announced he, Ennis, would withdraw from the race if the fans didn't settle down. On March 15, 1879, Rowell crossed the line to claim the honor of covering 500.1 miles in 6 days; to claim the world championship and the gold-and-silver-encrusted belt; and to claim, not incidentally, $20,398. The sportsmanlike Ennis, finishing second, earned $11,938, while the third man, Charles Harriman, received $8,679.

The celebrated Weston finally graced the Astley contests with his august presence from June 16 to 21, 1879, in the fourth championship. At 40, Weston was 16 years Rowell's senior. The race took place in London this time, giving Rowell home advantage as well. The bookies agreed Rowell was the favorite, marking down Weston as a ten-to-one longshot in the race. Unfortunately, Rowell injured his heel before the gun even went off and withdrew, so the anticipated walker-runner confrontation never occurred. Rowell's injury may have spared him an embarrassing defeat, though: Payse not only won, averaging around 7:40 per mile, he covered an astounding 550 miles to establish a 6-day go-as-you-please world record. Weston, who was never injured during his career (although, with sad irony, his final days were lived out in a wheelchair, the result of an encounter between the aged, walking Weston and a speeding taxicab), claimed that walking was the perfect preventive measure against leg injuries. He said it was "like a soothing massage." Yet, to average 7:40 per mile, he obviously moved faster than a normal walk in the Fourth Astley Belt. All that preventive "massaging" must have paid off.

The Fifth and final Astley Belt race returned to Madison Square Garden. It also established a new record, but not for distance: Rowell won $30,000 for "walking" 524 miles on the 8-laps-to-the-mile track. Rowell was also handed back his $6,500 entry fee because he had won, although this was apparently not a typical gesture. Weston did not enter the race; possibly the canny Payse sensed the impending public disenchantment with pedestrianism.

Although there were sporadic attempts to revive 6-day races up until the end of the 1920s in America, the Fifth Astley Belt was the climax of go-as-you-please racing. In December, 1881, Patrick Fitzgerald set a 6-day record of 582 miles, but received only $2,000 for his trouble. In 1882, Rowell set a fantastic 100-mile time of 13 hours, 26.5 minutes, and a 72-hour distance of 353.125 miles during the first half of a 6-day race, but inadvertently gulped down a cup of vinegar and had to withdraw from the event.

The public tired of spectating and betting. People wanted to exercise for themselves. Professional running soon became a means of public recreation, nearly analagous to modern "fun runs." Entry fees for "professional" sprint and distance races held in the American hinterlands were far cheaper than the $6,500 Rowell had to pay for the Fifth Astley Belt; they were about a nickel or a dime. Although that wasn't inconsiderable in terms of 1880 incomes, it was quite reasonable in light of the fact that *there were no public athletic facilities available.* Neither were there any school facilities nor

American academic athletic programs. For the interested amateur runner, pro track was the "only game in town."

This "pro" circuit offered material rewards in addition to the personal satisfaction derived from competition. Cash prizes were occasionally paid, but more often winners received merchandise prizes, such as pianos and grandfather clocks. This quasi-pro circuit offered events for women as well as men, although sprints (in full-length dresses!) were far more common for women than were distance races.

Women were still proving they could cover long distances without injury, although the competitive opportunities came less often, and the financial rewards stood far lower, than those accorded men. Amy Howard was the outstanding woman ped of the era. She was so strong that she often had to offer rivals generous handicaps to entice them to compete. In a 6-day go-as-you-please race held in 1881 in San Francisco, Howard offered a 20-mile headstart "to any . . . contestant hailing from the Pacific Coast," other than champion peds Millie Young, Madame La Chapelle, and Belle Sherman, to whom she offered only 10-mile advantages. A competitor had to cover at least 320 miles in this event in order to claim her share of the $1,200 prize money. (Just as the purse was a diminutive version of what male peds received, so was the minimal distance requirement; most male events demanded a 480-mile minimum before anybody got paid.)

Americans had more interest in women peds than did their English cousins. In England in 1885, Madame Englo attempted to cover 240 miles in 5 days, walking around a track. A steady rainfall frustrated her effort and may have accounted for the dismal spectator turnout, hence, the meager remuneration given the brave madame.

The circumstances of a clear public demand for running programs and facilities, a rapidly dying pro circuit, and the resulting pool of talented former pros with nothing to do combined to spawn amateur and collegiate running in the U.S. Interest in truly *amateur* distance running was augmented on both sides of the Atlantic by the emergence of the first great and genuine amateur runner since the ancient Greeks, Walter George of England.

The New York Athletic Club, founded on September 8, 1868, was the first great American amateur track club, while the Intercollegiate Association of Amateur Athletes of America (IC4A), begun on December 5, 1875, established the formal roots of collegiate track and field in this country.

The New York A.C. grew out of the tradition of amateur track clubs only recently begun in England, when the London Athletic Club was founded in June, 1863. While it took the British club nearly three years to hold its first track and field meet, the New York A.C. held the first indoor track and field meet in America only two months after its inception, on November 11, 1868, in the Empire City Skating Rink at 63rd Street and Third. This first indoor meet marked the first use of spiked shoes by American runners. Spikes had been introduced to the Yanks by Bill Curtis, who had traveled to England in September, 1868, and brought back the pointed news. There was only one pair of spikes at the first American meet, so everybody shared them, or tried to.

The English got off to an earlier start than the Americans in collegiate track as well, but, again, the U.S. quickly caught up, even if spikes were in short supply. The first collegiate track and field meet ever took place between Oxford and Cambridge in 1864. The inaugural American collegiate meet, the IC4A Championships, occurred at Saratoga Springs, New York, July 20 and 21, 1876. The colleges competing were Amherst, Columbia, Cornell, Harvard, Princeton, Trinity, Union, Wesleyan, Williams, Yale (the original members of the IC4A), Bowdoin, Brown, City College of New York, Dartmouth, and the University of Pennsylvania (later joiners of the confederation). Although team spirit was reportedly high, there were no team scores kept or team titles offered. Team championships would not be offered until 1881. Spectator interest was apparently extremely keen, especially in light of it being an amateur (no wagering) event. The *New York Times* noted that "The interest felt in many of the contests prompted the crowd to invade the course . . . and everything passed off capitally."

The first American collegiate track champion was a walker, T. A. Noble of Princeton, victor in the 3-mile strut. W. J. Wakeman of Yale set an American record in the 120-yard high hurdles with a 17.25-seconds showing. The mile run fell to Dartmouth's E. C. Stimson in 4:58.5. Stimson had earlier won the 3-mile race, the meet's longest distance run, in 16:21:00.5. Sprinting for Williams, H. W. Stevens also triumphed twice, running the 100-yard dash in 11 flat and the quarter-mile in 56 seconds.

Crowd spirits may have been elevated not only by the competition but also by an important spectators' innovation: the world's first organized cheering section, courtesy of Pennsylvania. The cry, "Hurrah-Hurrah-Hurray-Penn-syl-va-ni-a" echoed through the air. This fact may account for yet another track innovation introduced about this time, the use of a pistol to signal the start of races. Before 1876, races were started by an official calling out, "Go!" (although the New York A.C. was fond of using a big bass drum to send the athletes on their way). As rooting sections became more vocal and more equipped with noisemakers, the use of a starting pistol—which could, in a pinch, also be used to threaten the crowd into quietness—became clearly prudent.

The 1880 Amateur Athletic Union championship meet produced one startling result: It was won by a team consisting of one man. Twenty-one-year-old Lawrence Myers conquered the meet singlefootedly. Myers's size rendered his competence even more impressive. He stood 5'8" and weighed 112 pounds. Before he turned professional at the age of 24, he established the following American amateur standards: 10.0 seconds for 100 yards; 22.5 for 220 yards; 48.6 for 440 yards; 1:55.4 for the 880; and 4:27.6 for the mile.

Although the schools and athletes enjoyed the organized competition provided by the IC4A organization, the collegiate programs lacked in athletic training. With little competent coaching available, schools turned to former pro track men, offering them respectability and reliable income in exchange for their expertise. How frustrated some college athletic directors must have been in the late Victorian era, then, when it became apparent that the most talented distance runner was not a pro but a pure amateur, the great W. G. George of England.

Walter George earned the title "Champion of Champions" among runners in the 1880s, and no hyperbole was involved. He emerged on the athletic scene in 1878, when, at the age of 19, he told the English Moseley Harriers running club he intended to run a 4:12 mile. The contemporary mile record, held by Walter Slade, stood at 4:24.5! Understandably, the Moseley Harriers thought young George had perhaps been putting in a little too much roadwork for the benefit of his common sense.

In a way, the Moseley Harriers were correct. George never ran 4:12. His fastest official mile—eight years after his announcement—was 4:12.75, taking over 3 seconds off P. William Cummings's then current record of 4:16.2. George's mile record would stand *for nearly 30 years*, until Norman Taber of Cambridge, U.S.A., would run 4:12.6, in July of 1915. A "Champion of Champions" indeed!

A smaller man than the hulking Deerfoot, George had an excellent build for a miler. He stood 5'11½" and weighed 136 pounds. He almost undoubtedly

Walter George, "Champion of Champions" and the nineteenth century's most outstanding miler. (Illustration by George Guzzi.)

took his physique into his athletic calculations. Trained as a chemist, George was one of the most scientific trainers among early distance aces. His grueling "100-Up" exercise seems a forerunner of the "bounding" exercise and circuit training practiced by Great Britain's Sebastian Coe, world record holder in the mile in 1979. As George himself wrote of the exercise, "This action is exactly that of running, except that instead of the legs moving forward as each stride or leg action is performed, the foot drops back into its original position on the ground." It is interesting to note the modern tone of the introductory warning George penned for his readers' introduction to the exercise:

> Directly the correct form is lost the work should stop. Beginners should start the exercise slowly and on no account strain or over-exert themselves. Hurried or injudicious training, or fast work while the system is unprepared for it, induces breakdown and failure. On the other hand, slow, well considered, steady practice is never injurious, while breakdowns are practically unknown among those who start their training slowly and who gradually increase distance, time or pace as the heart, lungs and the muscular system throughout grow accustomed to the extra strain and revel in it.

Whether by virtue of scientific background or common sense or both, George had realized one of the great secrets of distance training: take it easy, don't strain—*train*. Of course, what runners of the day considered rigorous training sounds ludicrous to runners of the late twentieth century. George's training diary reveals that, although he did double workouts daily (when it wasn't raining!), he never ran more than 2 miles in any day and never all at once. A typical diary entry, dated October 26, 1882, says that in the morning he ran "1,000 yds medium," and in the afternoon he completed "350 yds fast twice." On the other hand, many of the workouts listed state either "Walk" or "Long Walk." The object lesson of pedestrians such as Payse Weston hadn't been lost on quick distance runners such as W. G. George.

Another thing George possibly learned from the spiffy Weston was a sense of sartorial style. George sensibly eschewed Weston's velvet garb, but usually competed dressed in a black silk vest and black silk running pants that reached down below his knees, where rested a contrasting light blue stripe of silk. Resplendent in handlebar moustache, his slick hair parted exactly down the center, Walt George was the zenith of Victorian running splendor.

Two years after announcing his intent of making the world mile record his own, George succeeded. On August 16, 1880, he ran 4:23.2 to claim the record, but not the time, that he'd intended.

1882 was a brilliant year for George, one paralleling Henry Rono's 1979 world-beating season. (In 1881 he'd *only* set the world record for 3 miles—14:42.8.) First, George established world marks at every standard track distance from three-quarter-mile to 10 miles; he lowered the mile record to

4:19.4 that year. He also won the English National Cross-Country crown and the (English) Amateur Athletic Association titles at the half-mile, mile, 4 miles, and 10 miles. The versatile George also made a strong bid for the A.A.A. steeplechase prize, but, with 2 laps of the 3-mile event left, he lost one of his shoes and his 60-yard lead.

Up to this point in his outstanding career, George was not running against professionals. Strong as his times were, the public held professional athletes in higher esteem than amateurs, no matter how talented. George's amateur status harmed him in ways other than public esteem. Amateur running clubs could not provide their members with the training that the pro circuit offered. Once a pro was accepted by his or her peers, he/she became privy to all kinds of training and racing tips. A race between George and American amateur Lawrence Myers illustrates this point. On November 30, 1882, a crowd of 60,000 braved the cold and snow at the New York Polo Grounds to watch George beat Myers in a three-quarter-mile race in a time of 3:10.5. No time was recorded for Myers, because he fainted 20 yards from the finish line. The hearty George accepted the crowds' and officials' congratulations, hied himself to his dressing room, and there collapsed, insensate, for 20 minutes. (Myers came back to life after 2 hours or so.)

Just as the go-as-you-please meeting between Weston the walker and Rowell the runner constituted the inevitable conflict between two drastically different approaches to pedestrianism, the races between George the amateur and William Cummings the professional bid to settle the argument as to which school of athletics was the better.

George initiated the contests. In an ad in the issue of *Sporting Life* magazine dated July 1, 1885, he stated he was "willing to run Cummings three matches, the distances to be one mile, four miles and ten miles for £300 a side, the winner of two of these races to take the £600." Cummings accepted.

In preparing for the first race, George ran what was arguably the most incredible workout of his era. In fact, it would have been literally incredible (like Glenn Cunningham's alleged sub-4 mile) had it not been witnessed by George's financial "angel," Richard Williamson (who was also a professional timekeeper), three *other* professional timekeepers, Sir John Astley, and a newspaper reporter. Admittedly, George had three runners serving as rabbits for him, but a first-lap time of 58.2 was remarkable under almost any conditions. Then came the second lap split: 60.4. The third lap passed in a slowish 68.4, and the observers' heads started to nod: the lad had gone out too fast and was dying. Oh well, it was only a time trial.

Then George kicked. He ran the last lap in 63.2. He had run the mile in 4:10.2! Moreover, when the track was measured afterward—largely because the onlookers were incredulous—not only was it found *not* to be short, it was 1.5 yards too long per lap. In effect, George had run a 4:09.4 mile! Because it was not an official race, it was not a record officially; unhappily, George never ran so fast again. Beyond what this story tells of George, it also points out to all athletes that, on any given day, they may find some magic in themselves, and should savor it to the fullest.

George, not surprisingly, won the first race, a mile, against Cummings. The time was a mediocre 4:20.2, although George later wrote he felt he could have run 4:12 or better had Cummings (who almost passed out from the exertion) been able to put pressure on him. (Perhaps Cummings would have done better had he engaged in a more extensive warm-up. The champion pro runner's "warm-up" consisted of one 15-yard sprint before the race.)

If the race pace was a trifle pedestrian, the crowd scene at the track in Lillie Bridge that August 31, 1885, was spectacular. The financial success of the race depended on paid attendance. Officials expected 10,000 interested persons to show up. Imagine their horror when 30,000 fans descended. When the track grounds were full, officials attempted to lock the gates and dismiss the crowd. The crowd instead dismissed the officials and smashed the gates. A group of professional prizefighters managed to keep the crowd off the track. They were no help to poor George, however, who arrived close to the 6 P.M. starting time, only to find a mass of humanity barring the way to his dressing room at the top of the grandstands. Worried about what the throng might do if George could not prepare for the race and the race not come off, officials found a ladder in a convenient coalyard, and George hied himself over the fence and into his quarters.

George lost the second match, the 10-miler, to Cummings, who won in 51:06.6. There may have been an extenuating circumstance behind George's poor showing: the fellow had apparently been poisoned two days before, when he unaccountably passed out seven times in one day. Money sport is not without its disadvantages to competitors, especially when most of the money comes from gambling.

The next meeting between George and Cummings was not part of their three-race series. It was the race that, with benefit of historical hindsight, running experts consider truly "The Mile of the Century," wherein George ran 4:12.75. When George had announced that he, as a youth of nineteen, would run 4:12, he'd already worked out a lap-by-lap pace schedule he confidently expected to execute. The splits he had laid down were: 59, 63, 66, 64. He had established this pacing schedule by June 1, 1878. On August 23, 1886, he ran splits of 58.25, 63.5, 66, and 65.

Yet, for all his methodicalness, the crowd by no means expected George to be the mile champion. While George had run with mechanical consistency from the instant old Jack White, the "Gateshead Clipper" himself, fired the starting pistol, Cummings had been running like a man with Lucifer on his tail. At the final lap he pulled away from the predictable George, but George didn't respond. He kept his pace. Cummings pulled a lead of nearly 10 yards and was still smoking. George kept his pace. The crowd was frenzied. George kept his pace. Cummings, as George knew any human must, lost it. He had begun his kick far too soon; George sedately passed the huffing Cummings on the backstretch. While the implacable champion miler was breaking the tape, Cummings was 60 yards from the finish line, passing out.

The rest of the great George's career was necessarily anticlimactic. Cummings eventually won their best-of-three series, beating George in the 4-mile run in 20:12.6. Neither runner was in very good shape at this time, though, and both put it down to overtraining!

Like other pure amateur runners, George found it hard to earn a living. He wrote a book or two, ran a sporting goods store for a while, tried his hand as a landlord, and so on. He always argued that he was better made for distances beyond the mile and once ran a 10-miler in 49:29 to validate that claim. Regardless of his problems in personal life, though, Walter G. George, "Champion of Champions," was the greatest runner of his day, whether professional or amateur, and he must have been a tremendous inspiration to the growing legion of true amateurs in the United States. In fact, the combination of George's example and the rising collegiate track scene almost undoubtedly created a heyday of amateur distance running in the U.S. and England. The Olympic ideal, revived in 1896, also put amateurism in an attractive light, as did the Boston (Athletic Association) Marathon.

Collegiate track in America was getting a big boost just as George's career was winding down. On January 21, 1888, the New York A.C. and sixteen other amateur athletic clubs formed the Amateur Athletic Union (A.A.U.), marking a significant organizational step forward for amateur runners, both collegiate and post-collegiate. Up until this date, only the New York A.C. and the IC4A had been organizing track meets in America. The rise of the A.A.U. took amateur track and field out of the domain of a handful of large and small Ivy League schools and offered it to the masses.

The rise of the A.A.U. also confirmed New York as the home city and birthplace of amateur track in the country. In 1877 the IC4A meet left scenic Saratoga Springs for the bustling Big Apple's Mott Haven Field, where the event stayed until 1903. Although the A.A.U. held its first outdoor championships in Detroit in September of 1888, its first indoor championships were held in Madison Square Garden on November 21, 1888, and the organization was soundly molded by the New York A.C.

II

The Modern Olympics and Track

1891–1919

As England and America pushed into the 1890s with amateur athletics established and spurred by public enthusiasm, France became the arena for activity complementary to that: the revival of the Olympic ideal. Born of French Baron Pierre de Coubertin's passion for world peace, the modern Olympics were based on the Baron's belief that "The foundation of real human morality lies in mutual respect—and to respect one another it is necessary to know one another."

Coubertin tendered his first proposal for a revival of the Olympics in a lecture delivered at the Sorbonne in 1892. The response was underwhelming. The idea seemed impractical, even silly. It was, however, only one Olympiad away from fruition.

Coubertin then convened a Congress on World Peace at Paris in 1894. The Olympics plan was the Baron's major, but not sole, program through which to achieve global stability and harmony. Skepticism stemmed from delegates thinking the idea too good and simple to be practical, but the Olympics finally catalyzed the Congress into action. A date was set—1896—and a place was set—Athens. Then the Olympic fever hit hard. Frenchman Michel Breal argued that the new Games should pay homage to the old by instituting a new race, the marathon, to honor the great Greek *hemerodromi*, as personified by Philippides. Breal put up a silver cup as prize for the winner of the first marathon and, *for the first time in history,* men and at least one woman began training to run 25 miles in competition: thus did poetry and imagination give birth to concrete fact.

Ancient Hellas may have been a land of poetry and imagination, but nineteenth-century Greece was a land that wanted a concrete victory in the first modern Olympics. Perhaps they knew that the Italians had staged two 50-kilometer races on June 24 and July 22, 1894, and that this experience would give the Latin runners an advantage in the 40K marathon at Athens. At the Pan-Hellenic Sport Celebration in March, 1896, the Greeks staged a marathon over the designated Olympic course. It was claimed by Harilaos Vasilakos, over eleven other Greek runners, in 3:18 flat. Two weeks later, on March 24, 1896, thirty-eight Greek distance men again raced the route. A runner named Lavrentis took 6.5 minutes off Vasilakos's mark by clocking 3:11:27 to take first place, and a runner named Spiridon Loues finished fifth in 3:18:27.

The modern Olympic Games began on April 6, 1896, at 10 AM.

Tommy Burke is MAD. So are Jimmy Connolly, Bobby Garrett, Artie Blake, and Ellery Clark. The whole U.S.A. Olympic Team is in angry disbelief because they've arrived in Athens not two weeks but ten minutes before the start of the first modern Olympic event. Nobody in the Boston Athletic Association had told them that the Games would be run by the GREEK CALENDAR. They'd figured they'd have seventeen days to get from Naples to Athens when they landed on the Italian Coast on what the rest of the world called April 1, 1896. But, oh no! The Greeks figured the date as April 12th or 13th, which meant there was no time to rest, no time to train, no time to do anything but get to Athens on the double. Jimmy Connolly of Boston is so steamed that he gets to the Games and triple-jumps 44 feet, 11¾ inches to become the first modern Olympic champ.

Tommy Burke, just as mad but a bit better rested than Jimmy, takes the medal in the 100 meters with a 12-flat blast, then runs 400 meters on the 333-meter dirt Olympic track in 54.2 to snatch another win.

Altogether, the first American Olympic team grabs nine silver medals out of the ten events the small team enters. No, they don't all finish second; first prize in the 1896 Games is a silver, not a gold, medal. Composed of men from the greater Boston area and sponsored by the Boston A.A. with enthusiasm from its president, George V. Brown, this U.S. team dominates the first Olympics and establishes an American tradition of track and field supremacy. Australian Edwin Flack, competing as a member of the English team, prevails in the only two running events not taken by the Yanks. He runs 2:11 for the 800 meters and 4:33.2 for the 1500, showing that Oceania will also be a force in the Games of the future. Tom Curtis of the U.S.A. takes the 110-meter hurdles in 17.6; Ellery Clark jumps 5 feet, 11-2/9 inches in the running high jump and 20 feet, 10 inches in the running broad jump; Bobby Garrett also doubles with a 36 feet, 9¾ inches shotput and a 95 feet,

7⅝ inches discus hurl; and Billy Hoyt poles his way to a 10 feet, 9⅞ inches vault: thus are the first modern Olympic standards established.

Olympic marathon history began at 2 PM on April 10, 1896, the final day of the first modern Olympic Games. Twenty-five official competitors toed the line for the start of the 24.9-mile course. There was also an interloping entrant huddled among them, a Greek woman named Melopene, who ran the marathon unofficially in 4:30 or so.

Greek Army Colonel M. Papadiamantopoulos fired his revolver! The twenty-six figures churned off into the rising distance; the course was uphill and rocky for the first half. There were mounted army troops and a horse-drawn ambulance following behind, with a few coaches or "handlers" trundling along on bicycles.

The Frenchman Lemeusieux bombed into the lead and was 3 kilometers ahead at the 15-kilometer checkpoint. He was trailed by middle-distance man Flack, Gyula Kellner of Hungary and Arthur Blake of the Boston A.A., who had never run anything even approaching 40 kilometers. Blake fell to the ground at 14 miles, while still hounding Lemeusieux, and never got back into the marathon. (His efforts were far from being in vain, however, because his track club inaugurated the Boston (Athletic Association) Marathon the very next year.)

Lemeusieux's efforts were interrupted when he was hit by the bicycle ridden by his coach. Flack had caught up with Lemeusieux shortly before the accident at the 30K point, and the two athletes gutted out a duel that left them both ragged. The Frenchman reentered the contest after the collision, but was no longer a factor in the race. Flack took the lead briefly, but was soon to be beaten by a runner playing the canniest but most nerve-wracking of all marathon strategies: running smoothly and evenly, coming from behind to take the lead only at the very end.

At 21 miles into the world's first marathon race, a little Greek shepherd, Spiridon Loues, overhauled the Olympic 800- and 1500-meter champion and chugged on to victory after a 2-mile shootout that sent the Australian to the hospital. It was a hot time in old Hellas that day! Loues needed police to push the manic crowds out of his way for the last 2 miles. Sixty thousand rabid spectators anxiously awaited him in the Olympic Stadium. When Spiridon hit the Olympic track the multitude did not merely explode, they nova-ed. King George I of Greece somehow managed to remain in the royal box, but Prince George and Prince Constantine leaped onto the track to accompany their humble countryman to the finish line. The classic democratic ideal of a commoner standing above an aristocrat on the game field was here incarnate.

History repeated itself. The Greeks hastened to offer twenty-four-year-old Spiridon rewards more substantial than the crown of olive leaves. He was offered free food, clothing, and barbering for the rest of his life. He was offered unspecified, but "handsome," sums of money from at least two wealthy men. George Averoff, a rich Greek merchant, offered his daughter in marriage and a dowry of one million drachmas. Loues, a married and moral man, refused it all in order to preserve his status as an amateur athlete, although he apparently never raced again. He had run the 24.9 miles in 2:58:50, a time that would not come close to qualifying him for the Boston Marathon today, but which must be appreciated in the context of his own competitive day. Greece's Harilaos Vasilakos finished second in 3:06:03, while Hungary's Kellner officially placed third in 3:06:35, after the third man over the line was disqualified for an irregularity. (The third man was Greek Spiridon Belokas, who hitched a ride in a horse-drawn carriage during the race—most irregular!)

Spiridon's approach to training bore almost no resemblance to modern technic, although his job as a water carrier probably helped him develop an excellent aerobic capacity from walking 15 miles daily beside his mule. Spiridon trained mainly by faith. He dreamed he would win the marathon race and restore Greek glory as his sacred duty. The day before the race he did nothing but pray before holy pictures and icons, eating nothing. Then, the day of the race, he consumed a complete chicken. No wonder Spiridon ran the marathon with "his face twisted in pain," according to original reports.

Greek joy at a Greek triumph in the revived Games was not to be denied by the champion's inconvenient moral code. When King George pressed Spiridon to accept *something* as a reward, he finally requested a horse and cart, "so I won't have to run after my mule anymore."

Neither did Art Blake's heroic effort in the 1896 Olympics go unrewarded; however, just as Blake didn't finish first (or at all) in the Olympic marathon, neither did his home club sponsor the first American marathon. Boston was edged out by some enterprising (and fast) New Yorkers who, in October, 1896, raced from Stamford, Connecticut, to the Knickerbocker Athletic Club at Columbia Oval in New York City. Thirty men, almost all New Yorkers, ran the 25-mile course in muddy conditions. Only one-third of the field made it to the finish, led by 24-year-old John J. McDermott in 3:25:55. This was also the world's first point-to-point marathon (as opposed to the Olympic, circuit-type course). Onlookers may not have known for certain what they were witnessing, but they were delighted. The *New York Times* reported that "Women who knew only that the first race of its kind ever held in the country was nearing a finish, [sic] waved their handkerchiefs and fairly screamed with excitement. Men dashed from their seats and down beside the track to get a look at the Americo-Marathon victor. There was a pandemonium of joy."

That pandemonious joy found a permanent home on April 19, 1897, in the greater Boston area, when the country's longest-running long run got under way. The start and finish areas would not be familiar to any who have run the race since it became a mega-event, nor would the distance be familiar to the modern marathoner. While today's Boston Marathon is 26.2 miles from Hopkinton to the Prudential Center in Boston, the first edition of the runathon was only 24.5 miles long, the distance between Metcalf's Mill in Ashland to the Irvington Street Oval in downtown Boston.

The size of the field might surprise the modern marathoner as well—fifteen men! Six of them had traveled from New York, seasoned veterans of the very first American marathon, including winner John McDermott. As almost always happens at Boston, though, the pre-race favorite was challenged by an "unknown" or two. McDermott was strong in the endurance department, but others in the field had more get-up-and-go: specifically, New York cross-country runner Hamilton Gray and Harvard trackman Richard Grant. Gray and Grant took the field out at a sprightly pace, soon leaving the runners behind with only dust.

Gray and Grant were also combatting dust. The runners weren't kicking up the suffocating plumes—the horse-wagons and bicycles that surrounded the frontrunners as an entourage were. (As will be seen, autos in this era were far too unreliable to work as escorts for the athletes.) Despite this turn-of-the-century air pollution, the two speed demons clung to one another for 15 miles. Then third-place McDermott made his move on a long downhill section, a strategy suggesting a lapse from the early leaders, since McDermott easily pulled away. Grant bravely battled back after the downhill into Newton Lower Falls, but by the time the duo reached the series of hills in Newton that would thirty-nine years later be dubbed "Heartbreak Hill" by ace *Boston Globe* newshawk Jerry Nason, McDermott had 500 yards on the Harvard man. Exhausted (possibly heartbroken?), Grant ducked under the shower of a street-watering wagon for some respite.

His only competition now far behind, McDermott allowed himself to walk three times during the final 10 miles or so. Hitting the Massachusetts Avenue homestretch, McDermott was himself almost hit by several automobiles making up a funeral procession. McDermott churned on, exasperated but unstopped, but several of the delicate horseless carriages, in appropriate funeral fashion, stalled. McDermott hit the tape in 2:55:10, although he was then suffering from a serious case of blisters. "This will probably be my last long race," he announced. At least seven other runners in the field must have felt the same way: only eight athletes finished the first Boston Marathon.

With the birth of the Boston Marathon following the founding of the IC4A and the AAU, many of America's most important amateur running institutions were in place. The next important cornerstone was laid on March 31, 1906—the Intercollegiate Athletic Association, which on December 10, 1910, changed its name to the National Collegiate Athletic Association (NCAA). Turn-of-the-century America was a great place to be an amateur distance man, and several American greats deserve special mention.

"There goes Shep!" the crowd would cry when Melvin W. Sheppard stepped his stuff for the Irish-American Athletic Club from 1904 to 1915. Mel had a couple other nicknames, both of them justifiable. One was "Peerless Mel" and the other was "the greatest track athlete of all time." Although not in Deerfoot's or George's class, Peerless Mel had no peer on the American cinders or boards during his prime. He won over 1,000 track races at distances between the 440 and the mile. Just as George had a miler's physique, Shep had an ideal body for his chosen distances: a deep, powerful chest and legs that resembled pistons in both appearance and movement. Sheppard set the world indoor 600-yard record for two consecutive years, finally leaving it at 1:13.8 in 1908.

George Bonhag, another Irish-American A.C. member, was not only an outstanding athlete, but also one of the sport's first dedicated statisticians, keeping track of records ignored by the fledgling AAU. Competing as one of Sheppard's teammates, Bonhag preferred running longer distances than his peerless friend. On February 16, 1911, Bonhag set a world record for 3,000 meters—8:35.0. He competed regularly at distances between 2 and 5 miles on the track.

Joie ("Chesty") Ray drove taxis in Chicago when he wasn't driving hard in a distance race on the track. Unusually versatile, Chesty (an appropriate nickname, as photographs of him attest) set records at distances from 1,000 yards to 2 miles as he competed for his club, the Illinois A.C. Although he set numerous American and world records during his competitive years (1917–1925), his most singular achievement was setting an *absolute* world record for the 2-mile of 9:08.4 while running on a flat (not banked) indoor track—with no spikes!—in the Brooklyn Armory on February 10, 1923.

Although track athletes were enjoying more and more competitive opportunities as a result of the IC4A, AAU, and NCAA, road-running distance men (for there were no women on the roads in America at this time) could count only on the Boston Marathon. The 1898 running of the fledgling classic again saw Ham Gray launch himself into an early lead and again saw the cross-country specialist gobbled up from behind by a more prudent pacer. A fellow named Ronald McDonald, wearing bicycle shoes and running his first marathon, came from the back of the twenty-one-man field to overtake Gray on Beacon Street in Brookline. The Boston College student made his surge on the Newton hills, at the top of which reposed his alma mater, and crossed the line 3 minutes ahead of the plucky but unplanning Gray. The hills established themselves very early in Boston history as the make-it-or-break-it section of the course.

The 1899 Boston Marathon brought big news: it was conquered by the heaviest man ever to claim victory. Lawrence Brignolia of Cambridge, Mass., a 173-pound blacksmith-sculler, ran 2:54:38 when he crossed the course's new finish line on Exeter Street.

America's premier marathon fell to foreigners for the first time in 1900, when an invading Canadian contingent swept Boston's first three places. The growing importance of the race was signified by heightened competitor nervousness, as demonstrated by the first "jumped" start in its history. James J.

Caffrey of Hamilton, Ontario, hit the tape in the record time of 2:39:44, nearly 2 minutes ahead of runner-up Bill Sherring (who would run 2:51:23.6 on the 4/10-mile longer "Olympic" course to claim marathon victory in the 1906 Athens Olympics).

Amateur athletics, seemingly established, were not well served by the 1900 Paris Olympics. Although they were official Games, the Paris contests are considered in retrospect the worst-organized and most vitriolic of any held up to and including the 1980 Moscow Olympics.

Much of the problem stemmed from holding the Olympics concurrently with the Paris International Exposition. The French knew little about track and field, and cared as little for it as they cared for Americans. In fact, Paris officials tried to bury the name "Olympic Games," fearful it might distract attention from the Exposition intended to showcase the might of French industry to the world. This accounts for the surprise of the American team that arrived in Paris that July. The Yanks didn't know they were coming to compete in the Olympics—they only found out these were *the* Games when they were handed their medals with "Olympics" stamped on them!

There were problems with the official facilities as well as with the French officials' attitude. The most obvious (to all but the organizers, apparently) physical problem was the minor detail of having no running track! The French had selected a rather divine setting for the Games, the grounds of the Racing Club of France in the scenic Bois de Boulogne. The grounds were simply too, too lovely to be marred by things such as cinder running tracks or dugout pits for the long- and high-jumpers. Called in at the last instant by France in an effort to at least *hold* "the championships" (as the officials referred to these particular Olympic Games), Baron de Coubertin wangled permission to set up a 500-meter running oval on the Racing Club's lawn. What the athletes' spikes did to the genteel lawn is anybody's guess; the spikes probably had about the same effect on the lawn as the completely uneven running surface had on the athlete's knees.

Other contestants also suffered, as did the marks recorded for other contests. "Makeshift" was the order of the day. No one-meter hurdles available? *Alors*, we will make do with telephone poles. No take-off area for the broad jump? *Eh bien*, mark one off over there, on that little uphill (yes, uphill) section. There is no sprinting course? *Zut!*, hold your sprints on those grassy drumlins. Finally, some of the best hurls by the hammer and discus men couldn't be judged because their implements sailed over what little open ground was left and landed in the idyllic grove beyond.

The American team arrived in Paris in far better spirits than did the 1896 team in Athens. The Americans had triumphed over the English in Britain's Stanford Bridge games on their way. The team's happiness rapidly drained away, however. Not only were the facilities ramshackle, the "sacrilegious" officials had scheduled some final events for a Sunday. Football great Amos Alonzo Stagg had raised $2,500 on his own to help bring his boys from the

University of Chicago to the Games. (Athletes were also sent to represent the U.S.A. by Yale, Princeton, Georgetown U., Michigan State, U. Penn, Syracuse U., the New York A.C., and the B.A.A.) Stagg complained that "Everybody here feels it is a most contemptible trick. Not a single American university would have sent a team had it not been definitely announced that the games would not be held on a Sunday."

After much arguing—exacerbated both by cultural differences concerning the proper use of Sunday and the fact that the preceding Saturday happened to be Bastille Day—the finals were held on Sunday as planned, and the Yanks still took home seventeen track and field silver medals (counting one first place in the tug-of-war). Even with dedicated Yankee Christians sitting out the finals, the only significant running event America lost that Sunday was the 1500, claimed by England's Charles Bennett in 4:06. On other days, England also scored with A. E. Tysoe's 2:01.4 victory in the 800-meters and C. Rimmer's 4,000-meter steeplechase win in 12:58.4. America grabbed the 2,500-meter steeple when G. W. Orton zipped through in 7:34.0.

Then came the marathon. It was probably very fortunate that the race was a late event on the card, so the athletes and officials would be too tired to dispute the result . . . very much.

The marathon route was originally planned as a point-to-point course, starting in Paris and terminating in Versailles. The major teams of course studied and practiced on the prescribed route. Imagine their surprise and consternation when they stepped up to the starting line and were told the course had been changed. It was now a circuit course around Paris.

The French runners, of course, knew the route well; possibly they knew it too well. France swept the first three places in the marathon, Michel Theato crossing the line at the end of 40 kilometers in 2:59. The New York A.C.'s A. L. Newton was the first American finisher, nearly an hour behind Theato. Because of the last-minute route change, officials admitted they had problems keeping all the athletes on the right course. A diplomatic U.S. newspaper suggested that "It may be that the chief reason for the Frenchmen's success in this event is that they were familiar with the course." Theato worked as a delivery courier for a Paris bakery, and undoubtedly knew the streets, and shortcuts, of the city well. Many other observers threw diplomacy away and said outright that Theato had cheated by cutting corners. Perhaps it was fitting irony that the Americans, who would host the next Olympics, would have their own "cheating" scandal to contend with in the marathon.

A touch of scandal even tainted the sacrosanct Boston Marathon in 1901. James Caffrey made it two-in-a-row with a new record of 2:29:23, but 1898 victor Ronald McDonald was in second spot until he hit Cleveland Circle, at which point he hit the dirt face-down. A physician who examined poor McDonald announced the runner had tried to wipe his face with a sponge someone had soaked in chloroform.

Acrimony struck the Marathon in 1903, when previous winners Sammy

Mellor (1902) and Caffrey traded the lead, insults, and almost physical blows for 17 miles. The lead changed 9 times during that first stanza. Once again, the Newton hills proved the strategic turning point, and Mellor left Caffrey far behind. Also far behind at that point, in ninth place to be exact, was John C. Lorden of Cambridge, Mass., dealing with bad cramps. Midpoint in the race, Lorden's cramps vanished and began, somehow, to plague Caffrey's legs. Lorden picked up the pace, zipped past Caffrey, who dropped out at 19 miles, and nailed Mellor on Beacon Street in Brookline to cruise home about 6 minutes ahead of the former winner.

In 1904, the Boston Marathon was won by New Yorker Mike Spring in 2:38:04, but the second-place man, Cambridge's Tom Hicks, was only 90 seconds in arrears. Both Spring and Hicks had gobbled up the luckless Mellor, who had (perhaps foolishly) led from the gun, in the last 3 miles of the race. Later that summer Hicks would post a marathon time of 3:28:53—not nearly as good as his Boston showing, but good enough to win the 1904 Olympic marathon.

The 1904 Games bore too strong a resemblance to the 1900 edition for any track and field fan's taste. Held in St. Louis, the Olympics were nearly as much subordinated to the World's Fair as the Paris contests had been to the International Exposition. Once again, the zenith of athleticism was considered a sideshow to industrial gimcrackery.

At least there were decent facilities this time. The problem was that the organizers made little effort to publicize or promote the Games. Neither France nor England sent any athletes to St. Louis; most of the athletes Germany sent were swimmers. Spectator attendance was better than at Paris; it could hardly have been worse. An average of 10,000 people witnessed the St. Louis Olympics daily. Only about 1,000 had come to the Games each day in Paris.

Even the most lackluster Olympics have their colorful moments, and St. Louis was no exception. Two footraces from 1904 deserve special mention in the sport's history: the 800 meters and the marathon.

The 800-meter final of the 1904 Olympics still stands as one of the most exciting 2-lappers in history. Although the field consisted almost entirely of Americans, intense rivalries existed amongst the Yanks. The Americans at St. Louis owed athletic allegiance primarily to their track clubs or college track teams. They were only secondarily loyal to the U.S.A. Team as a whole. The 800 final had representatives from the New York A.C., the Irish-American A.C., and the Milwaukee A.C.; Germany and Canada were also there.

At the gun, the Milwaukee and New York Athletic Clubs, championed by E. W. Breitkreutz and George Underwood, respectively, led a tight-knit pack through a yellow-hot first lap. The start of the bell lap saw Germany's John Runge pull about a one-step march on the battling A.C.s. Runge made his move too soon; he wilted from the consistent high speeds, not to mention from the tactically questionable idea of starting his kick in a 2-lap race at the start of the second lap. Howard Valentine, also of the New York club, took over from his sagging teamie, Underwood, and looked like he could guts out the lead until the end. The pacing had been so fast and foolish that the whole field was nearly burned out. The only man who hadn't made a stab at the lead was James D. Lightbody, who'd whipped the New York and Irish-American A.C.s—oh yes, and also the country of Ireland—in the 2,500-meter steeplechase final three days previously. Poor old Lightbody was probably knackered from the steeple effort and deserved to take the 800 easy.

He may have deserved to, but he didn't. With 50 yards left to the tape, Lightbody kicked mightily and blew by the whole pack, taking the silver in 1:56 flat. Two days later Lightbody underlined his versatility, not to mention his powerful quadriceps, by winning the 1500-meter final in 4:05.4, a new Olympic record by nearly a second. His 800-meter time was an Olympic standard by over 5 seconds. Perhaps even more important than Lightbody's unquestionable speed was his use of tactics. Even today, the 800 is considered a less "tactical" event than the 1500; power is supposed to be more important than strategy in the sprints. Lightbody's example gives the lie to that belief. What better way to win than to let the opposition exhaust themselves, then start to kick from the back of the pack so nobody sees it coming until it's too late to respond? It is now a classic tactic, and Lightbody owns the copyright.

The St. Louis marathon set no speed records, but broke new ground in the history of running "characters." The first manifest character was little Felix Carvajal, a Cuban who quickly became the semi-mascot of the U.S. Team. This Havana postman had raised money to come to St. Louis by running in circles around a public square in his home city. When a crowd gathered, Felix would mount a soapbox and plead for donations to send him to America to run the Olympic marathon. The donations got him at least as far as New Orleans and a hot dice game, which relieved him of his cash, but not of his dreams. A half-starved Felix hit St. Louis and was discovered by the American Team's hurlers, who gave him food and encouragement, as well as a few running tips (although what throwers knew about running is puzzling, if historically moot). Little Felix came to the marathon starting line decked out in a long-sleeved shirt, full-length trousers, and street shoes with heavy heels. Hulking Martin Sheridan, a discus thrower on "loan" to the U.S. Team from the New York Police Department, cut the sleeves and legs off Felix's getup—the temperature at the start of the race was in the mid-90s, and it was humid. It was also Felix's first race of any sort, a testimony to the relatively lax Olympic qualifying standards in those days.

Felix and the other runners did what they could to compensate for the heat, but there was little they could do about two other major problems: the accompanying caravan of bicycles, autos, and horse-drawn wagons that also served as moving chicanes, and the billowing dust kicked up thereby. One witness claimed the dust was so thick the convoy drivers often could not see the athletes they were trying to accompany.

The dust, traffic, and heat all contributed to the Keystone Kopish tone of the race, although some of the incidents were totally unamusing. (For example, U.S. runner Bill Garcia collapsed at 17 miles with a stomach hemorrhage brought on by breathing the dust; he very nearly died.) Many of the key events of the marathon would have done the creative genius of Mack Sennet proud, though. For example, two South African runners, hired to work the concession stands at the World's Fair, impulsively decided to enter the Olympic marathon. They showed the strength of South African distance men by finishing ninth and twelfth. Not bad: but the ninth-place man would have been higher had he not been chased a mile offcourse by an unusually violent dog.

Then there was irrepressible Freddy Lorz of the Mohawk A.C. Lorz was the race's early "rabbit," and, as rabbits tend to do, he burned out. Fred grabbed a ride to the finish with one of the autos; he shouted greetings and encouragement to the remaining competitors as the car sped by them all. Five miles from the finish, Lorz's car broke down, and he decided to jog on home to keep his muscles warm and limber. Big error! The crowd thought Lorz had blown the rest of the field away, so Fred thought he'd have a little joke and pretend he had. He confessed before Teddy Roosevelt's daughter, Alice "Blue Gown," gave him the medal, had his little laugh, and then got suspended for life by the AAU. He was reinstated when the other athletes testified his stunt was a joke, not an effort to cheat.

Felix Carvajal, meanwhile, was busy in an apple orchard, gobbling down green apples; the peaches he'd swiped from a spectator along the route hadn't sated his hunger. This was another big error. The apples gave Felix cramps and other problems well-known to marathoners. He pulled many pit stops in the home stretch; yet he finished his first marathon in fourth place.

Holding down the lead was Tom Hicks, an American citizen born in England. He was yelling to his handlers to have food ready for him at the finish. His handlers fed him something before he touched the tape: some egg whites, some brandy, and some 1/60-grain doses of strychnine! The drug was at that time legal for use in international competition. His senses deadened, Hicks didn't remember too much about the final 10 miles. He snapped the line in 3:28:53 and couldn't stand up to receive his acclaim. It is, by nearly one-half hour, the longest Olympic marathon in history; it was also arguably the most grueling.

The era of clowning in serious competition was fast ending. The sport's governing bodies became more determined to control their athletes, and, if they were uncontrollable, to bar them from competition forever. Fred Lorz was so grateful for his exoneration by the AAU that he ran the 1905 Boston Marathon flat-out (winning in 2:38:25) to prove himself a worthy athlete. He had to overhaul Sammy Mellor in the process, contend with bleeding feet, and (in a reenactment of Lemeusieux in the world's first marathon) shrug off a collision between himself and a bicycle right at the finish line (the stunned Lorz happily fell *over* the line)! Athletes only a little younger than Lorz received far sterner treatment. In 1906 British great, Alfred Shrubb, was suspended from amateur competition for life "for malpractices in athletics," which meant for taking too much expense money.

Shrubb was a record-setting machine whom changing politics barred from Olympic competition. Shrubb held the world records for 2 miles (9:09.6), 4 miles (19:23.4), 10 miles (50:40.6), and the 1-hour run (11 miles, 1,137 yards)—all set in 1904. He never ran more than 40 miles a week. He elected to skip the 1904 Olympics because the longest flat track race was beneath his distance—1500 meters. (However, Shrubb was an avid cross-country runner; why the marathon and/or the steeplechase didn't attract him is a mystery. Perhaps he wanted to run only on the track in his "peaked" year of 1904 and would have run the longer Olympic events in later Games.)

Shrubb's attitude about competing was as impressive as his records. He believed in strict self-reliance. He never used "rabbits." He even asked that his lap times not be called to him. He ran completely within himself. If any runner tried to take the lead, Shrubb advised: "You can allow them to almost come up to you. Then sprint for all you are worth. Jump right away." Shrubb knew that spirit was as important as physical strength in distance running. He kept his own spirits high, striving to break the spirits of his opposition. He most of all enjoyed setting new limits. He said that "Of all athletic forms,

Alfred Shrubb, who set four world long-distance running records in 1904. (Illustration by George Guzzi.)

running is perhaps the most taxing and the most exciting; that is, when carried to the extreme."

When England's A.A.A. suspended him for life, the diminutive (5'6", 119 pounds) Shrubb became a pro; he even ran an entire marathon on Madison Square Garden's 1/6-mile track. After a brief fling at professionalism, he became a college coach in the U.S. and then in 1920 was appointed the Oxford Athletic Club's coach—the first pro-turned-coach in England.

1906 was the first year in which a notable amateur runner was permanently suspended for alleged professionalism, and it was also the first and only year in which the modern Olympics were held in a non-Olympiad (4-year) cycle. The scheduling was unconventional, but the 1906 Athens Games were closer to the Olympic ideal in both sporting spirit and execution than were those in Paris and St. Louis.

These Games introduced two new Olympic institutions: team uniforms and national Olympic Committees. Until 1906, American athletes competed in the regalia of their athletic clubs; now they would all dress in nationalistic garb. Also until 1906, any athlete who could wangle passage to the Olympic site could take part in the Games (witness Felix Carvajal in 1904). The rise of national Olympic Committees established standardized selection processes for aspiring Olympians by laying down minimal athletic standards of Olympic performance. The sport's governing bodies were consolidating their power over the athletes' lives.

Three new events, the pentathlon, the 5-mile run, and the javelin hurl, were added to the Olympic program. Another throwing event, the discus, gave the first Olympic victory to a country that would become a mighty track and field power, Finland, represented by Werner Jarvinen, the first Olympic Finn.

The American Olympic Committee contributed another dubious "first" to the Games: the first American Olympic Committee selection mistake. Athletes were not selected by trials but by how well they were known by Committee members. This process left New York A.C. member Paul Pilgrim out in the cold. Pilgrim was a good 400/800-meter runner, but the U.S.A. already had the two defending champions in each of those events. Who needed Paul Pilgrim?

When the Committee discovered they had more money than originally expected, in a spirit of "what the heck," they asked Pilgrim to come along. Pilgrim won both his events (400—53.2; 800—2:01.2), the first and only athlete to sweep the "long-distance sprints" before Cuba's Alberto Juantorana won double-gold in 1976. Fate intended Pilgrim for the 1906 Games: he was nearly killed in a storm during the transoceanic voyage (saved by American hurler Jim Mitchell), and he never qualified for any other Olympics. He was happy to become athletic director for his athletic club, and served in that position until 1953.

George Bonhag emerged as another surprise winner for the Yanks, claiming silver in the 1500-meter walk. Bonhag had never strutted a metric mile before (nor since), but the Team needed *somebody* for the event. Bonhag won by attrition: the judges disqualified every other athlete for "lifting" (i.e., running). When it came down to a race between only Bonhag and the English walker, Wilkinson, the Englishman pretended he couldn't understand Greek when told he was disqualified. The chief judge was strapping-big Prince George, the same fellow who'd paced Spiridon Loues in his marathon victory a decade before. Prince George stood in the middle of the track in his full 6'5" glory, spread out his regal arms, and in English addressed Wilkinson when the walker came around again: "Leave! You have finished!" It was one of the clearest judgments in Olympic history, and Bonhag was staggering with laughter when he finally crossed the finish line.

American James Lightbody won the 1500 in 4:12 flat, but England's H. Hawtrey prevailed in the new 5-mile run in 26:26.2. Canada claimed marathon victory when William Sherring shook off American Billy Frank with a cry of "Well, goodbye, Billy, I must be going," at the 29-kilometer mark and ran home in 2:51:23.6. The Greeks gave him the traditional olive leaves and a nontraditional goat.

On April 19, 1907, Onondaga Indian Tom Longboat claimed Boston in 2:24:24, a new record. Running his first marathon, Longboat went out with hot-footed Bostonian James Lee. Ordinarily this would not have been a prudent tactic, for early leaders at Boston rarely win the race. Things were different in 1907. The fleet Longboat and Lee hit South Framingham just as a long, long freight train was pulling through the crossing spur track that cut across the marathon course. The rest of the pack had to wait for the choo-choo to go by! Longboat put Lee away at Auburndale and ran home to a new record. Reflecting on this race, the great Clarence DeMar said that "If Longboat had today's [1947's] race conditions—macadam roads and no accompanying cars—he might have set a 2:06 record for the old 24½-mile course."

Marathoning popularity doubled in America when another annual long race appeared on the calendar: the Yonkers marathon. The race was a 24- or 25-miler; it did not adopt the by-then standard marathon distance of 26.2 miles until 1935. John Hayes won the inaugural edition of the classic, running 2:43:00 on November 28th, 1907.

The Olympics returned to the Olympiad schedule with the 1908 London Games. These Olympics deserve a special place in marathoning history for two reasons: the establishment of the now-standard 26-mile, 385-yard distance, and the Dorando Pietri debacle.

The story behind the "odd" standard marathon distance is appropriately romantic and regal. The Princess of Wales was selected to start the race; the other royal grandchildren and Queen Alexandra wanted to see the start, too. The simplest solution, as far as the Edwardian English were concerned, was to move the starting line back to Windsor Castle, making a 40-kilometer race 26.2 miles. What was another mile to these commoner athletes?

The extra mile may have accounted for the second remarkable marathon incident in the 1908 Games, the celebrated disqualification of the first runner to enter the Olympic stadium, Dorando Pietri of Italy. Dorando, as he was known to all, had won the Paris Marathon the previous year, but experts thought American Johnny Hayes (one of the runners caught behind the freight train at Boston in 1907) had a better chance. Tom Longboat, running for Canada, was also a pre-race favorite, although American officials protested his entry because he'd been classified as a professional in the U.S.A.

The British disallowed the American protest, as they had been disallowing most American protests during the Games. Anglo-American political relations in 1908 were cool and athletic relations were even cooler. A reflective American coach later wrote that "Probably England was not as charitably inclined toward the American champions as she might have been, and it is equally true that the victorious Americans were not as modest as they should have been."

America claimed ultimate victory in the marathon, the result of a protest that British officials were compelled to honor. Sixty-five thousand people witnessed the officials dragging the exhausted and drugged Italian across the line, 34 seconds ahead of Hayes. (Dorando's handlers had given him a shot of strychnine during the race, according to first Olympic champion Jimmy Connolly, who was covering the Games as a reporter.) In fairness, the officials' compassion toward the lurching Dorando is understandable. A newspaper account of the event stated that Dorando "was practically delirious. He staggered along the cinder path like a man in a dream, his gait being neither a walk nor a run, but simply a flounder, with arms shaking and legs tottering." Hayes had gone out at a prudently slow pace, respectful of the unexpected 1.2 additional miles. His time of 2:55:18 became the new world best for the modern marathon. Dorando did not go uncompensated, though. He received a duplicate of Hayes' medal from Queen Alexandra; and, in the U.S., an aspiring young composer enjoyed his first hit song, entitled "Dorando," written about the plucky marathoner. The composer was Irving Berlin.

If Longboat's amateur status was suspect, so too was Hayes's. The press was told Hayes was a shipping clerk at Bloomingdale's department store in New York. He allegedly trained for racing by working out on Bloomie's roof. In fact, Hayes was paid by Bloomingdale's to train as a fulltime runner. His workouts were on a track outside Manhattan, not on a midtown roof. Hayes's club, the famed Irish-American A.C., had arranged this sweetheart deal. (Hayes, Dorando, and Longboat turned pro after the Olympics, although some feel Longboat had turned pro before them. Pietri beat Hayes in an indoor marathon in Madison Square Garden, and Longboat smoked Pietri twice in such events.)

It was a great Olympics for another Irish-American A.C. runner, Peerless Mel Sheppard, who took a double victory in the 800 (1:52.8) and the 1500 (4:04.4). England's E. R. Voigt claimed the 5-mile run with a 25:11.2 clocking.

Some old organizational problems were solved and new ones created in the 1908 Olympics. The American Olympic Committee selected athletes by means of trials in Philadelphia and Chicago, instead of by means of the "old-boy network." The International Olympic Committee (IOC) started the tradition of changing its mind: the Games were originally intended for Rome, but an impressive eruption by Mount Vesuvius suggested it might be smarter to move them elsewhere. Alas, London sports officials had never conducted anything like the Games, and most of the officiating problems in 1908 stemmed directly from inexperience. The IOC therefore wrought yet another change: officials for the Games would henceforth come from the international agencies that were responsible for each sport. In short, Olympic officiating suddenly became professionalized—and monopolistic.

The London Olympic marathon had been held in mid-July. It had undoubtedly been hot. The 1909 Boston Marathon was held in mid-April in New England. It was undoubtedly hotter.

This was the race called The Inferno, for the mercury hit 97 degrees in the sun. As a rule of thumb, runners reckon the temperature on a paved road to be 10 degrees higher than a thermometer reading. The Boston Marathon course is a shadeless one in mid-April, and the attrition rate in 1909 was staggering: 91 DNFs (Did Not Finish) out of 164 starters. The survivors were also staggering. Only winner Henri Renaud, who set a sanely slow early pace (he was 53rd at Framingham, 19th at the midpoint) didn't have to walk at all. His time of 2:53:36 was exceptional under the circumstances.

The 1910 running of the B.A.A. was a relatively tame version of the classic, hardly worth noting except for one special reason. It was claimed by Nova Scotia's Fred Cameron, an unexpected 2:28:52 victor, but the historical importance of the race rests on the man who finished second, the great Clarence DeMar, running his first Boston Marathon. The 21-year-old University of New Hampshire grad was, like Cameron, a dark horse, but a horse with a big kick. He moved from 24th at 6 miles to second (1 minute behind Cameron) at the finish line.

DeMar claimed Boston the next year, setting a record of 2:21:39. A great athletic career was in the making. Then DeMar stopped running completely. His physician had diagnosed a heart murmur in the young athlete and advised him against running altogether, claiming his life was at risk. So DeMar ran Boston in 1911, then quit for six years. He resumed competition not on the advice of a doctor, but on his own. He felt fine, and he ran even finer. When DeMar died of cancer in 1958, Dr. Paul Dudley White's autopsy revealed that the marathoner had tremendously large, broad, coronary arteries, but an otherwise normal and healthy heart. The enlarged arteries (which may have resulted from training or from heredity) must have contributed to DeMar's superlative endurance, but the murmur his doctor heard was apparently a functional one.

DeMar's medical problems were not uncommon; they arise even today from cautious, non-sports-oriented, medical practitioners. Several months before Peerless Mel Sheppard won the Olympic 800 and 1500 finals in London, the New York Police Department rejected his application to join the force because police physicians diagnosed him as suffering from arteriosclerosis and chronic endocarditis. In addition to his Olympic wins, Peerless Mel was six times U.S. 800-meter champ from 1906 to 1912. In DeMar's and Sheppard's cases, the murmurs of the heart were sweet ones.

Sheppard's speed wasn't enough for victory in the 1912 Olympics at Stockholm, although he shot through the first of the two laps in 52.4. Right on his shoulder going into the gun lap was Braun of Germany and "Ted" Meredith of the U.S.A., a 19-year-old student at Mercersburg Academy. Coming out of the final turn, Braun swung out to whip pass the Americans. Meredith got mad, picked up the pace, pulled past Peerless Mel, and nipped Braun by less than a yard at the tape. Ira Davenport, another American, was caught up in the spirit of the burst and also pulled past Braun. The hapless German wasn't dying; rather, this turned out to be the strongest 800-meter field in history. The London *Times* said simply that "A finer lot of men was probably never got together," and, considering that the first five finishers all broke the existing world record for 800 meters, it seemed a fair assessment. With a world record before the race of 1:52.9, the first five clockings were amazing: 1:51.9; 1:52.0; 1:52.0; 1:52.2; and 1:52.3. These were the Games that fortunately introduced electric timing to the Olympics.

The outstanding athleticism and officiating of the 1912 800-meter final typified the Stockholm Games, which were superbly organized and executed. They are considered the Games that "cemented" the Olympic movement, guaranteeing its permanence. Unfortunately, they are most popularly remembered as the Games in which Jim Thorpe was robbed.

Another positive mark of the 1912 Olympics is the victory of Finland in long-distance track events. The 5-mile run was supplanted in 1912 by two other events, the 5,000- and 10,000-meter footraces. Finland could have built an entire distance team from one family: Tatu, Hannes, and Willie Kolehmainen. "Little brother" Hannes won the so-called "Woolworth double" (the 5-and-10), but America and England could both justifiably feel they had contributed to the Finns' success. Hannes and Willie had journeyed to the U.S. in 1910 to pick up pointers from pro runners in America. At least one of the tactics they learned (whether from American pros or directly from the English) was Alfred Shrubb's pace-shifting ploy—the big, unexpected sprint to break an opponent's concentration and crush his spirit. Hannes didn't have to use this strategy in his first victory, the 10,000. He led from gun to tape, winning by 45 seconds over America's Lewis Tewanima in

31:20.8. Brother Tatu dropped out of the hot, fast race while holding down fifth spot.

Two days later, Hannes ran one of the most exciting 5,000-meters in Olympic history, clashing with France's Jean Bouin, who held the world record (30:58.8) in the 10-kilometers. The race was strictly between these two athletes, with everyone else running for third place. At the end of the first go-round, Bouin and Kolehmainen were alone in front. The Frenchman threw a few surges on the Finn, who went right along with him. Two laps from the end, Hannes took over the lead and tried a surge on Jean. Again, the two stayed together like a fly and flypaper. Bouin, in agony, drew out a 4-yard lead, which shrank to 2 yards by the final turn. Hannes's coach urged him to relax going through the last bend, for he could see Bouin was dying. Hannes took a deep breath, relaxed, then arrowed straight past the sinking Frenchman. Kolehmainen ran the 5K in 14:36.6, and Bouin in 14:36.7, the first time 15 minutes had been broken for the relatively new event.

Hannes's brother Tatu ran the marathon. He led it for 10 miles, but was forced by the heat to retire. The race conditions evoked the memory of the 1904 Olympics. The July heat was so oppressive that one of the runners, Portugal's Lazaro, passed out at the 19-mile point and died the next day. The U.S. fielded a topnotch team, but could do no better than third place, claimed by petite Gaston Strobino. After Tatu Kolehmainen dropped out, it turned into a race between Ken McArthur and Tim Gitsham, both of South Africa. A little bit of chicanery won the race for big Ken. Gitsham, thirsty from the long run, wanted to stop for a drink near the end of the race. "He said he would wait for me while I took a drink," Gitsham later said of his teammate, "but he didn't." McArthur, a practical mounted policeman in private life, replied, "I went out to win or die." He won in 2:36:54.8, an Olympic record.

Arnold Jackson of England set an Olympic record while running away with the 1500-meter final in 3:56.8, a time over 6 seconds faster than the previous Olympic standard. As Hannes Kolehmainen had done, Jackson drew the rest of the field along with him. The first five men all broke the mark by over 5 seconds.

The man who broke more marks than any other athlete in the Stockholm Games was the man whose heart was broken in return, the great Jim Thorpe. Thorpe took first place in the pentathlon (where one of his competitors was a young West Point student named George S. Patton, Jr.) and in the decathlon; he had to settle for fourth in the high jump and seventh in the broad jump. In congratulations, Sweden's King Gustav said to him, "Sir, you are the greatest athlete in the world," to which Thorpe replied, "Thanks, King." The next year, while playing professional football, Thorpe confirmed a story in a small New England newspaper that he had played minor league baseball in 1910. That meant he hadn't been an amateur in 1912. The IOC obviously couldn't stand for such indecorum and took away all Thorpe's medals, erased his records from the Olympic books, and made him an athletic "non-person" à la Stalinist Russia. The only people who remember him today are all the athletes, sportswriters, and fans in the world, for to be excellent means to be a professional.

While the politics of amateurism struck at Jim Thorpe, the politics of international relations struck at the Olympic movement. The Games were temporarily suspended under the shadow of World War I, but running continued in Boston. Arthur Roth of Roxbury, Mass. (a Boston neighborhood), was the first Bostonian to win the Marathon, and he had to beat Finland's Willie Kyronen to do it. His time of 2:27:16 was well off DeMar's record, but it was good enough to win.

DeMar came back to Boston to run in the 1917 B.A.A., but was beaten by the oldest man ever to win the marathon, 35-year-old Bill Kennedy of Port Chester, N.Y., who ran 2:28:27. DeMar earned third, running 2:31:05, less than a minute behind second-place Sid Hatch. Clarence had started slowly, picking it up at the halfway mark.

There was no Boston Marathon in 1918 because of World War I. Instead there was a ten-man military race on the marathon route, taken by Camp Devens. The Yonkers Marathon was likewise suspended, but for far longer. It would not be reinstituted until 1935. Yet 1918 was a highly significant year in marathoning history, for it was the year in which France's Marie-Louise Ledru became the first woman to run a full-length, 26.2-mile race.

Boston resumed the marathon in 1919. The race was taken by Carl Linder, a 29-year-old native of Quincy, Mass. Linder was New England javelin and decathlon champ, but won the marathon largely because fleeter rivals weakened in the day's heat. Ironically, Linder had been classified 4-F by the U.S. Army because he had flat feet. (A track team composed of DeMar, Sheppard, and Linder would surely have given the era's physicians something to mull over.) Only a touch over a minute behind Linder's 2:29:13 was the smallest man ever to run Boston, 4'10½"-tall Willie Wick, a neighbor of Linder's who was running his first marathon.

As the world faced the hard realities of global war, the sport's governing bodies became even more adamant in refusing to face the obvious reality of athletic excellence, professionalism. The paper chases of a century before had become an exercise in pursuit of something even more elusive than a slip of paper—the chimera of "pure" amateurism.

III

The Nurmi Era

1920–1932

The "War to End All Wars" left the Western world dazed and desiring diversion. 1920 was a year of naive optimism about humankind's future, a time of healthy national economies and wholesome international heroes. Compared to the ravages of the first modern war, the unrelenting progress of Paavo Nurmi on road or track seemed wholesome, anyway.

The war ended just in time to revitalize the Olympic movement. Rarely have any other modern Games so apparently been in the classic Olympic tradition of offering respite from Mars' hot breath. (The war may have been over, but its passions were not. Neither Germany nor Austria was invited to send a team to the Games.) Antwerp, in battle-scarred Belgium, emerged as the International Olympic Committee's quickly chosen host city. Belgium had never been a hotbed of track and field fervor. The lack of basic Belgium enthusiasm, combined with the understandable shortage of resources so soon after a major foreign occupation, produced makeshift Olympic facilities. The Belgian government built a new stadium at Antwerp specifically for the Games, but the contests attracted only 10,000 spectators at most, one-third the stadium's capacity, and that only when schoolchildren were admitted free of charge. Belgium bore a substantial financial loss on the 1920 Olympics, and the nation deserves a warm spot in the sport's history for being so sporting itself.

The accouterments may have been makeshift, but the 1920 Games were

44

not a replay of the 1900 Games at Paris. Arrogance and ignorance had spoiled the turn-of-the-century Olympics. In 1920, the spirit was willing but the state was weak. The running track and field areas suffered from the ground ravages of rapid stadium construction. The competitive conditions deteriorated further from heavy rains during much of the festival. For a hostess with only one year's notice, though, Antwerp emerged proud, and the 2,600 competing athletes at the Games had few complaints about the facilities or their treatment by officials, a marked contrast to the Paris debacle.

True to tradition, however, the U.S. team had grievances. This time, though, the gripes didn't stem from misreadings of foreign calendars, from misgivings over proper use of the Sabbath, or from mistakes in athletes' menus. The gripes pertained directly to the facilities commandeered for the team by the U.S. Olympic Committee itself.

The USOC booked passage for the team on the "luxurious" SS *Princess Matoika*, which had just come off duty as a WWI troop transporter. Some may see little difference between troops heading into shrapnel on the Rhine and athletes heading into an Olympic 10K final, but athletes see significant differences. Two days out of New York, the collective U.S. Olympic Team wanted to be shown cause why the collective USOC should not be unceremoniously heaved o'er the side and into the brine. The Committee replied that they had tried to charter a larger and more plush vessel, the SS *Great Northern* (also an Army boat), but the *Great Northern* wasn't shipshape. No one was tossed overboard, but tempers on the American team were tender when the *Princess Matoika* reached Europe.

The American athletes were also unhappy with their Antwerp lodgings, a former schoolhouse. One of the Americans, triple-jump specialist Dan Ahearn, found better lodging for himself elsewhere. USOC officials, apparently operating *in loco parentis*, ruled that all athletes must be in the bunkhouse by 10 PM, but the freewheeling Ahearn considered the rule "bunk" and flaunted it. The compassionate American officials, who clearly understood the temper of an athlete facing Olympic competition, tossed Ahearn off the team.

The incident became what is arguably the first obvious rift between athletes and officials in American running history; sadly, it is an incident maddeningly common more than sixty years later. The American athletes presented a petition signed by nearly 200 of themselves to the USOC, demanding Ahearn's reinstatement. The USOC rejected the petition. The athletes then said they would boycott the Games, to which a befuddled Judge Bartow S. Weeks (whose own athletic credentials, if any, are lost) replied that simply couldn't be done. A person must discharge his appointed duty. Why, what would the athletes do if the hard-working USOC itself shirked its duties?! One athlete called out that they would get a better Committee if Weeks et al. bailed out. Ahearn remained officially off the team, but competed in U.S. colors in his event anyway, with no protest or interference from the USOC. The USOC was adamant that Ahearn not be put back on the team but gave no rational explanation for why he obviously *was* back on the team.

The opening of the Games unfurled the new Olympic flag, designed by Baron de Coubertin. The five interlocking and multicolored circles (one color of which appears in every national flag) symbolize the five great land masses as the Baron saw them (Europe, Asia, Africa, Australia, North/South America).

The Antwerp Games did not exactly unfurl the blue-and-white flag of Finland, but they did run it up the victor's flagpole more often than any other, save for the Stars and Stripes of America. *This* was something new, and the Americans were not pleased. American track and field supremacy was challenged by a nation with one-twentieth the population of the U.S. Finland, however, was a nation that had Kolehmainen, Ritola, and Nurmi. Most of all, Finland had Nurmi, and America did not.

Possibly America could not have had Nurmi. He developed himself out of the Kolehmainen tradition. Hannes Kolehmainen established an example for all Finnish youth by winning every distance-running event except for the marathon in the 1912 Stockholm Olympics. His victories enormously enhanced the prestige of running the distances in the eyes of young Finns. Nurmi, however, received some direct coaching from his idol—coaching without which he might have remained a reasonably good athlete, but not an Olympian, let alone *the* Olympian of his era.

The patriotic Paavo entered the Finnish Army in 1918, finding plenty of athletic training facilities. Nurmi was born on June 13, 1897, so it must have been in 1908 that, at age 9, he joined his local boys' athletic club. In a year Nurmi was running the 1500 in 5:43; in two years he was running 5:03 for the distance. He did not much improve over the next decade, until he and Kolehmainen struck up a correspondence. Kolehmainen wrote that Nurmi's distance base was adequate (although he suggested it should be supplemented with long walks), but that there was no speedwork in his training. The Olympic ace urged the young contender to practice running at different speeds so he could learn how to run truly fast. As Nurmi said, "I had no idea of speedwork, so it was no wonder I remained a slow trudger for so many years. The slow progress in my results at that time was entirely due to the lack of speedwork in training." Nurmi's lack of injuries probably also stemmed from eschewing speedwork until his cardiovascular system was strong (particularly prudent in a man whose father died of a heart attack). Paavo demonstrated his endurance early in his army career, when he won the annual Finnish Army March, a 15-kilometer test, in 59 minutes. Nurmi's time becomes impressive when one realizes the soldiers were compelled to compete in full uniform, carrying a rifle and a 55-pound backpack. Thanks to Hannes Kolehmainen's advice, Paavo had the opportunity to demonstrate his newfound speed in the Olympic Games.

Nurmi lost his first Olympic final, the 5,000 meters, but lost like a champion to France's enormously popular Jacques Guillemot. The French distance man was so admired that Belgium's King Albert flew to Antwerp specifically to watch him compete. Guillemot possessed the kind of ebullient personality that stands out among athletes, who are normally shy and/or taciturn. More important, Guillemot was a war hero. He'd been gassed at the Front by the Germans and his lungs allegedly ruined. Guillemot's lungs must have been made of the same stuff as DeMar's heart, because the little (5'3") Frenchman became a world-class distance runner after the war, but had no reputation to speak of before the gassing. Although the Americans had marked Nurmi's potential in his 5K heat race, they were pulling for Guillemot in the 5,000 final. (Head Olympic Coach Jack Moakley, seeing Nurmi, felt America would have to wait until Nurmi retired to hope to win some distance events. His was a fitting and ironic observation in light of the Kolehmainen brothers' tutelage under American pro runners such as Jack Moakley.)

Nurmi was gifted but his personality was that of the quintessential athlete. In short, he was the opposite of Guillemot, a difference that may have cost him first place. Nurmi insisted on planning his races with a meticulousness that made Walter George appear lackadaisical. The problem in 1920 was that Nurmi simply lacked the requisite racing experience at the Olympic level to permit him to plan for all eventualities. He therefore shot into the lead on the third lap of the 13-lapper, hoping his speed and endurance would neutralize the knowledge of his more seasoned competition.

They didn't. Coming out of the final turn, Guillemot snuck up on Nurmi's elbow, dug down, and ran past the dying Finn. Guillemot hit the tape in 14:55.6, 19.6 seconds slower than Kolehmainen's world and Olympic 5K record, but 4.4 seconds faster than Nurmi's clocking. It was a fitting evening-up of Kolehmainen's whipping of France's Bouin eight years earlier, but the crowd roared happily mainly because Guillemot was a war hero, not a redresser of Olympic balance.

Paavo Nurmi learned his lesson, apparently the only athletic lesson (save one—"Never take a check as under-the-table payment"—that would haunt him and end his career) that he'd yet to master. He was ready for Guillemot when the 10,000-meter final rolled around.

It was not a dramatic race, no more than the sweep of a watch hand around the face and across the numerals of a timepiece is dramatic. Guillemot led and Nurmi won. It was not the most sporting of tactics, but Nurmi had acted as pacemaker for the 5,000, so it was not the least sporting either. Paavo's time, 31:45.8, was nearly a minute slower than Bouin's 8-year-old world mark, but everything else in the post-war world was also slower.

Albert G. Hill's triumphant time of 4:01.8 in the 1500 meters, was exactly 5 seconds slower than Arnold Jackson's 1912 Olympic best, but Great Britain won again anyway. It was an outstanding time for the 36-year-old Hill, but a heartbreaking one for American "Chesty" Ray, who'd hoped to score at least one distance victory for the U.S.A. Ray could take some consolation from

Hill's earlier win in the 800 meters, clocking 1:53.4. Few pure milers have the speed to run with an 800-meter Olympic champion and those who can, such as Peter Snell or Sebastian Coe, are incontestably superlative. Although Ray could run a good 1,000 yards indoors, he lacked the speed necessary to stay with "old-timer" Hill.

Chesty wasn't the only man lacking 800-meter speed at Antwerp. The high point of the Games on Saturday was a race between Olympic officials and a stray dog that had wandered onto the track. The fat track officials had no better luck than their contemporary football counterparts usually do: The dog won the 2-lapper and the crowd, composed largely of schoolchildren, was delighted.

Paavo Nurmi lacked nothing at Antwerp, as he superfluously showed in the 10,000 meter cross-country race, which offered a team as well as an individual title. Nurmi again squared off against Guillemot and, again, France took the lead at the start of the race. Unfortunately, poor Guillemot was beaten by the course before he was bested by Nurmi. He tripped over the kind of detritus (a rock, a root, a dozing rummy) common to a cross-country course, landed with a thud, and dropped out. Nurmi came home in 27:15.0— over three-and-a-half minutes faster than his winning 10K track time! It seemed too phenomenal to be true! It was! The course was very, very short, but the victory put Peerless Paavo in the record books for a long, long time.

Ironically, the distance event that nerveless Nurmi didn't enter was taken by his mentor. Hannes Kolehmainen came back to win the one distance

Paavo Nurmi putting in roadwork while visiting the United States in 1929 to compete in the Penn Relays. When competing, he almost always carried a stopwatch in one hand. (Photograph from the authors' collection.)

medal he was lacking, the marathon's. Hearty Hannes was the only athlete to set an Olympic distance record at Antwerp, checking in at 2:32:35.8 over the 26.2-mile route and slicing 4:20 off Ken McArthur's 1912 best. The first American, Joe Organ, claimed seventh spot in the 49-man field, but the American team took solace from the facts that Hannes had married an American woman and had run in various American championship meets competing as a member (God alone knows why!) of the celebrated Irish-American A.C. Possibly Kolehmainen heard about the money deals the Irish-American clubbers could get for certain selected members. As time would show, the star Finns' love for money at least matched their possessiveness of the Olympic distance events.

After the 1920 Games, Nurmi studied mathematics at the Helsinki Industrial School. Math would have an important influence on his athletic career, both physically and fiscally, in the years to come.

Together with his coach, Jaakko Mikkola, Nurmi decided he was not particularly interested in beating specific human rivals; rather, he intended to beat the inhuman clock whenever he ran. Paavo's training after his first Olympics aimed at mastering pace over given distances. His goal was not to run the same pace interminably. Nurmi intended to be a latter-day Deerfoot, mastering any pace over any distance.

In the manner of some more recent Finnish champions such as Lasse Viren, Nurmi did not race very hard during non-Olympic years. Instead, he tested himself with an impressive methodicalness, an approach to training quite at odds with the "devil-may-care" empiricism of his contemporaries. The few races Paavo did run during the off-years were contests where his whole concentration was absorbed by his stopwatch. He thoroughly ignored his human rivals. They were not nearly as tough as the steel innerspring of the stopwatch. The other athletes, imperfect beings though they were, nevertheless had feelings, and Paavo Nurmi was not the most popular athlete among his peers. If that bothered him, he never showed it.

While Nurmi trained scientifically to smash every distance record on earth, the fellows who ran the B.A.A. Marathon prepared for the 1921 version in their usual idiosyncratic styles. Johnny Connors stepped to the line with a lit cigar clenched in his maw. Connors ran the Boston Marathon for nearly a full decade smoking a stogie, earning the uncreative but apt nickname, "Cigar." Frank Zuna, a Newark plumber who won the marathon in record time (2:18:57), dressed for the race right on the starting line. Zuna wore his running togs under his business suit and had his competition shoes jammed in the suit's capacious pockets. His striptease in Ashland ended with a sigh of relief when the assembled throng realized Zuna hadn't lost his sense—the feller wasn't gonna run nekked after all. Neither did Zuna lose the race. Urged on by his friend Chuck Mellor, Frank powered away during the run up the Newton hills and finished over 3 minutes ahead of Mellor, who deserved the good-sport-of-the-race award.

Almost exactly two months after the Boston Marathon, on June 17 and 18, 1921, the National Collegiate Athletic Association staged its first outdoor track championships at the University of Chicago. As the *New York Times* reported of the event:

> An evenly balanced team which scored points in ten of fifteen events, without capturing a single first place, today brought national honors to the University of Illinois by carrying off first place in the National Collegiate Athletic Association meet at Stagg Field, a contest open only to champion athletes and entered by more than three score of the country's colleges and universities.

The *Times* also noted that "A slight rain before the meet made the track tricky." The times for the distance finals testified to that "trickiness." Eby, running for U. Penn., claimed the half-mile in 1:57.4. The Kansas Aggies' Watson came home in front in the mile run, clocking 4:23.4. Remig of Penn State hit the tape at the end of the 2-miler in 9:24.0.

On June 22, 1921, Nurmi grasped the award he'd gone after: a world 10,000-meter record. He ran 30:40.2 to erase Jean Bouin's old mark.

Nurmi showed off the results of his meticulous preparation during the two years after his Olympic debut. Only those who knew about the scientific underpinnings of Nurmi's training could see the method behind the apparent strategic madness in his races (one Finn said Nurmi ran "like a madman"). Running with a stopwatch in hand gave Paavo a certain clinical air. Nurmi believed in careful pacing, but what was careful for him was insanity for anyone else. He regularly ran the first lap in 61 seconds, storming away from the field with the apparent abandon of a Tom Longboat in the Boston Marathon. In 5,000-meter races, Nurmi would normally churn through the first 1500 meters in 4:08, leaving defeated 5K specialists in his wake and in oxygen debt. His training worked; by the end of 1922 he'd added the records for 2K, 3K, and 5K to the year-old 10K world record reposing in the Nurmi household.

Arguably the preeminent runner of the day, Nurmi was not the only consistent distance record-setter. Clarence DeMar won his second Boston Marathon in 1922, knocking off Frank Zuna's year-old mark by running 2:18:10, the fastest the 24.5 mile route would ever be run. Coming in second was a man destined to play a central role in distance running in the era: Ville Ritola, a Finn residing in New York's Bronx. "Willie" ran 2:21:44, but his greatest feats would not manifest for another two years. Third, behind "Willie," came Missassaja Indian Albert Smoke—appropriately named, for he, like "Cigar" Connors, finished with a lit stogie clamped in his jaw. His time was 2:22:49.

DeMar came right back and did it again, albeit in 2:23:37, in 1923. It was the end of the line for the old Marathon course, for the B.A.A. extended it to what the club thought was the full 26.2 mile standard distance in 1924 (the B.A.A. was off by 176 yards for a few years, then short by 1,232 yards for a few more years). It may also have been the end of the line for a dog that tangled with DeMar on Main Street in Natick. DeMar never stopped for anything, let alone a dog. He drop-kicked the bowser out of his way—out of sight, according to some witnesses (people drink a lot during the Marathon)—and went on to win without further incident.

In 1923 Nurmi won the world records for the 1500, the mile, and the 3-mile. Comparing Nurmi's record-breaking mile effort of August 23, 1923, to Walter George's own mile record set on exactly the same date, but in 1886, is interesting. Like the Englishman, the Finn prepared a precise lap-time schedule to which he knew he could adhere and which, when run in sequence, would render the former record "yesterday's news." The interest lies in the difference between the two champions' schedules: there wasn't much. George had planned to run laps of 59, 63, 66 and 64 seconds. Nurmi planned to run laps of 58, 64, 64, 63. George actually ran laps of 58.25, 63.5, 66 and 65. Nurmi actually ran laps of 58.6, 63.2, 64.9 and 63.7. Although Nurmi ran faster than George, George came closer to his intended mark. Nurmi's 4:10.4 was nearly 1.5 seconds slower than he'd hoped, while George was only 0.75 seconds off his target. Two lessons stand out from this comparison. First, great champions of any era plan their racing carefully while extending their personal limits by training superhumanly. Second, anyone wanting to set a new mile record ought to try it on August 23.

On graduation from the Industrial School, Nurmi took a job in the Helsinki electricity works. When it was too cold and snowy to run normal workouts, Paavo would walk an hour and a half to work to build his stamina. When Finland's weather warmed enough for the natives to be able to find—let alone run on—a track, he put in track work when he left his job in the late afternoon. Paavo Nurmi intended to equal his hero Hannes Kolehmainen in the next Olympic Games.

1924 was also a great year for Clarence DeMar, who readily conquered the new, longer (26 miles, 209 yards) Boston Marathon course. The 35-year-old DeMar ran 2:29:40 to complete his B.A.A. Marathon "hat trick" in an effort that veteran Marathon reporter Jerry Nason called "probably . . . his all-time Boston best in a seven-win career." Running strongly but prudently, Mr. DeMarathon stayed with the lead pack until the halfway mark, then charged to a 200-yard lead heading up the Newton hills. He added another 300 yards to his lead by the time he shot past Boston College on the downside of that heartbreaking hill collection. Frequent bridesmaid Chuck Mellor came in almost 5 minutes behind Clarence the Great, but Mellor must have caught DeMar's bouquet, because he would finally win the following year.

DeMar ran in the marathon at the 1924 Paris Olympics, but he was beaten by Finland's Albin Stenroos. Finland's Ville Ritola, competing for his homeland, ran in the 10K, the 5K, the 3K steeplechase, the 3K team race, and the

10K cross-country; he won the 10K and the steeplechase. Finland's Paavo Nurmi ran in the 1500, the 5K, the 10K cross-country, and the 3K team race; he was beaten by no one.

The story behind the distance events in the 1924 Games began two months before the Opening Ceremonies. In May, 1924, Ritola beat Nurmi's 10,000-meter world record by nearly 5 seconds. Finnish officials thought the smart thing to do would be to designate the 10K as Ritola's event and have Nurmi double in the 1500 and the 5,000. Ville and Paavo could slug it out between themselves in the 10K cross-country and the 3K team races, both of which were essentially team efforts anyway.

Two problems emerged with this plan. The first was Nurmi's ego. The second was the iron-bound Olympic finals schedule, which had the 1500 and 5K finals run within an hour of each other.

Paavo's ego proved less problematic than the impossible Olympic finals' scheduling. Nurmi had already won the Olympic 10K championship, but had lost the 5K in 1920. A true champion, he had hoped to defend his title in the upcoming Games, but Coach Mikkola suggested Paavo could make his point to the world by soundly thrashing whomever won the Olympic 10K title in the cross-country race later in the program. Nurmi was willing to run the 1500 and 5,000—the question then became whether he was *capable* of doing so.

Track experts questioned whether any human could pull off Nurmi's proposed effort. They questioned it even more in the case of Nurmi, who became injured late in April, 1924. Nurmi had adjusted his training in an effort to compensate for the injury. The only way to know for certain if Nurmi, let alone a fully healthy human being, could pull off the intended Olympic double was by empiricism: see if he could duplicate in a trial run what he proposed to do in the Games.

Nurmi took his tests on June 19, less than one month before the Olympics. Within 60 minutes, he ran 1500 meters in 3:52.6 and 5,000 meters in 14:28.2, proving he could do it. Boy, did he prove it. Not only had he run the requisite distances in the requisite time, he had also casually set two world records.

The Finns were more than delighted, for they strongly suspected the Olympic officials of deliberately setting up the "impossible" schedule to prevent Nurmi from grabbing all the precious marbles. The 5K, after all, is the most logical event for a miler to move up to, especially a miler who is also the Olympic 10,000-meter champion.

The 1924 Games were hosted by Paris at the express request of Baron de Coubertin, who planned to retire from the IOC the following year. The Games had originally been awarded to Amsterdam, but the city good-naturedly understood the importance to the Baron of seeing "his" Games in "his" city. This time Paris fully made up for the farcical 1900 Olympics. Three thousand athletes, representing forty-four nations, were viewed by daily crowds of up to 60,000 at the 1924 Paris Games, and royalty and heads of state sat with Baron de Coubertin as French President Gaston Doumergue declared the Games open on July 5. In fact, the organized splendor on opening day allowed no time for any competition.

Competition began the following day, with Ville Ritola claiming the 10K title by running 30:23.2, 12.2 seconds faster than his own world record. Two facts—one concrete, one possibly spurious—help put Ritola's Olympic run in proper perspective. First and indisputably, it had rained heavily the morning of the 10,000 meters, saturating the track. Ritola sliced 12 seconds off his world mark in the muck. Second, and arguably, rumors still persist that Nurmi ran his own 10K race on a private track at the same time as the Olympic final, clocking 29:58. Sober experts tend to dismiss this story; Lauri Pihkala, an outstanding Finnish newspaper reporter contemporary of Nurmi's, is among them. Pihkala, however, wrote that he believed Nurmi, "if trying *and pushed*, able in those days to run the distance close to 29 mins 30 secs." We must consider the tale mythic, then, but the myths that attach to a man reveal much about him. What is indisputably significant is that it *was plausible* for Nurmi to run 24 seconds faster than his detested rival on the same day and in the same hour. Many distance runners take great motivation from anger. Finnish officials forbade Nurmi from racing with Ritola in the 10K track race, but suggested Nurmi could run for second place. Paavo decided he would rather not.

Paavo Nurmi wanted to win. His tacit quarrel with Ritola was apparently the only time Nurmi ever focused on a human rival. He preferred to defeat time, not people. People were so *inferior* to the inexorable march of time; time ruled his life. He set his mile record thirty-seven years to the day after Walter George set his own mark. July 10, 1924 was the precise twelfth anniversary of Hannes Kolehmainen's classic duel with Jean Bouin at the Stockholm Games. It was to be, as of 1981, arguably the greatest day in the life of any one Olympic runner.

A trifle large for a distance man, Nurmi stood 5'8½" and weighed about 145 pounds. He ran with his chest as much as with his legs, thrusting his pectorals out in front of him, with a decided bounce to his stride. He held his arms chest-high, and stuck his elbows out at the sides. In short, Nurmi had rotten form. He landed on his heels, rather than his forefeet, as is characteristic of middle-distance runners (where speed is as important as endurance). The only classically positive point to his running posture was his head carriage. He ran with his head erect; that may have been the whole symbolic point, for Nurmi was a "heads-up" runner. He ran in the fashion of a jogger, but he had the personal style of a champion.

The Finnish guy with poor running form swept past the best middle- and long-distance stars the world could offer that July afternoon. First came the 1500-meter final. Nurmi would have preferred to run a mile rather than a "metric mile." There is no mile in the Olympics, so the 1500 it would be. Nurmi held the world record in the event, and few spectators doubted he would lose the Olympic 1500 championship; the drama derived from whether he could possibly recover in time to do the same in the 5K.

Nurmi's metric mile was a runaway. He took the lead 100 meters into the race, with eyes only for his stopwatch. It was just Paavo and his heart racing around the track after he took the pace from Douglas Lowe on the first turn. He clocked the first 400-meter lap in 58 seconds flat and the second in 63.6. Nurmi looked at the stopwatch following each lap and, following each peek at his heart, faintly smiled. The contenders in the field were gasping in his train as though his speed were befouling their life's air—which, in a manner of speaking, it was.

On reaching the penultimate lap, Paavo Nurmi again looked casually at his stopwatch, gently lobbed it onto the grassy track infield, and accelerated 40 yards clear of second-man Watson. He hit the tape in 3:53.6, precisely 1 second slower than his world best but 10 meters faster than the American, Watson. England's Henry B. Stallard claimed third spot, then passed out crossing the finish line, in decided contrast to Nurmi's casual mien after the contest.

Nurmi was indeed a superman, but some put too much stock in poor Stallard's condition as an index of the abnormal arduousness of the race. Stallard ran the race with a fractured foot bone and a torn arch ligament; to round out his condition, he had a septic throat. Small wonder it took physicians a half-hour to revive the brave man after he took an Olympic 1500 bronze medal! He was not the ideally fit Olympian. Nurmi's time speaks for itself, but one suspects Paavo ran fast enough to win yet not so fast he'd have nothing left for his first confrontation with Ritola several minutes later in the 5,000 final.

Ritola had become Olympic steeplechase champion the previous day, three days after claiming the 10K crown. He had had a full day to rest and prepare himself emotionally for the 5K showdown. In contrast, Nurmi had become Olympic 1500 champion that day. He had 45 minutes to get himself together for the 5,000-meter final.

He had hardly broken stride after breaking the 1500's tape. Finland's team manager helped hustle him into his sweatclothes and then into the locker room where a masseur worked on Nurmi, keeping all systems warm and supple while both of the man's hearts rested. Paavo Nurmi had taken an instant to recover his stopwatch before going incommunicado.

The finalists in the 5,000-meter footrace stepped to the line at 4:45 PM that July 10 afternoon. The gun fired, and they shot off.

The apparent strategy among Nurmi's competitors was to set a torrid pace that would deplete what wind he might have left. That hope soon evaporated. Sweden's Edvin Wide served as rabbit at the start, and Nurmi, Ritola, and Dolquès of France bunched up behind him. By the second lap these four were well clear of the "spectators" who were also running on the same track.

Dolquès dropped back after 1500 meters; Wide, after 2,500. Nurmi and

Ritola ran together, alone. It was a fast pace. The first kilometer had passed in 2:46.4. Two kilometers took 5:43.6. Three kilometers were passed in 8:42.6, and 4000 meters took only 11:38.8 of Paavo Nurmi's precious time. Nurmi knew exactly what the splits were; he knew them by heart, for he consulted his ticker at the end of each lap.

Nurmi and Ritola ran the second half of the race like an engine and caboose with no train in between. Two meters separated them. God alone knows at what kind of emotional distance they stood from each other. Witnesses reported Ritola clenched his teeth and fists ever tighter with each lap, and that Nurmi, although physiognomically impassive, looked at his clutched stopwatch almost anxiously as he reeled off the laps.

The gun lap: Nurmi again threw his heart to the infield and entered a controlled sprint. Ritola entered that world of hot pain, the uncontrolled sprint. The two meters of physical distance between them remained constant, as Paavo Nurmi intended. It was not enough that Ritola be beaten; he must be humbled.

The crowd, standing on their seats and screaming, expressed definite interest.

Five thousand meters passed in 14:31.2 for Paavo Nurmi, in 14:31.4 for Ville Ritola. Nurmi passed the finish line two steps ahead of his alleged teammate, passed into the history books, and, pausing only to collect his now-passive stopwatch, passed off the field with his sweats over his arm.

Nurmi's 5K time was exactly 3 seconds slower than his world record. His metric mile was exactly 1 second slower. Nurmi seemed under no compulsion to take 4 fewer seconds on the Olympic field that July 10 and, had he attempted it, he might not have achieved what he did. As it was, the world was left fumbling for explanations for Nurmi's "impossible" double. The most common explanation, which explained nothing at all, was that Nurmi was a "superman." One facetious reporter, Leonard Cline, offered by far the most original reason for Nurmi's success: "Every single person [in Finland] goes through, day after day, the ordeal of talking in Finnish. After that, why should one be surprised at anything the Finns accomplish?"

The Finns were far from finished with the 1924 Games. There was the 3,000-meter team race for a team championship. It constituted one of the comic moments of these dramatic Olympics and, somewhat atypically but perhaps not surprisingly, Paavo Nurmi stood at the center of the comedy.

Part of the humor derived from parody. America's "Chesty" Ray gave his impersonation of Nurmi's running style during the race. Ray, who as his nickname implies was himself gifted in the pectoral region, ran with an out-thrust chest and pointedly looked at his wristwatch every couple of steps. He had his laugh. He also finished eighteenth.

Part of the humor came from a comedy of errors. Nurmi took off at the gun, checked his watch after the first lap and found he was going too fast for his Finnish teammates. He dropped back, found Ritola and third-man

Katz, presumed they were securely hitched to him, and charged off again. The hitch ran into a hitch: Ritola and Katz couldn't keep up. Again Nurmi dropped back, found the two men once more, and once more hooked up with them. He drove them ahead of him for a few laps, became satisfied that the boys had finally learned the proper pace, assumed his lead at the head of the Finland Express, then, on the bell lap, zoomed to a 50-meter victory for Finland—for he had pulled Ritola and Katz through to second and third places behind himself.

Paavo missed his stopwatch, but it was useless to carry a stopwatch when racing across the irregular cross-country course. Paavo also longed for the familiar, regular quarter-mile track. Paavo, the watch, and the track all belonged together, the most invincible running "team" of the 1920s; but the cross-country race was on the 1924 Olympic program. The distance was right: 10,000 meters. The weather was right: 90 degrees and humid. It was an easy chance to win a fifth Olympic championship. Paavo felt himself made to win Olympic medals. He would run over grass, through water, indeed on TOP of water if necessary. His passion was the science of his sport. When he ran on the track holding his stopwatch, he ran with his heart in his hand. When he ran cross-country, watchless, he ran heartlessly.

Paavo ignores the runners dying behind him. False rumors spread that two Olympians had literally died. Twenty-four of the thirty-nine starters do not finish the race. The Frenchman Marchal collapses, insensate, 50 yards from the finish. He falls facefirst onto the infernal track cinders; when he is pulled away his face is covered with baked gore. The Englishman Sewell heads the wrong way around the track, is turned about by officials, and then nearly runs headlong into one of Nurmi's teammates. The shock is too much for them both: the athletes collapse and do not finish. A fifth runner, attempting to finish, runs into the stadium's concrete wall and splits open his scalp.

Paavo reaches the stadium exit in the 85 seconds it takes his closest rival, the hated Ritola, to cross the finish line. Then, unexhausted, nearly unintentionally, Paavo the human running machine almost smiles and turns and leaves the field. Paavo Nurmi has crushed every other runner under his spikes as relentlessly as the sweep of his heart's second-hand.

The 10,000-meter cross-country race served as a grim counterpoint to the 3K team race's good humor, and after the finish, the IOC forever removed the brutal cross-country contest from the program.

Officials kept the rugged marathon race on the program, and Finland won that, too, although America's great Clarence DeMar tried to prevent it. At 35, DeMar was an old man for Olympic sport. His third place finish was remarkable under his chronological circumstances. Ha! The fellow who *won*, Albin Stenroos, was 36! He legged the 26.2 miles in 2:41:22.6. DeMar ran 2:48:14. The two would meet again, and on Mr. DeMarathon's home court— Boston. Second man Romeo Bertini of Italy, a mere youngster at 30 years of age, ran 2:47:19.6.

The 1924 Games had been superlative, but also somewhat of a shock for the U.S.A. America garnered more first places than any other nation, twelve, but Finland came close with ten. The American public was understandably interested in the prowess of Finnish athletes, particularly in the prowess of Nurmi, and Paavo was more than willing to let them see him run . . . on the lucrative American indoor track circuit, nearly five months after his Olympic triumphs.

Interest in the running sport, undoubtedly impelled by the successful Olympic movement, spread across the globe. Sports officials from Czechoslovakia, attending the Games as observers, returned home very enthusiastic about the marathon race. In October, 1924, the Czechs instituted the Kosice Marathon, which turned 50 years old (they skipped a few runnings during World War II and didn't count those years) in 1980.

While the Czechs were hitting the open road, the American people turned their attention to indoor track. Most American track athletes gained a major portion of their experience bounding off the boards indoors. Joie Ray, of course, was a major indoor force in the U.S., although when Nurmi traveled to America in December, 1924, to compete on the indoor circuit, he made "Chesty" pay for his Paavo-impersonation during the Olympic 3K team race by stealing away Ray's indoor 2-mile record.

"Willie" Ritola was another ace undercover man who won a total of 14 AAU distance championships. Later in his life he won an American citizenship and wife. Although Nurmi either ignored him or toyed with him during the Olympics, Ritola was no man to be ignored or played with during the Olympiad's 3 year "off season." During the 1923 indoor season Ritola established world marks for 3 miles (14:14.8), 5,000 meters (15:01.4), and 4 miles (19:27.8). In the 1925 board season, "Willie" set a 2-mile world best of 9:03.8. He thrice lowered his 3-mile mark, finally settling on 13:56.2, a quarter-minute faster than Paavo Nurmi's 3-mile outdoor record! He bested Paavo in the 5K record, too, but only by 5 seconds (14:23.2)—but, again, Ritola set his mark while running on an indoor track; Nurmi, while enjoying the benefit of a full 400-meter outdoor venue. Ritola marched to a 24:21.8 5-mile record, finally eclipsing Alfred Shrubb's 1904 world standard. The next year, Ritola lowered the record for 5,000 *yards* to 13:39.0.

Miler Ray Conger, another great American indoor man of the period, is another runner whose history intertwines with Nurmi's. Talented at the 1000-yard run, Conger snared the AAU championship in the event three times in his career, ultimately clocking 2:11.0 (faster than the world outdoor record) only to have the race declared "unofficial" because AAU rules required "a border of boards, rope, cement or other material around the track," and there was no such border. At least Conger was not stripped of his amateur status for running on an unofficial track.

Nurmi came to America late in 1924 to try his foot at running on American wood. In retrospect, we also know he wanted to try his hand at collecting

American dollars, the kind passed under the table or inside a winner's watch. (A complaint among money-seeking top runners in those days was, "I got the works!" This meant they'd been given a real, working watch, one with the "works" intact inside it. If the "works" were inside the watch, there was no room for tainted "expense" money to be slipped to the athlete.) Nurmi was renowned for having an exceptionally low resting pulse rate, 40 beats per minute. He was only slightly less well-known for his high "appearance fees," or "travel expenses." One wag, a track official, combined these two data in the immortal quip, "Nurmi has the lowest heart beat and the highest asking price of any athlete in the world."

International rules permit an athlete to receive travel expenses when invited to compete in a foreign arena. Nurmi felt fully justified, in this era of boat travel, to request round-trip ocean liner passage from his home city, Helsinki, to the American city where he was invited to compete. Nurmi, however, demanded the same round-trip "travel expense" from *each* of the 24 host cities he visited during his American tour! (Nurmi was by no means the last "amateur" athlete to make such a request, but he very well may have been the first.) It must be noted that Nurmi's 1924 U.S. tour brought in gate receipts of *nearly one million dollars* for the indoor meet promoters. In fact, Paavo Nurmi helped establish indoor track as *the* money-making track and field circuit (far out-earning the outdoor version of the sport). Nurmi helped both the promoters and the sport make a lot of money. He undoubtedly thought it only fair in turn for the promoters to give a lot of quid to a pro . . . rather, to an amateur.

Nurmi gave value for value received. The double-hearted Finn lost only twice in fifty-five races that season, smashing upwards of thirty indoor records. He lost once to Ritola in a 5K showdown. (Ritola's victory bore a blemish: Nurmi pulled out of the race, a victim of indigestion generated by American veal pie. Popular history remembers Nurmi's favorite meal as dried fish and black bread, but the Finn's choice repast was actually oatmeal.) He lost once, at the wire, to top American half-miler Alan Helffrich of Penn State in an 880-yard battle around Yankee Stadium on May 26, 1925. At the end of his American sojourn, President Calvin Coolidge shook Nurmi's hand in the White House. If "Silent Cal" noticed the stigma of professionalism on the Finnish "shamateur," he kept quiet.

Nurmi opened his American visit with a repeat of his Olympic 1500–5,000 double on January 6, 1925, at the appropriately titled Finnish-American Games at Madison Square Garden. The crowd scene outside brought to mind the days of Deerfoot and George. The police and fire departments first tried reason, then *force majeur* on the overflow throng to convince them they could not get inside.

Inside were Paavo Nurmi, Joie Ray, and Lloyd Hahn (who would, one month later, erase the mile record Nurmi would establish that evening), all waiting to race a hard indoor mile. Nurmi, as was his wont, took off in the lead with the pack trailing behind, but, as was not his wont, lost the lead 3 laps from the end when Chesty and Hahn chugged by. Paavo bided his time, nailed the two Yanks on the last lap, and whipped home in a 4:13.6 world record. To cool down, he beat Ritola in the 5K.

Nurmi set a world record at the 2-mile, which required he run 22 laps on an unbanked indoor track. His time, 8:58.2, sliced 11.4 seconds off the outdoor standard; however, recall that Joie Ray's indoor 2-mile, set three years before, stood at 9:08.4, also well under the outdoor best.

Then Nurmi took his American loot and went home, but he left America a different athlete from when he came. It was not that he'd besmirched his amateur status. Only Nurmi himself knew exactly when he lost his amateur virginity. It was that his 55-race schedule (some put the total as high as 70 races) served as kryptonite to his superman status. Whether he had burned out a bit or his rivals become better athletes, or a little of both, Nurmi never again found it quite as easy to dominate a race as offhandedly as he had dictated the events at Paris.

The Boston Marathon remained a bastion of complete amateurism, the one major race in the world that pays no expenses to *anyone*, and the 1925 edition helped restore the scent of pure amateurism to America's air after Nurmi finally used one of his twenty-four boat tickets to go back to Helsinki. To date, that was the coldest Boston Marathon in history. The mercury showed 33 Fahrenheit degrees, if one cleared away the snowflakes from it. (It snowed before the start of the race.) Clarence DeMar was back from his Olympic effort and raring to win a fourth Boston in a row, but the Boston bride was to be beaten on this day by his frequent bridesmaid, Chuck Mellor of Chicago, running his fifth B.A.A. Marathon.

DeMar and Mellor slugged it out for almost the entire race. Chuck charged away at that most strategic part of the course, the Newton hills, but DeMar dashed right after him, catching him after the 6-mile flight over the strenuous steps. Mellor was prepared this year, however. He'd reserved a jot of strength for breaking away from DeMar. He'd also been chawin' away on a plug of "tabacee" the whole race. In case he got bored, he had that morning's edition of the Boston *Globe* stuffed down his singlet; it also doubled as insulation from the bitter weather. Mellor crossed the Exeter Street finish line at 2:33 into the race; DeMar was there at 2:33:37.

1926 goes into distance-running history mainly for marathon motives. Violet Piercy of England became the first woman known to race a 26.2-mile marathon, hitting the tape in 3:40:22. Clarence DeMar lay in wait at Boston that year to take another hit at Finland's Albin Stenroos, who'd outslugged the preacher/printer two years before in the Paris Olympics.

The two grand old men (aged 37 and 38, respectively) of marathoning were upset, in all senses of the term, by a grand young man of the event. John C. Miles of Nova Scotia wasn't quite 20 years old when he stepped to the marathon line. It was his first attempt at the event; the longest distance he had previously logged was 10 miles. Miles's name proved prophetic, however. Neither the distance nor the competition gave him any trouble, even though he'd eaten one of the worst possible pre-race meals (a complete steak). Miles hung with DeMar during the early part of the race, a smart thing to do in most marathons, but not in this one. The iron DeMar was having a rare off day. Stenroos vanished into the middle distance, and the determined Miles realized he'd have to hoof a bit harder if he were going to win. Once again the Newton hills provided the dramatic climax. Stenroos got a side-stitch striding up them, and Miles nailed him at Boston College on the downside of the roller coaster. He ran on to a new course record—2:25:40, exactly 5 minutes under DeMar's previous best. Stenroos finished second in 2:29:40 and DeMar claimed third in a slowish (for him) 2:32:15.

The IC4A celebrated its first half-century of organizing track and field with a big meet at Harvard Stadium. Befitting the Ivy League tone of the member schools, the celebratory banquet ranged from broiled chicken fermière to sultana roll with claret sauce. Twenty-five thousand spectators filled the stadium the next day to witness sprint demonstrations by former world champs Bernie Wolfers and Maxie Long (running in their civvies and accompanied by men on high-wheeled bicycles!), marching bands, and the unfurling of the new IC4A gold-and-white flag. As one journalist put it, "The hands of time were turned back and then abruptly it was a fine May day in 1926 and the serious business of crowning fifteen intercollegiate champions was begun." The star runner of the meet was Cornell's Henry A. Russell, who blasted the 100-yarder in 9.7 and the 220 in 21.0.

The first race ever entitled "the mile of the century" was the meeting between George and Cummings in 1886. The first "mile of the century" for the twentieth century was run at an American indoor meet in 1927, officially known as the Columbian Mile. Ace American boardman Lloyd Hahn (who held indoor records for the half-mile, 1000 yards, three-quarter-mile, mile, 1000 meters and 1500 meters at one time or another in his career) zipped 4:12.2 to beat Swedish Olympian Edvin Wide.

Clarence DeMar claimed the Boston laurels again in 1927, taking his fifth win in 2:40:22. The Boston Marathon at last became a full-length marathon. The course had been 176 yards shy of the mark when Miles ran his record the previous year.

On March 4, 1928, football great Red Grange served as official starter to one of the most officially weird footraces in history, Charles C. ("Cash-and-Carry") Pyle's ballyhooed "Bunion Derby." Presumably sane men were going to race each other from America's west coast to her east coast.

The Transcontinental Foot Race, as it was officially if not popularly known, consumed two months of time, 3,422 miles of distance, and goodness knows how many calories and injuries for the 300 men who ran in hopes of winning the $48,500 cash prize. An overtly professional affair, the Bunion Derby grew out of the pedestrianism tradition established in the nineteenth century. Onlookers wouldn't have known it, though, judging from the start: many runners sprinted off smartly, heedless of the 60 miles they would have to cover that day alone. Unfortunately, the majority of competitors in the Bunion Derby were not seasoned athletes. Neither were they sufficiently trained to undertake such an event. A handful, such as Peter Gavuzzi or Arthur Newton, were outstanding ultra-distance men. Earle Dilks, another of the few properly trained Bunioners, regularly ran 60 miles a day on Saturday and Sunday each week. (He had only one day per week off from his job at the B&O Railroad, so he could train hard only on Saturday afternoon and Sunday.) In fact, these three men showed each other how to race and train. The posture they developed was more conducive to shuffling than to running; it must have been very similar to Payse Weston's. South Africaner Newton had snapped Weston's 100-mile record in 1927 with a 14:43 clocking for the distance.

Gavuzzi, Newton, and Dilks sometimes trained together when Dilks got out of work early. They regularly covered 200 miles per week, running slowly and landing on their heels. Newton also smoked regularly; one wonders what kind of marks he might have set had he let his lungs clear out.

Newton had only one bad incident during the second Bunion Derby, and it had nothing to do with tobacco. He was run down by an auto driven by a parson. Newton's own father was a minister, and Arthur was unharmed by the accident, so found it in himself to forgive the man of the cloth in Terre Haute, Indiana.

In the first Bunion Derby he had to withdraw at Two Gun Camp, Arizona, suffering from inflamed Achilles tendons. C. C. Pyle immediately hired the biggest star in the race to stay on as a technical advisor, and Newton saved himself much of the trouble of running across the Mojave Dessert in 105-degree heat.

"Cash and Carry" Pyle was a showman in the P. T. Barnum tradition. He would set up a carnival at the end of each day's run to take advantage of the local spectators who'd been attracted by the Transcontinental Race. He took care of his athletes on the first race: There were no entry fees, and Pyle provided the support teams and vehicles himself. On the other hand, there was no prize money except for the winner, and athletes such as Dilks ran the race on leave-without-pay from their steady jobs.

Only 55 men out of the original 300 starters (actually a good survival rate) finished the Bunion Derby. First among them was Andy Payne from Oklahoma.

Pyle conducted the Bunion Derby from east coast to west the next spring, but made some changes in the procedures. Competitors had to provide their own support teams (although there was a man in a van who drove along with the race to mend the runners' shoes). They also had to pay a hefty entry fee. Some characteristics of the first Bunion Derby carried over to the second edition, though. Will Rogers, the great American humorist, served as official starter, and the race paid homage to the country's distance-running history by starting in New York's Columbia Oval, where the first U.S. marathon race finished.

The second Transcontinental offered a more dramatic finish than the first Bunion Derby for two reasons. First, New Jersey's Johnny Salo beat England's Peter Gavuzzi by less than two minutes after nearly 80 days of running almost 47 miles daily. Second, Cash-and-Carry Pyle skipped out without paying the Finnish-American Salo a penny of the promised prize money. In the closing years of the decade, Newton, Gavuzzi, and Dilks tried to revive pedestrianism-for-pay, even staging such stunts as snowshoe racing and racing horses. But Pyle's vanishing act proved prophetic: For the professional distance runner of the era, there was simply no money to take, no matter how much he ran. Only "amateurs" such as Paavo Nurmi were making substantial incomes from running!

Running always seems more special in an Olympic year, and 1928 soon erased the bad impression made by Pyle's second Bunion Derby. Lloyd Hahn set an absolute world record for the 880 at the IC4A indoor meet, running 1:51.4 on the ⅛-mile track to take 2/10 of a second off the world mark.

Clarence DeMar didn't improve his course record in the 1928 Boston Marathon, but he did add another notch to his "win" belt, making it even more improbable that another runner would ever equal, let alone exceed, his all-time number of Boston victories. The de-marvelous DeMar hit Exeter Street 2:37:07 after the gun had fired at Hopkinton. The irrepressible Chesty Ray, running his first marathon, claimed third spot in 2:41:56, just behind James "Hinky" Henigan. Ray nosedived after crossing the line, collapsing in the pile of blisters that had formerly been his two feet. All three men had great reason for pride that day. DeMar's reasons are obvious. Henigan rejoiced because it was the first time out of eight efforts that he'd been able to run the full distance. Joie Ray was happy with an excellent time for a distance longer than he was used to running and was ecstatic that he could now *stop* running.

Amsterdam offered the Games a home in 1928. That year first-place in an Olympic event gave the champion a gold rather than silver medal. Also that year women were finally allowed to compete in track and field events. For the U.S.A. team, fur flew before the athletes ever engaged in competition. Sprinter Charley Paddock, who had competed in the 1920 and 1924 Games, supplemented his income by charging fees for lectures he gave and articles he wrote about running. Some members of the USOC, notably George W. Wightman, charged that Paddock had lost his amateur status because of lecturing and writing! The USOC finally decided Paddock still had his amateur purity. After all, he had not been paid *to run*. Wightman resigned in a huff after the Committee vote that permitted the 1920 100-meter champion to remain on the U.S. Olympic Team. Wightman said his resignation stood as a protest against the perversion of amateurism. One presumes Wightman felt that members of other, purely amateur teams, such as Finland's, would be sullied by having to race against the dastardly Paddock who stooped to take *money* for his lectures on running. As was the case with Judge Weeks in 1920, history has lost track of Wightman's own athletic competitions—if any. Finally, at the Games themselves, the IOC dismissed an English protest of Paddock.

The inclusion of women in the track program also demonstrated the enlightened international attitude toward athletes and athletics. Women had been competing in swimming, tennis, and gymnastics for some time; now they were allowed on the oldest and arguably purest of athletic fields. Women were finally in *the* Olympics!

International protocol also drew attention in the Antwerp Games. The lesson of World War I—how foolish and destructive a force is national pride—seemed not learned. When Holland's Prince Hendrik reviewed the parade of teams in the opening ceremonies, the U.S.A. refused the customary courtesy dip of the Stars and Bars as the flag passed the head of state. Old Glory dipped for no foreigner! Besides, this was the greatest Olympic team the world had ever seen and would bow before no one. As Major General Douglas MacArthur, President of the USOC, boasted: "The opening of the Games finds the American team at the peak of form. We have assembled the greatest team in our athletic history. Without exception, our athletes have come through the long grind of training into superb condition. They are prepared both mentally and physically for the great test. Americans can rest serene and assured."

The 1928 U.S. Olympic Team was the worst team in history (although experts believe the 1980 Team, had it attended the Moscow Games, might have finally relieved the 1928 Team of that "honor"). The culprit was arrogance, such as was demonstrated by refusing to dip the flag and by the mania for counting national medal totals and drawing spurious conclusions about the comparative strength and moral fiber of nations thereby.

A more fundamental problem was organizational incompetence. George Wightman was not the only incompetent on the USOC. The tradition was established before 1928, but it had become very clear by that year: Coaches and officials for the American Olympic Team were selected on the basis of their abilities to make the right personal contacts, not on the basis of their abilities to make the right athletic decisions. Olympic pork-barreling was the reason why the American track and field squad had one head coach, ten assistant coaches, one head manager, three assistant managers, one head trainer, and five assistant trainers, all to direct the 84 men and women competing in track and field. The *New York Times* commented that "The boys themselves say they get orders from so many sources that they don't know which to take."

The USOC also decided to hold the American Olympic Trials less than a month before the Games opened. It takes an exceedingly rare athlete to hold a top competitive peak for a full month. History abounds with major champions incapable of such a feat. A competent coach would almost never suggest his athletes try to reach world-class condition twice in the same three-week period.

Bad coaching notwithstanding, Lloyd Hahn gave it the old American try in the 800 meters. He had tied his 1:51.4 personal and world best in the Olympic Trials, but, as the trials were held on an outdoor, quarter-mile track, Hahn obviously could go much faster. An inveterate frontrunner, he stepped out at the start in an effort to burn the finishing kick out of his rivals' quadriceps. Alas, Hahn's usually reliable tactic failed him this time, and England's Douglas Lowe snapped the wire in 1:51.8, the first man in Olympic history to defend the 800-meter title successfully. The race portended America's fortunes at Amsterdam.

There were only three running events for women in the 1928 Games, one of which was a 400-meter relay race, taken by the Canadian team in 48.4. American Elizabeth Robinson emerged as Olympic 100-meter queen with a 12.2-seconds clocking (2/10-second slower than Tommy Burke's 1896 performance at the same distance). Possibly the most remarkable women's track and field effort came in the discus when Helena Konopacka of Poland hurled 129'11¾"—a toss that would have won the event in the first three Olympic Games.

The discus may have been the most remarkable performance, but the women's 800 meters was probably the most spectacular, but unfortunate, event on the card. Japan's Kinue Hitomi held the world mark at 220 yards going into the Games, but there was no 200-meter event for women. (Neither was there yet a women's long jump, in which Kinue also held the world's best.) The sporting Kinue elected therefore to run the 100 and the 800. Beaten by Robinson in the former, she was determined to win the latter. She came close. She charged hard against the three German women running, à la Nurmi and the Finns, in a team train, grabbing second in 2:17.6 to Germany's Lina Radke-Batschauer's victorious 2:16.8. Both Radke-Batschauer and Kinue were under the previous world record for the event. What a great victory for women's athletics! The event also had a farcical turn. Remarking the haggard condition of many of the athletes after the 800, the questionably wise IOC decided women were incapable of running beyond 100 meters and removed the event from the Olympic program. (It was not reinstated until 1960!) The British Olympic Association protested that the state of collapse of the women in the 800 meters had been "grossly exaggerated," but the IOC ban stuck. With the benefit of hindsight, it seems reasonable to believe that some of the women *were* straining in the event, but that was because—like many of the men—they were not properly trained yet as athletes. It seems further fair to presume that the wretchedness of their condition seemed especially hideous to spectating officials precisely because it was so . . . so *unfeminine*. The poor girls were sweating! They were *breathing hard!* Some of them probably even *smelled* a bit unpleasant! Running "long distances," then, was *prima facie* destructive of a woman's good health, reasoned the IOC.

If Olympic officials were so concerned about athletes' good health, one wonders why American officials counseled Ray Barbuti and Herman Phillips to chug down sherry and eggnog between the semifinals and finals of the 400 meters. Alcohol is not high-performance fuel for distance running; alcohol in the bloodstream inhibits oxygen processing. The booze must have helped Barbuti to relax, because he squeaked through to the gold in 47.8, staying just barely ahead of Canada's hard-driving James Ball. A nip between races helped Barbuti nip Ball at the wire, handing the U.S.A. her *only* track victory, other than in the relays, at Amsterdam.

Running too many long-distance races may have deteriorated Paavo Nurmi's health if the Finn's constitution was judged strictly by the first-place results of the 1928 Games. Nurmi won only one Olympic gold medal, repeating his 1920 triumph in the 10K. He and Ritola ran neck-and-neck until the last lap, where Nurmi pulled away effortlessly to win in 30:18.8 to Ritola's 30:19.4. An excited General MacArthur exclaimed that "It's worth crossing the ocean just to see this."

Nurmi elected not to defend his 1500 crown, so the race was claimed by another Finn from Nurmi's hometown of Abo, Harri Larva, who trotted the metric mile in 3:53.2. Larva's easy victory and Nurmi's decision not to compete in the event raised plausible speculation that the Finnish team was under strict orders regarding which athlete would win what event, and perhaps in what time. The sentiment gained credence when Ritola beat Nurmi in the 5K final. The race seemed a reverse of the 10,000: Both athletes ran as a pair until the last lap, but this time Ritola surged ahead. Onlookers report Nurmi slowed and moved aside for "Willie" to pass him, but made certain Sweden's Edvin Wide was far enough back so that Finland would strike both gold and silver in the race. If Nurmi had enough steam to stay ahead of a charging Wide on the last lap, there's an outstanding chance he could have held off Ritola also.

Nurmi finished second in the steeplechase as well. Neither Paavo nor Ville, the defending champion in the event, much liked the water barrier. Ritola wound up taking a bath in it and retired from the final early in the going. Nurmi also took a few headers in the aqua, yet finished second to Finland's new steeple star, Toivo Loukola, who won in 9:21.8. Thus four separate Finns won four separate Olympic events—a great demonstration of Finland's track power. To round things out, Paavo Yrjola won the decathlon to field five gold medals for Finland. It was only one Olympic championship less than Nurmi alone won in his career. When the 1928 Games ended, so did Paavo Nurmi's Olympic career.

The Amsterdam Olympics ended, as was becoming traditional, with the marathon. America entered Clarence DeMar and Joie Ray, who had learned about the event three months earlier at Boston. Finland hoped to grab another gold, courtesy of Martti Matilainen, but was frustrated by a diminutive vegetarian dispatch carrier for the French Moroccan Army. It was a hot day and a tough course, and athletes began dropping out almost from the very start. The great DeMar didn't figure on this, his last Olympic Marathon, and he eventually finished twenty-seventh in a field of what had originally been 75 runners. Chesty Ray, on the other hand, was having a terrific day slugging it out with Matilainen. In fact, the U.S. team was pretty much expecting to see the Chicago cabdriver come home a winner, or at least snare second place. So was Chesty, who was as surprised as anyone else when El Abdel Baghinel Ouafi (whose name weighs more than he did) turned on the speed in the last couple of miles and came into the stadium 26 seconds ahead of Chile's Miguel Plaza. Matilainen claimed third. Ray was struck by severe leg cramps and gutted out a fifth-place finish. Medical reports indicate Ray suffered extreme pain in the last 2 miles, but the always effervescent Chesty explained his performance with, "I lost because I ran too slow."

After the Amsterdam Olympics, Nurmi set out to show he had lost nothing of his old pale fire. In October, 1928, he ran 11 miles, 1,648 yards in one hour, in the course of which effort he also sailed through 10 miles in 50:15.0. Then he went to the United States to race on the indoor circuit again. Undoubtedly, Nurmi traveled to all the American cities on his route "via Helsinki."

Once again, Nurmi conquered everywhere he went in North America, with one stellar exception: the Wanamaker Mile at the Millrose Games, the premier event of the most prominent indoor track meet in the world. American Ray Conger, who'd taken over from Lloyd Hahn as the nation's top miler, nabbed Nurmi on the final lap and—enthusiastically urged on by the manic, partisan crowd—blasted through to a 4:17.4 clocking, some 8 yards ahead of the Olympic great. The live band present in the arena immediately launched into a lusty rendition of John Philip Sousa's "Stars and Stripes Forever," and the crowd immediately launched themselves into a reasonable imitation of excited simian behavior. Both Nurmi and Conger went on to further personal victories. Conger was undefeated in the mile from 1929–1930 and 1930–1931. Nurmi continued to beat the other runners in Finland consistently, to smash Shrubb's 6-mile record, and finally to run under 9 minutes (just: by ½-second) for 3K outdoors. Both athletes retired the same year, 1932, but for very different reasons.

Finland sent two swift representatives to Boston in 1929. Willie Kyronen and Karl Koski were running to win the Marathon, but Johnny C. Miles was back in Beantown and back in form after dropping out of the 1927 race at 5 miles. The Ontario native nailed down his second B.A.A. victory after besting "Whitey" Michelson in a 10-mile toe-dance 'tween Wellesley and Coolidge Corner. Miles surged hard at the Brookline landmark, breaking Michelson and, fortunately, also breaking away from the fast-closing Finnish duo. Miles posted a 2:33:08 time to take nearly 4 minutes off DeMar's previous best.

Koski (2:35:26) and Kyronen (2:35:44) also ran in under Mr. DeMarathon's distance delimitation.

The great DeMar came back in 1930, nearly 42 years old, to claim his seventh and final Boston Marathon win. DeMar's record number of wins constitutes one of the most impressive performances in distance-running history and is a record that will almost certainly never be surpassed or even equalled. DeMar himself equalled and then surpassed Hans Oldag of Buffalo that Patriot's Day in 1930. He caught Oldag going into Newton Lower Falls, then marched away from him up the famed hills. On course-record pace up until 21 miles, Clarence wilted from the heat and humidity and checked into Exeter Street with "only" a personal record of 2:34:48. The two Finns again finished second and third, but in reverse order from 1929, Kyronen whipping Koski by nearly 2 minutes with a 2:36:27 marathon run.

DeMar failed to figure in the front of the 1931 Boston classic, but, precisely because of his "backrunning," he helped to dictate the eventual winner. Ever-popular, ever-loving (the father of four children) Hinky Henigan finally won the Boston Marathon in his tenth effort (and only his second finish). Henigan came to the Hopkinton line determined to win or bust. So did Finland's Karl Koski. Henigan and Koski offered a study in contrasts. Henigan sometimes ran emotionally, therefore, recklessly. Koski hewed true to the Finnish tradition of a schedule for everything and everything on schedule. The Finn reckoned that the man with the best schedule in the Boston Marathon was Clarence DeMar. It wasn't DeMar's day, and Koski lost time and distance hanging on Clarence's iron shoulders while Henigan and Dave Komonen dueled up front. Hinky was long gone by the time Koski stopped pacing off DeMar, and local Medford-man Henigan finally pinned down the prize that for so long had pranced pitilessly away from him: first place in the Boston Marathon in 2:46:45. Koski finished third behind second-place Fred Ward, Komonen was fourth, and DeMar rounded out the first five.

Los Angeles was the host city for the 1932 Olympic Games, but national pride failed to pull the Americans through to yet another Boston Marathon victory that year. Germany's Paul de Bruyn beat Hinky Henigan and came within an ace of taking away John Miles's course record by running 2:33:36 on the road from Hopkinton to the Hub City.

If the B.A.A. Marathon disappointed Americans, the Los Angeles Olympic Marathon promised more than ample compensation for thrill-seeking spectators. Paavo Nurmi was going to run the marathon. It was the only distance race in the Games in which he had not yet claimed his gold medal. Nurmi's hero, Hannes Kolehmainen, boasted a full set of distance medals; Paavo Nurmi would not be satisfied with an incomplete set for himself. Word drifted across the Atlantic of Nurmi's marathon training. Early in 1932 the twin-hearted Nurmi ran a 40.2-kilometer road race in his homeland in 2:22:03.8. Nurmi averaged 5:41.23 per mile for the race. By comparison, John C. Miles's Boston Marathon record constituted an average pace of

5:51 per mile, and Hannes Kolehmainen's Olympic Marathon record reduced to a 5:48-per-mile average. None doubted Nurmi possessed the endurance to keep his pace through the full 26.2-mile distance. Distance athletes began ceding the 1932 Olympic Marathon to the Finland Flash. Although America looked strong in the shorter distances at the 1932 IC4A Championships (which doubled as a U.S. Olympic Trials—the first and only time the meet was held on the west coast, to prepare athletes for the Los Angeles climate), no long-distance talent emerged to challenge Nurmi.

The politics of amateurism challenged Nurmi instead. They beat him. Nurmi journeyed with his team from Helsinki to Los Angeles only to discover he had been stripped of his amateur status by the International Amateur Athletic Federation (IAAF) for all those other trips he had made "via Helsinki." The IAAF never made public the reason for Nurmi's disqualification, stating only that they had "good and sufficient grounds" for believing him to have received excessive expense money. In fact, they had a cancelled check from one of Nurmi's American race promoters. Nurmi continued to race for three more years in Finland, which understandably refused to recognize the IAAF ban, but his Olympic career was finished. The IAAF ruling may have been a blessing in disguise to the Nurmi record. Peerless Paavo came to Los Angeles an injured athlete. Much later in life he revealed that he suffered such a bad case of Achilles tendonitis he could not possibly have completed a marathon that 1932 July. Let down by both his body and the international agency charged with looking after his best athletic interests, Paavo Nurmi retired gracefully if not uncontroversially from international competition never having lost any Olympic final—save only his first—he intended to win. (Nurmi proved equally tenacious and sagacious in his post-athletic career. He became a highly successful businessman as both a landlord with large holdings and proprietor of a sporting goods store.)

The greatest distance runner of his era, and perhaps the most eminent mileage-man of any period, Paavo is today remembered by the annual *Runner's World* magazine Nurmi Award, given to the man and woman who most closely replicate the Finn's fanaticism for always finishing whatever he started. His disqualification left the sport riddled with questionable distance victories for years.

IV

Scientific Running

1932–1939

In a story on the 1932 Los Angeles Olympics, the *New York Daily News* reported that "This track is the fastest in the world. All of the athletes say that they have never encountered one like it. It is like running on a springboard." While the ancient Greeks held their Olympic races on shifting sand in a deliberate effort to hinder athletes, the track meet organizers in the 1930s initiated serious efforts toward *helping* athletes establish world records. Walter George and Paavo Nurmi, each in his own way, had demonstrated that a gifted but scientifically trained athlete would invariably whip a gifted but sporadically trained athlete. Both George's and Nurmi's training was idiosyncratic, though. Few or no other athletes contemporary with them attempted to profit from their training principles. The athletes of George's day simply put little stock in hard training. They felt too much training injured an athlete instead of improving him or her. The athletes of Nurmi's day were probably more open-minded, but Nurmi refused to discuss his training methods. The era of great coaches, supported in many cases by largess from the political state, is the era examined by this chapter.

In terms of physical plant alone, the Los Angeles Games did the U.S.A. proud. They introduced the first Olympic Village, providing the athletes a communal retreat from the rigors of competition and the demands of press and fans. Just as important, perhaps even most important, the Olympic Vil-

Coach Bill Bowerman designed both the basic training program that put the "Ducks" of the University of Oregon track team at the pinnacle of college track and field and the famous waffle-soled running shoes that cushioned millions of runners in the 1970s. (Photograph courtesy of the University of Oregon.)

Arthur Lydiard, the coach who was synonymous with distance running in Australia and New Zealand in the 1960s and 70s, poses with one of his athletes, three-time Olympic gold medalist Peter Snell. (Photograph courtesy of The Boston Herald American.)

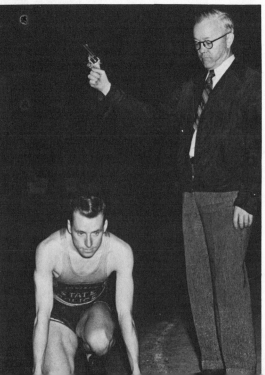

Coach E. C. "Billy" Hayes, America's first outstanding long-distance track coach, prepares to send Don Lash, America's first stellar collegiate long-distance runner, off on a 2-mile race. (Photograph courtesy of Indiana University.)

lage encouraged socializing between athletes from all teams of all nations. The Village therefore constituted a great stride toward achieving the non-nationalistic ideal of the Olympic movement. Housing all athletes in close but comfortable quarters promoted fraternity and understanding among them. The Olympic Village was a concrete homage to the fact that an athlete sufficiently superlative to ascend to Olympus has transcended citizenship in a mere state and has entered citizenship in a universal athletic discipline.

The Olympic Village comprised 550 housing units, 40 different ethnic kitchens, 1 hospital, 1 library, and 1 post office situated on 321 acres in Baldwin Hills outside of Los Angeles. The $2.5 million raised by California and Los Angeles to set up the Olympic facilities also paid for expanding the Los Angeles Coliseum into a 105,000-seat Olympic Stadium as well as for fitting the "fastest track in the world" inside the arena. Other unusually outstanding amenities provided included a country club, tennis courts, roque courts, a bowling green, an art museum, a rifle range, rowing course, a 10,000-seat auditorium and a 12,000-seat swimming stadium. Olympic facilities were becoming more refined, more complete, and—like the athletes themselves—more professional.

The only minor step backward from Olympic tradition came with the Opening Ceremonies on July 30, 1932. Ordinarily, the Head of State for the Olympic host city declares the Games open, but President Herbert Hoover, in true misguided fashion, decided it was more important for him to campaign than to open the Olympics. Vice-President Charles Curtis stood in for Hoover, and no one complained about the switch. In fact, the Opening Ceremonies offered at least one athlete the opportunity to vindicate the Olympic ideal of athletic brotherhood and sportspersonship: Britain's Lord Burghley, a hurdler, heard that Morgan Taylor, an American rival whom Burghley would be meeting in competition the following day, was marching with the U.S. team in the Ceremonies and even carrying the American flag. Taylor's action was unusual because athletes scheduled to compete the day after the Opening Ceremonies are excused from the frivolities so they may rest. Burghley therefore marched with the British team so as not to take unfair advantage of Taylor.

Perfect weather conditions throughout the Games enabled fan and athlete alike to concentrate solely on the competition, and several events and/or athletes produced very concentrated competition. Arguably the most sizzling clash of champions came in the event known as "The Killer"—the 400-meter run.

The 400 is either the longest sprint or the shortest distance race . . . as far as a spectator is concerned. To an athlete who is lunging out of the final turn, muscles wracked with lactic acid, mouth gulping huge draughts of air but delivering no appreciable oxygen to the body, there is no question about where The Killer belongs: It is the longest distance race. When Bill Carr and

Ben Eastman went upside each other's head in the 1932 L.A. finals, they crammed as much excitement into the race as goes into most marathons.

Carr and Eastman were bitter collegiate rivals. The short, swarthy Carr ran for the University of Pennsylvania. The tall, fair Eastman ran for Stanford; he also held the world's record in the 440-yard run, although he was considered an 800-meter specialist.

Eastman's coach, Cliff Templeton, steered his protégé toward the Olympic 400. Templeton was mad that Carr had beaten Eastman at both the IC4As and the Olympic Team Trials. Whereas the Finns would have insisted each athlete compete in only one event (or at least let his competitor win in "his" event), the hardheaded Yanks set two top middle-distance men to grinding each other up in only one race. (Such extravagance can be forgiven with benefit of historical hindsight. The U.S. grabbed eleven gold medals in 1932, making up for the disappointing 1928 team.)

Conditioned as an 800-meter man, Eastman and his coach reckoned he had more endurance than 400-meter specialist Carr; therefore, Eastman's best strategy would be to scream out of the hole when the gun went off, crush Carr with superior strength, then hold on and pray until the finish. It almost worked. Eastman darted through the first 200 meters in 21.7 seconds. (Gum-chewing Eddie Tolan of the U.S.A. took the 200-meter title in the same Games with a 21.2 clocking; Eastman's time was faster than all but two previous Olympic 200-meter finals.) Going down the backstretch, Eastman had a clear lead over Carr. Then Carr started to ramble. He used the same strategy on Eastman that he always had: Coming out of the far turn, he drew level with the flying but sagging westerner. Then Carr put the hammer down hard and walked away from his California rival, hitting the worsted in 46.2, with Eastman 0.2 seconds in arrears. Both men slid under the Olympic record of 47.6, and Carr finally beat Eastman's world mark of 46.4.

Although the gallery wouldn't know until the race was over whether Carr or Eastman would emerge triumphant in the 400, none doubted that an American would win the event. By the same token, almost no one doubted the Finns would win any of the long-distance track foot races. One of the few "doubting Thomases" was Poland's 10,000-meter specialist, Janusz Kusocinski, and it turned out he was right.

True to form, the Finns strove to turn the 10K race into a team effort. Lauri Virtanen and steeplechase great Volmari Iso-Hollo showed the blue cross of Finland in the one and two positions for the first 6400 meters . . . but Kusocinski lay third, right on their heels. After 6.4 kilometers, Virtanen could not maintain the pace and began gently to fall back. The Pole moved up onto Iso-Hollo's bustling tail, drawing even with the charging runner. Kusocinski then pulled ahead of the astonished Finn, who responded in kind. As often happens in a distance event, an unspoken truce of sorts settled on the two primary combatants, and they shared the pace silently for several more laps. At 8,000 meters Iso-Hollo unleashed a decisive bid for the lead;

Kusocinski went with him, but did not pass the flying Finn—not until the last lap, at which time he sailed past the steeplechaser on the backstretch and ran away from him all the way to the tape and an Olympic 10K record of 30:11.4.

The Finns were primed to revenge themselves in the 5,000 meters. Lauri Lehtinen and, once again, Lauri Virtanen poised to pound any Poles or other breed of interloper into potash beneath their flashing spikes. Once again, they almost pulled it off. Certainly they never put much stock in an American challenge in the event. The U.S.A. produced great sprinters, and there was that yearly marathon in Boston, but the Americans were the basic weak sisters of the long-distance races held on the track. America's Ralph Hill of the University of Oregon was nobody's sister, however, and he cut the Finnish daisy chain in half right from the gun. Lehtinen took the lead and Finland's perennial second-string-man Virtanen sandwiched Hill between himself and his teammate. Thus they ran, Hill the filling in a Finnish Oreo, until 1½ laps from home, when Lehtinen and Hill spurted and Virtanen once again faded. The Los Angeles fans, as the saying goes, "went bananas." Here was the U.S.A. straining cheek-by-jowl in a distance race with mighty Finland! Alas, try as Hill might, he could not edge past the lashing Lehtinen, who seemed to occupy every lane of the track every time the Oregonian strove to shoot by. The two athletes crossed the line in an excellent impersonation of Siamese twins, both of them checking in with an Olympic record of 14:30 flat, albeit exactly 13 seconds slower than Lehtinen's world record for the 5K.

The crowd held its collective breath and, in about as much time as it took for the runners to complete the race, the judges rendered their decision: They handed it to Lehtinen. Not surprisingly, this was not a popular decision in Los Angeles, but was at least a judgment of unimpeachable impartiality. Just as important, as far as American honor was concerned, the U.S. had clearly shown it could run with the Finns—and there was always next time.

In an Olympics fraught with surprising victories, the victor in the 1500 meters possibly created the most sensation of all. America's running legend, Glenn Cunningham, was among the star-studded field. So was 1928 gold-medalist Harri Larva and his Finnish teammates Eino Purje and Matti Loumanen. Canada contributed Phil Edwards; Sweden sent fleet Erik Ny, and Oxfordman Jack Lovelock represented his New Zealand homeland. The several other bodies also at the line were not accorded even a chance for the medals.

As in the 10,000 meters, the field initially ran true to expectations. Cunningham and Edwards took the pack out at a brisk tempo, then gradually pulled away from it. Going into the final lap the duo held a lead of some 10 meters over the balance of the field. Some of the backmarkers put on the expected rush this lap: Lovelock, who had been holding back waiting for Cunningham and Edwards to burn out, started his finishing kick from 400 meters out. Jerry Cornes, running for Great Britain and Luigi Becalli, running for Italy, went along with Lovelock. Everyone else simply straggled along, totally out of it. Although no one country dominated, it seemed certain the Anglo-Saxons were about to take home three medals. Then, unheralded, unsung, untiring Luigi Beccali ran away from the whole lot, setting an Olympic record of 3:51.2, a few steps ahead of Cornes and more than a few ahead of a sagging Edwards. Cunningham finished fourth.

It seemed an Olympics destined to humble the heirs-apparent to the various gold medals, but one athlete finally emerged to dominate the Games. Her name was Mildred Didrikson, an 18-year-old Texas woman who preferred to be called "Babe" and whose major ambition was "to be the greatest athlete that ever lived." She pretty much achieved her goal: When America's sportswriters elected Jim Thorpe the greatest male athlete of the first half of the twentieth century, they also voted Babe as the preeminent female athlete.

Didrikson stood 5'4" and weighed 110 pounds, and she performed as if she had the muscles of an ant her size. She intended to break world records. Informed she was restricted by Olympic regulations to competing in only three events, she complained, "I'd break 'em all if they'd let me." In her first event, the javelin throw, Babe saw a small flag down on the ground far out on the javelin field. She asked what the flag was. "It marks the distance for the world record in this event," came the answer. Babe smiled and let fly. On her first toss, the spear smote the ground 14 feet beyond the flag. She took the gold with a 143'4" hurl. Next Didrikson took on the 80-meter hurdles. She won and set her second world record of the Games: 11.7 seconds. Next, the high jump. Alas, Didrikson only equalled the world record in this one, leaping 5'5" into the air and over a wobbly little bar. She had to settle for a silver medal, for America's Jean Shiley tied Babe's jump. In the jump-off, both athletes cleared the 5:5 height, but the judges ruled Didrikson's feet were not the first part of her anatomy to pass over the bar (an arcane, but obviously enforced, rule in those days), so they handed the gold to Shiley.

It was Babe's first and last Olympics. She went on, as Babe Zaharias, to make the women's All-American basketball team three times, then turned pro—pro golfer, that is, and won seventeen consecutive golf tournies.

The American women took the 400-meter relay in 47-flat, and a woman living and competing in America, but running for her native Poland, claimed the 100-meter dash in 11.9. Her name was Stanislawa Walasiewicz, but she was known in the U.S. as Stella Walsh. Only the second woman in history to run under 12 seconds for the event, Walasiewicz ran 11.9 in each of her three Olympic races (two qualifying heats and the final), a consistency Nurmi must have respected.

As always, the marathon closed the Olympic program. It turned out to be an Olympics full of proud victory predictions. Kusocinski and Didrikson both promised victory, and both came through. Argentina's Juan Carlos Zabala did the same in the marathon, and he broke the Olympic record set by the immortal Kolehmainen in the process, running 2:31:36 for the 26.2 miles.

Englishman Sam Ferris followed 20 seconds back. In fact, the first four finishers climaxed within 1:05 of the winner, and twenty out of twenty-eight starters completed the full distance. They loved that California weather!

The Olympics were rolled up and put away for another four years, but athletic life went on. Not every great athlete in the world competed at Los Angeles. Nurmi, of course, was barred from international amateur competition. The American team was also poorer because the great U.S. miler, Gene Venzke, had missed making the Olympic Team. Venzke's nickname was "The Picture Runner," not because he was a film star but because he ran with perfect, flowing form. Why he didn't make the team remains a mystery. He started off 1932 with a world indoor record of 4:11.2 in the fabled Wanamaker Mile at the Millrose Games. The previous record (4:12) was held by Nurmi and Ray. The time stood as the third fastest mile in history, indoors, outdoors, or straight down a mountain. Later that indoor season, at the New York A.C. meets' Baxter Mile, Venzke let loose a 4:10-point-zip on the boards. At New York's Knights of Columbus ("KC") indoor meet, Venzke turned in a 3:53.4 1500-meter run that topped every Olympic 1500 time through 1928. Despite these achievements, Venzke still didn't make the Olympic team.

An outstanding American who made the Olympic team but who, like Venzke, made more of a name for himself in domestic competition was Joe McCluskey. Joe finished third in the steeplechase final at Los Angeles, although he was the unquestioned king of the AAU indoor steeple in the States, claiming the championship 8 times between 1932 and 1941. McCluskey held the world records for the indoor steeplechase at both 2 miles (9:46.8) and 3,000 meters (8:50.0).

While McCluskey was linked to an event, the steeplechase, Princeton miler Bill Bonthron was linked to another great runner, the incomparable Glenn Cunningham; but Bonthron was an outstanding runner in his own right. One of Bonthron's problems in gaining personal fame was his team-playing attitude. An excellent miler with a deadly finishing kick, Bouncing Bill preferred to run the longer distances and various relay legs for his beloved Princeton. He won the bitterly contested Princeton-Yale meets for the Tigers almost singlefootedly in 1932 and 1933, and was the major contributor to Princeton's championship AAU and IC4A distance relay teams in 1933. Bonthron finished second in a mile race with Olympian Jack Lovelock in 1933. Kiwi Lovelock merely set a world record of 4:07.6 staying ahead of the hard-kicking Princetonman, and Bonthron perforce contented himself with an American mile mark of 4:08.7.

Runners such as Bonthron possessed great physical gifts, but they possessed national and world records because they honed those gifts. Much of this athletic steel was tempered in the heat of top-notch competition; the always competing Venzke exemplified this approach to perfection. Good coaching, however, was becoming ever more important during the 1930s. Possibly the finest American coach of the period was Coach E. C. "Billy" Hayes of Indiana

University. Aware that even the sprints, such as The Killer 400 meters, placed heavy demands on an athlete's aerobic capacity, Coach Hayes introduced the idea of putting collegiate sprinters and middle-distance runners on a long-distance athlete's high-mileage base. The idea was analogous to the great distance runners relying on walking as a fundamental part of their training program. An athlete can keep up highly intensive physical exertion far longer if he or she has taken prudent time to build the ability to achieve such effort. Running while in oxygen debt is vastly destructive to the body. The more body there is to destroy, the longer the athlete can hold together before smooching the cinders. Coach Hayes's approach to conditioning was only a slight paraphrase of the old saying, "What goes up must come down." The longer a runner took to build to peak condition, the longer he would take to be torn back down by the stress of competition.

It sounded like a great theory. Coach Hayes provided the most concrete validation conceivable: the Indiana runners. Take the example of Charles Hornbostel. Most people called him Chuck, but everybody called him "fast." Like Bonthron, Hornbostel ran with a relay team's baton as if it were a lighted dynamite stick with a thumbnail-sized fuse. No slouch as a solo artist, Hornbostel swept away from the field in the 1933 New York A.C. indoor meet half-mile, the first of a four-in-a-row NYAC 880 winning streak for the Indiana boardman. He went on to equal Lloyd Hahn's 2:12.8 1000-yard indoor record in the 1934 Millrose Games and to establish a world's record of 1:11.3 for the 600-yard run in 1935. Hornbostel, Don Lash, and Fred Wilt rightly demonstrated Coach Hayes belief that runners could achieve speed by doing distance work.

In the 1933 Boston Marathon, a runner demonstrated that a "speed" athlete could easily run long distances. Leslie Pawson, a good friend of the ageless John A. Kelley, specialized in 2-mile and 10-mile races, but, that windy Patriots' Day, he set a course record, 2:31:01, in his charge to the Hub City. After he literally "breezed" in nearly 5½ minutes ahead of Canadian Dave Komonen, Pawson said: "I don't know how many minutes the head wind cost me, but you'll someday see this course run in 2:24." He wasn't quite right. The fastest time for the course Pawson ran was eventually 2:25-and-a-lot-of-change. Then road construction inadvertently shortened the route. It would not be until 1957 and the victory of the B.A.A.'s own John J. Kelley that the 26.2-mile Boston Marathon would be run in 2:24 or under.

It would not be until 1954 that the 4-minute barrier for the mile would be broken, either, but legend had it that Glenn Cunningham, the best miler in all of Kansas, had run a sub-4 mile in a meet in Chicago. The legend also said Cunningham's coach told him not to breathe a word of it to a living soul, "'cause nobody'd believe it." As with Paavo Nurmi's sub-30 ten-kilometer fable, the fact that such a tale attached to Cunningham indicates how prodigious he was. Considering that Cunningham almost had his legs amputated when they were hideously charred in a schoolhouse fire while he was still a

Les Pawson, the man who brought speed to marathon running, first claimed the Boston Marathon in 1933; he also won it in 1938 and 1941, and finished in the top 10 a total of eight times during his career. The photo shows him on his way to victory in the 1933 United Shoe Machinery Road Race, held on August 22 that year. (Photograph from the authors' collection.)

lad (and that the circulation in his legs remained impaired the rest of his life), the Kansan's miling talent must rank with such stratospheric four-lapmen as Herb Elliott and Jim Ryun.

Cunningham grabbed the national spotlight at the 1933 Millrose Games, but it was at the NCAA outdoor meet that spring that he grabbed the American mile record with a 4:09.8 clocking. He also tangled with Chuck Hornbostel in the NCAA championship half-mile, and lost to the Hayes-coached middle-distance specialist by about 1 foot; they were both timed at 1:50.9, a meet record and the second-fastest ever recorded for an American (let alone for two of them simultaneously). Cunningham finally took Hornbostel's measure in the AAU meet later in 1933, when they met in an 800-meter showdown taken by the Kansan in 1:51.8. Then Cunningham turned around and won the 1500 AAU championship from Gene Venzke in 3:52.3, becoming the first athlete since Chesty Ray in 1919 to pull off the 800/1500 "double" at the AAUs.

Glenn didn't slacken the pace in 1934. Track meet promoters quickly realized a match-up mile between Cunningham and Bill Bonthron would pack stadium seats with rabid throngs unseen since the days of Walter George and P. William Cummings. The first Cunningham/Bonthron confrontation came in the New York A.C.'s indoor Baxter Mile at Madison Square Garden on February 17, 1934. The press played the event as if it were a prizewinning sturgeon on a fishing line. The "hype" worked, for the anticipated ravening mob showed up and New York's Finest had to mount their horses to jockey the overflow-crowd back from the Garden's doors.

Excitement escalated as Cunningham and Bonthron hit the track early in the evening for their warm-up routines. Cunningham's routine began with a series of vigorous, almost grotesque, calisthenics. The Kansan's routine de-

Glenn Cunningham defeats Gene Venzke in the 1938 Penn Relays mile footrace. Venzke, the "Picture Runner," was esteemed for his excellent running form, but "Galloping Glenn" Cunningham was loved by track fans of the era for a flamboyance and courage that made him distance running's answer to Babe Ruth. (Photograph from the authors' collection.)

rived not from hyperactivity but from practical necessity. He needed far more warm up than any of his peers in order to get the circulation going in his tattered legs. The reception the Garden crowd accorded Bonthron and Cunningham so overwhelmed the normal flow of meet events that the finals for the 60-yard dash had to be delayed until the clamor subsided.

Finally it was race time. A "rabbit" took the pack through the first half-mile slightly under 2:14. At the end of the sixth lap of the 11-lapper, the powerful (5′9″, 165 pounds) Cunningham went into the lead with Bonthron trailing him as a tail does a comet . . . and so did unheralded but talented Gene Venzke who had moved from last to third place in 6 laps, almost unnoticed.

Knowing he couldn't match Bonthron's finishing kick for all the corn in Kansas, Cunningham strove mightily to burn the bite out of the "Pride of Princeton"'s legs. Had he surged earlier and more often, it might've worked; but Bonthron hung with Cunningham and, coming off the last bend, drew ever nearer to him, passing him about 2 centimeters in front of the tape. Bonthron hit the string in 4:14.0, meaning a 2-minute-flat half-mile for the two great runners (Cunningham received the same time as Bonthron), and Venzke came in perhaps 6 feet behind the dueling duo to claim an excellent third.

For the second week in a row the New York Mounted Police have to ticket ticketless track fans lusting for a view of the rematch between America's mile kings, Glenn Cunningham and Bill Bonthron, at the AAU Indoor Championships Meet. It is to be a metric mile, a distance nearly 370 feet shorter than an English mile; in short, a race made for a kicker like Bonthron, not an enduring plodder such as Cunningham.

Cunningham, ironically, goes down into a sprinter's stance awaiting the gun, while whippet-runner Bonthron simply bends forward slightly. BAF!, goes Johnny McHugh's pistol. Scrabble-scrabble-scrabble-scrabble-thudda-thudda-thud-thud-thud, go the runners' feet as they maneuver for balance and position in the first lap.

It's a replay of the Baxter Mile from last week. Cunningham paces off a "rabbit" for the first six laps, then goes into the lead—but, waitaminute, it's not Bonthron on his tail, it's Venzke! The Picture Runner's in between the Running Scar and the Pride of Princeton. Do the fans love it! Bonthron's falling back and back, but Venzke's imitating Elmer's Glue. Two laps from the end the glue breaks—and Venzke steals the lead! Glenn Cunningham takes it right back and is locomoting down the front straight as if Casey Jones had him by the ears. Bonthron rolls himself into a ball of speed and rumbles past Venzke and, improbably, catches Cunningham at the tape—ALMOST. This time, the Bear holds off the Tiger by the width of a newborn's whisker; they both get a 3:52.2 clocking, which just happens to be a world record, and Gene Venzke ambles home third in 3:52.5.

The 1934 B.A.A. Marathon was won by a man in whose shoes no one else could possibly have been: Ontario's Dave Komonen (who finished second to the speedy Leslie Pawson the previous year) crossed the line victorious in 2:32:53 while wearing a pair of racing flats he'd made himself. A cobbler by trade, Komonen duked it out with Johnny Kelley until the last 5 miles when the Finnish-born Komonen ran away with the race. Komonen became one of an extremely elite handful of marathoners to intervene in the Kelley-Pawson-Cote-Brown slug-outs that dominated the Boston Marathon between 1933 and 1948.

It was a hot spring and summer for miling in the U.S.A. Glenn Cunningham established yet another indoor mile record, 4:08.4, at the New York Knights of Columbus meet, but without pressure from Bill Bonthron. Cunningham and Bonthron clashed three more times before the leaves turned. Cunningham beat Bouncing Bill on the latter's home turf at the very first Princeton Invitational Meet. The quick Kansan set a world mile record of 4:06.7 while running with Bonthron and Venzke at his back and a lot of bandages on his injured left ankle. To sweeten his victory, he beat Bonthron by 40 yards.

Bonthron ran 4:08.9 for the mile the following week at the NCAAs in L.A.'s Olympic Stadium, but it was good enough to vanquish Kansan Cunningham. That meant each mile star had two victories over the other. There was one more race, the AAU championship 1500 at Milwaukee. Running from behind, as always, the pouncing Princetonian nipped the fleeing Cunningham at the wire in the 100-degree heat and recorded 3:48.8 for his efforts, a world 1500 mark.

Athletes establish records, only to see them broken by their peers. A mile record more than two years old seems carved in granite. Starting around 1934 (the records are unfortunately conflicting and confusing), Germany's Rudolph Harbig began a training program that, five years later, would result in two of the longest-lived records in track history. Harbig's records will be discussed at the proper time; but his training exemplified the new scientific methods beginning to permeate distance coaching. Harbig's coaches were Drs. Woldemar Gerschler and Hans Reindell, two exercise physiologists who trained their athlete for the glory of science and the Fatherland.

Harbig's pulse was 143; he had 10 seconds of rest left before launching into his third 23-second 200-meter run of the workout. He had two more 200s to run after this one. Harbig shoved the dreadful thought away, just as he forbade himself to recall what it had been like to run as a normal human being. GO! Harbig ran forward, entered the noble world of searing pain. All he could see was the track unfolding under his toes. His chest was a cell of phlegm; mucous poured from his nostrils, spittle ran from both corners of his mouth. STOP! Rest while jogging for 45 seconds. One more, and then one after that, then a simple 2-mile warmdown. Any superman could do it; any true Aryan would laugh at it. He would run two more hard intervals, then jog 2 miles, and survive, in fact, thrive. Science assured him he would.

Gerschler's and Reindell's interval training methods bear only casual resemblance to the interval training practiced in 1981. The doctors would refine the technology further. In the 1930s, Harbig *walked* between his hard track repetitions. By the 1950s, Gerschler had learned it is the "recovery" interval phase that strengthens the heart, *not* the flat-out "exertion" phase (which does strengthen the *will*, however). Consequently, significantly more benefits accrue from interval training if the runner keeps moving at a pretty good clip in between sprints. Harbig walked, though, and normally for about 5 minutes in between his hard 200-meter repetitions; he would jog for 5 minutes between some of his 300-meter repeats. Yet Harbig's training was easy compared to the 1980's middle-distance stars. He often trained only three or four days per week, and frequently only one of those days was dedicated to track workouts. The rest of the time Harbig ran over hill and dale, through mud and under low branches, as has virtually every other distance ace before or after him. The early, crude approach to interval training constituted an enormously important moment in the history of distance running because it was a method easily available to the great mass of runners and coaches. Nurmi, probably the first truly scientific runner of the modern era, kept his mouth shut. Herr doktor Gerschler couldn't wait to tell the world about his discoveries. The world received them gladly. So did the Third Reich.

1935 was a good year for Johnny Kelley. The man whose name has since become a symbol of the race finally claimed the Boston Marathon in 2:32:07. He ran the first 12 miles with Dave Komonen, of whose heels Kel' had seen much the previous April in Boston. Both Kelley and Komonen waited for early leader Tony Paskell to die, which he obligingly did, and Kelley sailed into the lead a mile later while Canadian Komonen dropped out. (Komonen got out of town before the marathon ended, but was so certain Kelley would win it he left Old John a note of congratulations before returning to Ontario.) From there on, Kelley's only competition was his own stomach: the glucose tablets he had been eating during the race for strength started to eat *him* instead. One mile from home, Old John "fingered" the problem, cleared out his stomach, and won. Not only had he bested Komonen, he had (probably unknowingly) triumphed over an athlete who would also eventually go into the legend books: Ellison M. "Tarzan" Brown, a Narragansett Indian running his first marathon race, and in a pair of patchwork shorts and singlet sewn together by his mom.

The Yonkers Marathon had lain dormant since 1917. The Chippewa Athletic Club decided to awaken it in 1935, and Kelley and the USOC were both glad the club did: the USOC, because the race served as a qualifying trial for the U.S. Olympic Marathon Team; Kelley, because he won it in 2:38. Leslie Pawson (2:40) and Mel Porter (2:40) also won a free trip to Berlin that November 28, while 120 other runners did not, and 10,000 spectators cheered wildly.

Johnny Kelley, who in later years earned the nickname "Old John" (partly to honor his tenacity and partly to distinguish him from John J. Kelley, another Boston Marathon champion), ran his first B.A.A. Marathon in 1928 at age 21, one month after running his first marathon ever, in Rhode Island. He finished seventeenth in the Pawtucket-to-Woonsocket trek, but dropped out of the 1928 Boston Marathon after approximately 24 miles (at Coolidge Corner, to be exact). Kelley decided then and there to stick to 6-milers and 10-milers and to leave the Marathon to the saps who ran every spring, as the uncreative local sportswriters put it. One of the top American road runners of the twentieth century, Kelley ran in literally hundreds of races (by the end of 1980, he had run 1,365 races and was still piling it on). Unlike his European and American track counterparts, Kelley never made a dime under the table, and—like every other American road runner of the day—had no idea how to train scientifically. As Old John put it: "We had no set program at all. We'd just go out and run easy. We didn't know anything about intervals or speedwork. We would run a race at Thanksgiving and then not run again until New Year's." Considering that the Kohlemainen brothers had traveled to the U.S. early in the century to learn the training secrets of American pro runners, it would seem as though that tradition had not been passed along to pure American road-running amateurs only two decades later.

Glenn Cunningham continued his winning ways in 1936. Like Harbig, the hulking Kansan drank neither alcoholic nor caffeinated draughts, nor did he smoke. Historians estimate Glenn ran over 10,000 miles during his career, much of that mileage aimed at restoring his legs' circulation. Like Old John Kelley and Alfred Shrubb, Cunningham understood the true meaning of the sport; he said: "People can't understand why a man runs. They don't see any sport in it, argue that it lacks the sight-thrill of body contact, the color of rough conflict; yet the conflict is there, more raw and challenging than any man versus competition. In track it is man against himself, the cruelest of all opponents." Cunningham's first victory of 1936 came in a race ballyhooed as one of those "mile of the century" meetings, but which went into the history books as "the typographical error mile."

It was the NYKC meet at Madison Square Garden. There were 16,000 drooling fans in the stands, every manjack of them expecting to see a world record for the mile—certainly for an indoor, 11-lap mile, and possibly an absolute record. The field was as elite as elite could be: only three runners, each one of them a champion. There was Joe Mangan, who had won the 1936 Wanamaker Mile, soundly beating the other two fellows who were in the "Casey" race. There was Gene Venzke, who had taken the 1936 Baxter Mile and the indoor 1500-meter record with a 3:49.9 clocking at the AAU champs. Finally, there was Cunningham, who was lagging behind Venzke and Mangan that season much more than he desired. To most track fans, it must have sounded like the perfect field, but a sophisticated track strategist might have anticipated what would actually result from the meeting.

What resulted was that nobody wanted to take the lead and get sniped at from the rear. It was like an Olympic final. Nobody really cared about the time; everybody was going for the win and the win alone. The three athletes circulated the track in a remarkable imitation of Alphonse and Gaston: "After you, my good sir." "Oh, no, after *you*." The split at the quarter-mile was 1:13.2. The split at the half was 2:34. Men can walk that fast, and the hooting crowd knew it. Finally Venzke jumped into the lead in the middle of the eighth lap and it started to look like a genuine footrace. Two laps later Cunningham nailed Venzke, rose up on his tippytoes, and arrowed for the finish. He won by about two steps in 4:46.8, with Venzke claiming second spot by one foot over Mangan. The time was so absurdly slow that people reading the result in the morning paper assumed the time was a typographical error, hence the name by which the event is remembered.

The colorful tradition of the Boston Marathon was enriched significantly by the 1936 winner—"Tarzan" Brown. Veteran Boston Marathon reporter Jerry Nason called Brown "perhaps the finest physical specimen to ever win [sic] the event." "Tarzan" demonstrated the quality of his physique from the start. There are always a few "crazies" who grab the lead and what glory they can for a few hundred feet at the start of the Boston Marathon every year; but every year they are always overhauled within the first mile by the serious, trained athletes. Brown took off like a serious "crazy," earning himself yet another soubriquet: "Chief Crazy Horse." Unlike less gifted maniacs, Brown held onto the lead. He was 600 yards ahead at 6 miles and 900 yards ahead at 16 miles, the foot of the Newton hills. "Tarzan" ran so far ahead of the gasping pack that the gentlemen of the press followed the bunched pack for 5 miles, thinking the leader must be among them.

One runner among that pack was Johnny Kelley, and thus was another Boston legend born. Old John was going to give it the old (Boston) college

Ellison M. "Tarzan" Brown cruises through Natick on his way to victory in the 1936 Boston Marathon. (Photograph from the authors' collection.)

try. Trailing by 900 yards at the foot of the dastardly series of hills, Kelley amazingly caught Brown heading up the last of the hills to, well, to Boston College. Always sporting, Kelley patted Brown on the back in a gesture of admiration and encouragement as he pulled out to pass the sagging "Tarzan." It was a friendly gesture, but a gross tactical error. Brown suddenly realized how much trouble he was in and lit off once more in a hell-for-leather sprint. It was too much for Old John; Brown's second charge crushed his spirit, and the last hill of the Newton series was instantly named "Heartbreak Hill" by the creative Nason. By the last mile-and-a-half, Brown and his two closest pursuers, Billy McMahon and Kelley, were all limping home, walking. "Tarzan" hit the tape in 2:33:40, although goodness knows what he would have run had he paced himself more prudently. McMahon held on to get second, but Kelley virtually crawled across the line, having fallen to fifth spot in the last 2 miles.

A stone mason by trade, Brown got most of his cardiovascular workouts while chopping wood. Distance-running experts believe that had he been scientifically, or even regularly, trained, "Tarzan" Brown might have gone on to be the world's greatest distance runner of his day. After his 1936 B.A.A. win, Coach Fred Tootell of the University of Rhode Island became curious about the American Indian's talent and timed him in a mile run on the track. Brown turned in a 4:20 performance. He ran it barefoot.

It is two months after the Boston Marathon and the emergence of a potentially astounding American distance athlete, "Tarzan" Brown. A crowd is gathered at the Princeton track to watch the man who is about to become America's first great distance runner indisputably establish himself in history. He is chasing the ghost of Peerless Paavo Nurmi in the 2-mile footrace. The runner is muscular and intense. He runs on the tips of his toes. He runs almost every track distance event; his friends urge him to cut back his versatility and concentrate on one event, but he ignores them. None can set the pace for him after the first three laps, so he runs on alone, holding his head high and lifting his knees almost up to it. A steady rain makes the track slow . . . but not the runner. He parts the tape in 8:58.3—1-point-3 seconds faster than Nurmi's world record. His coach, "Billy" Hayes, looks on. He is Don Lash.

The second of Coach Hayes's three greatest runners, "Iron Man" Don Lash was the first American distance hero. He ran everything from the mile to the 5,000 meters, but is best remembered as a 2-mile specialist. Up to and including 1936, only two Americans had times under 9:07 for 2 miles. Lash, with his record, was one of them. Wayne Rideout, who ran 9:03.5 also in 1936, was the other. That's how far ahead Lash was of any other American: over 5 seconds ahead, and his greatest efforts would not come for another year.

Then came summer and the 1936 Olympic Games at Berlin. America had strong reason to expect Olympic success. Aboard the S.S. *Manhattan*, steaming toward Europe, were such greats as Johnny Kelley, Tarzan Brown, Glenn Cunningham, Helen Stephens, Billy McMahon, Ralph Metcalfe, Archie Williams, Don Lash, John Woodruff, and a fellow named Jesse Owens. Awaiting them was Adolf Hitler's version of the Olympics . . . and glory.

As the time for the Games drew nearer, the brouhaha among the press, public, and politicians over whether or not a U.S.A. Team should compete in Nazi Germany intensified. The IOC had awarded the Olympics to the city of Berlin (not to the state of Germany—the Games are never awarded to a nation, only to a city) back in 1932. The Committee had not foreseen the rise of Hitler and his fascist programs and pogroms. An argument, one that would become sadly familiar over the next forty years, developed that participation in Games held within the boundaries of an enemy (or at least unpalatable) state constituted, at the least, a tacit endorsement of the political policies of that state. As would also become maddeningly common in the future, officials of the beseiged national Olympic committee, in this case America's own Olympic committee, proved naive and inept in their public statements. USOC president Avery Brundage (who competed in the decathlon in the 1912 Olympics) argued that sport should not be sullied with politics. Questioned about the propriety of sending a Team to compete in a nation openly anti-Semitic, he replied: "Frankly, I don't think we have any business to meddle in this question. We are a sports group, organized and pledged to promote clean competition and sportsmanship. When we let politics, racial questions, religious or social disputes creep into our actions, we're in for trouble." The U.S. Team went anyway.

That decision was nevertheless controversial. The American public directs attention to track and field only once every four years. Such an audience could hardly be expected to appreciate Brundage's arguments that sport transcended politics. Further, a significant proportion of the Americans whose interest in and knowledge of the sport extended to actual participation in and/or financial support of it were Jewish. Prominent newspapers such as the *New York Times* editorialized against Brundage's logic and against American participation at Berlin. With the enormous benefit of historical hindsight, one sees how unfortunate it was that Brundage and the USOC did not seize the opportunity in the midst of controversy to educate the American media and public to understand the true Olympic ideal: that "sport transcends politics" precisely because people who meet on the playing fields not only develop great personal character and integrity, they—perhaps more important—also develop mutual respect and understanding. From its inception by the Delphic oracle, the Olympic ideal aimed at the same goal as the League of Nations and the United Nations, with a far longer history of success than either of those two political institutions. Phrased thus, the argument in favor of the Olympics demonstrates the high, yet concrete, ideals of the Games. Phrased the way the USOC puts the argument, it sounds as if athletes just don't want to be bothered with politics.

Brundage didn't help matters much when he and the U.S. Team arrived in Berlin. "No nation since ancient Greece has captured the true Olympic spirit as has Germany," he observed. A defensible statement, its timing was politically unfortunate and its insight insufficient. Germany had indeed made a mighty effort to be the perfect Olympic host, but her motives were the antithesis of Olympic spirit.

The Olympic Stadium at Berlin, for example, was massive and stunning, designed with the active participation of Herr Hitler, who flatly refused even to enter the stadium that Otto March had originally designed. When inspecting the model for the approved stadium design, Hitler was informed by architect Albert Speer that the athletic field fitted into the stadium did not meet the dimensions required by Olympic standards. Hitler replied: "No matter. In 1940 the Olympic Games will take place in Tokyo. But thereafter they will take place in Germany for all time to come, in this stadium. And then *we* will determine the measurements of the athletic field." It was not what one normally considers a sporting observation. In a perverse way, however, Hitler enjoyed an excellent grasp of the deep meaning of the Games. Hitler perceived the Olympics as more than a showcase for the achievements of Nazi Germany and a propaganda *coup*. He perceived the Games as a means of placing the entire world under the same sort of spell that he wove in his highly ritualized and symbolic mass rallies. Hitler once wrote that, "The tradition of the Olympic Games has gone on for almost a thousand years. That proceeds, it seems to me, from a *mystery* comparable to that which is at the origin of Bayreuth. Man feels the need to come out of himself, to commune with an idea which is beyond his comprehension." To spare foreign visitors from communing with an idea only too fully within their comprehension, Hitler ordered the removal of all anti-Semitic posters and the cessation of all anti-Semitic activities during the Games.

America's Olympians had a good time while sailing to Europe, perhaps too good a time. Johnny Kelley favored the Team with his rendition of "Now Is

The Hour" during one of the shipboard parties. That was okay. What wasn't okay was Eleanor Holm-Jarrett's love of champagne. A gold medalist in the 100-meter backstroke at Los Angeles, the USOC kicked Holm-Jarrett off the Team for imbibing alcohol on the boat. She had "broken training." As in 1920, the other athletes requested she be reinstated, and, as in 1920, the USOC refused. Avery Brundage contended that to reinstate a delinquent athlete such as Mrs. Holm-Jarrett "would wreck the American Olympic team," although the question of how the Team could maintain high morale when (a) treated as if it were populated by children, and (b) its petitions for Holm-Jarrett's reinstatement were continually rejected by the very Committee that is supposed to be responsive to the Team's collective wants and needs, never seemed to have occurred to Brundage and the Committee. (The Committee also suspended two boxers from the Team shortly after arriving in Berlin. The official reason for the suspension was that the athletes were homesick, hence it would be unfair to subject them to intense international competition. In fact, the boxers were thieves; they had been caught shoplifting and no one argued for their reinstatement.)

Hitler's Olympic motives were base, but the execution of them was lofty. On July 21, 1936, Germany initiated the tradition of runners relaying the Olympic flame from the Temple of Zeus at Olympia to the host city's Olympic stadium. Three thousand runners passed the magnesium torch to one another through seven different nations. When the torch reached the Berlin stadium on August 1, Hitler declared the Games open in front of 110,000 spectators. Trumpets rang, canons sang, the Olympic flag flew, and 3,000 white pigeons (one for every torch-bearer) soared into the heavens. Then the parade of Olympic teams began and politics once again interfered with athletics. National teams sympathetic to the Nazi regime, such as the Bulgarians and the Austrians, gave the fascist salute as they passed the reviewing stand. Those teams either opposed or neutral to Nazi Germany gave either the Olympic salute or no salutation at all; the U.S.A. Team was among these (again refusing to dip its flag in honor of the head of state) and was rewarded with jeering whistles from the observing Berliners. After the parade the crowd sang "Deutschland Uber Alles," and Chancellor Hitler received Spiridon Loues, winner of the first marathon race ever, in his box. Always humble and direct, Loues wore the traditional clothing of the Greek peasant. He carried an olive branch from Olympia, and he cried. As he presented the branch to Hitler, the good Loues said, "I present to you this olive branch as a symbol of love and peace. We hope that the nations will ever meet solely in such peaceful competition." Hitler shook Loues's hand with his notoriously limp Nazi handshake.

The Nazis prepared well for their athlete-guests, spending about $30 million in 1936 currency. Considering it was money spent as much for political propaganda as for sport, the cash must have been considered well used by the leaders of the thousand-year reich. The amenities of the Los Angeles

Games were raised to the *n*th power by the Germans. The stadium seated 110,000. The swimming stadium seated 18,000. There were the expected tennis courts, ethnic kitchens, and practice fields, but there were also six gymnasia and a railroad station. There were steam rooms and sauna baths, and also—not coincidentally—a bungalow from the L.A. Olympic Village allegedly installed as an historical monument to the first Village, but really set up to show how much more magnificent were the German equivalents.

Once all the political baloney was out of the way, the Games truly began . . . only to get quickly bogged in politics. The first event on the program, the shotput, was won by Germany's Hans Woellke, and Hitler made a show of congratulating the first champion of the Games as an example of Aryan manliness. IOC officials took Hitler aside and pointed out that according to Olympic policy, he got to open and close the Games, and that was *it* as far as his official participation in the Olympics was concerned. Yet Hitler continued to receive German medal-winners in his private room underneath the stadium stands.

America's best 5,000 meter runner competed in the 10-kilometer race. Dashing Don Lash ambled home in eighth spot in the 10K final, which was taken by Finland's Ilmari Salminen in 30:15.8 with relatively little drama. Arvo Askola claimed the silver and Volmari Iso-Hollo the bronze in a clean sweep of the 6.2-mile run for Finland.

The American women's 400-meter relay team cruised home to a gold in 46.9, and Missourian Helen Stephens of the U.S.A. ran a wind-aided 11.5 seconds for the 100-meter dash to take home even more precious metal. The rustic but quick Stephens said her speed training consisted of "chasing rabbits on the farm back home." Her closest competitor at Berlin might as well've been a rabbit. Stephens finished an amazing 10 yards ahead of her closest competitor in the 100-meter final.

Babe Didrikson unfortunately failed to pass on her spark to the American competitors in the 80-meter hurdles, and Italy's Trebisonda Valla (who also excelled in the long and high jumps) won in 11.7 seconds, although she equalled the world record of 11.6 in a semifinal round.

The Nazis were not overjoyed to see the Americans win anything, of course, but it was the result of the 100-meter final that began to add insult to injury for the Fascists. The Germans had remarked the Americans' "black auxiliaries" as they called them—that is, the black Americans on the Team—from the Opening Ceremony. A fundamental tenet of Nazism of course was the supremacy of the so-called Aryan race over all other races. Jesse Owens broke both what little plausibility there may have been to Hitler's racist theories and a passel of records. After the Games were over, Hitler would comment to confidants that it was unfair for Aryans to have to compete against people "who had descended from the jungle" because such jungle-people obviously had stronger physiques than did civilized men and women.

One of Owens's performances at Berlin exceeded his normal capabilities:

in the 100-meter final, Jesse grabbed the lead right from the gun, holding on for both dear life and a gold medal at the finish. Normally, Owens got off to a sedentary start, then ate up the track, and the competition, midway through the dash. Whether as a result of peaking for Olympic competition or of being piqued by the Nazi Olympics, Owens was 2 yards ahead of the pack by the 50-meter mark. The track was mucky from the rains that afflicted most of the 1936 Games, yet Owens still equalled the Olympic 100-meter record of 10.3; he was 1/10-second off the world mark—which was held by a man named Jesse Owens. Ralph Metcalfe, the huge, strapping sprinter also from the U.S., likewise shone in the race. Getting off to an abysmal, and atypical, slow start, superpowerful Metcalfe charged, thundering from last to second and to a silver medal, 1 meter or so behind the bouncing Owens and 1 meter ahead of Holland's Martin Osendarp.

As Jim Thorpe did in 1912, Paavo Nurmi in 1924, and Babe Didrikson in 1932, Jesse Owens simply dominated the Olympic Games. His coach, Larry Snyder, had taken pains to make sure the "Tan Streak" from Ohio State didn't compete as often in the indoor season as he, Owens, would have liked. Snyder also worked with the Tan man on his sprint starts. In the past, Owens had trouble taking his eyes off his rivals while awaiting the gun. Coach Snyder got him finally to concentrate on the gun instead of on the guys, and Owens could then dominate the races right from the start, instead of employing his normal tactic of an electric kick thirty yards from the tape.

Owens's next gold medal came in the long jump, in which he competed between running preliminary rounds of the 200-meter sprint. Holder of the pending world record (26′8¼″) in the event, Owens certainly anticipated no problems in getting through the *qualifying* round, but he twice in a row fouled (by overrunning the takeoff board) in his qualifying efforts. Very likely

The immortal Jesse Owens, who won four gold medals in the 1936 Berlin Olympics. He is shown here practicing his broad jumping aboard the S.S. Manhattan, en route to the Games. (Photograph from the authors' collection.)

Owens, who owned what Coach Snyder called "a high tension nervous system," was too geared up from his hyper sports activity to calm down and qualify. Then one of those moments that validate and sanctify sport occurred. Luz Long, Germany's top long jumper, came up to Owens (who had only one more chance to qualify for the event) and suggested the American draw a line in the dirt a ways back from the takeoff board and make his jump from there. Long said, "You'll be sure not to foul, and you certainly ought to jump far enough to qualify." Owens took off a foot behind the board and qualified with a foot to spare. In the finals, he and Long traded the leading mark back and forth until Owens put the gold away for good with an Olympic record leap of 26'5¼". Long took the silver with 25'9²⁷⁄₃₂", and he extended Owens a friendly and sincere congratulation. (Hitler then privately congratulated Long, but didn't send Owens so much as a posey.)

Owens's third gold medal came in that other sprint, the 200-meters. It was no contest; Owens also held the world record in this contest. He set an Olympic best of 20.7, finishing 4/10-second ahead of the silver medalist, America's Mack Robinson—the biggest winning advantage in 200-meter Olympic history. After this performance, the German crowd gave Jesse Owens, the black American, a standing ovation. Observers failed to see Hitler anywhere in the crowd.

To round out his collection of medals, Owens took the first (hence longest) leg on the victorious American 400-meter relay team.

The 800-meter field promised a lot of excitement and a fast time; the field delivered on the former, but not on the latter. The race went down in history as the greatest 800-meter broken-field-running championship ever. Coach Billy Hayes's middle distance ace, Chuck Hornbostel, was entered, and so was University of Pittsburgh frosh John Woodruff, who had terrific speed but almost no international competition experience. The U.S.A. coach told young John to beware of the tricks of the Europeans, such as being boxed into a strategically poor position in the jostling pack. At the gun, Canada's Phil Edwards took the lead and poor Woodruff took it on the chin—he was boxed in behind the backmarkers in the pack right at the start of the 2-lapper. Unable to maneuver around his blockers, Woodruff hit on the unique tactic of coming to a full stop and allowing the rolling chicane to run away from him. Now he had a nice clear track. Astoundingly, Woodruff then not only caught up with the pack, he raced into the lead! While paying off the interest on his thus-incurred oxygen debt, Woodruff again fell into the persistent Edwards's clutches; further, Italy's Mario Lanzi also took advantage of the sag in the pace to try to snag a gold or a silver medal for himself. Once more Woodruff was in the box, and it was the last turn of the race: Edwards in front of him, and Lanzi at his right elbow, closing the door on the outside of the corner.

The peripatetic Pitt freshman took a flying leap in front of Lanzi, freeing himself from the pocket but adding many feet to the 800-meter distance he was theoretically running. Woodruff stormed past Edwards, finally claiming a 5-meter lead and a clear track between himself and the tape . . . and then started to die badly. Lanzi came on. He zipped past Edwards and zeroed in on Woodruff. As the American struggled for the wire, the Italian ran relentlessly, the distance between them shrinking rapidly. The shrink wasn't rapid enough, however, and Woodruff became Olympic 800-meter champ with a mediocre clocking of 1:52.9. Lanzi became semi-champ, and Edwards was semi-semi-champ.

Hopes for yet another American victory soared in the 5,000 meter footrace; 5K was much closer to Don Lash's distance than was the 10K. Unfortunately, the Finns ran away from Lash in the shortie just as they had in the longie. It was about to be a clean sweep for Nurmiland until leader Ilmari Salminen (winner of the 10K) tripped over some of his own countrymen's feet on the penultimate lap, handing victory to Finland's Gunnar Hockert in 14:22.2, while Finland's 1932 5K king, Lauri Lehtinen, came in second and Sweden's John Henry Johnson appeared in third spot.

Jesse Owens dominated the Berlin Games as an individual athlete, but the 1500-meter final dominated the 1936 Olympics as an event. It is considered the greatest metric mile in Olympic history. All the stars were there: Glenn Cunningham, Gene Venzke, and Archie San Romani for the U.S.; defending champion Luigi Beccali for Italy; Eric Ny for Sweden; Jack Lovelock for New Zealand; ageless Phil Edwards for Canada.

England's Jerry Cornes set the pace at the gun, but it mattered little; the leader of the first lap rarely leads through to the wire in the Olympic 1500 final. Great Glenn Cunningham waited nearly a full lap to swing out and thunder by Cornes. Lovelock went right with him. The Rhodes Scholar from New Zealand had taken Cunningham's (and Bonthron's!) measure in several mile races and had planned his strategy for the Olympic final "for years." The massive Cunningham ran the third 400-meter lap in nearly 60 seconds flat. Not only did Lovelock stay with him, Ny and Germany's Schaumberg caught up and interposed themselves between the cannonballing Cunningham and the lashing Lovelock. Ny died after a lap, and the order going into the last circuit was Schaumberg, Cunningham, Lovelock, and Beccali coming up fast. Suddenly, sensation! Three hundred meters from home, Lovelock let out all the stops. Cunningham stomped down hard on the 2,000-or-so-horsepower housed in his hulking frame, and Beccali tromped the go-pedal too, but they both lost at least 3 yards to the vanishing Lovelock while shifting gears. Beccali's devestating kick had won him the 1500 gold medal four years previously, but at Berlin it could not dent the sprint of Cunningham or Lovelock. Cunningham ran as though chasing an angel and pursued by demons, but the sheer force of his attack seemed to carry Lovelock ahead of him on its shock wave. Lovelock ran those last 300 meters in 42.8, and the last 400 in 57.8, parting the tape in 3:47.8, taking a full second off the world's record held by Bill Bonthron. Cunningham held on for second in 3:84.4, and Beccali took a gallant third; Archie San Romani was fourth and evergreen Phil Edwards fifth—not usually significant positions, but, that day, the first five men broke the Olympic 1500-meter record set by Beccali only four years previously.

Lovelock demonstrated that years of advance planning paid off in victory. Defending marathon champion, Juan Carlos Zabala of Argentina, had already been in Germany for six months when the marathon race started, closing the Berlin Games. Zabala had trained rigorously on the official course, and acclimated himself to the German weather, which that day was particularly hot. He took off like a house afire at the gun, but burned out at the halfway mark and dropped out at 32 kilometers. Tarzan Brown worked his way up to third position, dealing with soreness in his ankles as a result of taking a 40-kilometer stroll with one of the American race-walkers several days before his own event. Brown eventually dropped out, as did Billy McMahon. America's Old Johnny Kelley finished in eighteenth spot, running 2:49. The day belonged to the son of the Rising Sun—Japan's Kitei Son, to be precise. When Zabala doffed his running shoes, Son and England's Ernest Harper sailed into the lead. Harper seemed to have taken a fatherly interest in Son. He had kept him from chasing off after the nickle-rocket Zabala in the earlier stages, assuring the Korean-born Japanese that Zabala would soon fold. Shortly after Harper's prediction came to pass, the Englishman sportingly encouraged the 21-year-old Tokyo student to speed up, pass himself, and take the lead. Son took the advice. He also took the marathon title in 2:29:19.2, with the 29-year-old Britisher claiming the silver medal. Japan's Shoryu Nan, also born in Korea, was the bronze medalist, and then the Olympics were over. There would be no 1940 Games at Tokyo.

To round out the athletic year, Glenn Cunningham stepped over to Stockholm after the Games and took on Harbig, Ny, and Lanzi at 800 meters. Galloping Glenn won in a world-record time of 1:49.7. Cunningham also continued to win in 1937. He ran as a member of a relay team that also included Jimmy Herbert, and he consistently beat Venzke, San Romani, Beccali, and athletes of equally lofty quality. Cunningham also beat Don Lash, but '37 was the beginning of Lash's "purple period," the era of his preeminence among American distance runners. Nearly invincible indoors or out, Lash was AAU indoor 5-kilometer king in both 1938 and 1939, in which latter year he left the U.S. 5,000-meter record at 14:31.0. (One wonders where Lash might've left the record had he been pressed in his races; during his competition seasons, the Indiana runner routinely ran 3 miles nearly every Monday "in 14:30 or faster." In both competition- and off-seasons, Coach Hayes had Lash walk 6 miles every Sunday. The first scientific American coach understood how valuable "old-fashioned" walking is to a distance training program.) Dashing Don ran his fastest mile in the 1937 Princeton Invitational, finishing second to Archie San Romani with a 4:07.2. San Romani recorded the same time—it was a close race. Glenn Cunningham came home in third, 2/10-second behind Lash.

"Iron Man" Lash's fundamental racing strategy lived up to his *nom de guerre*: "Go faster when you feel tired. Run third 440 of mile and seventh 440 of 2 mile very fast." A 54-second 440 man, Don Lash certainly knew what "very fast" meant, and in him was melded whippet-like speed with (thanks to Coach Hayes) impressive cardiovascular endurance. The world 2-mile record and seven national cross-country championships *in a row* were some of the results. He was the first American distance cinder hero.

Jimmy Herbert of New York University came on the national scene in 1937, becoming one of the most outstanding 600-yards/meters specialists of all time. He also was one whale of a quarter-miler and relay-team-runner, in addition to being a tireless worker who put himself through college while simultaneously supporting his widowed mother.

At nearly 6' tall and 155 pounds, Herbert possessed an ideal body for his chosen distances. His form was virtually flawless; sportswriters called it "silky." No wonder he scored so easily in the Columbus 500-meter Invitational Race held in Brooklyn; his time was 1:06.6. Later that indoor season Herbert defeated undefeated Eddie O'Brien in the Prout 600 at the Boston Garden; the time was 1:14.4, a Boston Garden record that would stand forever. Then Herbert beat both O'Brien and a more-seasoned John Woodruff in the Millrose Games 600 in 1:12.6.

Herbert ran quarter-miles mainly as part of the relay-team effort. He sometimes would run his 440-yard leg in 48.4, *which was faster than the contemporary world record for the distance.* (Herbert undeniably possessed enormous speed, but quarter-mile races begin with standing starts, not the flying starts enjoyed by relay runners.) In 1940 Herbert set a world record of 1:10.8 for 600 yards; in 1948 he defeated the great John Borican, who had stolen the record from him in the Chicago 600. By the time this stunning middle-distance man retired in 1948, he had won the Millrose 600 five times in ten years.

The 1937 Boston Marathon field embraced more former winners of the classic than any other up to that time: Leslie Pawson, Old Johnny Kelley, Bill Kennedy, Clarence DeMar, Dave Komonen, Paul DeBruyn, and Tarzan Brown. None of them won, however. That privilege went to an amateur boxer and former snowshoe-racing champion, 24-year-old Walter Young, who legged 2:33:20 after a 23-mile running argument with Kelley on a hot, sunny Patriots' Day. Old John, who exhausted himself by trying to pull out a big lead on the very fit Young, limped home second in 2:39, and Pawson got third with 2:41:46.

Classic races of course draw stellar fields and often offer memorable competition. The Boston Marathon was incontestably *the* classic American road race. Greater controversy surrounded determining *the* classic American track race. Curiously, indoor track events acquired higher status than their faster outdoor counterparts. This phenomenon resulted from America's strong indoor track tradition; the closest European parallel to this tradition occurs at the Bislet Stadium in Oslo, Norway, and for the same reason: the crowd is seated right down at the edge of the track, resulting in intense intimacy for spectators and intense encouragement for competitors. (Moreover, indoor track in the U.S. drew bigger crowds than outdoor track, which meant there was more under-the-table-money to be taken on the boards than on the cinders. That is why Nurmi ran indoors in the U.S.) Possibly the Wanamaker Mile at the fabled Millrose Games deserved recognition as *the* American mile race . . . but there was also the Baxter Mile at the NYAC indoor meet, the Columbian Mile at the Knights of Columbus games, and the mile run at the Dartmouth Invitational meet in the Davis fieldhouse. At least there was no controversy over who was the main American miler of the day: Grandstanding Glenn Cunningham won his fifth Wanamaker Mile in six starts in 1938, clocking 4:11 for the 11 laps. Then Cunningham ran on the oversized (6.73 laps to the mile) track at the Davis fieldhouse during the Dartmouth Invitational and established an *absolute* world mile record of 4:04.4! At the Knights of Columbus meet, Cunningham claimed the Columbian Mile in 4:07.4 (the fastest ever run on a standard indoor track).

There was no contest concerning the ultimate 600-meter run, though. It was the Casey 600 held at the K.C. Games in Madison Square Garden, and Cunningham decided to try for a double victory by running it in the 1938 version of the games. It turned out to be the greatest Casey 600 in history.

Sixteen thousand spectators listened as the meet announcer intoned the traditional fanfare for the event, "All out for the Casey 600!" It was a clash between Cunningham and Jimmy Herbert; Wes Wallace and Howie Borck, the only two men to have beaten Herbert at his specialty all season were also there, while Boston University sent Doug Raymond to round out the field.

Herbert immediately took the lead as if it were his birthright, while Galloping Glenn was stuffed into fourth spot because of a poor start. Raymond and Borck intervened between him and the disappearing NYU ace. Herbert kept the lead for a lap, and then (as is one of the beauties of the slam-bang 600) it was time to sprint for home. Borck pulled past a hard-kicking Raymond and set sail for Herbert, but Cunningham drafted along right behind him. Herbert, who had led from the start, was tiring; Borck's speed and Cunningham's raw power ate up the wood and the distance separating them both from the lead. The crowd jumped up and down on their seats, swung from the rafters, and generally raised hell. Herbert, in deep trouble, seemed to *ooze* toward the tape, his toes clutching into the track as a desert plant's roots dig desperately into arid soil. He made it; he had held off his attackers! Herbert rent the worsted in 1:11.1, 2/10-second under Chuck Hornbostel's world record. Borck slid in ahead of Cunningham, earning 1:11.2 (also under the old record), while Glenn recorded 1:11.3 ("merely" tying the old mark). It was hard to reckon who were more exhausted: the runners or the spectators!

At least two athletes tendered outstanding performances in the 1938 Boston Marathon. One of them was winner Leslie Pawson, who had first to beat a determined Johnny Kelley and last to withstand a rip-snorting charge by Baltimore's Pat Dengis to emerge the victor in 2:35:34. The other of them was the legendary Clarence DeMar who, *at age 50, finished seventh* in the B.A.A. Marathon.

Middle-distance man John Borican was an artist both on the track and off; like Johnny Kelley in his later years, Borican painted pictures when he wasn't paining the competition. He was voted the best indoor runner of the 1939 season. He starred in both half-mile and 1000-yard footraces, but was also thrice AAU pentathlon champ and once the AAU decathlon champion during his career. He set eleven indoor track records in 1939, the main ones being: at 800 meters (1:49.2), at 880 yards (1:49.8), and at 1000 yards (2:08.8), in which latter effort he beat Glenn Cunningham by a step. In 1940 the artistic Borican broke Lloyd Hahn's 15-year-old world mark for ¾ of a mile by racing 3:02.6 at the Millrose Games, beating Archie San Romani and Wayne Rideout, as well as the ghost of Hahn, in the process. Later that year he stole the AAU 1000 championship away from John Woodruff in 2:13, while taking the 1941 Millrose 1000 from Gene Venzke in 2:13.9. He stole the world record in the 1941 Casey 600 in a blistering 1:10.2, beating Jimmy Herbert, then also claimed the 1000 in the same night by running 2:10.3. In the 1942 Navy Relief All-Star meet, Borican drove the 880-yard record down to 1:50.5, nearly a second under Hahn's best time. Sadly, this illustrious athlete died before the next indoor season, at age 29, claimed by pernicious anemia.

Tarzan Brown won the 1939 Boston Marathon breaking every record for speed the course could offer. Not only did he establish a Marathon record of 2:28:51 (over 2 minutes faster than Pawson's 1933 best), he also set new standards for passing through every checkpoint along the route. He did it by pacing himself evenly and letting former winners Young and Pawson set the tempo for him for the first 17 miles. Legend has it that Brown so dominated the field he had time to take a short swim en route on the humid day!

The 1939 track season was gallant Glenn Cunningham's last great one. He took the Baxter Mile (his fifth win), the Wanamaker Mile (his sixth win), the B.A.A. indoor mile (his ninth win), and walloped Don Lash and Greg Rice in a 2-mile showdown in 9:11.8.

On the international scene, Germany's Rudolph Harbig went on his scientific record-breaking rampage. He ran the 1000 meters in 2:21.8. He ran the 800 meters in 1:46.6. He ran the 400 meters in 46-point-zilch. The 400-meter record lasted until 1948, and the 800 record remained until 1955. These were astounding feats, even considering the hiatus in competing and training incurred by World War II. He was reported missing in action at the Soviet front early in 1944.

V

Running During and After WW II
1940–1949

The onset of World War II disrupted sport but did not halt it. Athletes and fans alike went on short rations during the decade, but seemed ultimately toughened by the situation. Although the war reduced opportunities for competition, the runners and events that were able to go on maintained a high level of competitive quality.

Charging Chuck Fenske of the University of Wisconsin whisked by Glenn Cunningham in the 1940 Wanamaker Mile at the Millrose Games, tying Cunningham's "normal" world indoor record of 4:07.4. Glenn himself was second with a 4:07.7 clocking, and hugely popular Gene Venzke third in 4:08.2. Next week, Fenske did it again, running precisely the same time in the Baxter Mile, with Lou Zamparini second at 4:07.9, Venzke third and Cunningham fourth, both of them turning in identical 4:08.8s after Venzke willed his way past the careening Cunningham at the wire. To round out his best year by far, the fleet Fenske hoofed 2:59.7 for three-quarter-mile on a dirt track, the first man in history to break 3 minutes for the distance.

Gerard Cote of Quebec was only the second man in history to win four Boston Marathons; Clarence DeMarathon, winner of seven, beat him to the honor. Cote started his string in 1940, breaking Tarzan Brown's record with a 2:28:28. Cote turned in an heroic catch-up effort. Lying fifth at mile 13.1, he speeded up and passed Tarzan Brown, Leslie Pawson, and unheralded but

95

obviously fit Scotty Rankin by mile 21. One mile later, John Kelley was no longer leader, and Cote was on his way to the laurels. As indefatigable historian Jerry Nason noted, 3 miles from Exeter Street Cote was 1:15 off Brown's record. By the Exeter Street finish line, he was 23 seconds under it—a mighty finishing kick for a race so long, and especially so taxing after the hills.

Gerard Cote just kept on a-winnin' marathons in 1940. He claimed "the other" American marathon, the Yonkers runathon, in 2:34:06.2.

The 1940 IC4A Championships Meet deserves special mention because it waved bye-bye to the former west coast members of the athletic association. The East was too far for athletes from those schools to travel. The University of Pittsburgh team won the title without having a single athlete win an event. The Pitt Panthers were the Shakespeare of the cinders: they "did nothing outstandingly, but so many things *well*."

Nostalgia reigned at the AAU Championships in Fresno, California, later that spring. Glenn Cunningham was ending his career, at age 30. Alas, he ended it on a bittersweet note. The sweet: he ran the fastest 1500 meters of his life—3:48.0—and missed the world's record by 2/10-second. The bitter: he lost to Walter Mehl, who established a new American record of 3:47.9. Galloping Glenn then went on to earn his Ph.D. and enter the Navy as an officer in World War II. As brilliant a thinker as he was an athlete (if one may make that artificial distinction), Cunningham's philosophy was: "Proper relaxation makes possible recuperation while running, I think. Pace judgment is important, and you must work on it constantly until mastered. Rest is as important as work." What Babe Ruth was to baseball, Glenn Cunningham was to running the distances on the track, a hero, a myth.

Heroes go, to be replaced by others. Greg Rice trounced Don Lash's venerable 2-mile record at the New York K.C. meet, tearing off an 8:56.2 and beating Walter Mehl. At the AAU meet where Cunningham ran his fastest 1500, Rice laid Willie Ritola's fastest 3-mile mark to sleep with 13:55.9. Mehl and Don Lash might as well have been asleep themselves during the race. Rice whipped Mehl by 100 yards and Lash was another 20 yards down from that! Rice also cruised past Hannes Kolehmainen's 3-mile American best. He pushed the 2-mile record to 8:52.0 in 1942; by the end of the season he had gone under Nurmi's 1925 record 11 times. Hampered by injuries during much of 1943, Rice came on strong at the Cleveland K.C. Meet with another world 2-mile record: 8:51.0. He retired at the end of the 1943 outdoor season to devote himself to the U.S. Merchant Marine, beaten in his last race by Gunder Haegg. In his running career, he won five straight AAU 5,000-meter titles in a row from 1938 to 1942. (As of 1981, two other athletes, Fred Wilt [1949–1951] and Matt Centrowitz [1979–1981], had won *three* in a row.)

The years 1941 to 1945 were the years of the first great milers' rivalry of the modern era. One finds it hard to mention Swiss great Gunder Haegg without also thinking of his countryman Arne Andersson. Haegg had the endurance. Andersson had the speed. They both had the determination. In

Don Lash, Greg Rice, Joe McCluskey and Finland's Taisto Maki start the 3-mile run in the 1940 Finnish Relief Fund Meet at Madison Square Garden. Rice prevailed in the world record time of 13:52.3. (Photograph courtesy of the University of Notre Dame.)

1941, the world outdoor mile best was 4:06.4, although Cunningham's Dartmouth indoor record stood at 4:04.4. By the time Andersson and Haegg were done with each other in 1945, the record was 4:01.3. It belonged to Haegg, but very possibly would never have been achieved without the impetus of Andersson, who held both the mile and 1500-meter marks in 1943 and 1944. On the other hand, 1942 and 1945 were Haegg's peak years for success. During 82 days in the summer of 1942, Haegg set ten world records in seven different distance events from the metric mile to the 5K. (The latter record was especially good; Haegg was the first person to crack 14 minutes for 5,000 meters, running 13:58.2, over 10 seconds under the old standard.) In 1945 Haegg put the mile mark away and lowered the 1500-meter best to 3:43.0. Ranked above Andersson because of all his world records, Haegg enjoys esteem by many track historians as arguably the most outstanding middle-distance runner yet. A large body of opinion also holds either Haegg *or* Andersson would have been the first athlete to crack the celebrated 4-minute barrier for the mile. Unfortunately, both of them were forcibly retired from competition at the end of 1945 for failing to heed the lesson of Paavo Nurmi. They got nailed for taking money under the table, but are today remembered for having been nearly a decade ahead of any other miler in the world.

Meanwhile, back in the States, Les MacMitchell emerged as a middle-distance star when he ran a 4:10.2 mile in the 1941 B.A.A. Games at Boston Garden, coming in third behind Walt Mehl and a runner named Munski. He finished second in the Wanamaker Mile, one step behind Mehl this time and in front of Fenske and Munski. Returning to Boston Garden later in the season for the Hunter Mile, MacMitchell tromped not only Mehl, Fenske and Munski, but also Olympic champ Luigi Beccali. In 1942, MacMitchell, running for NYU, set a new collegiate mile best of 4:08, but was beaten in the AAU championships by Gil Dodds, 4:08.7 to 4:08.9. He never successfully returned to track after his World War II stint in the Navy.

Les Pawson returned to the Boston Marathon successfully in 1941 for his third and final victory in 2:30:38. Johnny Kelley made a valiant effort to fend off the 36-year-old Pawtucket, Rhode Island, native, but settled for second best in 2:31:26. Kelley, who in 1980 described Pawson as "one of my closest friends," consoled himself with having been beaten by a buddy.

Friendship was also significant between Dodds and another super American distance man, Lloyd Hahn. Even as a teenager, Dodds knew he could run very fast. One afternoon while walking along a road in his hometown of Falls City, Nebraska, 13-year-old Dodds imprudently threw a rock at a passing car. The man driving the car braked to a stop, sprinted after young Gil, and gave him a boot in the butt for his mischief. The driver was Lloyd Hahn who, when introduced to the budding high-school track star under more cordial circumstances, agreed to coach the youngster.

After an undistinguished college career, Dodds took Hahn's advice that he move to Boston, join the B.A.A., and hook up with Hahn's own former coach, Jack Ryder. That was in 1941. In 1942, Dodds came into his own. He ran the 2-mile at the Millrose Games, earning second place behind Greg Rice, falling 3 yards short of Rice's 8:53.2. He claimed the AAU board mile championship with a 4:08.7, defeating favored Les MacMitchell. Dodds chopped 2/10-second off his mile time in the Navy Relief Meet, but MacMitchell ran even faster, at 4:07.8, to relegate upstart Dodds to second spot. Dodds was ranked number one among American mile men in 1943, but retired from track to become a minister in 1944. Surprisingly, he returned to the cinder path in 1947. (Religion, of course, in no way excludes athletics, as champion pole vaulter Rev. Ralph Richards, the "vaulting vicar," knew.) He ran 4:09.1 for the mile his first time out, showing the old talent remained. Dodds took the Wanamaker Mile, the AAU mile, and the NYAC 2-mile (in 9:05.6) that season, then moved on to Canada where he ran his swiftest mile yet: 4:06.8. With the Olympic Games once again in the offing, Dodds set his sights on qualifying for the 1948 U.S. Team, and ran the 1948 Wanamaker Mile in 4:05.3 (equalling Gunder Haegg's American best) to test his fitness. Sadly, the mumps laid Dodds low shortly thereafter, ending his athletic career.

Illness often ends runners' stories, but it occasionally turns out to be the opening chapter in running success stories. Take the case of Bernard Joseph Smith. A milkman by trade in the Boston suburb of Medford, Smith was by avocation a marathoner. He awoke the morning of Patriots' Day, 1942, feeling sick and woosy and not at all like running competitively for 26.2 miles. Sage Mrs. Isabel Smith sensed vitality under her hubbie's affliction, and talked him into giving it a go anyway. After all, the 27-year-old Smith *was* the AAU marathon champion; he clearly possessed the mettle to snare a B.A.A. medal.

Mrs. Smith was right. Mr. Smith set a new Marathon record of 2:26:51 on the 44-degree day, over a minute ahead of runner-up Lou Gregory. If it sounds like a tall story, chalk it up to Smith's height: at 6'2", no taller man has ever won the Boston Marathon.

Few American milers have ever had a longer career than Fred Wilt's, whose powers peaked from 1942 to 1955. Wilt was another of Coach Billy Hayes's wondermen; his longevity as an athlete testifies to the sound conditioning principles underlying Hayes's coaching theories. Wilt earned both the Big Ten and NCAA 2-mile crowns in the summer of '42, but lost to both Greg Rice and Gil Dodds in his initial 2-mile indoor efforts in the east (Millrose and NYAC meets). Wilt patriotically put his track career on "hold" so he could fight in World War II, but was back chasing the best foreign 2-milers in 1949, going head-to-head with American mile great Don Gehrmann. He left the American indoor 2-mile standard at 8:50.7, with fans gasping for breath at any meeting between himself and Gehrmann.

Gerard Cote got his second Boston Marathon victory in 1943, outrunning Johnny Kelley by 1:35 to hit home in 2:28:25. Running with an injured Achilles tendon, Cote was lucky to finish, let alone to win. Cote went on to "double" at the Yonkers Marathon, winning with 2:38:35.3.

Coach Billy Hayes died in 1943, leaving behind him the legacy of the Indiana training program, which would eventually blossom into increasing American effectiveness in international long-distance competition. As Hayes's pupil Fred Wilt summarized the value of the coach's work: "He had a system of training which recognized the individual differences among runners and took into consideration the physiological factors. He constantly searched for better

Gil Dodds, running in the regalia of the Boston Athletic Association, leads Rene Gustafsson in an indoor race. Notice the shoes worn by the athletes of the era. (Photograph courtesy of The Boston Herald American.)

methods, paid particular attention to the training of others, continually re-examined his own system, and was always willing to change his methods in favor of something better." The Earle C. (Billy) Hayes Trophy, created in 1945 and presented annually to the team that wins the National Collegiate Cross-Country Championships, immortalizes this great coach.

Gerard Cote apparently needed no more added effectiveness to his own long-distance ability. He made it two-in-a-row at the 1944 Boston Marathon, once again beating Old John Kelley with a 2:31:50. Old John was only 12.6 seconds too late that year. They were both fortunate to finish. Jerry Nason counted no fewer than seven surges thrown by the battling duo during the last 3 miles.

At last and huzzah! The next year, 1945, John A. Kelley of Arlington, Mass., stopped finishing second and won the Boston Marathon for the second and final time. Kelley altered his strategy to take his second Boston Marathon in 10 years. He let other guys set the pace for a change, waiting until mile 16 to make his move. He didn't take the lead from Lloyd Bairstow until mile 23, from which point it was figuratively (but, contrary to popular opinion, *not* literally) downhill to the finish line and a 2:30:40 victory.

World War II was over by the time of the 1946 Boston Marathon, and that was exactly why winner Stylianos Kyriakides of Greece ran it. Old John

Leslie Pawson, Gerard Cote and Johnny Kelley fight for the lead in the 1943 Boston Marathon. Cote won. (Photograph courtesy of The Boston Herald American.)

probably didn't mind finishing second yet again (in 2:31:27), because Kyriakides was running the race to publicize the plight of his Greek countrypeople. They were starving; Kyriakides himself was a former victim of malnutrition. His time, 2:29:27, was excellent, but his motive for running was more so, and the American public responded sympathetically and outpouringly to the Greek's cause. His victory also encouraged more foreign athletes to enter the B.A.A. race.

It was also in 1946 that B.A.A. president Walter Brown interdicted the big parade of automobiles that had come to accompany the runners. As of 1947, only three official buses would be permitted on the Marathon course, and the runners could finally breathe.

With near-boring predictability, Gerard Cote, who finished third at Boston that year, took the 1946 Yonkers Marathon in 2:47:53.

Although World War II played hob with the progress of distance running in most respects, it did result in at least one salutory phenomenon. American GIs stationed overseas passed on their love of marathoning to Oriental athletes. The Koreans became especially interested in long-legging and sent Yun Bok Suh to the Boston Marathon in 1947 with funds donated by American servicemen. He went on to run 2:25:39, a course record, and become both the first Asian and the shortest man (5'1") to win the classic footrace. It was a gutty run for Bok Suh. While engaged in a thrilling fight for the lead with European marathon champion Mikko Hietanen of Finland at the Newton heartbreakers, a ferocious fox terrier attacked the Korean and knocked him down on his knees. The accident must have released an adrenal rush within Bok Suh, for bloodied, and with one shoelace broken, he rose up, swept by Hietanen, and kept the lead all the way to the finish, beating the Finn by 4 minutes.

Another great marathon tradition sprang up in 1947, the biannual Enschade (Holland) Marathon, largely inspired by Czechoslovakia's Kosice Marathon. The first running of the 26.2-miler happened on opening day of a track meet between Holland and Czechoslovakia, and the Enschade and Kosice races have ever since been considered kindred competitions.

In Germany in 1947, Adi Dassler decided to contract his name and put it on the athletic-shoe company he had just founded. Adidas was the result.

Gerard Cote enjoyed win number four, his last, at the 1948 B.A.A. Marathon, but he didn't much enjoy the company he had during the competition. He and Ted Vogel ran at each other's side for 23 miles, trading insults, frustrations, and almost physical blows. Vogel didn't like Cote's habit of following closely on his heels or, when leading, of physically blocking anyone trying to take over the pace. Cote didn't think much of Vogel, either, and demonstrated his disdain by distancing himself from Ted at 23 miles, sprinting to a 44-second victory over him with a 2:31:02 clocking. Third-place Jesse Van Zant was 5 minutes behind the leaders as testimony to the torrid pace they set, if not to the hot words they exchanged.

The running world was looking better in 1948. The Olympic Games were going to be revived, and a new distance-running king was starting to make his mark in Europe. To disseminate all this good news to track-hungry Americans, a new magazine hit the newsstands and, although its contents were (and are) far from sacred, it earned a justifiable reputation as "the Bible of the sport": *Track & Field News*.

Three athletes dominated the 1948 London Olympics: young Robert Mathias of the U.S.A., all-talented Fanny Blankers-Koen of the Netherlands, and superhuman Emil Zátopek of Czechoslovakia.

Zátopek is now widely recognized as the first modern exponent of interval training, but there was much—indeed, almost everything—that was not realized about Emil when the London Games began. The hiatus of the war had interrupted the running world in more ways than one. Not only had competition and training opportunities dried up during the Big One, so too had sources of information concerning who was getting hot and who was getting old on the international circuit. The first notable observer to recognize Zátopek's talent was Paavo Nurmi himself, who had become coach to another flying Finn, Viljo Heino. Heino held the world record for 10,000 meters (29:22.4), which he set as part of his 1948 Olympics buildup. A month before the Olympics, Zátopek came within 2 seconds (1.6, to be precise) of Heino's 10K mark. Moreover, Zátopek had beaten Heino in a 5-kilometer race at the 1947 Finnish National Games in front of Heino's home crowd. The defeat seemed to have been instrumental in Heino's decision to move up to the 10,000 and marathon exclusively, but he was about to learn a lesson distance runners even in 1981 still were learning—there's nowhere to hide from speed; it will inevitably inhabit every distance.

Observing Zátopek training in the Olympic camp, Nurmi remarked exactly that fact. Seeing the torturous training (and tortured running form!) of the Czech, Nurmi declared that he, Zátopek, was the only athlete at London who understood what hard training meant . . . and where it would lead.

Zátopek could have been born fully-formed from the head of Nurmi; the two shared much in common, yet were distinctly different in terms of temperament. Nurmi was taciturn, while Emil was more friendly, open, and cordial than perhaps any other athlete of any era (Bill Rodgers comes close). As with Nurmi, Zátopek discovered the training benefits of military service. Not only were there time and facilities for training, there were also heavy, ungainly combat boots to make training even more difficult. He would regularly run 8 miles after a hard day of military drilling. He wore the boots year-round, tromping through forests and performing windsprints (albeit untimed ones—unlike Nurmi, Zátopek foreswore the use of a stopwatch in his training or racing). Questioned about the apparent absurdity of training as a fast runner while wearing leaden equipment, Zátopek replied that, "There's a great advantage in training under unfavorable conditions, for the difference is then a tremendous relief in a race."

Other athletes, before Zátopek and since, embraced much the same phi-losophy, but none with the devotion of the Czech. He ran 20 × 400-meters in his army boots. Before entering the service, his interval work consisted of 10 × 200-meters in 26–28 seconds, and/or 10 × 400-meters in 60 seconds flat. Oc-casionally he would run a workout of 10 × 100 meters in 13 seconds each. What were such workouts to a man used to carrying a torch along with him to light his way through his post-drill 8-mile runs?

Such workouts constituted another step forward in scientific running. This was science born out of inspiration, although, of course, drenched with per-spiration. Gerschler and Reindell hit on the idea of interval training as a re-sult of their theoretical and empirical knowledge of human physiology. Emil Zátopek arrived at the same conclusion thus: "It seemed to me that, if you wanted to run fast, you had to *practice* running fast." Another significant difference between Zátopek's approach and Gerschler-Reindell's was that Zátopek was a long-distance runner; the Germans' boy, Harbig, was a middle-distance athlete. Zátopek knew what Heino didn't: running means *speed*, regardless of the distance. If one isn't going fast, why run?

The 1948 London Games were far from establishing new heights of mo-dernity in terms of Olympic facilities. A major war had just ended. Although the war had ended on favorable political terms for the British, it had left London and the English national economy in disarray. In fact, many English protested against hosting the Games at all. The protests failed, but London lacked both the will and the wherewithal to erect splendid facilities in the mold of Los Angeles or Berlin. Old facilities, such as Wembley Stadium, would just have to do . . . with maybe a new coat of paint and a little cleanin' up, o' course, guv'. True to their stiff-lip-and-spine tradition, the British came through magnificently, as had the Belgians in 1920. The only ones who weren't surprised by their success were the English themselves. Various Olym-pic Teams arrived in London only a few days before the Games were sup-posed to start, only to find apparently nothing prepared for them! There was not a jot of news about the Olympics in the British press; there were no signs in London directing athletes and spectators to salient Olympic spots; there wasn't *anything*! It was the reverse of the 1900 Paris Games, when the ath-letes did not know the meet they were attending was the Olympics. In 1948, athletes showed up expecting to compete in the Olympics and began wonder-ing if they had not instead arrived at a low-key international track meet.

Fifty-nine nations had sent nearly 4,500 athletes to London, and their col-lective anxiety dispersed on Opening Day. It was 93 degrees and sunny, and King George VI and 83,000 of his subjects jammed into Wembley Stadium to welcome the revived Games. As at Berlin, a flock of pigeons was released; but, unlike at Berlin, the birds this time seemed to betoken peace, not to herald an impending holocaust. (Understandably, neither Germany nor Japan sent a team to London.)

The galleries remained packed for the entire Olympics, people forgetting the pain of war and cheering the champion athletes before them. The athlete who received the most cheers was undoubtedly Holland's Fanny Blankers-Koen, the only athlete—male or female—to win more than one gold medal in 1948. She won four and almost undoubtedly would have won more had she not been restricted to competing in only three events. It was the same rule that frustrated Babe Didrikson. Blankers-Koen won four golds because she was permitted to compete as a member of Holland's 400-meter relay team in addition to her three individual events. A lucky thing for the running world that Holland's Olympic swimming coach told her, back in 1935, that the Netherlands already had enough waterbabies and that she'd be better off going out for the track team!

Blankers-Koen went into the London Olympics holding the world records for the long and high jumps. She didn't enter either of these events at London, and the winning result in each of them came nowhere near her marks, hence the assumption that the 30-year-old Dutch mother of two would have won a few gilded medals more had she been permitted unlimited competition. Instead she entered the running events: the 100- and 200-meter runs, the 80-meter hurdles and the women's relay race. She swept the cinders clean. She ran eleven races during the eight days of the Games and won them all, the heats as well as the crucial finals.

Her victory in the 100-meters surprised few. She was the world's best in that event as well as in the jumps. She only equalled Stanislawa Walasiewicz's (Stella Walsh's) Olympic record 11.9 (Helen Stephens's 11.5 does not count because wind-aided), although her record stood at 11.5. With the London weather staying in the mid-90s for most of the Olympics, even the sprinters must have wilted a trifle.

Blankers-Koen's second gold came in the 80-meter hurdles, in which she also held the world's record. Again, Fanny's Olympic performance fell short of her personal best. She won in 11.2 seconds, 2/10-second slower than the world standard . . . but a full ½-second faster than Babe Didrikson ran 'em in 1932.

Then came the 200-meter footrace final, the first such in Olympic history for women. Blankers-Koen did not hold the world record, but she won anyway, many yards ahead of the panting pack, becoming the first woman triple-gold-medalist in Olympic history.

She became the first woman quadruple-gold-medalist when she anchored the victorious Netherlands' 400-meter relay team. The winning time, 47.5 seconds, was the slowest since the inaugural Olympic running of it in 1928, but the heat and the war hiatus precluded record-breaking in 1948. Like everyone else (except perhaps Zátopek), Fanny Blankers-Koen was content simply to win.

Seventeen-year-old Bob Mathias set what must have been a new Olympic record for courage when he became the youngest Olympic champion ever in track and field, let alone in the man-killing decathlon. He began training for the ten decathlon events only four months before the London Games began. His original plan had been to qualify for the 1952 Olympics, but when he won the U.S. decathlon championship—only his second decathlon competition *ever*—two months before the Olympics, he was bound to go to London. Strongest at the hurdles, discus, and high jump, young Mathias had no cause for shame as a runner, although he was not nearly a candidate for even a national ranking on the flats. His times for the London decathlon running events were: 100 meters: 11.2; 110-meter hurdles: 15.7; 400 meters: 51.7; 1500 meters: 5:11.

The power of running while relaxed and enjoying oneself was one of the alleged benefits conferred by the fartlek form of training, the take-it-as-it-comes workouts practiced by Zátopek and the Swedes, Haegg and Andersson. At the 1948 Games, the power of relaxation and enjoyment gained yet another proselytizer—sprinter Mel Patton of the U.S.A. Tagged as a favorite to win the 100-meters, Patton instead finished only a distant fifth; outstanding hurdler Harrison Dillard of the U.S. won in 10.6 seconds. While resting up for the 200-meter final several days later, the despondent Patton received a visit from Marshall Smith, who was then sports editor for *Life* magazine. A friend, Smith asked Patton what had happened in the 100; Patton replied he must have been tense and so "tied up" during the race. He didn't seem to relish the impending 200-meter final that would happen in a few minutes. The insightful Smith decided to try some sports psychology. Seeing Patton needed to cheer up and relax, he invited the sprinter to travel with him to Paris for a good time on *Life's* expense account after the Olympics were over. Patton brightened immediately, jumped up, went out to the starting blocks, grabbed the lead at the gun, and held it for a full 21.1 seconds, enough to win the gold.

A great American middle-distance man, Mal Whitfield turned in one of the most memorable 800-meter runs in Olympic history at London. Whitfield seemed destined to dominate the 1948 800. He won his one preliminary heat in 1:52.8, but it had been warm and dry in London then. The day of the 800-meter final was cool and rainy. When the dust had cleared after the starting gun, Whitfield was in third spot behind France's Robert Chef D'Hotel (honest!) and Jamaica's Arthur Wint, famed for his 9-foot stride. Starting the gun lap, Whitfield trucked past the two former leaders and assumed command, running with the smooth, nearly arrogant style that became his trademark. Wint, a big favorite before the race, faded like the London sun; heading down the back straightaway he was in fifth position. Then, as if he had waked from a doze, the Jamaican used his 9-foot boots to bear down on Whitfield with nearly unbearable physical and psychological pressure. Whitfield held out with 2 yards to spare, running 1:49.2 to Wint's 1:49.5. The former Olympic best had been 1:49.8, set by England's Tom Hampson

Marvelous Mal Whitfield, two-time Olympic gold medalist at 800 meters. Whitfield's powerful physique was apparently natural; he claimed never to have lifted weights as part of his training. (Photograph courtesy of Ohio State University.)

in 1932. Third-place man Hansenne of France equalled Hampson's old mark in a very fleet and wet field.

The longer the race, the more effect a soggy track has on its results. The 1948 1500-meter final was a case in point. Stripped of their amateur status, Haegg and Andersson were prohibited from running in the Games, but they'd left a lethal light-footed legacy among Swedish milers. Basically, it was a question of which Swede would win, and the answer was a bit surprising under any circumstances other than the wet ones prevailing in Foggy Old London. The fastest man lost to the strongest man. Sweden's Lennart Strand had speed, and his compatriot Henri Eriksson had muscles. Strand cagily waited to take the lead in the metric-mile final. At the critical 1-kilometer mark, the Swede made his bid, but "the Swede" was Eriksson, not Strand. Splashing through the slush going down the backstretch and heading for the final turn, Strand decided to draft behind Eriksson, confident that his own finishing kick would finish off the hard-charging Henri. Ordinarily it would have been a good idea; that day, it wasn't. Eriksson kept on in front, his slow-twitch endurance muscles moving through the mud more efficiently than Strand's fast-twitch speed muscles. Then suddenly Holland's Slijkhuis was trying to muscle his way past Strand. Strand pulled the unsophisticated but effective tactic of moving into the Netherlander's path to block him physically from passing. Crash! The two athletes collided at the line and fell over it. Strand held his second place, while Slijkhuis slid into the bronze. Gold-medalist Eriksson recorded 3:49.8, and experts believe he would have taken Jack Love-lock's Olympic record had the track been dry. Of course, had it been dry, perhaps Strand would have taken Eriksson.

The medals are delivered at the end of the final events, but the champions smelt for them beforehand. A 5,000-meter trial for the 1948 Olympic final is suddenly turning into a donneybrook with 1 lap to go. The two leaders have been running nearly arm-in-arm for 24 laps. They'd probably made a pact beforehand to run that way. A trial is not the time for guts and gore.

Look! This Swedish fellow, Ahlden, just foolishly decided to spend himself on a cheap, pointless win by sticking it to the rest of the field on the last lap. How dumb! Look at 'im, he's just pulled out 20 or more meters on that other bloke, and ev'eybody else is waddling along behind like a duck, content to finish and qualify.

Blimey, the blighter's cracked! The guy's taking off after the Swede! Lookit how he runs, like he's just swallowed some lye and had a wad of steel wool dropped down his shorts! His head rolls from side t' side like a clapper in a bell on a ship in vomitous seas. This Zátopek is cracked! But he's catchin' the bugger! There's nothin' the Swede can do, oh, it's gonna be close, it's gonna be soooo cllllloooose . . . Blast! The Czech got within a bloody FOOT-STEP of him, but didn't nip 'im. How's that for guts? Make up mor'n 20 meters in half-a-lap. What a hell of an athlete! Stupid, but a hell of an athlete!

Ahlden's time for the 5K qualifier was 14:31.2; Zátopek's, 14:31.4. The third-place finisher was 11 seconds behind them, and the final qualifier another 19 seconds back. The winners of the other three qualifying rounds all ran over 15 minutes for their races.

Emil Zátopek was not stupid, however, although undeniably gallant. He knew how much psychological leverage the winner of a race, any race, gains over those he beats . . . even if he wins by treachery rather than by virtue of hard training. Alas, Zátopek's own arduous training still required competition experience to bring his talent to full fruition.

One wouldn't have known it from watching the 10,000-meter final. Nurmi probably knew who would emerge the victor; everybody else thought it would be Nurmi's pupil, Viljo Heino. That was the way it looked at the start, too. Heino was off into the lead and Zátopek was running in twenty-seventh spot with his usual badly informed form. By the tenth lap, though, Zátopek was on Heino's heels, the two slushing lightly through the drizzle. For six laps the Finn and the Czech paced each other; then Zátopek moved decisively away, picking up 30 meters on Heino in less than 1 lap. Crushed both physically and psychologically, Heino immediately stepped off the track and retired from the race! Zátopek had such a tremendous lead he could afford to coast the remaining 8 laps. He didn't. He picked up the pace instead! It must have felt better than running in combat boots while carrying a torch. He lapped the tail-enders; goodness, he almost lapped second-place man Evert Heinstrom of Finland, who appeared near passing out from the exertion required to avoid such an embarrassment. Zátopek hit the tape in 29:59.6, 48 seconds and 300 meters in front of France's Alain Mimoun, who'd sneaked past the dying Heinstrom. It was the first sub-30 10K final in Olympic history.

Having claimed the 10K, Emil seemed a sure bet for the 5K. The Europeans who knew his track performances considered him more of a 5,000-meter specialist than anything else; they accorded his 10K win to his fundamental strength. It was in fact the Czech Locomotive who was willing to take the lead at the start of the 5,000 final—"willing," because it was windy and steadily raining. The man in the lead not only took the psychological pressure of setting the pace, he also accepted the physical debility of serving as windbreaker for those stalking him. So of course Zátopek took the lead at the gun.

The first lap was slow, nearly 70 seconds, and the pace did not much hasten with succeeding laps. By the eighth lap it was plain Zátopek was having trouble getting a grip on the track. Although his normal running style indicated agony in the upper body, his legs usually swept smoothly under him. Not so in this race; his limb rhythm faltered, and a pursuing predator summoned the courage to pounce. At 3.5K, Belgium's Gaston Reiff swept into the lead, picking up the pace by 4 seconds per lap. Reiff was an inflated 1500-meter runner with excellent steady-state speed, but little kick. The next man to put Zátopek down a notch, Holland's Slijkhuis, was also a miler, but one with a superb sprint. With 1 lap remaining, the two milers were 60 and 30 meters, respectively, ahead of Zátopek, who had clearly failed in his "double" effort.

Well, the failure was clear to everybody except the Mad Czech. Three hundred yards from the wire, Zátopek pulled out the stops and bore down on the two milers like a 40-ton semi about to bunt a couple of Datsuns into the boonies. His eyes were barely-open slits in a tank turret; his lips were pulled back in the predatory anger of a Mako shark. This was not a comfortable man. He walloped Slijkhuis and set sail for Reiff, who was sweating out his shrinking lead, probably wishing he had spent a little time sprinting in combat boots in practice. Comes the tape! Comes the Czech! Reiff holds on—*just*. He gets the gold in 14:17.6, a step ahead of Zátopek's 14:17.8. The Olympic record, set when it wasn't raining, had been 14:22.2. Slijkhuis has the bronze in 14:26.8. Remember, Zátopek was 30 meters back of him a lap from home.

For closers, the British laid on one of the wickedest Olympic marathon courses yet devised by mad gods or Englishmen. In an Olympics rife with upsets, Argentina's Delfo Cabrera upset at least two marathoners: the former leaders, Belgium's Etienne Gailly and Korea's Yun Chil Choi. Gailly held the lead for 17 miles, at which point Yun Chil Choi relieved him of it. With a mile to go, excitement swept the crowd—a new leader! The Belgian got a second wind and rushed past the Korean, zooming for home and a gold medal. The second-wind effort cost the Belgian dearly, apparently, because he turned into a wet noodle when he hit Wembley Stadium for the final track-lap. In spurted upright Cabrera, the proverbial man out of nowhere, and nipped the folding Gailly in the last 400 meters to become 1948 Olympic marathon champion. His time, 2:34:51.6, was excellent for such a rugged course.

Politics refused to let go of the Olympics. As the 1948 Games closed, several Hungarian and Czechoslovakian athletes (*not* including Zátopek) requested political asylum, not wanting to return to Soviet hegemony. No longer could athletes claim disinterest in political affairs. Here were the athletes themselves confronting a political issue in the traditional athletic manner—by demanding asylum from it!

Almost the only thing to stop Sweden's Karl Gosta Leandersson in his charge to Boston Marathon victory in 1949 was one of Massachusetts's deservedly feared crazed motorists. While passing through Auburndale in an unchallenged lead, Leandersson had to triple-jump out of the way of a driver who suddenly pulled out of a side street and onto the Marathon route, nearly striking the swift Swede. Leandersson had ten days previously broken the Marathon course record in a training run; nobody expected him to be bested, and he wasn't. The practice session (and/or the near-fatal mishap) must have taken some starch out of the Swede, for he checked in at 2:31:50, a fine time, but no record.

As a closing note for the decade, on June 12, 1949, Emil Zátopek set his first world record. Running in the Czech Army Championships at Ostrava, he clocked 29:28.2 for 10,000 meters, 7.2 seconds faster than Heino's previous best.

VI

Zátopek and Bannister

1950-1955

As 1950 opened, America got a hint that it would be the home nation for a great miling duo to rival the Haegg-Andersson match-up earlier in the decade. Dynamic Don Gehrmann of the University of Wisconsin emerged as a runner able to push fast Fred Wilt to his maximal oxygen uptake.

Gehrmann and Wilt were so closely matched that, in their first famous clash, it took the judges *eleven months* to decide who beat whom! At the fabled Wanamaker Mile in the 1950 Millrose Games, the two tracksters snapped the wire in identical 4:09.3 clockings. Science hadn't as yet perfected a means of resolving such disputed finishes; it devolved to the human officials to decide. The officials specifically entrusted with eyeballing the mile finishers rendered a split decision. Two favored 2-mile specialist Wilt, two favored mile-ace Gehrmann, undefeated in collegiate miling during all of 1949. Chief Judge Asa Bushnell broke the tie by voting for Gehrmann, and then the politicking began. A month later the Metropolitan AAU registration committee "corrected" the ruling, saying Wilt was the winner and Gehrmann was second. The committee pointed out that there had been two judges charged with checking the winner, one judge with checking second place, and one judge for third place. The third-place judge had cast the tying vote for Gehrmann. The committee said he should not have been brought into the discussion; had

110

he been left out, it would have been 2-to-1 in favor of Wilt. Bushnell put in two appeals, finally going all the way to the National AAU Convention in December, 1950. In the interim, Gehrmann had decisively whipped Wilt at the Chicago Daily News Relays, running 4:09.5. This may or may not have influenced the ultimate decision, but Gehrmann was reinstated as the winner of what proved to be the "longest mile" in running history.

A long foreign domination of the Boston Marathon continued in 1950, as Korea's Kee Yong Ham earned the laurels with a run of 2:32:39, leading a Korean team to the first three places in Beantown.

More eastern schools than ever competed in the 1950 IC4As. Yale's Wade won the mile in 4:10.3, a fine time in this era.

In August, 1950, Zátopek lowered his 10K record while running on Nurmi's home track at Turku, Finland. The result: 29:02.6. The split for the first 5K: 14:37.0; for the second: 14:25.6. Thus did Zátopek establish the pattern that made him dominate the distances. The Czech was ready, willing, and able, to run the second half of his races faster than the first.

Johnny Kelley triumphed in the 1950 Yonkers Marathon, winning in 2:45:55.3.

This was an era of unparalleled optimism and naiveté not only in sport but in all other aspects of life. As Roger Bannister, the man who smashed through the most important barrier in sport, the 4-minute mile, put it: "The 1950s was an age of exploration and attempts to smash physical barriers in a world liberated from war, a world in which we were no longer soldiers, or bombed, or rationed." The war ended long before the decade began, but the advent of an entirely new decade numeral seemed to wipe clean the slate of consciousness and to cause most people to view the world in terms

Wisconsin's Don Gehrmann battles Fred Wilt in the 1950 Wanamaker Mile. Both runners hit the tape in 4:09.3; after deliberating for eleven months, officials finally declared Gehrmann the winner. It is considered the "longest" mile footrace in history because of the decisional hiatus. (Photograph courtesy of Howard Schmertz.)

of black and white or, more precisely, in terms of "free" and "communist" blocs and values.

What could have been more symbolic of the age than a world-class miler/ 2-miler who was also an FBI agent? G-man Fred Wilt as much symbolized 1950s distance running as Micky Mouse symbolized popular culture. (Perhaps significantly, steeplechaser Horace Ashenfelter was also one of J. Edgar Hoover's finest.) Almost unchallenged in American distance running, Wilt battled mightily in the mile runs against Don Gehrmann. Gehrmann usually won the contests; when he wasn't in the race, it was normally a Wilt runaway. Wilt took the 1951 AAU indoor mile championship in 4:09.4 without Gerhmann there. Then he had the supreme satisfaction of ending dashing Don's streak of thirty-nine straight indoor mile wins when the FBI man collared his arch-rival in the Columbian indoor go-round with a time of 4:08.4.

The 1951 Boston Marathon was claimed by a native of Hiroshima, Japan. Shigeki Tanaka ran 2:27:45 on a course somewhat shorter than 26.2 miles due to road construction. The 19-year-old Tanaka was one member of a four-man Japanese team sent to conquer the marathon for the Land of the Rising Sun. The fourth-string runner on the foursome, Tanaka not only blew away from his teammates, but was the only one of them to finish in a medalist position. America's John Lafferty finished second in 2:31:15, and Greece's marathon champ, Athanasios Ragazos, earned third in 2:35:27.

1951 was a good year for the marathon event. It was the year a former 10-kilometer specialist, Englishman Jim Peters, decided to "move up," challenging himself with an additional 20 miles. He ran his first marathon in his homeland, England's Polytechnic Harriers Marathon. Not only did he win, he ran 2:29:28 to become the first Briton to break 2:30.

The astounding Zátopek made a concerted effort to come back from a bad skiing accident (of which many contemporary track experts were unaware) toward the end of 1951. In late September he launched an attack on Viljo Heino's world marks for the 1-hour run and the 20,000-meter run. Running on the track at Prague, Czechoslovakia, Zátopek went after both records in one run, as was common. He ran the first 10K in 31:06. Heino's 1-hour mark was surpassed by 240 yards, for a total of 12 miles, 269 yards. He ran the second 10K in 30:10! Down went Heino's 20K personal best of 1:02:40. Zátopek, characteristically, knew he could do better still. Two weeks later he tried again, this time at Stará Boleslav. The first 10 kilometers passed in 29:53.4—6.2 seconds swifter than his 1948 golden Olympic performance! (Unplanned, but perhaps predictably, Emil set a world record for 10 miles en route: 42:12.) The second 10,000 meters passed in 29:58.4. The hour, passed in 12 miles, 810 yards! The 10-mile standard would stand for 10 years, and the 1-hour best remained the world's reference for 12 years. Zátopek was back.

Gehrmann and Wilt were also back on the track in 1952, with Wilt giving a bit more than he got in return from the fast Wisconsinite. Wilt beat

Gehrmann in both the Columbian Mile (second year in a row) and the Baxter Mile. Gehrmann, who loved the ½-mile as well as the mile, set a Madison Square Garden ½-mile best of 1:51.0. Earlier in the board season he'd smashed John Borican's thirteen-year-old 1,000-yard world record by zipping 2:08.2 at the AAU championships.

At the IC4A champs that year, Wilt ran up against fellow gumshoe "Nip" Ashenfelter in an invitational 2-miler that produced an indoor record of 8:50.7 for Wilt. Only two other men had ever run the distance faster; they were Gaston Reiff and Gunder Haegg, and they both did it outdoors on a 4-laps-to-the-mile track.

Horace "Nip" Ashenfelter had earned his way to that IC4A invitational. Foremost a steeplechaser, the nimble Nip had a running repertoire as flexible as his frame. From 1952 to 1956 he won a total of 13 indoor and outdoor long-distance AAU championships. He was ranked the second-best indoor distance runner in the world in 1952. From 1953 through 1956, inclusive, Ashenfelter ranked Number One.

Guatemalan Doroteo Flores, who'd never before completed a marathon, emerged as Boston Marthon champion in 1952, arriving at Exeter Street in 2:31:53. Flores's time must be appreciated in the light of the hot 88-degree weather.

Six weeks before the 1952 Games, Jim Peters let loose with the world's fastest time for the marathon, 2:20:42, rendering him, in the words of Olympian Chris Brasher (who would help pull Roger Bannister through the 4-minute barrier two years later) "the absolute clear favorite for the [Olympic] marathon." Peters's mark came in the same Polytechnic Harriers Marathon, run from Windsor Castle to Chiswick, in which he'd made his runathon debut.

A caveat, here, regarding "world records" for the marathon: there are no such things. Marathon courses differ profoundly from one another. Many, perhaps most, are run point-to-point (the Boston Marathon exemplifies this; so does the current New York marathon route, and so did the Polytechnic Harriers's route), meaning an athlete may be aided by a strong wind at his back. Conversely, he or she may encounter a hindering headwind the whole way. In short, *no* impartial international sport authority accepts "world records" for marathon running because of the sheer impossibility of comparing marathon performances and ascertaining the precise accuracy of the course. (The reader will notice how often and for how long the venerated Boston course was "off.") Understanding these points, note that Peters sliced 8:46 off his previous effort on the same course in one year! He paid the price for it. He was so exhausted throughout the body of the contest he kept feeling like "an awful fool" and promised himself it would be his last marathon. He broke his promise. He would compete in the Olympic marathon.

Athletes around the world were tuning up for the Helsinki Games. Germany's Herbert Schade flirted with Gunder Haegg's 5-kilometer record of 13:58.2 by running 14:06.6. In England, Gordon Pirie also showed strong 3-mile and 6-mile form, running the latter distance in 28:55.6. Algerian Alain Mimoun (who ran for France in the Olympics) turned in a 29:38.2 10K performance as indication of his own fitness and gilded intentions. Zátopek prepared for Helsinki by coming down with the flu.

The Czech Locomotive went to Kiev shortly before the Games and finished third in the 5K behind Soviets Kazantsev, who ran 14:13.2, and Popov, who ran 14:18.0. Zátopek recorded 14:22.0. He barely whipped Anufriev in the 10K, breasting the worsted in 29:26.0. The track world reverberated with rumors that Emil would foresake the 5,000 meters at Helsinki to move up to the marathon. The rumors were only half-right.

The rumors of war in the decade proved slightly more accurate than those of Zátopek's leaving the 5K behind. The 1952 Helsinki Olympics constituted the first Cold War Games. The Soviet Union intended to compete for the first time and to use her anticipated success as a weapon in the Cold War. Pjotr Sobolev, secretary-general of the Soviet Union's Olympic Committee, stated before Helsinki that "Sport will be a weapon in the fight for peace and for the promotion of friendship among all peoples." The Soviets had a strange way of demonstrating their support for Olympic sport. They refused Finland's request for permission to allow the Olympic torch relay runners to cross Estonia. As part of the request, the Finns specifically stated they would welcome the use of Soviet citizens as runners for that leg of the relay. A spy could hardly infiltrate Mother Russia as part of the event—as if the notion of Finland, which had lived under Soviet hegemony for years by then, sending a spy to the U.S.S.R. while carrying a lit magnesium torch were not sufficiently ludicrous. The Soviet refusal meant a several-thousand-mile detour around the Baltic Sea and over the Arctic Circle, which the taciturn Finns accepted. It probably helped them with their training.

None doubted that the Russian Bear would come to Helsinki loaded for, well, bear. The Soviets had sent a counsel of coaches to observe and take notes at the 1948 London Olympics. Their photos and memos resulted in a multi-million-ruble Soviet Olympic program. By embarrassing contrast, the USOC had only $350,000 in hand two weeks before the Games were to begin. The USOC had projected costs of half-a-million-dollars more than that. The American public wanted to beat the Russians at the Olympics, but it was an era of apathy. The public seemed to care more for personal entertainment than for political entanglement. A solution suddenly presented itself; Bob Hope and Bing Crosby offered to help put the Olympic Team on "the road to Helsinki" by hosting a 24-hour telethon. Out of $1,000,020 pledged during the TV "marathon," the USOC actually collected over $350,000. They were a few dollars short, but the Team took off for Finland on schedule.

Sixty-seven nations sent nearly 6,000 athletes to compete at Helsinki. Several of the Soviet Union's best men and women athletes did not attend the Helsinki Olympics because the Russians considered them "politically unreliable." Neither did a Chinese delegation of any sort parade or compete at Helsinki, because the IOC accepted applications from both Nationalist China and the People's Republic of China. Both countries were miffed at the acceptance of the "false" China, so neither appeared. The IOC refused to recognize East Germany as a sovereign state and so rejected its application; however, West Germany appeared and competed.

In addition to leaving "unreliable" athletes at home, the Soviets made a further political statement by setting up a separate Russian "Olympic Village" to prohibit mingling of Eastern and Western athletes. This from a nation that had stated her intentions to use "sport . . . for the promotion of friendship among all peoples"! More likely, the Russians worried about the "unreliable" political effect of permitting their athletes free intercourse with those from the Western Bloc. As Roger Bannister, whose only (and undistinguished) Olympic competition came at Helsinki, wrote years later: "In all the avalanche of criticism of international sport, it is often forgotten that every athlete who participates becomes a bulwark back in his own country against accepting complete lies about another nation. Once you have competed on the track and queued for food and joked in the shower room you can no longer be persuaded that a foreigner has two horns and a forked tail." The Soviets themselves apparently were so persuaded, because they eventually opened up their camp fully to other athletes toward the end of the pre-Olympics training period.

The IOC itself went through a political shake-up, albeit of a very peaceful nature. Former USOC president Avery Brundage was elected over England's Lord Burghley to replace retiring IOC head J. Sigfried Edstrom of Sweden. Brundage became the first American so honored.

Politics were not alone in casting a pall over the Olympic buildup. The weather also did its worst, as heavy rains soaked the Olympic track. It was so mushy by Opening Day that the runners despaired of setting Olympic records.

The Helsinki Stadium was jammed well beyond its 70,000 capacity (in fact, 80,000 spectators witnessed the events) when the always spectacular Opening Ceremonies began on July 19, 1952. Possibly the turnout was the Finns' way of compensating for their nation's declining Olympic fortunes. The golden days of Hannes Kolehmainen and Paavo Nurmi had faded from memory. The exquisite bronze statue of a naked, running, Paavo Nurmi, executed by Waino Aaltonen, graced the stadium entrance. It seemed, sadly, more a reminder of past glory than a harbinger of future successes at that juncture in Finnish sporting and political history. If only the bronze could come to life, no matter how briefly.

In a way, it did. The parade of thousands of uniformed athletes passed by smoothly in the incessant Opening Day rain. (Unfortunately, the parade also turned what was left of the Helsinki track into a fair imitation of a hog wallow.) Now it was time for the Torch Bearer to appear, the final runner in the unusually long relay bearing the Olympic flame. As had become traditional, the host nation maintained strict secrecy surrounding the last runner's identity. Then he stepped from history's shadows and could not possibly have unleashed more furor and emotion had he held aloft not the Flame but a fused atom bomb. It was Paavo Nurmi! Baldheaded, fifty-five years old, and sprinting out of the stadium tunnel as if Ritola were trying to snatch away the torch! He now had a belly, and a bank account crammed with money, but the old elbows were still out a tad too far and the stride smoother than French silk.

Pandemonium! One of the most exciting and revered moments in modern Olympic history! The highly disciplined, meticulously dressed Olympic athletes went berserk. Everyone, including the Soviets, broke ranks and ran to the edge of the track to feel Nurmi's aura as the living Olympic legend bounded past, head and torch held erect and high. For the first time in recorded history, Paavo Nurmi ran on a track without his mechanical heart, holding aloft instead the fire that inspired his biological one.

A roar from archangels enveloped the throng. Reporters thought it mere applause. Historians note no Games before or since ever heard such a tumult.

The Flying Finn ran nearly a full lap of the stadium, halting finally in front of the huge bowl that would nurture the flame for the duration of the Games. He thrust the torch into it, and there was light. Then Paavo Nurmi passed the still-burning torch to a gaunt old man in running clothes. The crowd wiped rain and tears from their eyes and recognized the second Torch Bearer: Hannes Kolehmainen! The first-ever Flying Finn sped off with the torch and scrambled up the 272-foot Olympic tower atop which he ignited the second Promethean beacon. The circuit was at last completed. The flame Kolehmainen had kindled in Nurmi had now been passed back to him. The Games were open.

The 1924 Olympics were the Nurmi Games; the 1952 Olympics belonged to Zátopek, the man Roger Bannister termed "without doubt the greatest athlete of the postwar world." The first footrace of the Helsinki Games was the 10,000-meter final. Without the culling process of preliminary heats, thirty-three athletes stepped to the line on the first day of Olympic competition. Zátopek, the defending champion, started from the second row, as Australia's Les Perry scatted off into a 40-yard lead after 2 quick laps. The third lap came at a more prudent pace, and the Soviet Union's Aleksandr Anufriev, whom Zátopek had only barely beaten during his Russian tour, assumed the lead. It lasted for 2 laps. At 3,000 meters, Emil Zátopek showed ahead. No sooner had Zátopek taken the pace than Gordon Pirie darted up in a bold bid for an early breakaway. Pirie's breakaway broke down. Zátopek passed him as if he were a gnat. Soon France's Mimoun pushed Pirie down into third spot and settled himself into Zátopek's regular 71-second laps. The Czech Locomotive was more punctual than Amtrak, and Mimoun could live with the pace, at least for awhile.

The 5-kilometer mark passed in 14:43.4, and then Zátopek picked up the pace, not with a surge but with a sustained pace raised to a higher octave than the initial 5K. Mimoun started to sag. Three laps into the new gear Pirie lost all contact with the two leaders. At 8,000 meters the Beast of Prague threw in a hard pickup and dumped the Frenchman. In near perfect unison, the spectators began to chant, "Zá-to-pek! Zá-to-pek!" He pushed the last lap down to 64 seconds, hitting the tape a good 100 meters ahead of Mimoun in 29:17.0 (meaning Zátopek's second 5K took only 14:33.6 of his time). He was 42.6 seconds under the previous Olympic 10K best, which he had set in 1948. Zátopek deadpanned disenchantment with his performance, declaring: "I am disappointed. I was not fast. I was bad, very bad. I will try to do better in the 5,000-meter run." Emil Zátopek, who had been fluent in six languages since age 12, knew how to use every one of his six tongues cunningly.

Mimoun claimed second in the 10K, while Anufriev of Siberia came home third, becoming the first Soviet track-and-field Olympic medalist. Americans Curtis Stone and Fred Wilt finished twentieth and twenty-first, respectively. Zátopek pulled the first five men after him in under his old record—not bad for a "disappointing" run. Recalling the race nearly three decades later, Zátopek remembered it as "relatively easy." Mimoun almost undoubtedly had different recollections.

Marvelous Mal Whitfield took time off from flying bombing missions in the Korean War (he had flown 27 of them as a tail-gunner by the time the Olympics rolled around) to repeat as Olympic 800-meter champion. Both his style and his time equalled his 1948 performance: 1:49.2. So did the second-place finisher's; Jamaica's Arthur Wint again had to settle for silver, just as in 1948. Whitfield, who just barely whipped Wint at the tape, shook his old-time rival's hand; after the shake, Wint crumbled to the Olympic lawn, the victim not of a hearty hand clasp but of a hard 800 meters. Germany's Heinz Ulzheimer, although losing to Wint in the race, beat him to the collapsing part. The East German was already curled up moaning on the infield.

Australia's Marjorie Jackson came to the line in the 100-meter final having equalled the world mark of 11.5 set by Fanny Blankers-Koen in her semifinal heat. She did the same in the final, breaking the wire three yards ahead of the competition. America's Mae Faggs claimed sixth spot. Then the 20-year-old Australian typist turned around and doubled in the 200 meters in nearly a replay of her 100-meter performance. She equalled the world standard of 23.6, held by Stanislawa Walasiewicz, in the elimination heat, but had to content herself with establishing only an Olympic—not a world—record by winning the final in 23.7.

Then came a playful prelude to what would become arguably the greatest Olympic distance race in history, to date. Among the athletes running in one of the 5,000-meter semifinal rounds were Emil Zátopek, the Soviet Aleksandr Anufriev, England's Chris Chataway, and America's Curtis Stone, with whom Zátopek had become very friendly, as was characteristic of the good Czech. Anufriev took the field out at a relatively sedate speed. Zátopek shared the pace-making task with the Siberian after a couple laps, but seemed to be encouraging Anufriev to slow down even more. Perhaps Emil recalled vividly his last Olympic 5K qualifying heat, where he'd thrown away both common sense and perhaps a gold medal in a brave but imprudent race with Ahlden. It seemed clear Zátopek was trying to impart the point that the first five finishers qualified for the final and there was no sense wasting auric effort just *qualifying*. Then it suddenly seemed as though Emil had taken the finalist-selection chores on his own, constantly rolling, shoulders. At 2K he let loose a burst of Czech Locomotive steam, and the four fastest mortals in the field went after him. After two more laps, Zátopek deliberately fell back in the field to have little talks with his friends. He passed some time with Chris Chataway, then fell even further back to talk with and encourage Curt Stone, struggling along in eighth place. What did Emil say to Curt when they finally were running shoulder-to-shoulder? The lighthearted Zátopek suggested that Stone "Hurry up—or you'll miss the bus!" Then Zátopek picked it up again and rejoined the leading foursome. He made a big show of counting heads—one, two, three, four, five—and raised five fingers into the air for them all to see. "See? There's no reason to bust our butts now, his gesture proclaimed. As Nurmi had done in the 3-kilometer team race in 1924, Zátopek encouraged and hustled each man in his manifest charge along with words and gestures. Seeing that Anufriev was gathering himself to tear off on the final lap, Zátopek grinned and gave the Soviet a little shove on the back, as if to say, "Go ahead and take it; it's yours." Then Emil flagged down third man Bertil Albertson of Sweden and they crossed the line together. Anufriev won in 14:23.6, while Zátopek and Albertson checked in with 14:26.0. It was by far the slowest 5K qualifying trial. West Germany's 5K ace, Herbert Schade, ran 14:15.4, taking 2 seconds off the Olympic record in his own heat. Anufriev shook Zátopek's hand afterward and thanked him repeatedly, but one doubts Zátopek conducted himself as he did during the heat merely to receive gracious words of praise. Although highly amusing to watch, Zátopek's qualifying antics permitted him to slip into the 5,000 meter final without revealing what kind of condition he was truly in, a significant strategic point in his favor.

The weather clears. The heavens step aside as Zátopek, Schade, Mimoun,

Chataway, Reiff, Anufriev and Pirie step to the 5,000-meters' line. Sixty-six thousand spectators crouch, watching.

Chataway chats away in the rabbit role, spending the first lap in 65.8; his miler's muscles know the pace. Schade shoves him aside imperiously, but with a hint of anxiety. Running from the front, the German unreels laps of 67.6, 67.8, 68 and 68. Zátopek moves up, takes the pace for 68 more seconds, then Schade shoves him back into the ruck. Zátopek struggles back to the lead, his head rolling, his eyes rolling, his tongue rolling. In German, he shouts to Schade: "Herbert, do two laps with me!"

The pack bides their time, letting the German and the Czech get the tedious running out of the way before the real race begins.

The real race begins 2 kilometers from home. Schade shifts up and storms away from Zátopek. Chataway and defending star Reiff smell blood and pounce after Schade, ignoring the fading Zátopek. Pirie, running forcefully and exhaling each breath powerfully, shoulders Zátopek aside and runs past Schade and the group to take the lead.

Pirie's lead lasts approximately one step. Schade cuffs the Englishman back to where he belongs. Mimoun, who's been slip-streaming Zátopek, finally realizes it's time to move or get left in the red track dust; he sprints and joins Schade's stalkers.

At 4500 meters the order is Schade, Chataway, Mimoun, Zátopek and a fading Pirie. Defending gold medalist Gaston Reiff gives up the chase in nervous exhaustion and steps off the track.

The final lap: Schade, Chataway, Mimoun, along with Zátopek who is in agony. One of these will win; the rest are dead or dying. At the sound of the bell Zátopek punches maniacally, leaping the entourage in a single bound, his eyes barely visible under his brow's furrows. He can't shake his attackers! The strategic kick gains him NOTHING, costs him nearly everything. In 100 meters Chataway sails past him, Schade in his shadow. 200 meters from the medals Chataway, Schade and Mimoun run inside each other's shorts. Zátopek is two meters behind them, his speed unequal to their's, his massive strength drained. Schade asserts his right to the lead. Chataway disputes it, taking command heading into the final turn. The crowd is frantic, howling wildly.

Then the howls coalesce. They are screaming, "Zá-to-PEK! Zá-to-PEK!" From somewhere deep within, the Czech Locomotive has summoned the courage of the angels! Chataway, who in two years will push Bannister through the 4-minute barrier, leans hard into the turn, balancing himself for a devastating sprint. It never comes. Zátopek springs like Blake's tyger, his jaws slavering, his driving leg pummeling the dirt track. Panicked by Zátopek's fury, Schade and Mimoun blast past Chataway. It's too late. Zátopek is all over them and away, his upper and lower bodies almost going in different directions as he powers through the turn far wider than any of the others.

Chataway, passed by three desperate men in the space of four footsteps, brushes against the turn's pole and crashes to the track.

Zátopek's face is crucified with noble effort, his eyes closed, his mouth agape. Mimoun claws the air with his arm thrusts, as if to grasp Zátopek's singlet and halt him. Schade, in third, glares angrily through his eyeglasses, his top speed gaining him naught on Zátopek's courage.

"Zá-to-PEK! Zá-to-PEK! Zá-to-PEK!" The Beast of Prague breaks the tape, after breaking the field, in 14:06.6. Mimoun crosses second in 14:07.4. Schade, third, in 14:08.6. Zátopek takes nearly 9 seconds off Schade's still-wet Olympic record. The final lap takes 57.9 seconds, and many years of pain and determination. Emil Zátopek has his 5K gold. The rest of him is steel.

The brave Chataway recovered to finish fifth in 14:18, behind Pirie, also 14:18.

Skill obviously ran in the Zátopek family. While Emil was running the most stunning Olympic distance race ever, his wife Dana was coolly winning a gold medal in the javelin toss—and on her first throw! Like hubby, she set a new Olympic reference, 165'7". Like hubby, she was humanly exuberant afterwards; she turned a few cartwheels.

To top off the excitement, Emil instantly announced his intention to compete in the marathon run three days hence. Only Hannes Kolehmainen, in 1912, had duplicated the long-distance track double pulled off by Zátopek. No one in history had ever seriously attempted an Olympic distance *triple*. The closest correlative was Nurmi's 1924 Games, where Nurmi did not face nearly the depth of competition as Zátopek in 1952. It seemed as though the Mad Czech had finally blown his mind, but, as Zátopek said, "If I didn't think I could win, I wouldn't have entered."

Zátopek's marathon announcement counted as less of a surprise than the Helsinki steeplechase results. While the Soviets could not, in their first Olympics, expect to sweep the track clean of gold medals, the U.S.S.R. Team felt they could reasonably expect one or two track golds if they concentrated on specific events, especially events in which the Yanks never had much strength. The steeplechase, 3,000 meters of constantly changing physical motion, seemed the ideal event. No American had ever won it. To make matters even more optimistic for the Ruskies, one of their own athletes held the world's best time in the event (but not the world record; international sports bodies had not begun to recognize a world record in the steeplechase). Vladimir Kasantsev had run 8:48.6 on cinders, over hurdles, and through water. No American had ever broken 9 minutes. That was before Horace Ashenfelter had a little chat with Finnish steeple expert Olavi Rinteenpam.

FBI man Ashenfelter was a dedicated G-man, who only trained after working hours. The 29-year-old New York A.C. teammate of Fred Wilt's practiced his steepling in a park, bounding over barriers he or nature had made—it wasn't the same as running on a real steeplechase track. In pre-

Games practice at Helsinki, Nip approached Rinteenpam, whom the Americans had nicknamed "Rin-Tin-Tin," for some pointers. The obliging Finn helped Nip immensely. He explained the European system of steeplechasing, which concentrated more on clearing the water barrier as quickly as possible than getting gracefully over the hurdles. "Rin-Tin-Tin" pointed out that the Americans, possibly because of their strong intermediate hurdling tradition, would sail serenely over the hurdles, only to wind up taking a big bath in the water beyond; while the Europeans would put one foot atop the water-hurdle to propel them to the farthest, and shallowest, edge of the water.

The FBI agent took good notes. The burly Kasantsev ran 8:58 in his own steeplechase trial heat, 5.8 seconds under Iso-Hollo's 1936 Olympic record. Seven other qualifiers also broke the old mark, and chief among them was Nip Ashenfelter, who also erased Kasantsev's standard by running 8:51!

Outstanding trial times may or may not demoralize the opposition, but they almost always take a lot out of the grandstanding qualifier (as Zátopek had learned). Medals come in the finals, not in the trials. Kasantsev could remain confident as he stepped up for the steeplechase final. Ashenfelter had run his qualifying round 15 seconds faster than he had ever run before, while Kasantsev had qualified easily by running 9 seconds slower than his personal best.

Nip darted into the lead 3 laps into the 7-lapper. Kasantsev appeared satisfied to follow in his wake, at least until the final lap when, as virtually everyone expected, the Soviet blew by the American hauling down the back straight. The only obstacle between Kasantsev and the first track gold medal for Mother Russia was the final water barrier. That's just when Soviet hopes dampened. Ashenfelter, refusing to say "die," cleared the barrier perfectly, leaping off with his left foot, kissing the top of the vine-covered hurdle with his right foot, and imitating Superman in a flight to the shallow end of the pool and a quick push-off with his landing left foot. Rin-Tin-Tin had saved the FBI man's neck; Kasantsev, losing his physical and emotional balance when Ashenfelter drew even with him, took a dip in the briney. By the time the Soviet was clear of the water, Ashenfelter was 5 meters clear of *him* and charging for the tape. Nip hit the wire over 25 meters ahead of Kasantsev, checking in at 8:45.4! Kasantsev barely held off England's John Disley to salvage the silver in a race that savaged Iso-Hollo's old record. The first six men were all under the old mark. Kasantsev gave Nip a sincere, warm bear hug in congratulations. Horace Ashenfelter singlehandedly created international respect for American steeplechasing.

Some may have suspected Ashenfelter's steeple win rested on more than Finnish coaching. (Those who knew Ashenfelter's coach at Penn State, Charles D. "Chick" Werner, were especially suspicious. An assistant U.S. Olympic coach in 1952, Werner also worked with such athletes as Curtis

Stone, Barney Ewell, Ed Moran, and Ashenfelter's brother, Bill.) Hanging around top milers such as Gehrmann and Wilt certainly couldn't have hurt Nip in the speed department.

An American who had run the steeplechase in 1948 (and who had taken an even bigger swim in the water than had Kasantsev) was Occidental College's Bob McMillan. Embarrassed by his big splash in the London steeplechase, where he literally had fallen on his face, McMillan decided to run the 1500 meters at Helsinki. A miler moving up to the steeplechase sounds gutsy and promising; a steeple runner moving down to the mile sounds gutsy, but disastrous. It wasn't.

McMillan had won the American metric mile trials in 3:49.3, his first under 3:51 for the 1500. He seemed profoundly over his head in the Olympic 1500. Roger Bannister was running. More important, Germany's Werner Lueg, who had tied the world 1500 record with a 3:43 blast, was running. Their times were much faster than McMillan's best.

They were off! McMillan quickly gained his rightful place in the field—dead last. While Lueg legged off into the middle distance, McMillan slugged it out for next-to-last place with Luxembourg's Joseph "Josey" Barthel, who had respectable 800-meter speed but who had only managed to dip under 3:51 for the 1500 but once in his career, when he ran 3:48 in his Olympic qualifying trial.

On the third lap, Barthel picked up his knees and the pace and, to everyone's amazement, stuck himself between Lueg and Bannister. Barthel's pickup must have inspired McMillan. Possibly he reasoned that, if he had been running stride-for-stride with Barthel in last place, then he could run stride-for-stride with him in dispute of the silver medal.

McMillan took off mightily and latched onto the slipstream of the leading trio. He was right on Bannister's spikes! Heading down the backstretch of the last lap, Lueg signalled the engine room for a fuller head of steam and stormed off. Then there was an excited cheer from the assembled multitude, and Lueg in desperation turned his head to see who, or if, anyone was closing on him. History repeatedly shows taking a quick peek over the shoulder a serious tactical blunder. Barthel slithered past on Lueg's blind side and was gone—and so was McMillan! He sprinted the final 100 yards in just a touch over 10 seconds! Bannister and Lueg got splendid looks at Barthel's and McMillan's disappearing backsides as the American bore down on the Luxembourger. They hit the tape simultaneously. Both Barthel and McMillan tallied 3:45.2, but Josey got the gold and Bob got the silver. Barthel became the first Luxembourger gold medalist, and McMillan became an exonerated steeplechaser-turned-speedster. Lueg held on for the bronze, and Bannister finished fourth. The first eight athletes all broke Lovelock's 3:47.8.

The American women's 400-meter relay team broke both the Olympic and world records for the event, striking gold in 45.9, a half-second faster than the German team's former world standard, and a full second better than the Olympic referent, also held by the U.S.A.

The final running event of the Helsinki Games blazed its way into memory for a number of reasons: It was Zátopek's first marathon. It was also the first race he had ever run without his characteristic grunts and feints, as if he were about to faint or die. (One infers that Zátopek's groaning and bobbing had more basis in tactical thespianism than in practical pain. He would run "normally" in the 1956 Melbourne marathon, too, in which race he was obviously enjoying himself and not intent on seriously competing.) Jim Peters, the world's fastest marathoner, was of course entered, as was defending champion Cabrera, 1952 Boston Marathon victor Doroteo Flores, America's Ted Corbitt, and Sweden's Gustaf Jansson, a highly experienced European road-man. The weather cooperated in raising anticipations: warm and with a slight breeze; the meteorology was good, although not perfect, for running a marathon race.

Zátopek planned to learn how to run a marathon by sticking with Jim Peters during the race. As the Czech put it, "I didn't want to follow a nobody." Zátopek knew the Englishman was supposed to wear number 187. (Throughout the 1952 Olympics, Emil Zátopek himself wore number 903.) Never a man to leave anything to chance, Zátopek approached Number 187 before the start, stuck out his hand, and said in English, "Hello, I am Zátopek." Number 187 shook his hand and replied, "I'm Jim Peters." Check.

The Pakistani, Aslam, who ran barefoot, took the field through the lap of the stadium track, but Peters hauled past Aslam and chugged off into the distance, clearly intent on running away from the field as quickly as possible. He later revealed his concern that he would be "nobbled" (blown away) early in the race by the various track runners' manifestly superior speed. (Peters had moved up to the marathon because he lacked sufficient speed to compete on the track internationally.) He admitted the pace he set at Helsinki was much too fast.

Peters pushed through the first 5 kilometers in 15:43. His British teammate, Stanley Cox, ran in company with Jansson and Zátopek, 19 seconds back. Peters's coach, aghast at the pace, called out to his athlete to "take it steady."

Peters hit the 10K mark in 31:55; Jansson in 32:11; Zátopek in 32:12. At 10 miles, Zátopek and Jansson were up even with the Britisher after running several steep hills on the out-and-back Olympic course. The three ran abreast for the next 2 or 3 miles. Peters and Jansson were in the depths of concentration. Emil Zátopek wanted to be in the depths of conversation. He tried to speak with Jansson, but the Swede spoke only his own tongue, which Professor Zátopek did not. The Czech of course knew English, so he turned to Peters and inquired: "The pace, Jim, the pace—is it good enough?" Peters, playing a game, replied: "It's too slow, Emil." Zátopek, who had

Emil Zátopek enters the Helsinki Olympic Stadium to complete his sweep of the 1952 Games' long-distance gold medals by winning his first marathon (2:23:03.2), a feat almost certain never to be duplicated. Although hard to tell due to the quality of the photograph, Zátopek is grinning broadly as he lopes onto the track for the final lap inside the stadium. (Photograph courtesy of Track & Field News.)

never before competed beyond 20,000 meters, asked: "You say 'too slow.' Are you sure the pace is too slow?" Ever the tough cockney, Peters eloquently answered, "Yeah."

That was when Emil Zátopek put the hammer down hard and blew away from Jim Peters for good, shrugging his shoulders a little bit as he vanished. Jansson went with him; by 20 kilometers they were 10 seconds ahead of the Englishman, both of them clocking a split of 1:04:37. They reached the halfway point, turned, and ran back into the wind toward the 5 kilometers of hills waiting for them 15 kilometers from the finish line.

At 25K Zátopek and Jansson had 30 seconds on the failing Peters. Emil made his move. He ripped through the 30K checkpoint in 1:38:42, *taking 12 seconds off the world record* (held by Moskatchenkov of the Soviet Union, who was somewhere back in the pack by now) *for that distance!* Jansson was down nearly half-a-minute by now. Five kilometers later he was down 65 seconds on the Czech Locomotive. (The brave Peters cramped up at this point and had to retire from the race.) Zátopek broke 40K in 2:15:10, 2¼ minutes ahead of second-man Gorno of Argentina, who had overhauled Jansson. Zátopek rolled his red Czechoslovak singlet up under his arms to bare his belly to the breeze, but he took no fluids during the race.

The Beast of Prague seemed somehow tamed when he arrived in Helsinki Stadium. He no longer needed to fake distress; Zátopek was in pain, ennobled by it. Whether it was the pain of an athlete running a marathon or of a humble man confronted with 70,000 mad people chanting "ZÁ-TO-PEK! ZÁ-TO-PEK!", one cannot know.

In a gentle motion Emil Zátopek lifted his arms and breasted the tape. It was an Olympic record: 2:23:03.2, over 6 *minutes* faster than Kitei Son's 1936 effort.

"ZÁ-TO-PEK! ZÁ-TO-PEK! ZÁ-TO-PEK!" Everyone had waited for Emil to come home, including the Jamaican 1600-meter relay team (who had sliced over 4 seconds off the world record in winning relay gold). The Jamaican team hoisted Zátopek on their eight shoulders and the crowd drowned him with acclaim. Zátopek was in his sweats and eating an orange when silver-medalist Gorno came in at 2:25:35. (Jansson earned the bronze in 2:26:07. Ted Corbitt finished forty-fourth in 2:51:09.) Zátopek offered Gorno a slice of the orange, then offered the world his opinion of the 26.2 miles. Perhaps thinking of Peters's "It's too slow, Emil," Emil said that "The marathon is a very boring race." Then the Helsinki flame flickered, and died. Zátopek had his third Helsinki gold medal, and his third Helsinki Olympics record.

Possibly Ted Corbitt would have placed higher in the Helsinki marathon had he not run it in crepe soled shoes. Almost undoubtedly he would have placed higher had the race lasted a little longer . . . say, 24 or so miles longer. Racing since 1939, Corbitt had always preferred ultra-distance events to "sprints" such as a marathon run. He'd developed a strong distance base as a schoolboy, running the several miles back and forth between the family farm in Dunbarton, South Carolina, and the local school. Young Corbitt *had* to run to school, because he was black. Only whites were permitted to ride the school bus.

He ran his first marathon in 1951, placing fifteenth with a 2:48:42, at age 31. Between 1951 and 1979, Corbitt had completed 193 races of the marathon distance or beyond; he had also logged over 120,000 training miles in the same period. He returned from Helsinki extremely impressed by Emil Zátopek (not surprisingly) and became one of the first American long-distance athletes to emulate the Czech's training, especially the twin emphases on interval workouts and resistance workouts (running uphill, running in heavy boots, and so on). Corbitt won his last marathon in 1962 when, at age 42, he claimed Philadelphia's Shanahan Marathon. That same year, Corbitt helped start the New York Road Runners Club. As of 1981, he was still actively competing and still measuring and certifying courses. Although perhaps not a paragon of speed, Ted Corbitt stands as a paragon of courage, deserving recognition as one of the greats in American distance running history.

Corbitt was not the only distance runner to find a new means of training as a result of the 1952 Olympics. While waiting to board his flight home to England at the Helsinki airport, Gordon Pirie encountered Woldemar

Gerschler who was "the first man who ever suggested that [he] could do *more* than [he] was trying to do." Gerschler took Pirie under his wing— although initially only by mail, because Pirie could not afford to travel to Germany—and taught the English runner his and Reindell's new approach to interval training. When they worked with Harbig in the 1930s, Gerschler and Reindell quite reasonably focused on the *sprint* phase of the interval workout. As Zátopek had learned, if a runner wants to run fast, he or she should practice running fast until good at it. Zátopek, blessed with both iron will and body, took shorter recovery intervals than the German doctors had given Harbig. Whether as a result of further scientific inquiry or of watching Zátopek (or both), Gerschler and Reindell learned that the recovery interval is even more important than the sprint interval. It is during the jogged recovery that the heart muscle gains strength. Harbig had walked between his sprints, which did nothing to enhance his endurance. By sticking to a precise schedule for both the sprint *and* the rest phase of interval training, and by keeping the pulse rate within a certain range in each phase, the athlete simultaneously improves his/her speed and endurance in the same workout. Further, the willpower required to keep moving during the "resting" interval helps train the athlete's determination for facing the rigors of competition.

This was the "new" interval approach into which Gerschler initiated Pirie. Within a year, "Puff-Puff" (so named because of his blown-cheeked exhalations during a race) Pirie set British records for 3K, 2 miles, 3 miles, and 5K, as well as a world mark (28:19.4) for 6 miles.

Zátopek was also setting world records. By the end of 1952 he possessed the global standards for 15 miles, 25K, and 30K.

1953 was Fred Dwyer's big year as an American miler. He was ranked Number One on the indoor mile circuit—in itself, a notable achievement, but Dwyer made it even more so. How? He ran for Villanova, which had no indoor track on which to practice! In 1954 Dwyer went on to win the AAU outdoor mile championship. When his college career ended, Fred became coach at Essex Catholic High School in Newark, New Jersey, where he shaped a promising young miler named Marty Liquori, turning him into a sub-4 high school miler. Dwyer later moved on to a collegiate coaching post at Manhattan College.

The object example of Emil Zátopek winning all the long-distance marbles at Helsinki understandably caught the attention of many international distance coaches. Gerschler (who was really more researcher than coach) was one; Nikiforov of the Soviet Union was another. Nip Ashenfelter wasn't the only fellow who could learn quickly by observing the best. The Soviets copied superlatively well. Gordon Pirie was perhaps the first post-Zátopek athlete to bear fruit from Zátopek's methods, but Vladimir Kuts quickly eclipsed him. Under the tutelage of Coach Nikiforov, Kuts began interval training over distances far longer than anyone else attempted in that era (up to 2-kilometer pickups, or down to 100-meter sprints). Dubbed "Iron Man" by track experts, Kuts unofficially bettered Pirie's 3-mile record toward the end of 1953. He beat Zátopek's best 5K time that same year, serving notice that Soviet distance men were serious international distance competitors. Zátopek was not sitting still either and set world records for 10K (29:01.6) and 6 miles (28:08.4—11 seconds faster than Pirie's, and set on the way to the 10K mark) in 1953. Like Zátopek, Kuts possessed extraordinary courage as an athlete. He always preferred to control a race from the front, as he would demonstrate in the 1956 Olympics. Coaching undoubtedly contributed to his success, as perhaps did political fervor, but the man possessed indisputable raw talent and stands as one of the very first *modern* (as opposed to postwar) distance runners.

Marvelous Mal Whitfield, owner of 2 Olympic 800-meter gold medals, had his best season ever in 1953. He was almost invincible in the 600-yard run indoors, claiming the 600 title at the New York K.C. Meet, the Chicago Daily News Meet, the Buffalo 174th Armory Games, the Boston A.A. Games, and the AAU Championships. Whitfield set the all-time Madison Square Garden 880-yard record at the New York "Casey" meet—1:50.9 (just missing the world record for 800 meters on the way to the tape). He won numerous firsts as a member of the Grand Street Boys Club relay team that year as well, perhaps the most remarkable performance of which was the team's 3:14.4 mile, an absolute indoor mile relay record, anchored by Whitfield's strong legs. The two-time Olympic 800-meters champion went undefeated in every race he finished (save only his first, in 1954), including a double victory in the Millrose Games in the 880- and 600-yard runs. Whitfield remained ranked the Number One 600 runner in the world for 1955 and retired at the end of the 1956 season at age 32.

Marathoners, as well as tracksters, set records in 1953. Japan's Keizo Yamada smoked the Boston Marathon (short) course in 2:18:51. Not until 1956 would officials discover the course to be nearly a half-mile short due to new road construction since 1951. Yet it was wind and competition, as well as the shortened road, that contributed to Yamada's blazing time. Behind the tiny (5'2", 108 pounds) Japanese runner was a 25-mile-an-hour tailwind and European road aces Veikko Karvonen (Finland) and Karl Gosta Leandersson (Sweden), who finished 28 and 45 seconds, respectively, behind Yamada. The other members of the Japanese team finished fourth, sixth, and eighth.

Leandersson, who had won the Boston Marathon in 1949, went on to the Yonkers Marathon in 1953 to notch another roadathon win. He ran 2:48:12 on a full 26.2-mile route.

Because there were more track meets than road races for Americans in the 1950s, more track than road records emerged from the decade. Nip Ashenfelter ran wild in 1954, setting three indoor track records, two of which formerly belonged to Paavo Nurmi. In the 2-mile run at the Millrose Games,

G-man Nip went through the 3K mark in 8:17.7, over 8 seconds faster than Nurmi's 1925 best. At the New York A.C. Games he set a 2-mile mark of 8:50.5 to erase Fred Wilt's record by 2/10-second. Finally, at the AAU champs he hit the 4K mark of the 3-mile run in 11:27.4, again taking another former Nurmi record. Ashenfelter continued to compete until 1957, when he retired to devote full attention to sleuthing.

Emil Zátopek rang in the New Year, 1954, by ranging wildly through the midnight streets of São Paulo, Brazil, on his way to winning the 4.4-mile San Sylvestre Midnight Run over a field of 2,140 other runners.

Superstrong half-miler Tom Courtney began a three-year winning streak in the New York Pioneer Club's Invitational Half-Mile run in 1954, winning in 1:52.7. (He would eventually leave the meet mark at 1:52.2.) Extraordinarily large for his event, the Fordham runner possessed surprising agility, which helped account for his string of indoor track successes. Before retiring in 1957, Courtney tied Mal Whitfield's indoor 600-yard record at the 1957 B.A.A. Games and John Borican's 1000-yard record at the New York Casey Meet the same year.

The Flying Finns finally finished first in the Boston Marathon in 1954, when European marathon champion Veikko Karvonen ran onto Exeter Street ahead of arguably the finest Boston field assembled up to that time; the runners included Jim Peters (who cramped up in West Newton), Delfo Cabrera, and John J. Kelley, the pride of the B.A.A. and AAU marathon champion. Karvonen cavorted home in 2:20:39 after Peters cramped up and let him by.

The Yonkers Marathon that May fell to Ted Corbitt and his crepe soled walking shoes in 2:46:13.9.

When the American marathons are over, spring is close at hand. In the spring of 1954, a medical student at Oxford University named Roger Bannister called on a cobbler from Wimbledon for a special project. Bannister needed a pair of special racing shoes. He told the cobbler: "They should be light. I need them only for three races, for 12 laps." The cobbler did a good job, but Bannister modified his craftsmanship even further. The prospective physician filed the shoes' spikes with graphite "so they'd slip more easily out of the cinder track."

Bannister had at least three good reasons for taking such care in preparing his spikes. First, he was used to making his own athletic preparations, for he trained without benefit of a coach. (He was, however, "guided" by Franz Stampfl, the Austrian who coached Bannister's Oxford teammate, Chris Chataway.) Second, the tracks on which he intended to race, most notably Oxford's Iffley Road track, demanded such precautions. Modern track experts estimate that tracks such as Iffley Road reduced times by about 1 second per lap as compared with modern, all-weather surface tracks. Third, the shoes fitted into Bannister's plan to become the first miler to crash the 4-minute barrier, a quest in which he was hardly the only contestant. Wes

Santee, the great American miler, had started to train with super-speedy Mal Whitfield in an effort to sharpen his own speed for an assault on 4 minutes. Australia's John Landy, after four times dipping under 4:03, moved to Europe in April, 1954, publicly intending to become the first sub-4 man. Time, always precious to a competitive runner, was particularly so to Bannister that '54 spring. If he didn't get the record, someone else was going to do it instead. Gunder Haegg probably would have claimed it nearly a decade previously. The war and the Europeans' concentration on metric, instead of English, distances combined to conspire to keep Haegg's 4:01.4 the world standard for an unnaturally long time.

On the other hand, World War II ultimately resulted in a postwar era highly supportive of "impossible" athletic efforts. As Bannister remarked of his successful assault on the 4-minute barrier: "It happened at a time when there was much less sporting activity than there is today [in 1979]. We had turned away from the end of World War II—rather a gloomy time—and people felt free to take part in sport, climb mountains and sail boats, and it represented the mood of that particular era."

More time was available to concentrate on sport, but not for a medical student. Bannister could train only one hour a day. He had an absurdly low distance base by 1981 standards for a miler, but dedicated himself to high-quality track workouts. In the two-and-a-half weeks before his sub-4 effort, Bannister performed seven interval workouts on the track, three of which were essentially time trials (880 in 1:53.0; ¾-mile in 3:00, pacing with Chataway; and 2 ¾-mile separated by 8 minutes' rest, the first in 3:14, the second in 3:08.6, neither of them with any pacing help). Ten of the days during the final weeks before the assault were devoted to naught but rest. Bannister's preparations were consistent both with the vicissitudes of his medical studies and the philosophies of Franz Stampfl, who argued that "The athlete who believes that all normal social life and entertainment must be abandoned in the interest of rigorous and continuous training is a man devoid of imagination and proper understanding of the value of recreation. A colorless, Spartan life in which all other interests are sacrificed to a single ideal is no existence for a man intent on achieving physical and mental fitness." On five of his ten days of rest, Roger Bannister went rock climbing.

Although proud of coaching himself, Bannister turned to Stampfl for advice increasingly during the final preparations. The two athletes who would help pace Bannister in his attempt, Chataway and Chris Brasher, both regularly received Stampfl's tutoring; it was only natural for an anxious athlete to want some comforting advice in his time of greatest trial. In retrospect, one sees Stampfl as an excellent choice. He was one of the first coaches to understand that, as he wrote, "Training is principally an act of faith. The athlete must believe in its efficacy. . . . He must be a fanatic for hard work and enthusiastic enough to enjoy it." The 4-minute mile earned the title "the most important barrier in sport" because, with the benefit of historical

Roger Bannister, one step away from the finish line and immortality on May 6, 1954, as he finishes the first sub-4 mile footrace. Years later he revealed that the coaches of his day thought an athlete would die if he attempted a sub-4 mile. Asked his own feelings on the subject, circa 1954, Bannister replied, "I was prepared to die." (Photograph from the authors' collection.)

hindsight, one clearly sees the barrier was far more psychological than physiological. Athletes in 1981 know that, to achieve a given time for a given distance, the athlete must first *believe* he or she can do it. The flood of milers cracking through 4 minutes after Bannister opened the gate was the first concrete example of the importance of self-confidence in distance running, and Coach Stampfl preached the gospel of self-confidence to Roger Bannister.

The target date was May 6, 1954, at a meet between Oxford and the British Amateur Athletic Association at Oxford's Iffley Road track. All day Bannister worried about the wind. If it were too strong, he planned to postpone the attempt another ten days, saving it for the White City Stadium Meet. Stampfl advised him not: "If you don't try today, you might not get another chance," Stampfl said portentously, the ghosts of Landy and Santee haunting his little speech. "With the proper motivation your mind can overcome any sort of adversity. In any case, the wind might drop." Bannister, Chataway, and half-miler (in 1:56.7) Brasher decided to give it the old Corinthian try. Brasher would handle the early pacing chores, Chataway would take over on the third lap, then Bannister would scoot for home; anyone who could go with and/or pass him was welcome to kick in also.

For the record, the other runners in the event were G. F. Dole and A. K. Gordon of the Oxford team, and W. Hulatt of the AAA team. There was a wind, but a reasonable one. The attempt was on! . . . only to be stymied by a false start by Brasher.

The gun! Bannister felt impatient with Brasher: first the false start, then the fellow didn't seem to take it out nearly fast enough. Bannister later recalled that "I was so full of running and so impatient that I couldn't believe he was going fast enough." He was: 57.4 for the first lap, perfectly meeting the scheduled pace.

They passed 880 in 1:58, 2/10-second under Haegg's world mark. Stampfl looked into Bannister's taut face and yelled, "Relax!"

Long-distance man Chataway took over from the fading Brasher on the third lap, and "the red (headed) fox of Oxford" took Bannister through the ¾-mile mark in 3:00.4. Three hundred yards from the tape Bannister went into his kick. Nobody went with him. All that stood between him and his goal were 300 yards of dirt track and decades of negative mental conditioning. Describing the moment, Bannister reflected: "There was no pain, only a great unity of movement and aim." He arrowed at the tape, snapped it, then "felt like an exploded flashlight. I knew that I had done it before I even heard the time. I was beyond speech. . . . There is a certain oblivion at that point."

The crowd waited in that oblivion, aching to hear the result of the race. The meet announcer was the puckish Norris McWhirter, a pretty fair relay runner and who, with his identical twin Ross, would eventually found and edit *The Guiness Book of World Records*. After Bannister snapped the tape and the assembled crowd held their breath, McWhirter announced:

"Ladies and gentlemen, here is the result of event number nine, the one mile. First, number 41, R. G. Bannister, of the Amateur Athletic Association and formerly of Exeter and Merton Colleges, with a time which is a new meeting and track record, and which, subject to ratification, will be a new English native, British national, British all-comers, European, British Empire and world record. The time was three . . ."

No one heard the rest of the statement. There were cheers.

Bannister's achievement was tantamount to man landing on the moon in terms of the international excitement, wonder, and optimism it created. That which the species had been taught for generations to believe impossible—a mile run in less than 4 minutes—was possible. The fact that another athlete ran under 4 minutes less than two months after Bannister rent the so-called barrier negated any discussion of Bannister as a superhuman. On the complete contrary. Men cheered that May day precisely because the young medical student had shown the strength of human imagination. Roger Bannister had willed himself to go through an alleged barrier, and the rest of humankind followed him.

There were also cheers for Emil Zátopek on May 30, 1954, when another of Haegg's venerable records bit the track dust. Running in Paris, Zátopek won the 5,000-meter event in 13:57.2, one full second faster than Haegg's twelve-year-old-best. Two days later, in Brussels, the gold-and-steel Czech set new world records for both 6 miles and 10,000 meters in the same 10K race. He cruised through the 6-mile point in 27:59.2 and hit the 10K tape in 28:54.2. Zátopek was the first to run under 28 minutes for 6 miles and under 29 minutes for 6.2 miles.

On June 21, John Landy set a record of his own. Racing at the Turku, Finland, track (home of Paavo Nurmi), the Australian miler broke Bannister's mark by 1.5 seconds, recording 3:57.9. There were now two sub-4 milers in the world. There had to be a race between them.

There was. It was called, like so many before and since, the "Mile of the Century," and it came on August 7, 1954, at the British Commonwealth (or Empire) Games in Vancouver, British Columbia. It was a meet in which not only would the world's two fastest milers meet, but in which eventually the world's premier miler would have a grotesque meeting with the world's greatest marathoner.

A certain irony prevailed in the meeting of the world's only two sub-4 milers. Bannister's mentor, Franz Stampfl, emphasized the importance of mental preparation in an athlete. Australian coach Percy Cerutty, who sheparded John Landy to preeminent miler status, was also one of the first "psychological" coaches, indeed, even more so than Stampfl, who emphasized scientific interval training as much as emotional preparation for an event. Aware that Bannister probably possessed speed superior to his own, Landy ran from the front in an effort to deplete Bannister's kick. Landy led from the gun. He ran the first lap in 58.2 seconds; the first half-mile in 1:58.2. He entered the bell lap in 2:58.4, with Bannister a full 5 yards behind him. He went through the 1500-meter mark only 1/10-second slower than his own world record for that distance. He led right up until the final 80 yards, at which point he turned his head to take a peek at Bannister over his shoulder. That was when the Oxonian charged past the Australian. As Bannister remembered the moment: "Landy looked the right way for what he was trying to do, which was to take his last chance of seeing where I was; he looked three-quarters of the way 'round. He looked 'round the bend and could have seen me if I'd been behind him. It was the moment I'd always learned to attack. . . . I had to run extra distance to get the element of surprise." As Landy remembered it: "You rarely get two chances in a mile race, and any move should be sudden and decisive. When a runner is passed, he should be 'jumped' as unexpectedly as possible and given no chance to bridge the gap or fight back. Franz Stampfl has likened the effect of the shock this produces to a blow in the stomach, and I can vouch for this in my race against Roger Bannister in 1954." Bannister blazed the final straight, coming home in 3:58.8 to Landy's 3:59.6—the first mile footrace in which two athletes broke the 4-minute mark. In 1979, Bannister reflected: "In retrospect, probably I let the gap grow too large [between Landy and myself]. . . . If I hadn't managed to beat Landy, the four-minute mile would have been unsubstantiated." That latter thought likely gave impetus to Bannister's legs and bravery. His powerful finishing strength also moved

Landy to reconsider his own racing strategy. While Landy had traditionally run the first half of a mile race faster than the second, he thenceforth trained to run the second half approximately 3 seconds faster than the first 800 yards. Zátopek's long-distance running strategy was filtering down to the middle distances.

Several weeks after the Empire Games, a new American biweekly sporting journal called *Sports Illustrated* appeared on the newsstands for the first time. On the cover was a picture of Roger Bannister besting John Landy in the world's first sub-4 showdown.

Yet another showdown occurred at the Empire Games on the same day as the Bannister-Landy shootout. On August 7, 1954, marathoner Jim Peters ran his last race. The marathon race was the final event of the games, in parallel to the Olympics. The Canadians laid on a devilish course. Not only was it unusually hilly and not only was the temperature in the 90s, the course was nearly ¾-mile *long*. Peters had been incorrectly warned that the course was only about ⅛-mile long, so he intended to win the race in around 2:20. He remembers that "I knew I was capable of 2:15 but not in that heat." His teammate, Stan Cox, intended to push Peters to the limit that day because Cox had never beaten his friend in a marathon. As he had done at Helsinki, Peters flashed into a raging lead to crush the spirit of any potential competition. He arrived back in the Vancouver stadium in 2:22, a full 3 *miles and 15 minutes* ahead of second-place Joseph McGhee. Peters's brazen will and the brazen sun had taken their toll: the scene was worse than Dorando Pietri's in the 1908 London Olympics. By conservative count, Peters collapsed twelve times in trying to complete the final 440 yards of the marathon. Chris Brasher, who had earlier witnessed his friend Bannister whomp Landy, later recalled Peters's distress. "He collapsed, got up and collapsed all again. It was a hell of a scene, one of the most horrific in athletic history. I was on the side of the track and saw it all. They took his temperature right there and his brain temperature was about 107 or 108 degrees. It is something that is still absolutely unbelievable in medical circles. He was on the verge of cooking his brain."

Officials quite sensibly withdrew the insensate Peters from the race 200 yards from the finish line. (Joe McGhee finally won in 2:39:36.) The first marathoner ever to go under 2:20 (his best mark was 2:18:40.2) finally opened his eyes in the resuscitation ward of the Vancouver Hospital to find his friend Stan Cox, exhausted, in the bed next to him and to find his attending physician was the first miler ever to break 4 minutes—Roger Bannister. After such an ordeal, Jim Peters decided to hang up his "plimsoles" (flimsy canvas-and-rubber shoes roughly as sturdy and protective as 1981's beach slippers).

After one last race, Dr. Bannister followed Peters's example and hung up his special spikes. On August 29, 1954, Bannister won the European 1500-meter Championship at Berne, Switzerland, then retired from track, still

Wes Santee of Kansas duels with Gunnar Nielsen of Denmark in an indoor mile race at Boston Garden. Santee prevailed in 4:03.8, a world indoor record. Note the tape across the runners' shoes to keep them in place during competition on the boards. (Photograph from the authors' collection.)

at the peak of his powers. On retiring, he founded the Four-Minute Mile Club, membership in which obviously rested on running under 4 minutes for the mile. Once an athlete had done that, he would receive a tie designed (and entirely paid for) by Dr. Bannister, and which bore the subtle legend "4mm" on it. There was also a personal letter of congratulations. One infers Bannister presumed very few runners would pass the entry exam for the club, but several hundred have qualified since 1954. They have not all received ties.

Arnold Sowell was an American athlete who was at the peak of his own powers as the 1955 indoor season rolled around. Blessed with a 9-foot stride, Arnie ate up both the boards and the competition in ½-mile runs. From 1955 to 1957, Pittsburgh Arnie had a streak of 20 straight indoor victories at distances from 800 meters to 1,000 yards. His main competition came from Tom Courtney, whom Sowell beat 8 times in a row. Ranked Number One in the world at 880/1000 yards indoors, the versatile Sowell also anchored the Pittsburgh 2-mile relay team, ran cross-country, the 100-yard dash (9.8), 220-yard dash (21.1), 440-yards (47.0), and competed in the long jump (23′).

Emil Zátopek began 1955 by declaring his intention to "move up" in distance events. He intensified his training by running between 30 and 90 interval laps daily, with a jogged half-lap between each! He also practiced Walter George's "hundred-up" exercise, demonstrating the consistency of at least a few venerable training methods throughout history.

Miler Wes Santee deserved some credit for pushing Bannister through the 4-minute barrier. Although the Kansas native never broke 4 minutes himself, it was not for lack of either effort or talent. The Kansas University star had gone undefeated in the mile since high school, until he encountered Denmark's Gunnar Nielsen at the Washington Star Games in January, 1955. Santee had outkicked Nielsen the day before in an indoor mile at Philadelphia (winning in 4:10.5 to the Dane's 4:12.0). Nielsen returned the favor at Washington, prevailing in 4:09.5 to Santee's 4:11.5. The next week, on January 29, 1955, Santee beat both Nielsen and fellow Kansan Glenn Cunningham's world indoor record by whisking 4:03.8 for the mile. Then came the Millrose Games's Wanamaker Mile, where Santee faced not only Nielsen but ferocious Fred Dwyer. The front-running Santee sailed through the 1500-meter mark in 3:48.3, taking down yet another Cunningham record (by 1/10-second). Nielsen surged by the sagging Santee just then. As Santee and Dwyer shifted into their finishing-sprint gears, they tangled going through the final turn and Nielsen romped home free in 4:03.6. Santee held on for second spot, but lost his world indoor mile mark.

The Baxter Mile at the New York A.C. Meet featured a near replay of the Wanamaker Mile, minus the wrestling match in the last turn . . . and with a different winner. This time it was Dwyer who waited until the hard-charging Santee slumped on the penultimate lap, sailed by, and hit the tape in 4:06.2. Nielsen, who had paced along with Santee, claimed second, and the tired Santee was third. At the AAU indoor championships the next week, Santee beat Nielsen in 4:07.9, then went on to victory in the New York "Casey" mile, the Milwaukee mile, and the Cleveland mile. Wildman Wes went on to establish his all-time personal best mile mark, 4:00.5, in winning the Texas Relays outdoor mile later that spring.

Shortly thereafter the AAU stripped Santee of his amateur status. He had accepted double payments for expenses from one of the indoor meet promoters, and the AAU had a copy of the check to prove it. A runner with Olympic aspirations, Santee of course appealed the decision. While his appeal was pending, he ran the 1956 B.A.A. Meet in the Boston Garden. To prevent the other amateurs at the meet from potential contamination by competing against a pro (if the AAU decision were not reversed), Santee ran a mile "race" solo, clocking a remarkable 4:11, unpaced and unpushed. The AAU's decision was upheld, and Wes Santee's career was over.

While the AAU was discovering Santee's cancelled check, the Japanese were prevailing in the 1955 Boston Marathon. Lying tenth at Wellesley, Hideo Hamamura picked up the tempo going over the Newton hills, picked off leaders Eino Pulkkinen of Finland and Nick Costes of Massachusetts (who would go on to win the Yonkers Marathon in 2:31:12.4 the next month), and put on the laurel crown at Exeter Street, coming in with a 2:18:22 record run.

On October 22, 1955, a record-breaking athlete-coach team was forged when Percy Wells Cerutty met Herbert James Elliott, who would become, as of 1981, the greatest miler in all history. Cerutty had been invited to lecture on sports theory at a high school in Western Australia. The school reciprocated by staging a track meet for Cerutty's delectation. The coach took special interest in the 17-year-old who won the mile, unchallenged by older and/or stronger lads, in 4:26. The miler was Herb Elliott, and Cerutty wanted him to be his athlete. He told the youngster: "There is not a shadow of a doubt that within two years you will run a mile in 4 minutes." (Elliott was probably confident in his own prowess by this time, having lost only one mile race, to an upperclassman, during his high school career. It would prove to be the only mile loss Elliott *ever* suffered.) Elliott went on to take the state mile championship later that year in 4:20, but two months later broke a couple of foot bones and was sidelined for the next track season. He and Cerutty would meet again.

VII
Running on Road and Track
1956–1960

Running entered more popular paths in the second half of the 1950s. This was especially so in America, where a healthy economy and a quiet political scene combined with burgeoning communications media to make larger and larger numbers of people aware of new pastimes they might enjoy. Although racing on the track remained the preeminent form of running competition, the growth in the number of marathons across the globe influenced similar growth in sub-marathon length road races as the decade drew to a close.

Villanova University continued to defend its claim to collegiate track sovereignty in the U.S. in 1956 whenever Charles Jenkins hit the boards to run a fast 600 yards indoors. The heir-apparent to marvelous Mal Whitfield, Charlie ranked Number One in the world in the 600 from 1956 to 1958, inclusive. 1956 was also the year he laid Whitfield's 500-yard record to rest at the NYAC meet with a scintillating 56.4 effort.

Foreign domination of the Boston Marathon continued into its eleventh straight year as Finland's Antti Viskari beat Boston's John J. (the Younger) Kelley by 19 seconds, 2:14:14 to 2:14:33. Viskari's teammate, Eino Oksanen, also had a quick race in 2:17:56, and so did evergreen Nick Costes, running 2:18:01. In fact, all of the times were just a little too fast, even though the cool conditions and slight pursuing wind favored fast times.

Suspicious officials belatedly remeasured the course and discovered they had lost half-a-mile of it somewhere (to road construction, in fact). The venerable B.A.A. Marathon route was then restored to its full 26.2 mile glory.

Young John Kelley won the Yonkers Marathon in 2:24:52, an American marathon best, the following month. With that victory, Young John inaugurated a remarkable *eight wins in a row* at Yonkers.

Gordon Pirie vindicated Gerschler's and Reindell's new interval training methods on June 19, 1956, when he set a world record for 5,000 meters at the Bergen track, beating Vladimir Kuts in the process. His time, 13:36.8, took nearly 4 full seconds off the mark established by Hungary's Sándor Iharos the previous year.

Marathon opportunities burgeoned in America in 1956. The Pikes Peak Marathon began in August of that year. A race with a somewhat misleading name, the "marathon" actually covered 28.2 miles, exactly 2 miles longer than a normal marathon. Further, the route climbed 14,110 feet in its first 14.1 miles, then plummeted 14,110 feet in the next 14.1 miles! Even further the marathon consisted of two separate, but contiguous, races—up the mountain and/or down the mountain. Entrants did not have to run in both events, but many did. The ascent and the descent provide distinct challenges. In the climbing race, the oxygen pressure drops by 30 percent from the base to the top of the mountain. Not only does the cumulative fatigue of steady climbing inhibit the runners, so does the decreasing availability of oxygen. In the descending race, athletes not only have to contend with gravity and unexpected rocks, they also have to be aware of stragglers still coming *up* the trail in the climbing race! It is a wonder that so few have been injured during the race's history.

On October 26, 1955, Emil Zátopek set two world records in the course of one 25,000 meter race. The records were for 15 miles and 25 kilometers. Toward the end of 1956 he suffered a hernia as a result of his preparations for the Melbourne Olympics marathon. The Czech Locomotive was injured by running with his wife, Dana, perched on his steely shoulders! Finding there were limits to the effectiveness of resistance training, Zátopek underwent surgery six weeks before the Games. The doctors told him to take two months off before trying to train again. As Zátopek recalled the moment many years after: "But the Olympics were only six weeks away, so I went directly from the hospital to the track."

Australia has summer when the Northern Hemisphere nations receive winter. The timing created some controversy in the U.S., where Olympic officials split into two groups: one that wanted to hold the Olympic Team trials at the normal time during the American summer, the other that wanted to defer the trials until six weeks before the Games. In light of the fact that most Olympic aspirants were also college undergraduates, the first group won. It would hardly have been fair to either winners or losers in the trials to force them to defer making college plans until late October.

Political problems followed the calendar confusion leading up to the Melbourne Games. The Australians announced they would permit no separate quartering of any national teams. Translation: The Russians had to live in the official Olympic Village in 1956. Then there was a rebellion in Hungary, followed by Soviet "aid," and squabbles over rights to the Suez Canal in the Middle East. Worried about mounting political influence on the Melbourne Games, IOC head Avery Brundage griped that "In ancient days nations stopped wars to compete in the Games. Nowadays we stop the Olympics to continue our wars."

The USOC once again found reason to bounce an athlete off the U.S.A. Team after the troupe arrived at the Olympic site. Hammerthrower Cliff Blair got the heave-ho because he continued to work as a correspondent for a Boston newspaper, reporting on the Olympics for the periodical. That meant Blair was not an amateur athlete, because he received payment for writing about sports.

It rained hard and blew hard in the two weeks before the Opening Ceremonies, but the weather came right (as it always seems to do) when it was time to open the Olympics. A temperature in the 80s and a crowd of 103,000 awaited the 4,000 athletes from 67 countries at the Olympic Stadium.

In counterpoint to the Finns, who had asked the legendary Nurmi to bear the Olympic flame to the Opening Ceremonies, the Australians asked a promising 19-year-old miler to undertake that honorable task. His name was Ron Clarke, and he would go on to become one of the true giants of long-distance running. Like Nurmi, he would win the Olympic gold medal due him but, unlike Nurmi, he would not receive it during the course of any Olympic Games.

Young Clarke's performance in bearing the torch foreshadowed his performance in international competition in succeeding years. The flawed torch dripped burning naphthalene on his bare arm as he lapped the stadium's track. He neither flinched nor sprinted the distance, but ran with steely dignity until he could ignite the Olympic urn and extinguish his own torch. A then current Australian great, John Landy, took the traditional Olympic oath on behalf of all the assembled athletes. Then it was time to run.

The long-distance track events belonged to Vladimir Kuts in the 1956 Melbourne Olympics. The 29-year-old Soviet military officer nearly dominated his first and last Olympics. One says "nearly" because he lacked the obvious versatility of a Nurmi or a Zátopek, and his Ukranian taciturnity certainly did not capture the world's affection as had Zátopek's ebullience. Rather short and stocky (5'7¾", 159 pounds) for a long-distance man, Kuts enswathed his training regimen in secrecy. He told some enquirers he trained twice a day; others, that he trained only six times a week. One either concludes Kuts trained only 3 days a week or that he mastered obfuscation. He claimed to train during the summer months as if every workout were a race;

he eschewed speedwork the rest of the year. One fact stands certain. Kuts felt he required a complete massage after each workout, and his masseur accompanied him to all races throughout his career.

Kuts and his coach, Nikiforow, copied Zátopek's training methods, but not his racing tactics. Kuts emphasized long intervals (up to 2 kilometers) in his race preparations. He always strove to run the first half of an event faster than the remainder, in contrast to Zátopek and to what was becoming the accepted racing practice of the day. His victory in the Melbourne 10,000-meters final illustrated his strategy perfectly.

The 10K final quickly evolved into a two-man race: Vladimir Kuts versus Gordon Pirie, one of only two men ever to defeat Kuts. Kuts ran the first 400-meter lap in 61.4 seconds, then ran a series of 68-second laps, aggregating a 4:27 first mile. Pirie, who had won international mile races in addition to his distance specialties, went with him. The rest of the field was outclassed from the gun.

Starting the fifth lap, Pirie clipped Kuts's heel, although whether intentionally (to throw off his concentration, not at all uncommon a tactic in international competition) or carelessly was unclear. Kuts took off, going through the next 220 yards in 30 seconds flat, with a fifth lap total of 65 seconds—in a 10,000-meter race! Kuts pulled out 10 yards on Pirie with that surge. Puff-Puff struggled and closed the gap, but refused to take the pace. Two miles passed in 9 minutes flat.

More incredibly, the halfway mark of 5 kilometers equalled Zátopek's Olympic record for the distance: 14:06.6. Kuts and Pirie ran 100 yards clear of the balance of the field by that point.

Tired making the pace, Kuts moved wide and waved Pirie to pass him. Pirie declined. Kuts took off again and Pirie stuck with him, but with more puffing than usual. Again Kuts offered the Englishman the lead. Again Pirie, somewhat unsportingly but perhaps realistically, declined. The Alphonse-and-Gaston routine, not unknown in world-class distance running, continued until Kuts exasperatedly came to a dead stop on lap 20. Pirie, nearly in a trance and having let Kuts do his thinking for him for the previous 20 laps, saw no choice but to accept the lead.

Kuts let Pirie have his little lead for 100 meters, then hit the old Ukranian throttle hard and vanished by Puff-Puff. It was a devastating tactic. Pirie was finished, gave up trying and caring, and drifted down to eighth spot by the race's end. Kuts claimed the tape and the gold medal in 28:45.6, 15.2 seconds slower than his own world mark at 10K, but over 30 seconds faster than Zátopek's former Olympic best. The second 5K had taken 14:39, an indication of how much faster Kuts ran the first half of his races than the second half of them. Hungarian Josef Kovacs won the silver medal, and Australian Allan Lawrence, the bronze. Kovacs pointedly refused to shake Kuts's hand afterward, but Kuts remained gracious, saying of the crowd that they "were very kind, and I appreciated the way they applauded me."

Pirie had a few post-race words of his own: "Kuts murdered me. It wasn't the fact that he beat me; it was the way he beat me that hurt. I hope I never have to compete against a runner like him again." Yet Pirie would compete against the very prototype of the type of runner he claimed to detest in the 5,000 meters. The runner would be Vladimir Kuts.

The middle distances sizzled at Melbourne, as evidenced by the 800-meters final. While the 10K final resulted in the anticipated two-man race, four contenders lined up for the 2-lap shootoff: Arnie Sowell, the Pitt Panther, and Tom Courtney, the Fordham Flash, for the U.S.A.; Derek Johnson for Great Britain; and Audun Boysen for Norway. There was a strong Australian wind whipping down the front straight, the one that led to the finish line, yet each of the four men was also strong. Courtney and Boysen both boasted 1:46.4 credentials for the 800. Sowell was a 1:46.7 man, but had consistently beaten big Tom in national half-miles. Johnson not only had 800-meter strength, he also possessed great sprint speed and athletic versatility. He ran the 100-yard dash in 10 flat; the 440 in 47.7; he competed in the intermediate hurdles and the steeplechase.

The gun sounded, and after some indecision, Courtney swept into the lead. Sowell, trying to get up momentum for the run down the windy front straight, took the pace over from his teammate going down the wind-aided backstretch. Courtney tucked in behind him, followed by Boysen and Johnson. There were other runners, somewhere.

Sowell clocked 52.8 for the first 400 meters with the trailing threesome nibbling on his spikes. The order remained static for the next ¾-lap, until the final turn. Courtney expected Arnie to die after leading for so long; he moved out into lane 3 going through the final bend in anticipation of Sowell's demise. Then 180-pound Tom got nervous and moved out *hard* before Sowell obligingly fell back. His momentum straightened out for the windy straightaway; Courtney imitated a double-A fuel dragster coming out of the hole. He had swung a bit wide to pass Sowell and was just moving back into lane 2 when medium-sized Derek Johnson flew through the gap between the two Yanks. Johnson had planned to wait till the last 50 yards to set free his sprinter's speed for a surprise strategic strike but, like Courtney, had gotten nervous and let go the leash sooner than he had planned. His timing could hardly have been better. Courtney's sprint was spent and his leg muscles awash in lactic acid as he ran into a strong headwind. Johnson had a yard on him as the tape loomed. At 50 yards from home, just where Johnson had planned originally to attack, Courtney swiped the Englishman's strategy. Perhaps borrowing on the energy of his next four or five lifetimes, Courtney achingly closed the distance between himself and Johnson, tossed back his head and gulped sheer pain, then hit the wire 2 feet ahead of his rival in an Olympic record 1:47.7. He then fell directly on his face on the track. Johnson made it to the track infield before passing out.

Officials postponed the awards ceremony an hour so the gold and silver medalists could recover and compose themselves. Courtney commented after the rest: "When Johnson got a yard ahead of me, I thought the race was all over. I thought I had lost. I don't even remember what happened after that. I ran out of steam 30 yards from the tape, and then the Lord really helped me the rest of the way. I just kept lunging and lunging for the tape, wondering all the while why it never got any closer. I was completely fagged out. My legs were like rubber. I didn't pass out at the finish but I could hardly stand up. I knew rather vaguely that I had hit the tape but to make sure I had won I asked Johnson." He had pulled the three athletes behind him in under Mal Whitfield's former Olympic 800 standard, while fifth man Mike Farrell of England equalled it.

The 5,000-meter run was the next distance final at Melbourne. The field boasted more depth than that for the 10K: Kuts, Pirie, Chataway and Derek Ibbotson of England, and Laszlo Tabori of Hungary. The last three runners, amazingly, belonged to Bannister's Four Minute Mile Club, sub-4 athletes all. The field may not have intimidated Pirie, who preferred at that stage in his career to let others handle the pace for him and then kick past them 300 yards from home, but Kuts—although swift for a distance man—could not expect to live with many sub-60-second laps.

Consequently, Kuts contented himself with pacing the field through the 2-mile mark in 8:47, a mere 4:23.5-per-mile average. He never gave the other athletes a chance to take his measure at speed. He crushed them with his strength and psychology. Fifteen yards ahead of a pack allegedly faster than he, the Soviet started to pick up the pace and hit the tape 40 yards clear of second-man Pirie, who had fought back past Ibbotson in the homestretch in an argument over the silver. Kuts clocked 13:39.6 to break another Zátopek Games record, this time by 27 seconds. The race constituted yet another mass assault on Olympic references; the first five men all slid under Zátopek, while almost unquestionably owing him a huge training debt.

As at Helsinki in 1952, the Melbourne steeplechase final proved surprising and exciting. Sandor Rozsnyoi, the Hungarian who held the steeplechase world record (8:35.6) was in the race, but so was England's remarkable, underrated Chris Brasher, the half-miler who'd helped pace Bannister to the first sub-4 mile. An unusually tough athlete, Brasher also encountered unusual tribulations in his career. Hindered by numerous diseases, including bronchitis, he had at one time been chosen as a member of a team to climb Mount Everest. If he were healthy, he clearly had the speed and the timber-topping ability to excel in the steeple.

He was healthy at Melbourne, and crafty. The 28-year-old Cambridge alumnus hung back in the early going, allowing Norway's Ernst Larsen to make the pace. Two laps from home Rozsnyoi made his expected move to the fore, to be supplanted by the Soviet Union's Seyon Rzhishchin 200 meters later. Brasher waited in fourth spot. He picked it up on the last lap, sailing over a hurdle and between the battling Rozsnyoi and Rzhishchin going through the final turn, splashed through the water, and was away, clear by 10 meters at the tape. He established an Olympic record of 8:41.2, but officials tried to disqualify him, claiming he had interfered with Larsen at one of the barriers. The summary disqualification was of course protested and ultimately overturned, and Brasher became the only one of the Bannister-Chataway-Brasher trio to win any Olympic medal. A relieved Brasher commented, "Boy, it's really hard to win these medals." Then, perhaps venting feelings of inferiority he had developed after years of running in Bannister's and Chataway's shadows, he complained of the steeplechase that "This is a race for peasants." Coming one Olympiad after Zátopek's dour observation on winning the marathon, it began to seem that the gold medalists in what were commonly considered the two most arduous long-distance events held vastly different opinions of them than did the general public.

Surprises stormed out of the 400-meter final as well. A U.S. athlete had taken the event in eight out of thirteen races in modern Olympic history. It seemed reasonable to presume an American would prevail at Melbourne as well. Fastest of the Americans was Lou Jones, who held the world record, 45.2 seconds, for the 400, established in winning the Pan-American Games's single-lapper. Jones also copped the win in the U.S. Olympic trials, with Jim Lea and Charlie Jenkins qualifying in that order behind him. Lea failed to make it into the Olympic final, but Jones's speed so overmatched that of any other contenders that American hopes for gold remained high. A powerful runner, Jones could easily bull his way through the home-straight headwind that hampered the runners in the 800-meter final.

American high hopes sagged when Jones drew the high (outside) lane for the final. That meant Jones would take off far ahead of everybody else, a result of the staggered start used in the sprints and middle distances. In turn, that meant Jones would have no idea where his competition was; he would have to race "blind" and hope for the best, while every other competitor would know exactly where Jones was.

At the start Jones abandoned his knowledge of pace to Olympic-inspired nerves; he shot out of the blocks and leaned hard into the first turn as if it were the 200-meter final. Two-hundred-fifty meters into the race Jones had over 7 meters on the rest of the field, but could see second man, Soviet Ardalion Ignatiev, out of the corner of his eye. Jones later recalled: "It made me freeze. Running in the outside lane, I never should see anyone coming so close to me, and it sort of frightened me."

Fear makes an athlete tense his muscles, or "tie up," inhibiting his or her ability to move smoothly, hence, to run fast. Jones tied up just then, and Ignatiev took over the lead, going straight for the gold. That was when Charlie Jenkins made his move. Aided by the Soviet's imprudently fast pace in pursuit of Jones's even more imprudent starting kick, Jenkins smoked by the dying Russian 20 meters from home. Germany's Karl Haas moved up on Jenkin's elbow and that seemed to give the Villanova speedster all the incentive he needed to scat for the wire, the gold, and a 46.7 clocking. Haas held on for second, while Ignatiev had to split a bronze medal with Finland's Zoitto Hellsten when they dead-heated for third. Jones came in fifth, awarding Jenkins a big bear hug for his efforts.

The Australian crowd probably would have liked to hug bouncing Betty Cuthbert. Cuthbert, whose trademark was a constantly open mouth to gulp air as she sprinted, followed in the spikesteps of Fanny Blankers-Koen and Marjorie Jackson, scooping up all the women's running marbles in her Olympics. The 18-year-old Cuthbert equalled the Olympic 100-meter record in winning that event in 11.5; ironically, the athlete whose time she tied was her countrywoman, Marjorie Jackson. Moving up to the 200-meter event, Cuthbert beat the Olympic standard (23.7) but fell short of her own world mark (23.2) in winning her second gold medal in 23.4 seconds. Finally, Cuthbert anchored the Australian 400-meter relay team victory in the Olympic record time of 44.5.

The last day of Melbourne competition belonged to the metric mile and the marathon. A fantastic field showed up for the 1500-meter final. Not only was Australia's own John Landy, then the world record holder for the mile, contending, but so were four of the nine other men in history to run under 4 minutes for the mile: Ron Delany, Gunnar Nielsen, Laszlo Tabori and Brian Hewson.

None expects a world record in Olympic competition, although they occasionally come. In the Olympics, the medal stands paramount over the world marks. Few thought much of it, then, when England's Hewson and New Zealand "iron man" Murray Halberg took the field's measure for the first lap while Landy galloped along in last place. At the end of 2 laps, Landy enjoyed the company of Nielson and Delany in the last three spots in the twelve-man field. Australia's Merv Lincoln had paced the second 400 meters, with Halberg and Hewson stuck on his tailpipes. Going into the bell lap, Lincoln took off in an attempted runaway. Landy pulled up into fourth spot behind him, Halberg, and Hewson. The old Olympic finals shuffle began in earnest 300 meters from home. West Germany's Klaus Richtzenhain— a genuine "Who?" in a field such as this—took over the lead from Hewson, who had just taken it from Lincoln. Meantime, Ireland's Ron Delany moved from sixth at 300 meters to third at 200 meters to second at 150 meters, Landy behind him and Richtzenhain in front of him.

Delany claimed sole possession of the gold 100 meters later, zapping the German 50 meters from the tape. Delany, who trained and studied in the U.S.A., ran the final 400 meters in 54.2 to win the gold and set an Olympic mark of 3:41.2, exactly 4 seconds under Josey Barthel's previous reference. Richtzenhain held on, just, for second from a driving Landy, who won the bronze. The generous Delany commented afterwards that "I would still be running miles in 4:05 if it weren't for John Landy." Interviewed independently of Delany, and unaware of his comment, the gracious Landy stated his belief that "Delany could easily run the mile in 3:55"—that is, 3 seconds faster than Landy's own world record.

Emil Zátopek ran in—but did not actually *compete* in—the Melbourne marathon. Hampered by his hernia operation, the Czech invalid seemed actually to enjoy himself for the first time in any Olympic final. No groaning, no rolling shoulders, just smiles and an easy pace took him home in sixth place. Five places ahead of him, France's Alain Mimoun (himself an invalid from sciatica in 1954 until a pilgrimage to the Basilica of St. Theresa of Lisieux cured him) broke the tape in 2:25-flat to win his own gold medal. He had collected a raft of silver medals in the races where Zátopek won his golds. Mimoun fell nearly a full 2 minutes short of Zátopek's Olympic marathon record; if that bothered him, he did not show it. Waving aside trainers who wanted to wrap him in warm blankets, the swarthy French-Algerian waited patiently by the finish line for someone else to arrive. His friend finally crossed the line to cheers equalling those accorded the triumphant Mimoun—Emil Zátopek, running in his last Olympic race. A smile broke on both their faces, and Zátopek and Mimoun embraced at the finish line. Only one noteworthy distance-running authority had proclaimed his belief Mimoun could win the marathon at Melbourne. That authority's name was Emil Zátopek.

Inspired by the 1956 Olympics in his home country, Herb Elliott decided to see what Coach Cerutty could do for him. In December, 1956, the young miler hied himself to Cerutty's training camp at Portsea, Australia.

In 1981, Elliott reflected on his relationship with Cerutty, forged in his sojourn at Portsea, from which all women were banned, consistent with Cerutty's fundamental idea of the athlete-as-Stotan. ("Stotan," a word coined by Cerutty, derived from stoic and spartan.) Elliott recalled that Cerutty "was not a coach who took any interest at all in the details of training. He was only interested in my mentality and enthusiasm and he knew when that was there I would try hard and if I felt that slipping then he would get me enthusiastic again." Cerutty claimed his training methods constituted a refinement of those he learned from the great Swedish coach, Gosta Holmer, the father of fartlek, when Cerutty and Holmer met at the Helsinki Olympics. (A Swedish word that means "speed play," fartlek is a training exercise in which the athlete runs over a variety of different terrains at widely varying speeds. Its object is to keep the mind and spirit fresh while giving the body a mighty workout, for the emphasis in fartlek is more on speed than it is on play.) In retrospect, though, one infers Cerutty planned his training schemes partly on the methods of Gosta Holmer and partly on the thinking of Friedrich Nietzsche.

Cerutty summarized his training doctrine thus: "The amount of experience, of effort, of pain, and suffering that results in perhaps a work of art that lives, or a book that becomes a classic, is stupendous. So it is with track. The weak fall by the wayside, and the strong train on. The champion of the

Australia's Herb Elliott, the greatest miler yet, running in fifth place during the 1960 Olympic 1500 meter final at Rome. Directly behind Elliott is France's Michel Jazy; temporarily leading the field is Jazy's teammate, Michel Bernard. Elliott took the gold medal (in a world record 3:35.6) and Jazy took the silver. (Photograph courtesy of Track & Field News.)

future will be found training on. The thing that marks the super athlete is his capacity to suffer, and stand up to continued suffering. The days of easily earned success have passed in track. By the champion's ability to stand up to punishment on the track and in training you will know him. Suffering! He thrives on it!" Cerutty worried that the conveniences of modern living rendered most people soft and unfit in all senses of the terms. The excellent athlete, in Cerutty's theory, was the natural person, the one who trained and raced as nature intended him or her. Like Zátopek, Cerutty scorned the stopwatch, and so Cerutty's athletes also scorned training by one.

They did not scorn the stopwatch in competition, however, and in January, 1957, Elliott took 14 seconds off his personal record for the mile in interclub competition at Melbourne, running 4:06. On February 2, he beat Ron Clarke in a mile race run on a football field; Elliott ran 4:04.4. In the Australian Championships in March, Elliott (now 20 years old) ran 4:00.1.

Such rapid progress came at some cost. To train at Portsea meant, in Elliott's words, "to live like an animal." Cerutty emphasized not only running, but also weight-lifting, swimming in horrendous Australian surf, eating an uncooked vegetarian diet, and running up sand dunes until the athlete vomited. Although Elliott only ran over 60 miles in a week for one week during his career (that was a 100-mile week "just for the hell of it," as he put it), the mileage he did run must have been extremely intense. Reminiscing about the Portsea days, the great miler recalled: "You couldn't afford once in a training session or in a race to let a guy get past you once the chips were really down, because it just might be too easy to let it happen again some other time. . . . Now, I'm not saying I'm right, but that was the sort of attitude I had." The attitude almost undoubtedly sprang from Percy Wells Cerutty.

John J. Kelley's attitude of patience and persistence paid off in the April, 1957, running of the Boston Marathon. For the first time since 1951, the course covered the full 26.2 miles. For the first (and, as of 1981, sole) time in history, the B.A.A. Marathon was won by an actual member of the B.A.A. Boston Athletic Association President Walter A. Brown took such joy in the occasion he gave Young John an engraved gold watch (presumably with "the works" still intact) in addition to his medal and laurel crown.

Young John set a Boston record of 2:20:05, and his namesake, Old John, helped him do it. The Elder offered the Younger the shelter of his home the evening before Patriots' Day. As Young John remembered it in 1981: "Old John had me at his house in '57 the night before the marathon and, for the first time, I was completely relaxed. The phone would ring. John would answer it, wink at me, then tell somebody on the line, 'I'm sorry, you can't talk with him. He's gone to bed!' I was never so relaxed and rested for a Boston race as that year, thanks to Old John." Nerves were apparently Young John's only real competition for, in the race itself, no other athlete caused him the slightest worry. He cantered into Exeter Street around ¾-mile ahead of runner-up Veikko Karvonen (who had won in 1954). Then he went on to win his second consecutive Yonkers Marathon,

John J. ("Young John") Kelley, who won the Boston Marathon in 1957, shown winning the 1959 Pan-American Games Marathon in 2:27:54.2, four minutes ahead of the runner-up. Young John was the best American marathoner of the 1950s. (Photograph courtesy of The Boston Herald American.)

in 2:24:55.2, the next month—without sleeping over at Old John's the night before.

America got her first sub-4 miler on June 1, 1957, when Don Bowden, a junior at the University of California at Berkeley, ran 3:58.6 to win the mile at the Pacific Association AAU Championships in Stockton, California. Bowden, who claimed he felt dead tired before the race, had run the third fastest mile at that point in history. The 6'3", 162 pound Bowden ran the first ¼-mile in 59 seconds flat—not too surprising in light of the fact he had held the national schoolboy 880-yard record (in 1:53) while in secondary school. Bowden apparently ran his sub-4 on courage, for there was little pressure on him from other athletes in the event. The second-place finisher clocked 4:12.8.

An American track collegiate powerhouse finally came to the fore in 1957. Villanova University began its domination of the IC4As that year, led by Ron Delany, Charlie Jenkins, and Don Bragg. From 1957 to 1972, Villanova would win eleven IC4A team titles (losing to Penn State in 1959 and to Maryland University in 1965, 1966, and 1969).

While Percy Cerutty in Australia was helping Herb Elliott become the world's greatest miler, a coach in New Zealand began in 1957 to turn another athlete into arguably the greatest miler/half-miler of all time. The coach was Arthur Lydiard, and his runner was Peter Snell. Elliott was rangy and tough; Snell was big and strong, actually preferring the 800 meters (or the 880 yards) to the mile. Lydiard made certain Snell, as every other athlete he coached, received enough of a distance-running base mileage to complete a marathon if the athlete wanted, or needed, to. Lydiard had Snell run intervals, hills, and cross-country to sharpen his speed, but he still emerged as the first known coach to emphasize a gradual building of strength from a sound distance base. In this regard, Snell was the real modern heir to the training methods of Payse Weston and Walter George.

Herb Elliott ran his first sub-4 mile in January, 1958. He barely made it, recording 3:59.9; but five days later he hoofed the four laps in 3:58.7, one-and-a-half seconds slower than Derek Ibbotson's world record.

As usual, the three weeks leading up to Patriots' Day in Boston in 1958 saw the newspapers crammed with front-page and feature stories about the impending B.A.A. Marathon. Young John Kelley's win the previous year set area fans anticipating a DeMaresque winning streak by the local favorite. On race day the sports scribes got a juicy story to send over the wires. Three prospective marathoners were denied numbers because the perfunctory pre-race physical examination "concluded" they all had heart murmurs. The "invalid" athletes were Ted Corbitt, John Lafferty, and Al Confalone. The three made quite a post-race story, too. Deciding to compete without numbers, they started 100 yards behind the official field and finished, unofficially, in sixth, seventh, and ninth spots, respectively!

Young John ran true to his old form that day, which meant he finished second, beaten this time by Yugoslavia's Franjo Mihalic. Mihalic ran in a skullcap he made by sewing a Hotel Lenox table napkin to a sun visor to protect his bald pate from the sunny, 84-degree day. He ran 2:25:54, over 5 minutes off Young John's record, but nearly a full 5 minutes ahead of Young John (2:30:51) himself that day, while Finland's Eino Pulkkinen came home in third with 2:37:05.

On August 6, 1958, Herb Elliott set a world record for the mile while competing in Dublin, Ireland. He ran 3:54.5! In reducing Ibbotson's world mark by 2.7 seconds, the astounding Australian lowered the mile record by the largest amount in a single race in the twentieth century, as of 1981; it stands second only to Walter George's 3.45-second reduction of the record in 1886.

Road running in the U.S. started to hit its stride in 1958. Midwestern America, the heartland of track and field in the nation, essentially ignored road racing during this era, but the east and west coasts increasingly embraced this aspect of the sport. The University of Chicago Track Club stood as the sole notable exception to this rule, but their members had to travel to either coast to find competition on the roads.

England's Diane Leather was the premier female miler of the era. The 25-year-old Leather (5'9½", 130 pounds) set the women's mile record of 4:45.0 in 1958, in addition to finishing second in the European Championships' 800 meters. Coached by Mrs. D. Nelson and John Le Masurier, Leather competed for the London Olympiades Athletic Club and depended on her strength to break the field at the start of a race.

No matter where a woman traveled in America in the 1950s, she would not find a road race she could enter. There were no formal rules barring women—there did not need to be, because the idea of a woman running on the roads was literally unthought-of and unheard-of in the twentieth century. The decade of the 1960s would usher in changes in social and athletic values, but neither the men nor the women of the 1950s ever considered staging co-ed road races. Much about road racing in the U.S. during this period was lackadaisical and low-key compared to racing on the track.

I did not expect the race to be 10 miles. I knew there was a race, but I was hoping the race was going to be a 5. They had 5-mile races, 10-mile races and then a 12-mile race. Those seemed to be the major races around. I hoped it would be a 5, and with a 5, I said to myself, Billy Squires can run with anyone. It turned out to be a 10 miler.

A mile race on the track was lined up and the formality of it, a big mile, was that you were introduced. The crowds had programs, and they knew who you were. On the roads we lined up, people with all kinds of different clothing, with sweat clothes; they'd hand their clothes to someone, throw them to the side; whereas in the big stuff your clothes were taken off at a certain time, everything was put away. You were manicured, you were out in an elite society. This road race was like a training session where there were a whole bunch of people from different areas and where we were just going to go out for a jolly run; but there was a police car out there, leading us like Indianapolis. The police car and a motorcycle, and the police car had the siren and off we went and there were probably about, I'd guess, 200 people there, which was a big race for those days. I won it; 57 minutes.

Even in their earliest incarnations, sub-marathon-length road races in America emphasized socializing nearly as much as competition. Most road races would start at a school gymnasium, snake through back-country roads to avoid tangling traffic, and end in the center of a town. The gymnasium would serve as a post-race gathering place for the runners and their families, while the in-town terminus would give the athletes some encouraging spectators (usually between 300 and 500) and publicity while only minimally inconveniencing townspeople. Because traffic control was in its primitive stages during 1950s' road races, the truly slow runners at the back of the pack took care to run way over on the right shoulder of the road to permit autos to pass them.

Most road races offered prizes of some sort. Nearly every road race featured three trophies, one for the overall winner and two for special local athletes, such as the first townsman to finish, the first military veteran, and/ or the first member of a civic organization or club. In addition to trophies, a high-class event offered ten or so merchandise prizes donated by whatever merchants the race director could convince to part with something valuable. (Sometimes crafty merchants used their "prizes" as a marketing ploy. Occasionally a runner would win an automobile tire, for example, show up at the tire dealer's for his prize, and be treated to a spiel as to why he should buy a matching tire to make a pair.) Road race prizes ran the gamut of variety from meat or poultry to motorcycles or pianos. Neither t-shirts nor beer appeared on the lists of prizes and accoutrements of 1950s' road races. A special race would offer juice, soda, coffee, and cookies to athletes and their families after the competition, usually back at the gym where everyone had left his sweat clothes.

Miler Ron Delany preferred a racing strategy with a kick, taken from Roger Bannister's mold; the Villanova mileman normally let other athletes take the pace for the first 3½ laps and would then breeze by them to take victory; hence his nickname, "The King of Kick." The 1956 Olympics' 1500-meter final perfectly demonstrated the winning Delany technique.

Delany's favored tactic was used against him in one of the last races of his career. Running in the Columbian Mile at the New York K.C. meet, on March 7, 1959, Delany squared off against Hungary's Istvan Rozsavolgyi. Delany surged into his patented kick 2 laps from home in the 11-lap indoor mile. Then "Rozy" let loose his own, patent-pending, kick, and galloped by the Gael a lap-and-half from the wire. The Hungarian held the Irishman off until the homestretch, where Delany dug down deep and Rozy slipped on something on the boards, allowing Delany to go by, winning by 2 feet in the world indoor record time of 4:01.4 to Rozsavolgyi's 4:01.8. In the same meet, University of Houston frosh Al Lawrence (who hailed from Australia) broke the world indoor 2-mile mark with his 8:46.8 effort.

Three weeks later, on March 28, 1959, Delany won the mile at the Chicago Daily News Relays in 4:06.4, noteworthy as Delany's thirty-fourth consecutive mile win and his *fortieth* consecutive track triumph. The King of Kick retired at the end of the 1959 indoor season, having set five of the world's eight then-fastest indoor mile times.

Finland's Eino Oksanen started a winning streak of his own at the 1959 Boston Marathon, which he would claim thrice in three successive, successful *entries*. Oksanen did not win the 1960 race; he did not enter it. On Patriots' Day, 1959, Oksanen, popularly called "The Ox," muscled his way past Young John Kelley in mile 25. A detective on the Helsinki Police Force, The Ox had been trailing his man for the previous 12 miles. A marathoner with a powerful finishing kick, Oksanen pulled out over a minute on Kelley by Exeter Street, winning in 2:22:42 against Young John's 2:23:43, while Canada's Gordon Dickson just nipped 1954 champion Veikko Karvonen at the tape in 2:24:04.

The great comeback story of 1960 belonged to miler Jim Beatty, who, disgusted by his constant injuries, retired from track in 1956. Late in 1959, Beatty (who was half-Italian) moved from Charlotte, North Carolina, to Los Angeles, California. The climate and the coaching, courtesy of Los Angeles T.C. mentor Milhaly Igloi of Hungary, revived 25-year-old Beatty,

Eino Oksanen wears number 1 in the Boston Marathon, as befit an athlete who would win the event three times during his career. In this 1962 race, the Finnish ace shares the pace with his countryman Paavo Pystenen and U.S. Marine Lt. Alex Breckenridge. "Ox" won in 2:23:48; Paavo came second in 2:24:58; the Marine finished third in 2:27:17. (Photograph courtesy of The Boston Herald American.)

and he won the 2-mile at the Los Angeles (Indoor) Invitational Meet in 8:57.0. In the New York A.C. meet two weeks after, Beatty bested Dyrol Burleson in the Baxter Mile, winning in 4:05.4, Beatty's fastest mile to that point.

Finnish domination of the Boston Marathon continued in 1960, but it was Paavo Kotila, not The Ox, who carried the blue cross of his homeland to victory in 2:20:54. The victory was especially embarrassing for Americans that year, because the 1960 Boston Marathon served as part of the qualifying process for a marathon berth on the 1960 U.S. Olympic Team. To salvage some Yankee pride, Gordon McKenzie of New York claimed second in 2:22:18, and Jimmy Green of the Boston A.A. took third in 2:23:37. For the first time, Young John Kelley had to drop out of the race; Young John injured his ankle the previous winter, then had a blister burst open on one of his feet at 16 miles. Discouraged and out of contention, Kel' dropped out.

The USOC had decided members of the Olympic marathon team would be chosen on the basis of aggregate performance in both the Boston and Yonkers marathons. To qualify for the Rome Olympics, Young John would have had to win Yonkers (which he had been doing steadily since 1956) *by 20 minutes over the runner-up*. Man O' War probably could not have beaten a field of Olympic hopefuls by 20 minutes; Young John's predicament was preposterous, and athletes, race officials, and the popular media (spearheaded by the Boston *Globe*'s sports editor, Jerry Nason) howled in outrage. The USOC relented. If Young John won Yonkers "in good form," he could go to Rome.

On May 22, 1960, Young Johnny Kelley took the Yonkers Marathon in the record (Young John set the old one, too) of 2:20:13.6 Kelley got to go to Rome.

Gordon Pirie called 1960 his "greatest season ever"; the 29-year-old Englishman finally broke 4 minutes for the mile and lowered his times for 6 miles and 10 kilometers. Pirie was peaking for Rome.

It was the Roman Emperor who declared an end to the decadent classic Olympic Games. There was some irony, then, in staging the 1960 Olympics in the city from which the decree ending the original Games was issued. The irony went further: The Italian Organizing Committee raised over $30 million to finance the Rome Olympics by drawing money from Italy's weekly soccer lottery, with the blessings of the IOC, which same organization eagerly banned from competition any athletes who dared receive tainted lucre. Even more decadence emerged. Knowing that Rome in summer does not entice tourists to stay very long in her unbearable heat, and wanting as much tourist money as possible, the Italian Organizing Committee moved the track and field portion of the Olympic program from the early part of the Games to the end portion of them. By saving the most popular events for last, the Romans ensured top tourist attendance for the duration of the Games.

Once the track races got underway, it rapidly became clear only one athlete had a chance to impress a personality on the Games as Zátopek or Owens had done. The athlete was America's Wilma Rudolph; her teammates called her "Skeeter," and the French called her "La Gazelle." Indisputably the fastest woman at Rome, the 20-year-old Tennessee native had been told by physicians while a child she would never walk properly in her life. They were wrong.

The seventeenth child in a family of twenty-one people, Rudolph contracted double pneumonia and scarlet fever at age four, leaving her left leg in ruins. As President Theodore Roosevelt had done, Rudolph absolutely refused to accept her debility and started her own exercise program to find the strength doctors told her she could not hope for. By age eleven she was walking normally. By age eighteen she was competing on the track team at Tennessee State University under the guidance of Coach Ed Temple. By age twenty she had three Olympic gold medals for sprinting. The first of them came in the 100-meter final. Rudolph had already equalled Australian Shirley de la Hunty's world-record 11.3 seconds in her qualifying heat at Rome. She came out of the blocks in the final with "all that harnessed energy explod[ing] into speed," as Coach Temple put it, to scorch the "century" in 11-point-zip. The gold was her's, but not the world record. There was too much of a tailwind, officials ruled.

La Gazelle took her second piece of Roman gold in the 200-meter final. She ran 24-flat, totally unchallenged throughout. Then she anchored the American women's 400-meter relay team in their gold medal effort. The Americans also tied the world record, 44.5 seconds, in taking the gold. The entire relay team came from Tennessee State, calling themselves the Tiger Belles, and were very familiar with each other's baton changes.

Run last (and first) in the 1928 Amsterdam Olympics, the women's 800-meter run was reinstituted at Rome. The Soviet Union's Shevcova-Lysenko won in 2:04.3, tying her own world record and taking the only women's running event at Rome not won by Wilma Rudolph, who did not enter.

The most productive athlete on the track at Rome, Rudolph was perhaps not the most surprising. New Zealand's Peter Snell, running in the 800 meters, was. Snell boasted no international reputation whatsoever before the Games. He turned in a mediocre qualifying heat time of 1:47.2, good enough to make the final but not sufficiently impressive to permit hope for a medal; yet if Rudolph's example showed anything, it showed that true champions generate their own hope; they do not look to find it in the opinions of others.

Snell looked to his own brutal physical strength for hope in the final and found it. Running at Rome simply to gain international experience, the 21-year-old Snell found himself glued to the backside of Belgium's Roger Moens (world record holder, at 1:45.7) going into the home straightaway. Although Snell would go on to earn a deserved reputation as a "strength" runner, he used the same crafty strategy just then that Bannister used against

Landy. Moens turned his head to see how much lead he had; there was an explosion on his blind side and the Belgian no longer had the lead, because Peter Snell had driven past him and was homing in on the tape. The New Zealand warhead blasted the wire in 1:46.3, 1.4 seconds under the old Olympic record and a full 2 seconds under Snell's own former personal best. The world had now heard of Peter Snell. In the future, the world would learn he preferred to start his finishing kick unnaturally far from the line— usually at the 500-meter mark in the 800 meters. Such a tactic requires far more than physical strength. It demands inhuman courage.

His left arm, withered since childhood, flaps in apparent uselessness, nearly hiding the silver feather of New Zealand that glistens on his uniform's black chest. Murray Halberg has just broken open the Rome 5-kilometer final, turning himself into a champion.

Twelve hundred meters from the finish Halberg invokes his sub-4 miler's speed, running the tenth lap in 61 seconds flat, digging into the air with his right arm, into the Roman earth with the fangs on his feet. He's raced 20 meters clear of the field; he's entered perdition unseen since Zátopek. He must survive for 800 meters more, he must live with no oxygen for another half-mile. He runs the next 400 meters in 64 seconds. Germany's Hans Grodotzki closes. Halberg's eyes close; his mind digs down into his soul; he will NOT give in, give up, give out. He springs from the final turn a wraith, 9 meters ahead of the German. He floats on the will of a champion down the final straight, his red cells imploring him for air, his visage steeled. Hal-

New Zealander Murray Halberg was a miler who moved up to the 5,000 meter run in the 1960 Olympic Games and ran an astonishing race there to win a gold medal. The photograph shows the red-headed Kiwi triumphing in the 1954 Ben Franklin Mile at the Penn Relays. His time was 4:10; his nearest competition was 35 yards behind. (Photograph courtesy of *The Boston Herald American.*)

berg tears the tape 6 meters ahead of Grodotzki. His time is 13:43.4. He has been able to breathe for 10.5 minutes of it.

The 400-meter final proved as much a challenge to modern timing technology as it was to the athletes involved. America's Otis Davis was 24 years old and a relative novice in world-class competition; he'd gone to college on a basketball scholarship. He equalled, then broke by 4/10-second, the Olympic 400 record in his qualifying heats. Breaking away with the gun, South Africa's Mal Spence spent the first 200 meters in 21.2 to Davis's 21.7, but by 300 meters, Davis was ½-second clear of Spence. West Germany's Carl Kaufmann was moving up, however, bombing through on the inside of the final turn of the one-lapper. Davis ran the last 100 meters in 12.3, Kaufmann in 11.6 (considered the fastest 400 meters closing kick in history by many experts). They dead-heated at the wire in 44.9 seconds, and then everybody waited for the finish photo to develop. The photo showed Davis ahead by about one-third of an atom, making him the gold medalist, the world record holder for the event, and the first man ever to crack 45 seconds for the 400. The second man in history to do it was Carl Kaufmann.

Herb Elliott went into the 1500 final coming off a 3:41.4 win in his qualifying race, 3/10-second slower than Ron Delany's victorious final time in 1956. Observers at the time assumed Elliott had run unwisely fast to shore up his confidence, but apparently he also intended to demoralize his competition. Years later, the great miler observed: "I believe that in any race you let a guy beat you—and you do let him beat you if you are not absolutely psychologically tuned up to winning at all costs—that creates a precedent that allows you to get beat in the race you care about."

The Australian's main competition in the final came from France, in the persons of Michel Bernard and Michel Jazy. Bernard took the lead for the first 2 laps. He flew through 400 meters in 58.2. (Elliott said of this point: "I felt as though I had run two laps, already.") Bernard ran the first 800 meters in 1:57.8. Elliott was in fourth place, clocking 1:58.8 for the 800, and then it was time to move. Crossing the line at 800 meters, Elliott went up on his toes and conjured a sprint that rivaled Kaufmann's 400 meters' do-or-die. Elliott ran the next 100 meters in 13.2 seconds. The rest of the field ran it, on average, in 14.7. Elliott ran the next 200 meters in 28.8, allowing himself a breather. He was now over 2 meters clear of second man Istvan Rozsavolgyi of Hungary. Then the amazing Elliott decided to *kick*. He ran the last lap in 55.6 seconds. One hundred meters from home, he had a full 10 meters on Jazy, who'd taken the silver position from Rozy going down the backstretch. By the time Elliott parted the tape, he had over 20 meters on Jazy. Elliott had run the second 800 meters in 1:52.8, had broken his own world 1500-meter record with a 3:35.6 (4/10-second under), and had run the equivalent of a 3:52.6 mile (a time that would not be equalled or surpassed for 6 years)! In 1981, the master of the mile offered an observation that seemed to summarize this race: "I had a dual goal in my running, that was to win and to achieve excellence, so I was never happy with a slow, tactical time. If the race were slow I would get in front and pull it up again. I couldn't stand a slow race. A lot of people seem to get screwed up on tactics. There is only one tactic in a race and that is to always be in a position where you can win it."

Soviet domination of the 10,000 meters continued. Pytor Bolotnikov claimed victory in the fast but relatively uninteresting contest in 28:32.2, 13.4 seconds under Kuts's Olympic standard. Significantly, tiny Max Truex became the first American to place in the top six in the 10,000 final. Truex chopped 45 seconds off the American 10K record to clock 28:50.2. He finished four spots ahead of Gordon Pirie.

The Olympic marathon winner's stand had normally been the province of track runners, regardless of the hordes of road specialists who took to the event in the U.S.A. The 1960 Olympic marathon introduced the age of the strict marathon ace in the person of Abebe Bikila of Ethiopia. A member of Emperor Haile Selassie's Royal Guard, Bikila was so unknown in international circles that many sportswriters thought his name was Bikila Abebe for several years after his victory. Not only was Bikila unknown, his marathon running dress was unheard-of. The fellow ran the entire race barefooted.

Bikila ran behind Belgian marathon champion Aurele Vandendriessche and England's Arthur Keily until the 20-kilometer mark, at which point Bikila and Morocco's Rhadi ben Abdesselem, a soldier like Bikila, blew away from everyone else. The two ran in tandem until nearly at the stadium, where Bikila went into a sprint and pulled out a 125-meter victory in 2:15:16.2, 7:47 under Zátopek's former Olympic reference and 25.4 seconds ahead of Rhadi ben Abdesselem. (Young John Kelley, the first American, finished in 2:24:58.) The 28-year-old Emperor's Guardsman clearly was unstressed by his ordeal. The barefoot man commented: "The marathon distance is nothing for me. I could have kept going around the course another time without difficulty. We train in shoes, but it's much more comfortable to run without them."

VIII

American Distance Running
1961–1965

The United States entered the decade of the 1960s with a fat economy and a flabby citizenry. In 1961, the President's Council on Physical Fitness and Sport issued the results of a lengthy study of the nation's fitness posture, finding it decidedly weak and sagging rapidly. The new president, John F. Kennedy, projected a strong vigorous personal image, and he wasted little time in using the Council's study. Particularly incensed by the decline in physical fitness among the American armed forces, President Kennedy reactivated a hoary tradition among Marine commissioned officers: the 50-mile hike in full battle gear. The program spurred a new fad among citizens: 50-mile hikes, minus the battle regalia. Any American president enjoys an inestimably strong personal influence on the values of the American people. While Dwight D. Eisenhower was president, the public were essentially sedentary. With the advent of the fitness-minded Kennedy administration, the public took a greater interest in *participating* in active sports and taking pride in one's body. Although President Kennedy was not a runner, he nevertheless deserves an honored position in the history of American distance running because of the favorable cultural climate for participation sports he helped create during the early 1960s. Hiking 50 miles certainly lays the foundation for cardiovascular fitness—and consciousness.

What happened to Young John Kelley in the 1961 Boston Marathon *should* have happened to a dog, but didn't. The great Finn, Eino Oksanen, returned to Boston after a year's absence, and he, Kelley, and Englishman Jim Norris slugged it out for the first 16 miles of the marathon. As they headed through Newton Lower Falls, a black dog attacked the runners, knocking Young John down. "Ox" Oksanen, thirty-two pounds heftier and perhaps nimbler than Kelley, jumped into the lead while Norris kindly stopped his own race to help Young John back up.

The bowser must have been related to the one that knocked down Yun Bok Suh in the 1947 Boston race, because Kelley responded exactly the same as the gutty, tiny Korean: he fell, bled, got back up again, and over-hauled his competitor to take the lead! Norris fell back shortly after the first Newton hill, but Young John and the Ox battled step for step until a half-mile from home, when Oksanen pitted his muscle against Kelley's speed and won out, coming in with 2:23:39 to his credit. Kelley ran 2:24:04, and Norris took third in 2:25:46.

Unhappy news emanated from the gallant Norris's homeland in the spring of 1961. British athletic officials had banned Gordon Pirie from inter-national amateur competition forever. Like many others before and after him, Puff-Puff got caught taking money under the table.

The immortal Herb Elliott retired at the end of the 1961 track season at age 22 and almost unquestionably still with many prime competitive years left him. Undefeated in the mile since high school, Elliott suffered only one mile loss in his *entire* career.

Thanksgiving Day, 1961, became one of the most important dates in road running history when 19-year-old Smith College sophomore Julia Chase at-tempted to compete in the annual 5-mile Turkey Trot Road Race held in Manchester, Connecticut. The New England record holder at 400 and 800 meters had tried to enter the event the previous year, but was rejected by officials because not "pre-registered." She saw the same officials allowing men to make post entries. Chase sent her entry in early in 1961, only to have it rejected for the same reason B.A.A. officials kept women out of the Boston Marathon: AAU rules forbade "mixed competition." Chase's coach, George Terry, scrutinized the salient AAU regulations and found they only concerned track races. Road racing was "beneath" the AAU's attention. There was no concrete reason for not allowing women to run . . . other than the obvious reason that cultural bias dies hard. Chase showed up in Manchester anyway, not to cause a fuss, just to run. She went right to the starting line, and, wonder of wonders, found two other women ready to race there, too! One was British Olympian (at 800 meters at Rome) Chris Mc-Kenzie; the other was local citizen Dianne Lechausse. They had heard about Chase's determination and decided running the Turkey Trot would be a good idea.

Chase found a few other folks waiting for her, too: newshawks from the *New York Times*, A.P., U.P.I., *Time*, and *Life* shouldered aside reporters for New England regional periodicals. The Manchester Turkey Trot was no bush league roadathon. It was, after the Boston Marathon, the most important road race in New England.

Race directors hustled the women to the back of the pack, behind the 137 official runners. All three women finished and in good form (although McKenzie, anticipating a move Frank Shorter would employ 20 years later, ran the last 50 yards on the sidewalk to avoid retaliation by the AAU). Chase would have finished number 128 overall, had she been "official." The next day's New York Times succinctly stated: "All the women went the distance. Two of the men failed to finish."

Chase had been inspired to run by Young John J. Kelley. She inherited his fighting spirit. In January, 1962, she petitioned officials at the Boston Knights of Columbus indoor track meet to include a women's half-mile run on the program. The officials finally agreed, but worried about finding enough women to run the race. They received 142 applications when word got out! As meet director Ding Dussault put it: "It looks as if the girls were right when they said the track promoters were the ones who didn't encourage women athletes. I have enough inquiries to fill a meet just for women."

A talented athlete as well as a gifted grassroots politician, Chase spent 1963 under the tutelage of California coach Mihaly Igloi, running 80 miles' worth of speedwork weekly. She trained for a while in 1964 with nationally ranked 10,000-meter runner Billy Mills, and Mills marvelled that this female 800-meter specialist was putting in more mileage, and just as hard, as he! Julia Chase almost became the first woman to run the Boston Marathon. She had planned to run in 1965 but injured her back in an auto accident. Swept up in her academics, Chase finally returned to the roads in 1981.

On January 27, 1962, New Zealander Peter Snell set a mile record of 3:54.4. Whether one should be grateful or petulant that Snell and Elliott never met in a mile race remains controversial. True, the result would almost unquestionably have been electrifying . . . but one of them would have had to lose.

On February 10, 1962, two of the world's great milers finally competed in the same meet. Both Peter Snell and Jim Beatty were running in the Los Angeles Times indoor meet at the Los Angeles Sport Arena. It was Snell's very first effort on the indoor circuit, while Beatty reigned as one of the true kings of the boards. Alas, they did not compete in the same race. Snell ran the 1000 yards, Beatty ran the mile. (In light of Snell's professed preference for the half-mile over the mile, it seems only natural he should have selected the shorter, faster event for his first indoor race.) Big and powerful, Snell led from the gun in his event. He went through the half-mile mark in world indoor record time—1:50.2!—and set a world best for 1000 yards when he parted the tape—2:06.0. Canada's outstanding middle-distance specialist, Bill Crothers, finished second in 2:07.4.

Later that night, Jim Beatty became the first man to run a sub-4 mile indoors. The indoor track world's first sub-4 was much faster than the outdoor track world's first sub-4. Beatty ran 3:58.9 and also checked through the 1500 meters in 3:43.2 to take another world standard. Beatty's ½-mile split was 1:59.7, nearly 10 seconds slower than Snell's clocking through the same distance in the 1000. On the other hand, Beatty and his coach Mihaly Igloi had not begun to prepare for the record until October, 1961, after Beatty had lost his conditioning due to several weeks' layoff with a hip injury. Obviously returned to fitness, Beatty dominated the mile on the 1962 American indoor circuit, winning the coveted Sullivan Award.

Peter Snell moved on to the Japanese indoor track circuit in March, 1962. Running indoors at Tokyo on March 17, Snell raced to victory in the mile in a slowish 4:06.7. On March 18, the potent New Zealander showed he had lost none of his speed: he ran the half-mile in 1:49.9, eclipsing his own indoor 880 world record set at Los Angeles.

Bill Crothers, the athlete Snell whipped in his first indoor race, was also running his first indoor season. A pharmacist from Canada who raced with a strap on his eyeglasses to keep them in place, Crothers came south to race in America because his homeland no longer offered him suitable competition. He would have had trouble finding competition regardless of where he lived; he went nearly undefeated for his entire career. Crothers ran the 500, 600, 1000, and also legs of a mile relay. Undefeated in these events in 1963, he set an American half-mile record of 1:50.0 at the 1963 Millrose Games. In 1964 he lost only one race, in which he fell and lost 35 yards, then checked in with the same time as the winning runner, Jim Dupree, but perforce settled for second place—1000 yards in 2:11.9. Perhaps Crothers's best performance came in the 1964 New York "Casey" meet, where he won the Casey 600 in 1:09.7, then turned around 90 minutes later and ran the final quarter-mile anchor leg for the East York Track Club mile relay team in 47.2 seconds!

From 1963 to 1966, Bill Crothers ranked Number One in the world among indoor half-milers, and, as of 1981, stood as arguably the greatest indoor middle-distance runner of all time.

Ox Oksanen completed his hat-trick at the 1962 Boston Marathon, winning for the third and final time in 2:23:48. His countryman, Paavo Pystynen, claimed second, and U.S. Marine Alex Breckenridge was third. Young John Kelley, having an off day, stated his belief after the race that Oksanen's victories deserved ranking above Clarence DeMar's because achieved against far tougher fields; yet historical objectivity demands the observation that no one knows how fast DeMarathon would, and could, have run against fleeter competition. Athletes from one era cannot realistically be compared against runners from another.

Eino Oksanen was frustrated in his bid for a fourth Boston Marathon title in 1963, but the frustrator was neither of the two Ethiopians whom pundits thought would blow all other runners into the tullies. Olympic marathon champion Abebe Bikila and his compatriot, Mamo Wolde, shared and held the lead for 21 of the 26.2 miles, but that was when Belgium's Aurele Vandendriessche overhauled them, taking the Boston laurels. Wolde's reasons for folding are unknown, but Bikila was plagued with leg cramps and ran like a wooden soldier for most of the marathon. Vandendriessche then romped to Exeter Street in the record time of 2:18:58, while Young John checked in with 2:21:09. (Interestingly, the Massachusetts Society for the Prevention of Cruelty to Animals assigned a van to troll beside Kel' during the 1964 race to prevent a recurrence of his 1961 altercation with the pooch.) England's Brian Kilby came third with 2:21:43. Where were the Ox and the Olympic marathon king? Oksanen was fourth in 2:22:43, while the brave Bikila came in fifth, 2:24:43.

In May, 1963, Peter Snell psychologically hobbled an entire field of ace American mile men at Modesto, California. Snell's competitors consisted of Marine Cary Weisiger and Los Angeles Track Club teammates Jim Beatty and Jim Grelle. There were also two bunny rabbits in the event: George Jessup, who agreed to pull the field through a hot half-mile split, and outstanding miler Bob Seaman (a teammate of Beatty's and Grelle's), who would pace the third lap.

It was a big race for the Yanks, a casual one for the Kiwi. LATC Coach Mihaly Igloi intended one of his boys to win. A track strategist in the mold of Walter George, Igloi reckoned if the LA Club could control the pace to hit the splits he had calculated weeks beforehand, an LATC runner would inevitably blast Snell into the infield. There would be no team tactics such as boxing the big miler in; instead it would be team spirit and strict adherence to schedule that would melt Snell as he ran.

Snell's advisor, Arthur Lydiard, griped before the race that Snell "has been niggling in his training. He is not as fit as he has been, but if an American is to beat him tomorrow night, he must run at least a 3:56. I feel that no American runner can beat him. His great quality is that he insists that he will not be beaten." The day of the race, Lydiard commented somewhat more charitably: "If Peter wants to train, I believe he can do a 3:48. I really mean it."

Peter did not run 3:48 that Modesto night. He did not even establish a world record. Rabbit Jessup took the field through the first 440 in a leisurely 58 seconds; Snell's split was 59.3, good only for sixth place at that juncture. Jessup passed the 880 in 1:59.1, and the serious milers (other than Snell) started getting nervous. It was quick, but not nearly fast enough to carve the kick out of Snell's meaty thighs. Weisiger got scared and took over on the third lap, drawing the pack through the three-quarters mark in 2:59.4, but a 60.3-second third lap barely warmed up half-miler Snell's blood. He was 0.8 seconds back of Weisiger, loose and ready. Weisiger tried to kick from 440 yards out. It was an intelligent, sustained burst, rising ever higher, not a flatout windsprint that would leave him on his face with 200 yards left, but against Peter Snell it was ridiculous. The brawny New Zealander moved easily out of fourth spot, cruised past Beatty like a shark passing a school of shad, and rested briefly behind Weisiger and Grelle while they had a little race for themselves. Then, going through the final turn, it was time to race for real. Snell hammered the go-pedal as if he'd inherited John Henry's genes. He nailed both Grelle and Weisiger in one swell swoop, moving *18 yards* ahead of them both in the space of that one turn! (He said after: "I felt I had to sprint around the bend because the homestretch on this track is very short and I want room to run.") Up on his toes and pulling away resoundingly, Snell hit the wire in 3:54.9. It was ½-second slower than his world record, but significantly faster than second-man Weisiger (3:57.3), third-man Beatty (3:58.0), or fourth-man Grelle (also 3:58.0). It was, in a word, Snell.

Tom O'Hara twice lowered the world indoor mile mark in 1964. He took Jim Beatty's record on February 13 at the New York A.C. Games's Baxter Mile by running 3:56.6, exactly *2 seconds* faster than Beatty's 11-lap mark; a 55-second final 440 must have helped O'Hara do it. On March 6, 1964, the 21-year-old Loyola runner ran 3:56.4 to win the Bankers Mile at the Chicago Daily News Relays. In both his record races, O'Hara captured the 1500 meter record en route (3:43.6 and 3:41.6, respectively). The battles between O'Hara and Beatty in the 1962 through 1964 indoor track seasons reminded fans of the Wilt/Gehrmann duels of the early 1950s in terms of quality and intensity. O'Hara ran in the 1964 Olympics with little distinction, then retired shortly thereafter.

New Zealand's Peter Snell, caught in his most familiar pose: muscles bulging and on his way to victory— in this case, the 1964 Olympic 1500-meter final. (Photograph courtesy of *Track & Field News*.)

One of the true kings of distance, iron man Ron Clarke, treated American indoor track fans during the 1964 season with a rare board appearance. Although Clarke's first American indoor efforts were not distinguished by his standards, he apparently became enamoured of running under the ceiling, because thereafter he made annual trips to the U.S. to race indoors. A runner who thrived on the most intense competition he could find, Clarke took to the sweaty, screaming arena of indoor racing with its staggering variety of contests and continuously clashing personalities. Like Kolehmainen, Nurmi, and Zátopek, Clarke felt a true distance runner competes at all the distances, not merely at the one in which he is most likely to win. The man the American crowds watched run the boards early in 1964 was the man who held five world long-distance records: 3 miles (13:07.6), 5 kilometers (13:34.6), 6 miles (27:17.6), 10 kilometers (28:15.6), and 10 miles (47:12.8). Clarke ran everything from the 400 meters to the marathon (personal best of 2:20:26.8); he was truly a runner's runner, but a champion without a crown of laurels. For all his manifest courage and talent, Clarke never won an international title, never triumphed in the Olympic Games. Occasionally guided by Les Perry, Clarke primarily coached himself, and therein perhaps lay the reason for his lack of titles. Clarke believed training carries on year-round, *as does racing*. Clarke often berated himself for lacking the fundamental speed, the kick, of many of his competitors; but this man who lacked a kick also refused to court a peak. By the 1960s it had become clear the athlete who wanted desperately to win a given race, such as an Olympic final, could markedly increase his or her chances by focusing all training toward that event. This process is called peaking, and explains why notable Olympic champions had little or no success in non-Olympic years. Instead of peaking, Clarke persisted in staying in shape constantly, while continually intensifying the quality of his daily training. Thus he would improve year to year, but rarely have available the rested reserves necessary for victory in modern, excruciating, championship racing. Of course, a palpable champion such as Clarke needed no material affirmation of his status; he himself affirmed it daily in his training, his racing, his being.

Geography also impeded Clarke in the pursuit of championships, just as it hampered all other long-distance runners from Australia and New Zealand. It is absolutely necessary for an athlete to have top-level competition to achieve his or her highest potential fitness. Because Oceania's seasons are the exact opposite of Europe's, northern hemisphere runners were understandably uninterested in traveling to compete on the underside of the world in between their own northern peak competitive seasons. This situation meant that the Oceania runners had to go to Europe and America to hone their talents. Leaving aside the havoc such a long journey wreaks on a highly fit person (far worse than the jet lag a normal person experiences), the trip is costly. European and American track-meet promoters were, and are, eager to pay expenses for top middle-distance runners such as Snell and

Iron man Ron Clarke winning one of innumerable races, the 3-mile championship in the 1967 AAA Games held at White City, England. His time was 12:59.6. (Photograph by E. D. Lacey, courtesy of Track & Field News.)

Elliott. The half-mile and the mile have always been the most glamorous and popular running events; patrons will pay good money to see the world's best milers. Promoters were considerably less eager to pick up the tab for a long-distance specialist. Clarke competed much more often on the (affluent) American indoor circuit than on the European outdoor circuit. The fat American indoor promoters were more willing to pay his way than were the hungry European outdoor organizers.

1964 was an Olympic year and most runners other than Ron Clarke were primed for their best performances during it. (Clarke was *always* primed for his best.) The sixth annual US-USSR dual meet at Los Angeles in July promised to portend the outcome of the fourth quadrennial Cold War Games, also known as the 1964 Tokyo Olympics. On July 25, 1964, 18-year-old American Gerry Lindgren ran away from the Russians in the 10,000-meter footrace. Young Lindgren had been putting in 30 miles a day for two full months leading up to the meet. Fifteen laps into the 25-lapper he made his move, responding to a surge by Leonid Ivanov. The American crowd, understandably, expressed some enthusiasm over Gerry's bravado; but Lindgren misunderstood all the commotion and thought the partisan fans were warning him the Russians were coming, the Russians were coming! He therefore scatted off into the middle distance, claiming victory by 120 yards with a 29:17.6 clocking. It was the first American long-distance running victory in international competition in modern history.

Unfortunately, it also stood as Gerry Lindgren's signal victory in his racing career. He sprained his ankle two days before the Tokyo 10K final and finished ninth, a miraculous, but certainly frustrating, performance. In 1965, Lindgren nearly tied with Marine Billy Mills in the AAU championship meet at San Diego, losing by a step. (Lindgren defied the NCAA in racing at the meet. The huffy NCAA decreed any athlete under its jurisdiction who competed in the AAUs would be ineligible for further collegiate competition.) Their time for the 6-mile run was 27:11.6—exactly 6 seconds under Ron Clarke's world record. In the early 1970s, Lindgren joined the International Track Association "pro track" circuit. Bedeviled by injuries and indecision concerning his career, Gerry Lindgren sadly and mysteriously vanished in 1981.

Aurele Vandendriessche from Belgium made it two in a row when he won the 1964 Boston Marathon in 2:19:59 over the largest field that had ever taken off from Hopkinton: 301 runners. Finland's Tenho Salakka slogged through the slush and snow behind Vandendriessche to take second in 2:20:48, and Canadian professor Ron Wallingford came home 3 seconds later to claim third.

On May 23, 1964, 27-year-old Dale Greig became the first woman to break 3:30 for a full marathon. Greig ran 3:27:45 on a hot day over a rough route at Ryde, Isle of Wight.

U.S. Marine Billy Mills leads schoolboy wonder Gerry Lindgren with one lap remaining in the 1965 AAU 6-mile championship run. Mills won by one step, but both he and Lindgren recorded the same time—27:11.6, a world record. (Photograph by Eli Attar, courtesy of Track & Field News.)

On June 5, 1964, Jim Ryun ran 3:59 for the mile at the Compton Invitational Meet in California. Ryun was 17 years old, the first sub-4 schoolboy in history. Even more impressive, young Ryun was hit and knocked down during the race. He passed through the first lap in 59.2, bunched among the leaders; then a group of runners burst from the back of the pack to jockey for position at the front. At 600 yards into the race, Ryun was jostled by these surging runners, stumbled, slipped into the inside of the track, and just caught himself before falling. Afflicted with a hearing problem, Ryun's sense of balance was less than perfect (his history would be spotted with stumbles and falls, some of them tragic). Later, Ryun reflected on that instant: "On the infield, I could feel Coach [Bob] Timmons intensify *my* mental toughness and I quickly rebounded by getting right back into the pack and picking up the pace." That was when leader Dyrol Burleson started a mighty surge, the pain and pleasure of which, Ryun said, helped him forget anxieties over nearly falling. The youngster held on to finish eighth in a field studded with mile studs: Burleson, Jim Grelle, Archie San Romani, and Tom O'Hara.

The Kansas air seems to breed great American milers, and young Jim went on to finish in the last qualifying spot (third) in the Olympic Trials 1500 by 1 foot over Jim Grelle. It proved not to be a great Olympics for teen-aged Americans. While Gerry Lindgren was spraining his ankle, Jim Ryun was coming down with a cold along with his Tokyo roommates, Dyrol Burleson and Bill Dellinger. The cold eliminated Ryun during the semifinals of the Tokyo 1500.

The Games came to Asia in 1964. To honor the occasion properly, the host city of Tokyo left nothing to chance. In October, 1963, Tokyo officials hosted 4,000 athletes at the International Sports Week, using the same facilities and procedures they would exactly one year later in the Olympics. Authorities also practiced the opening and closing Olympic ceremonies to make sure the timing was precise. They used schoolchildren as the audience, filling Tokyo Stadium to the brim.

The Tokyo hosts provided a polished Olympics program. None of the participants needed do anything other than compete—and worry. Just before the first distance final, the 10,000 meters, onlooker Peter Snell commented: "The worst possible outcome I can foresee is victory for an American. The Americans are traditionally masters of the short track events and we other nations are naturally not too keen to see that mastery extended to the longer races." Participant Ron Clarke looked to former steeplechase champion Chris Brasher for his appraisal of the Americans' chances for victory in any of the long-distance events. Brasher gave a succinct summary of his estimate of the Yanks' chances: "Not in a lifetime, old boy, not in a lifetime."

I knew he was gonna win when I saw him. I could just feel it, like a thunderstorm coming in August. Even on the other side of the world, I could tell. He's a United States Marine.

It's our new color set, and everybody on it looks kind of orange, but I can tell they're moving fast. The guy announcing from Tokyo says 10,000 meters is a little over 6 miles! I can't run two blocks in gym class. I ask Dad and Grandpa how anybody could run for 6 miles, let alone so fast, and they don't know, either. Dad's a football fan, and Grandpa's a baseball nut, and they only know about sprinting.

The TV guy keeps saying it's very surprising to see Billy Mills doing so well, right up there lap after lap with the Australian guy who has a crewcut as short as Billy's and as much muscle in his shoulders, too. There's a little tiny guy from Tunisia right behind these two big guys, but everybody else that everybody thought would do great before the race is pretty much out of it. The guy who won it last time is 'way back, and so is the guy who won the 3-miler the same year. That guy Lindgren, who's only three years older than I am and who beat the Commies in this same sorta race this summer's got a sprained ankle, and he's out of it, too.

The Australian guy's name is Clarke; the announcer just said it, and I'll remember it 'cause he looks like Clark Kent half-changed into Superman. They just said he's the world-record holder for running this far. I'll bet he is. He looks like he eats barbed wire for lunch. He keeps trying to run away from our guy, but Billy always catches up with him. Even I know why, from junior varsity wrestling: Billy's got nothing to lose. Clarke has everything to lose.

It's the last lap and Dad's put down his Scotch and Grandpa's beer's getting warm and these guys are running even faster than before. Billy and Clarke are shoulder-to-shoulder just ahead of the little Tunisian guy whose name's Mohammed Something and now I'll remember it because that's the name of his god or something. It just got like football, and Dad's shouting! Mohammed just put his arms between Billy and Clarke and shoved 'em both aside! They both almost fell. Geez, they oughta slug that little bastard! They're both really mad, and Clarke's right on Mohammed's heels but Billy's about 3 yards back and there's only a turn and a straightaway to go.

HE'S GONNA DO IT! I KNEW IT! Lookit him go, he's got his lips pulled back away from his teeth like our shepard, Rinty, when he's gonna bite Mr. Granger the mailman. Dad's screamin' like it was Jimmy Brown about to score for Syracuse. HE GOT HIM! There's the little thread, he's gonna do it, he's got his hands up in the air and a big smile on his puss and he's got leg muscles the size of our Buick and the announcer says it's a new Olympic record and no American's ever done anything like this before.

They're interviewing him now and his father was a Sioux Indian and he is a Marine lieutenant and he has an Olympic gold medal for running 6 miles. You can't get any more American than that.

Marine lieutenant Billy Mills ran the Tokyo 10K final in 28:24.4, 7.8 seconds under Pytor Bolotnikov's previous Olympic reference. Mohammed Gammoudi of Tunisia, who probably put in more stellar performances in fewer races than any of his contemporaries, held on for second place. A disappointed Ron Clarke came third; when asked if he had worried about Mills before the race, the world-record holder snapped: "Worry about him? I never heard of him."

American Indian Billy Mills finally came through on the promise of Louis Bennet, the celebrated Deerfoot of the nineteenth century. He had, in one half-hour, validated American distance running to the rest of the world. The 26-year-old Marine's experience before the 10K final symbolized the American distance-running experience in international competition. As the boxer-turned-runner put it: "No newspaperman as much as said hello to me" before the final. He also commented that Gammoudi's shoving "was a break for me. Luckily, I was knocked outside where the track was firmer, not so chewed up as on the rail. I found better traction and I was able to pick up immediately." The track had been soaked by rain before the race, which of course made Mills's time all the more impressive but may also help explain Clarke's bronze-medalist finishing position.

Yet another historically significant point may explain Clarke's fate in the Tokyo 10K. It was the first clear American victory in an Olympic long-distance race, but, as important, it was the first time that "kickers" had stayed the full distance with endurance machines such as Clarke or Zátopek. Much was made of the fact that Mills took nearly 50 seconds off his personal best time in the space of one race; but nearly overlooked in the celebratory frenzy after the gold was the fact Mills had run his 25th and last lap in a tick under sixty seconds and on a slow track! The era when runners were grouped into "fast" sprinters and middle-distance specialists on one hand and "slow" long-distance aces on the other closed with Billy Mills's gold medal at Tokyo, much as Deerfoot had halted the tactic of trolling along till the last lap then dashing madly for the wire. Those who would employ that tactic thenceforth would either have the sprint of a 100-meter star or the willingness to settle for losing.

Mills set the track world on its ear. Peter Snell's performance at Tokyo helped that world regain at least a little equilibrium. Ron Clarke had entered the 10K as world-record holder (28:15.6), but lost. Snell entered the 800 meters as world-record holder (1:44.3) and prevailed. Both athletes had another thing in common. Both were racing against the best in the world.

Although Snell preferred the half-mile over the mile and had virtually no serious challengers in the world of 800 meters, he went into the Tokyo Games far more prepared as a miler than as a 2-lap specialist. In 1964, a year after Coach Lydiard complained the runner was getting lazy and out of shape, Snell started putting in 100-mile weeks to establish the firm distance base needed for superlative miling. (Ironically, Snell was at the time working as a salesman for a New Zealand cigarette company and had to beg permission to take time off from work to train as an athlete.) Given a 42-beat resting pulse by nature, Snell apparently enjoyed fundamental speed and endurance, hence his stellar and unpressured performances in the half-mile. To run twice one's favored distance, although rarely demanding twice the usual distance base, demands the athlete have *confidence* in his or her ability to run the whole longer distance at competitive speed. Maybe Snell's body did not need 100-mile weeks, but his personal confidence almost undoubtedly required them. Like many other world-class talents, Snell's self-confidence, although normally stratospherically high, occasionally plummeted drastically.

Snell's emphasis on the Tokyo 1500 stemmed from his fears he had lost some of his essential speed as a result of aging; yet when he moved from his 100-mile weekly distance base to speedwork on the track, his worries seemed nonsensical. In one workout two months before the Games, Snell ran twenty 440s in an average of 61.5 seconds each. Snell's self-doubts seemed unfounded, but one fact remained indisputable. Because the mile is the glamour event of track, international meet promoters have much more expense money to offer the world's preeminent miler than they can offer the world's best half-miler. Further, like other record holders before and after him, Snell may well have felt his mile mark somehow besmirched if he did not have an Olympic 1500 gold medal to accompany it.

Finally, the last athlete to pull off the 800/1500 double in the Olympics was Peerless Mel Sheppard at London in 1908. It would be nice to be the first man in 56 years to execute that difficult double, and against far stiffer competition than faced by Sheppard.

Although Peter Snell wanted the 1500 the most, he had to run the gauntlet of the 800 first. That increased the psychological pressure on him. Snell commented: "Now that I was committed to the 800, I had to ignore the 1500 to avoid holding any reserves back that might be needed to get me home in the 800. I was in a rather confused state."

Snell finished third in his preliminary heat for the 800, running 1:49.0, while Kenya's Wilson Kiprugut won the heat in 1:47.8. Snell reflected that "My time was pleasing in relation to the effort it took." A hint of the effort at Snell's command came in his semifinal heat, which he won, totally unstrained, in 1:46.9.

Snell's performance in the 800-meter final recalled that of American John Woodruff's in 1936. He was boxed in. Having drawn lane one for the final, Snell decided he would let Kenyan Kiprugut set the pace and would slide in behind him for the first lap. Kiprugut took the lead, but did not go out nearly as fast as Snell had expected. Everybody else in the field went right with the Kenyan, therefore, and American Tom Farrell moved up on Snell's outside, boxing the meaty middle-distance man in behind Kiprugut.

Snell used a modified Woodruff tactic. He didn't come to a dead stop, he merely slowed significantly and let the human chicane rumble away from him. Snell then accelerated hard and passed everybody but leaders George Kerr of Jamaica and Kiprugut (both of whom had broken Snell's Olympic 800-meter record in their semifinal heat). He pulled out of their slipstream heading down the final back straight, then accelerated heartily through the ultimate turn. Peter Snell won his second straight Olympic 800 championship in the Games' record time of 1:45.1, 1.2 seconds under his old mark and a full second below Kerr's and Kiprugut's shared semifinal record. It was also the second fastest 800 meters in history, trailing only Snell's world record 1:44.3; but the New Zealander said of his Tokyo run: "This one here is the finer performance. That [the world record] was with a pacemaker. This was against the world's best."

It certainly was: the great Bill Crothers inveigled himself past Kiprugut and Kerr zooming for home and claimed the silver medal some three meters behind Snell. Kiprugut held on for the bronze, historically significant in that his was Kenya's first Olympic placing. Poor Kerr came fourth, racing against the best in the world.

America finished in both the gold and the silver in the women's 100-meter final. Tennessee State University roommates Wyomia Tyus and Edith McGuire ran together for much of the Tokyo final. Tyus had equalled Wilma Rudolph's 11.2-second world record in one of her preliminary heats, then blasted to a victorious 11.4-second final, 2 meters ahead of her roomie, McGuire.

To console herself, McGuire took the 200-meter gold medal, cracking Rudolph's Olympic record (but *not* world record) by a full second in clocking 23-flat. Where was Tyus? She didn't run the 200. Why not? It was too long a distance for her!

Evergreen Betty Cuthbert, who had taken both the 100 and the 200 at Melbourne, moved up to the 400 for Tokyo. It did not look like it had been a wise choice. In her semifinal heat she was beaten by up-and-coming British middle-distance star Ann Packer, who ran 52.7 to Betty's 53.8. Things looked glum for the Australian at the start of the final as well. It was a windy day and the lane Packer drew, Number Six, offered her partial shelter from the winds because of its proximity to the viewing stands. The wily Cuthbert therefore devised a moving windbreak of her own, Australian teammate Judy Amoore, whom Cuthbert drafted shamelessly—and sensibly—down the windy front straight and then pulled out and passed down the tailwind-aided backstraight. Cuthbert ran home 2 meters ahead of Packer, establishing the Olympic mark of 52 flat for the inaugural running of a woman's 400 meters in the Games.

Billy Mills accepted the fact that nobody wanted to talk to him before he made his mark by winning the 10K final, but his teammate, Bob Schul, refused to stand for lack of recognition. When Schul hit the Olympic

Village, anyone who spoke English knew he had arrived. The 27-year-old asthmatic sub-4 miler proclaimed: "I'm the man they have to beat. I have turned in the fastest time in the world this year and I expect to win."

What Ohioan Schul expected to win was the 5,000 meters. Although a swift miler, Schul and virtually every other miler had elected to move up to the "old milers' " distance, the 5K, rather than run an Olympic 1500 final against Peter Snell. Snell's presence in the Tokyo metric mile did not make the 5K any easier; indeed, the field bristled with quality: Schul held 1964's best 5K time, as well as the world record for 2 miles (8:26.4). Ron Clarke was in the field, as was Mohammed Gammoudi. France's outstanding miler, Michel Jazy, moved up to the 5K for Tokyo. This field did more than bristle with quality—it *growled* with it.

It made no difference. Schul, who was coached by Mihaly Igloi of the LATC, won anyway, making the U.S.A. two-for-two in the long-distance events at Tokyo. The early pace, although set by Strongman Clarke, was slow, owing to an extremely muddy track. The athletes were soon as spattered with muck as the windshields of semis are splattered with bugs on a warm Alabama highway. Jazy and Germany's Harald Norpoth hung on Clarke's shoulder, Schul was a couple meters back. At the tail of the pack, Schul's American teammate Bill Dellinger, of the University of Oregon, slogged along.

The order remained essentially static until a lap-and-a-half from the wire, when an American singlet zoomed to the front. It was Dellinger! The formerly leading quintet of Clarke, Jazy, Norpoth and Schul lit off after him. Jazy, the fastest miler of the bunch, shot ahead going into the last lap, but Schul's knees were churning the air and he reached the Frenchman 75 meters from the tape. Bob Schul ran his last lap in the 5K in 54.8 seconds,

Bill Dellinger, who won a bronze medal in the 1964 Tokyo Olympics' 5-kilometer footrace. He went on to take over from Bill Bowerman as head track coach at the University of Oregon, where he has maintained the Ducks' high performance level. (Photograph courtesy of the University of Oregon.)

one of the more astounding statistics in track history. Norpoth popped by Jazy for the silver . . . and Dellinger nipped him at the line for the bronze! Schul's time, 13:48.8, was lacklustre by contemporary world-class standards, but excellent in the light of the mud that passed for a running track. "One of my easy races," laughed Schul, holding his gold medal. Uncle Sam must have been laughing somewhere, too. Billy Mills and Bob Schul, as well as Bill Dellinger, had delivered on the promise tendered by Gerry Lindgren. Americans could now run the long distances with the best in the world.

Foiled by lack of experience in the 400 meters, England's Ann Packer triumphed with a plethora of power in the 800 meters. A 400-meter specialist, the young British schoolteacher agreed to try the 400/800 double for the honor of Great Britain, as well as for the favor of her fiance, Robbie Brightwell, who was captain of the English Olympic Team. She moved wide going through the final turn to avoid a rolling roadblock comprising four other runners, then hammered down the runway to take the gold in the world record of 2:01.1, 1/10-second under the world mark and 3.2 seconds under Shevcova-Lysenko's former Olympic record.

The American women didn't exactly blow it in the 400-meter relay final. They dropped it—the baton. Composed of Willye White, Marilyn White, and gold medalists Wyomia Tyus and Edith McGuire, the team entered the final as confident as Bob Schul, but a fumbled baton exchange handed the gold to Poland. Their time of 43.6 seconds would have been both an Olympic and a world record, but officials mysteriously disallowed it later. (The team was not disqualified nor were any changes made in the awarding of medals.)

The American runners did so well at Tokyo that the stadium band tired of playing "The Star-Spangled Banner" and concocted a truncated rendition to satisfy both protocol and the demands of human endurance. American Uan Rasey, a spectator at Tokyo who played lead trumpet in the M-G-M Studio Orchestra quickly caught the change, started bringing his horn to the stadium with him, and appended the remainder of the national anthem each time the Tokyo band played its bowdlerized version.

Peter Snell bowdlerized the 1500-final field, cutting out all the spirit from possible upsetters' hides with one indomitable, nearly incredible, final lap. It was the first important metric mile Snell said he enjoyed. Until the Tokyo Games, he continued to prefer the 800/880 over the 1500/mile. On the other hand, he had longed to win the Olympic 1500 ever since watching Herb Elliott's victory at Rome.

Snell stepped to the line after having run two qualifying heats for the 800 and the 800 final, and two qualifying heats for the 1500 (one in 3:46.8, the slowest qualifying time at Tokyo, and one in 3:38.8, the fastest qualifying time at Tokyo by nearly 3 *seconds*). Snell may not have been well-rested, but he was psychologically pumped up as a zeppelin—and as explosive.

Michel Bernard took the field through the first 400 meters in 58 flat.

American miler Dyrol Burleson hung on the Frenchman's shoulder, the rest of the pack bunched tightly behind. Going into the second lap, Bernard gestured to Burleson to take over setting the pace. The American refused, and there was a hiatus in the tempo for half a lap until Snell's teammate, John Davies, got fed up, accelerated, and sprinted away, Snell on his heels. The second lap passed in 62.5 seconds, testimony to the folderol among the previous leaders. The pace quickened thereafter, dipping down to 58.8 for the third lap. It wasn't fast enough to shake everybody else away from the New Zealand Express, though, and Snell again found himself boxed in heading into the ultimate lap of his ultimate race! Snell took his time to assess the situation calmly for half a lap more; this was not the time to slow down to pull himself out of the box! Heading through the penultimate turn he prepared to throw a body block on his capturers; but first he looked behind to see who was hemming him in, discovered to his delight it was polite Englishman John Whetton, extended his arm "rather like a motorist's hand signal" (as Snell later put it), and sprinted out of the cage as the sporting Whetton moved aside to permit him egress. "As simply as that, I was out," Snell recalled.

He was out and he was *off*. With 200 meters remaining him, Snell sprinted more than 10 meters clear of the field by the tape. His last lap, for half of which he was balked, took 52.9 seconds! Czechoslovakia's Josef Odlozil outsnookered Davies for the silver medal, so the other Kiwi in the race had to settle for the bronze. Both Odlozil and Davies hit home with identical 3:39.6 clockings. Peter Snell clocked 3:38.1.

Ageless Abebe Bikila returned to the Olympics to claim his second straight marathon gold medal. Bikila ran in shoes this time. Possibly that is why he ran the world's best marathon time—2:12:11.2—over 3 minutes under his previous Olympic best.

Bikila's footgear may have helped him, but the presence of Ron Clarke in the field undoubtedly also spurred the enduring Ethiopian to new heights. Iron man Clarke took the field out at a sub-5 minute pace, unheard of in marathons of the day, reaching the 5-kilometer point in 15:06, 11 seconds ahead of Bikila and 2 seconds ahead of Ireland's Jim Hogan. Clarke hit 10K in 30:14, with Hogan right next to him and Bikila a couple steps behind. Fifteen kilometers passed in 45:35, then Bikila decided it was time to run fast and *surged away* from the pack! By 25K he was 15 seconds ahead of the game Hogan and nearly 2 minutes clear of the dying Clarke. Bikila breezed home over 4 minutes ahead of silver medalist Basil Heatley of England. Leonard Edelen was the U.S.A.'s first finisher, running 2:18:12.4 to take sixth place. Ron Clarke came ninth in 2:20:26.8, and America's Billy Mills was the fourteenth finisher in 2:22:55.4.

The 1964 Olympics were over, but the Olympians themselves were not done with the athletic year—at least Peter Snell was not. The month after the Tokyo Olympics, he decided to do some fast running in Aukland, New

Abebe Bikila, the fabulous
Ethiopian distance runner who won
the 1960 Olympic marathon barefoot, shown claiming his second
straight Olympic marathon gold
medal at Tokyo. (Photograph
courtesy of Track & Field News.)

Zealand. On November 19, 1964, Snell ran a 1000-meter race in 2:16.6, a world record for 1 kilometer. On November 23, 1964, the Kiwi king ran the mile in 3:54.1, a world record. *Track & Field News* proclaimed him Athlete of the Year for 1964, as the magazine had done for 1962, making the zippy New Zealander the first person in history so honored.

1965 started off with a new American marathon: the Mission Bay Marathon in San Diego.

Ron Clarke ranked Number One in the world in long-distance running in 1965, and he returned to the American indoor track season at the start of the year to demonstrate his claim to sovereignty. It was a short stay. Clarke only raced two races. In the 2-mile run at the Golden Gate Meet in San Francisco, the awesome Aussie won in 8:34.8, topping both Billy Mills and George Young. *The next night* Clarke ran another 2-mile race at the Mason Dixon Meet, winning in 8:35.4. Then he went back home. In the balance of the year, the iron man lowered his personal mark for 2 miles to 8:24.8. He set the world standard for 10 miles in 47:12.8. He became the first long-distance runner in history to set *six world records for six different events in one year*. Clarke's 1965 marks were: 3 miles in 12:52.4; 5 kilometers in 13:25.8; 6 miles in 26:47.0; 10 kilometers in 27:39.4; 20 kilometers in 59:22.8; and 12 miles, 1006 yards in the 1-hour run. Not surprisingly, Clarke received both the Indoor Athlete of the Year and the Athlete of the Year awards from *Track & Field News*.

In 1965 the finish line of the Boston Marathon course was moved from Exeter Street to the newly completed Prudential Center on Boylston Street.

Will Cloney, the race director, moved the Hopkinton starting line back 389 yards to ensure the distance remained totally accurate, and he must have been glad he took such pains because Japan's Morio Shigematsu christened the "new" course with a record time, 2:16:33, as he led a team of five Japanese runners to an astounding 1-2-3-5-6 finish. Only defending champion Aurele Vandendriessche, who ran 2:17:44 to take fourth, cut into the Orient Express.

Ron Daws of the Twin Cities Track Club in Minnesota established American track records for 15 miles (1:18:10) and 25 kilometers (1:21:07) in the course of one 15.75-mile race in 1965. The 28-year-old Daws went on to become one of America's finest marathoners, although he did not begin to run the 26.2 miles until 1966. His first marathon took 2:40 of his time. By 1967 he had won the National Marathon Championship and the Pan-American Games Trials marathon, in qualifying for the Pan-Am Games team. Daws finished third in the 1968 Olympic Trials marathon and earned a trip to the Mexico City Games, in which he finished twenty-second in 2:33:53. The Minnesotan eventually became the coach of outstanding New Zealand long-distance runner Lorraine Moller. In 1981, he became her husband.

Kenyan Kipchoge Keino takes the high-altitude Mexico City Olympics' 1500-meter final from America's great Jim Ryun. Keino, running capless, hit the line in 3:34.9; Ryun in 3:37.8. (Photograph by E. D. Lacey, courtesy of Track & Field News.)

He ran with loose shoulders and an orange cap that could probably be seen from the moon on a clear day; he was Kipchoge Keino from Kenya, bursting on the European track scene in 1965 to set a world record at 3,000 meters (7:39.6). He would go on to greater glory at many other distances, most notably the mile, in a career that would span eight years. Keino, in company with Abebe Bikila, helped establish the African continent's claim as a distance-running power. The African continentals, in turn, had been fired up to competitive running by former U.S. middle-distance great, Mal Whitfield. Whitfield had been sent to Africa in the early 1960s by the U.S. State Department as a cultural ambassador. His enthusiasm and athletic knowledge helped Africans from all nations channel the fantastic aerobic strength they developed from their agrarian lifestyles into world-class track performances. Mal Whitfield deserves honor not only as a two-time gold medalist at the Olympics and a peerless board runner, but also as the man who awoke an entire continent.

In the 1965 AAU Championships mile run held at San Diego, Jim Ryun lowered his personal record for the mile in a 3:55.3 victory. The man who finished second to the 18-year-old wonder was Peter Snell. It was the Flying Kiwi's last season. The 26-year-old wonder announced his retirement shortly thereafter, closing a career in which he set eight world records.

No sooner does one mile great retire than one or more come up to take his place. Jim Ryun seemed the most obvious heir to the magic feathers of Peter Snell, but it was France's Michel Jazy, returning to the mile after moving up to the 5K at Tokyo, who lowered the mile world record. On June 9, 1965, Jazy ran 3:53.6, exactly ½-second under the mark set by the man Arthur Lydiard, and others, believed could ultimately have run 3:48 had he chosen to train for it.

IX

Running for Health
1966–1970

In January, 1966, the first issue of a poorly printed but richly enthusiastic sports magazine came on the market. It seemed like a typical venture by an ambitious college student, which it was. Young Kansan Bob Anderson, frustrated by the lack of information on long-distance running available to Americans, started publishing *Distance Running News*. There would be only one further issue of it that year, each issue selling one thousand copies. The magazine would eventually flourish, becoming *Runner's World* in 1970, the first entry in the popular American running media race.

While Anderson was cranking out *Distance Running News*, Dr. Warren Guild was working on a program at Boston's Peter Bent Brigham Hospital that would eventually *make* distance-running news. Dr. Guild poured over three years' data on his cardiac patients in 1966, deciding they showed two things. First, that his experimental program of prescribing exercise instead of rest for heart attack victims speeded their recovery from the attacks. Second, the data implied, but did not demonstrate, that regular aerobic exercise (exercise that raises the pulse rate but that does not bring on undue exertion and oxygen debt) probably functions as a means of preventing heart disease. In practical terms, this meant Guild had his patients jogging daily around the Fenway section of Boston, less than 1 mile from the Boston Marathon finish line.

Dr. Kenneth Cooper, the father of popular aerobic exercise and one of the most important authors behind the modern running boom. (Photograph courtesy of Dr. Kenneth Cooper.)

Dr. Guild's findings, initially of interest only to cardiac patients and Guild's medical peers, caught the attention of U.S. Air Force Lt. Col. Kenneth Cooper, M.D., who had run the Boston Marathon in 1962 (where he finished 101st, and last recorded runner) and in 1963. A cardiologist and former collegiate half-miler, Dr. Cooper was developing a program to enhance fitness among Air Force recruits. He was naturally interested by Dr. Guild's studies, and paid him a visit at Peter Bent Brigham Hospital to see firsthand how aerobic exercise helped both cure and prevent heart problems. Dr. Cooper's visit with Dr. Guild, in combination with Dr. Cooper's own research on enhancing fitness both in normal Air Force recruits and in astronauts, would result in the 1968 publication of Cooper's first book,

James F. Fixx, author of The Complete Book of Running, *is another writer whose work promoted running for the masses.* (Photograph courtesy of *The Boston Herald American.*)

Aerobics, which in turn would have a profound effect on distance running in America.

Iron man Ron Clarke came to the U.S. in February, 1966, to run the 2-mile footrace at the Los Angeles Times Indoor Games. As a result of advance publicity of Clarke's entry, the meet sold out a week ahead of time, and 13,477 track fans stood cheek-by-fanny under the wood to watch eight international stars run the boards for 2 miles. In addition to Clarke, the field included Kenya's Kipchoge Keino, Hungary's Lajos Mecser, the Soviet Union's Viktor Kudinski and New Zealand's Bill Baillie. Clarke went into the race holding *seven long-distance world records* for everything from the 2-mile run to the 1-hour run. Because Keino was in the race, Clarke hoped for a slow pace: "Two miles is a bit short for me, and Keino is 4 to 6 seconds faster than I am over the distance. Maybe I should steal his orange cap."

Clarke got his wish. The first 440 took 67.7 seconds. The iron man took over at the half-mile point, tossing a searing surge at the strolling pack. Clarke had not abandoned his pre-race strategy. He still hoped for an overall slow pace; he just wanted to soften up and shake down his competition with his own fantastic breed of endurance that could withstand short bursts of acceleration, just as Zátopek had often done. Unfortunately for him, Clarke coasted too much after each surge. His tactic took the stuffings out of Keino, but not out of Baillie, who whipped past Clarke ("He surprised the very devil out of me," Clarke said after) with a quarter-mile to go and scooted home in 8:37.4 to consign Clarke to second-man status. After the race Clarke delivered himself of what must have been the summation of his feelings about being long-distance running's perennial pacemaker: "There are times when being forced to set the pace is maddening. You feel like turning around and punching the fellow who's running right behind you."

The 1966 Boston Marathon certainly punched out American distance runners once again. The Japanese, in the person of 25-year-old Kenji Kimihara, won again, this time in 2:17:11. The race stands as historically significant because a woman ran for the first time. Twenty-three-year old Roberta Gibb Bingay completed the course in 3:21:40, an oustanding time for a woman in that era. She finished, unofficially, 135th in a field of 415. (Perhaps the second most outstanding thing about Bingay's performance was the comment race director Will Cloney made in attempting to emphasize to the press that no woman could be part of the Boston Marathon: "Mrs. Bingay did not compete in the Boston Marathon. She merely ran along the official route while the race was in progress.") Bingay perforce competed "unofficially" because the B.A.A. could not accept women in their race. The club and its officials were constrained from accepting women in the marathon for two reasons. AAU rules forbade women from running long-distance events on either track or road on the belief a woman could not physiologically stand such stress, and the same set of rules prohibited "mixed competition" (men and women running in the same race together).

*Roberta Gibb, the first
woman known to have run
the Boston Marathon, shown
here finishing a road race in
1981.* (Photograph courtesy
of Roberta Gibb.)

Bobbi Bingay originally planned to run the Boston Marathon in 1965, but injuries forced postponement of her marathon debut for a year. (She suffered from two sprained ankles, possibly the result of her chosen footgear— nurse's shoes! Her choice was dictated by circumstance. There were no running shoes for women available at the time. In the 1966 Boston Marathon, she wore a pair of boy's size-6 running shoes.) Aware that regulations barred her from competing in the marathon (as a result of the letter accompanying her rejected race application in February, 1966), Bingay decided to run the first part of the event incognito in a blue hooded sweatshirt. She emphasized both immediately after the race and in succeeding years that she had not run Boston to make a radical feminist statement. As she wrote shortly thereafter: "I ran the Boston Marathon out of love . . . Running expresses my love of Nature, my delight in being alive. Yet it was a love that was incomplete until it was shared with others."

On July 17, 1966, Jim Ryun brought the world record for the mile back to the United States, the first athlete to do so since his fellow Kansan, Glenn Cunningham, in 1934. Running unpressed in the Compton Relays at Berkeley, California, the 19-year-old Kansas freshman finished nearly 7 seconds ahead of the field in his 3:51.3 performance, taking 2.3 seconds off Michel Jazy's former world standard. This was the year young Ryun claimed both the Sullivan Award as the world's greatest indoor half-miler and miler and the *Track & Field News* Athlete of the Year accolade.

New Zealand's David McKenzie set a course record of 2:15:45 in winning the 1967 Boston Marathon, but, once again, women runners in the field received most of the news media's attention. The feminine noun was plural at Boston in 1967; it was the first female "field"—two women—in the race's history. Roberta Gibb (now divorced, she dropped Bingay from her name) ran as she had the previous year: fast, despite having the flu (3:27:17, which would have been good for 266th place), and without a number. The other woman in the field, Katherine Switzer, ran far more slowly, but sporting number 261 on her sweat suit.

Inspired by Gibb's run at Boston in 1966, the 20-year-old Switzer decided also to run the marathon. In later years she claimed to have been unaware that rules prohibited women from running the Boston (or any other) Marathon, but this seems improbable. Almost no story published about Gibbs's 1966 venture failed to point out the regulations forcing an "unofficial entrant" status on her. Switzer tendered an entry blank signed "K. Switzer" and did not show up for the pre-race physical examination at Hopkinton, both of which facts suggest at least a degree of duplicity on her part. Although Switzer received her race number, it was awarded improperly. Several miles into the race, an official, crusty Jock Semple, recognized Switzer as a woman and, in a rage, strove to remove the number from her. In a greater rage, Switzer's boyfriend, hammer thrower Thomas C. Miller, strove more successfully to remove Semple from the marathon course. In a remarkably unsporting gesture, runners who had completed the race linked arms and prevented Gibb, who arrived in 3:27, from crossing the finish line in 1967. (Switzer claimed to have completed the race in 4:20:02.) Although a colorful moment in running history in general and in Boston Marathon history in particular, the Gibb/Switzer "field" at Boston in 1967 did *not* confer official-entrant status on women. Switzer did *not* run in the race officially, no more than had Gibb.

Jim Ryun lowered his personal, and world, record for the mile to 3:51.1 on June 23, 1967, in the AAU Championships. All Ryun's outdoor records were established on *dirt* tracks. One can only speculate how fast he might have run on today's synthetic track surfaces. He also set the world 1500-meter record at 3:33.1. In fact, en route to receiving his second straight *Track & Field News* Athlete of the Year award, the maturing Jayhawk established an American 880 indoor record (albeit on an oversized, ⅛-mile track) of 1:48.3 and claimed the NCAA indoor mile championship in 3:58.6.

The fabulous Doris Brown inaugurated her succession of World Cross-Country Championships in 1967. Incontestably the greatest woman distance runner of the late 1960s and early 1970s, the 24-year-old native of Gig Harbor, Washington, won the first World Cross-Country Championship, held in Wales in 1967. She also won the second, third, fourth, and fifth. (Only Norway's Grete Waitz, the heir to Brown's mantle of preeminence, has come close to the feat to date.) Prevented by high school league rules from running track as a schoolgirl, young Doris had the Tacoma, Washington, Parks Department to thank for starting her on her competition career. The Tacoma P.D. hosted a Junior Olympics in 1958. Brown took second in the 50-yard dash

Doris Brown Heritage as she appeared in 1979. In the light of her five International Cross-Country championships and numerous records and national titles, history recognizes her as the greatest female American distance runner to date. (Photograph courtesy of Doris Brown Heritage.)

and first in the long jump and the 75-yard dash, which was the longest race open to girls at the meet. Her talent caught the eye of a local track club, and soon schoolgirl Brown was competing in the long jump for the Tacoma MicMac Team.

Her next big chance came in 1959, when the MicMac's female quarter-miler was away competing in the AAU Nationals. The club needed a woman to run the 440. Doris Brown ran it. She ran 59.4, a national record! Politics handed the developing distance star yet another opportunity. With the 800 meters back on the women's Olympic program in 1960, the event was of course quickly embraced by the U.S. Olympic Women's Program. Brown ran the 800 and set the national record, 2:19-and-some-change. Running at the U.S. Olympic Trials, she lowered her mark to 2:13.4, but finished second to Pat Daniels. Only Daniels went to the Games, for neither woman had achieved the Olympic qualifying standard for the event. (Every nation may submit one competitor for an Olympic event, even if no citizen of the nation has achieved the Olympic qualifying standard.)

Brown finally went to the Olympics in 1968, after establishing the American 800-meter record, 2:02.2, while racing in England. She also set the American mile mark the same year. An outstanding middle-distance, as well as long-distance, athlete, her fastest 1500 meters came in the 1971 U.S.-U.S.S.R. meet at Berkeley, California, where she raced the 4-lapper in 4:13. Her ultimate indoor mile time was 4:39, while her swiftest indoor 880, 2:07, was a world record.

Brown held numerous indoor world and American records, and competed in the 1500 meters at the 1972 Munich Olympics, where she unfortunately tripped on a lane curb and broke a foot. She often traveled with American teams touring overseas. She was a member of both the 1967 and 1971 U.S. teams sent to the Pan-American Games. A remarkably consistent runner, she claimed second in the 800 meters at both meets.

Doris Brown (now Doris Brown Heritage) herself provided much of the information herein, and perhaps most telling was a datum she omitted. On May 29, 1976, Doris Brown Heritage ran her first marathon at Vancouver, British Columbia. She ran it in 2:47:34.8, then the world's fastest time for a woman's marathon debut. This gracious and modest athlete felt she owed her success to Dr. Ken Foreman, the coach who infused her training with both a strong distance base and interval track work, to sharpen her speed. Originally a junior high school teacher after her graduation from Seattle Pacific University in 1964, she became track coach at her alma mater in 1969 and, in 1981, was made U.S. Women's Olympic Development Coach in addition to her other duties. Doris Brown is the great godmother of American women's distance running.

University of Arizona ace George Young started his own undefeated string with a victory in the 2-mile (in 8:43.4) at the 1968 All-American Games in San Francisco. It would be 1970 before lissome George lost another race, scoring *Track & Field News*'s Indoor Athlete of the Year trophy for both 1968 and 1969. Young won the bronze medal in the steeplechase at the 1968 Mexico City Olympics. In 1969, he tied the world indoor 2-mile record of 8:27.2 set by Australian Kerry Pearce the previous year on the very same track in San Diego. This gutsy distance runner finally retired in 1972 at age 34, after failing to qualify for the 5-kilometer final at the Munich Games—his fourth consecutive Olympics.

Another Australian, Ralph Doubell, made his indoor track debut in 1968. Unlike fellow Australian Kerry Pearce, Doubell was a middle-distance specialist. In his first indoor effort, at the Boston Garden, he ran the world's fifth fastest time for 1000 yards—2:07.7. He moved up to second all-time fastest at the distance in 1969 by legging 2:06.3 at the Los Angeles Times Meet. Doubell set the world indoor half-mile record of 1:47.9 the same year. In 1970 the Aussie finally claimed the world 1000-yard record in 2:05.5.

Jim Ryun ranked Number One in the world in the mile in 1968, ready for the Mexico City Games. Ryun ran the last mile race ever run in the original Madison Square Garden in 3:57.5. As testimony to Ryun's popularity, over 15,000 fans attended that final, USTFF, meet (although nostalgia over the fate of the old Garden may have brought at least a few of them out). The previous year the same meet drew 2,500 people.

On December 3, 1967, Derek Clayton of Australia became the first man to break 2:10 for the marathon. Clayton ran the 26.2 miles at the prestigious Fukuoka Marathon in 2:09:36.4 to defeat favored Japanese runner Seiichiro Sasaki as well as occidental greats Dave McKenzie and Mike Ryan. Unusually big for a marathoner at 6'2" tall and 160 pounds, Clayton hit on "his" event by trial and error instead of design. He would have seemed to possess the ideal frame for a middle-distance man. Clayton thought so, too. In his biography, he and author Paul Perry wrote: "In the beginning, I wanted to become a champion miler. I owe my zeal for the mile to Herb Elliott. . . . I wasn't running yet, but after watching Elliott conquer the field in that incredible [Rome Olympics] 1960 run, I decided running was the sport for me." Lacking the requisite fundamental speed to excel at the middle distances, the tough Australian (who was born in England) kept moving up in distance until he found the marathon. Running in his first marathon only four weeks after moving to Australia in 1961, the monochromatic Clayton clocked 3:00:02 in what was essentially a training run with his track club teammates. He would go on to become the greatest male marathon runner of his era.

When Ambrose (Amby) Burfoot won the 1968 Boston Marathon in 2:22:17 and led a record 890 starters to the Prudential Center, he accomplished more than returning the Boston Marathon crown to America. The 21-year-old Wesleyan University student forged another link in a near-mythic chain of great American distance runners, just as the outstanding Finns have forged such a chain (starting with Kolehmainen and currently extending to Lasse Viren). The American chain started with Clarence DeMar, who taught Old John Kelley a thing or seven about marathon runnings. It passed from Old John to Young John, when John J. spent the night at John A.'s home before John J. won the 1957 Boston Marathon. John J. moved the chain along when he became a high school track coach and took on an athlete named Amby Burfoot. It passed along even farther when Amby Burfoot took a new roommate at Wesleyan, a skinny blond fellow named William (Bill) Rodgers. In the next decade, the American distance chain would continue to run unbroken, as Bill Rodgers became mentor to the only teenager ever allowed to run for the Greater Boston Track Club, and who earned the soubriquet "the Rookie" as a result of his age—Alberto Salazar.

Oregonian Kenny Moore lived too far out west to be part of the New England marathon chain, but that didn't stop him from qualifying for the 1968 Olympic marathon team. One of the major personalities in the history of modern running, Moore matriculated at the University of Oregon from 1962 to 1966. Coach Bill Bowerman hadn't recruited Moore to become one of the celebrated Oregon "Ducks." Kenny had little reputation as a runner when he entered college, but his tenacity earned Coach Bowerman's attention and, ultimately, respect. It took another two years for Moore to win over the Oregon fans. Running the 2-miler at the 1964 University of Oregon/Oregon State dual meet (collegiate track's answer to the Harvard/Yale game), young Moore sliced over 12 seconds off his personal record to clock 8:48.1 and win the race. The stands instantly emptied as Oregonians isolated and lionized the tall (6'¼"), thin (143 pounds) Moore, who less than 9 minutes before had been so lightly regarded his name "wasn't even on the program," as he remembered it. Moore went on to establish improved personal marks in the steeplechase (8:49.4), the mile (4:03.3), and the marathon (2:11:35.8, set finishing second at Fukuoka in 1970). He finished fourteenth at the Mexico City Olympic marathon in 1968, and fourth at the Munich Games marathon in 1972, only 31.4 seconds short of the bronze medal. In between those two Olympics, he convinced a fellow distance runner to move up to the marathon; the fellow's name was Frank Shorter. Still an active competitor, Kenny Moore perhaps deserves even more veneration as, in company with Peter Lovesey and Brian Glanville, the best modern writer on the sport of running. One can only wonder how many athletes, in addition to Shorter, Kenny Moore has intentionally or inadvertently inspired, how many lives he has infused with quiet hope and grim courage.

Dr. Ken Cooper published his book, *Aerobics*, in 1968. When it was published, the best marketing estimates concluded there were 100,000 people at most running or jogging in the United States.

The American Medical Joggers Association was founded in 1968. As the name implied, the group consisted of medical personnel who actually participated in running. Coming on the heels of the interest in Cooper's *Aerobics*, the rise of AMJA helped lay the basis for a body of sophisticated sportsmedicine practitioners in America to look after all the neophyte joggers in America. Equally important, the personal experiences and clinical data collected by AMJA members resulted in concrete, empirically verified, information about what actually happens to the human animal under the sweet duress of running. American medical science had finally discovered running.

The U.S. Olympic Trials always abound with the predictable and the astonishing. Kenny Moore was not the only new runner to attract attention at Eugene, Oregon, in 1968. A brash Villanova frosh named Marty Liquori finished second to the fabulous Jim Ryun in the 1500-meter trial run. Liquori did not rank as a true unknown, only as an athlete untested in international flame. In 1967, he became the first schoolboy ever invited to run the Wanamaker Mile at the Millrose Games. Later in 1967 he ran his first sub-4 mile (3:59.8) to finish seventh in the AAU champ race where Jim Ryun established his ultimate American mile mark of 3:51.1. Hamstrung by inexperience, Liquori finshed dead last in the Olympic 1500 final at Mexico City. At age 19, Liquori was the youngest man ever to make the Olympic metric-mile final.

Liquori almost did not go to the Olympics; he and some others were at Mexico City by grace of a fortunate fluke. The runner who finished fourth in the Olympic Trials 1500 was Villanova's Dave Patrick, a 3:56.8 miler who had beaten Jim Ryun in the 1967 NCAA championship 800-meter run. The Trials at which schoolboy Liquori qualified for the Olympic Team were actually the second set of U.S. Trials held in 1968. In the original Trials, Patrick whipped the whole field to win the metric mile, easily reserving his berth for Mexico City. For various technical reasons, USOC officials were unhappy with the Trials' results. They polled the athletes and asked if they wanted another Olympic Trials. Not surprisingly, the majority of athletes wanted them—because, after all, a majority of athletes had failed their initial qualifying attempt. Here was a second chance! An experienced athlete, Patrick recognized the futility of trying to hold his athletic "peak" all through the interval between the Trials and the Games. He'd planned to get a little soft after the Trials, rest, and firm up just in time for the Games. He also, unplanned, injured an ankle. In the second Trials, Liquori beat him, and Patrick never saw Mexico City. Considering other distance runners' reactions there, he may have counted himself lucky.

None of the distance runners at the Mexico City Games was happy. The problem was the air: there wasn't enough of it. Situated 7,349 feet above sea level, Mexico City left athletes who were used to breathing fully oxygenated air gasping. Mexican officials, concerned about the effects of their Games' altitude on athletes, held an international track and field meet in 1965 to gather empirical data. Attending physicians discovered no undue strain on sea-level trained competitors, *provided their events could be com-*

Kenny Moore (right) and Frank Shorter (left) deliberately tie in winning the 1972 U.S. Olympic Team Marathon Trials. Moore went on to become America's preeminent running sportswriter, and Shorter went on to a gold medal at Munich and a silver medal at Montreal. (Photograph courtesy of Kenny Moore and Sports Illustrated.)

pleted in two minutes or less. Heavy exertion carried beyond 120 seconds placed the human organism under extreme duress, the physicians and the stopwatch concluded. In retrospect, the experience of the 1968 Olympics opened a new chapter in training for long-distance events. The athletes found that training hard at high altitude markedly improved their performances when they moved back down to sea level. It was a discovery made long before by the African nations, albeit inadvertently. There *is* no sea level in the country of Kenya, for example.

The Mexico City Olympics were not only the first Games held at high altitude, they were also the first to select a woman to light the Olympic Flame. Twenty-year-old hurdler Norma Enriquetta Basilio ran into both the Olympic Stadium and the history books on opening day of the 1968 Olympics as she arrived to ignite the pyre symbolizing the Olympic traditions of peace and universal brother-and-sisterhood.

Unfortunately, political turmoil from the world beyond sport again marred the Games. This time the athletes themselves brought politics into the arena. Earlier in the year a California-based group of black Americans began to urge all blacks to boycott the 1968 Olympics as a protest against racial prejudice in the United States. Although unprecedented in terms of Olympic history, the idea carried all too much precedent in terms of contemporary American history. The late 1960s in the U.S. was a time of citizen-initiated demonstrations against the Vietnam war and in favor of civil rights. In short, although totally contrary to traditional Olympic ideals, the boycott idea was harmonious with all the other political confusion and naiveté literally running riot in the country at the time. The boycott movement failed, but it apparently influenced at least two athletes at Mexico City. America's Tommie Smith won the 200-meter final in 19.8 seconds, breaking his own world record of 20 seconds flat. (The thin air at Mexico City proved conducive to setting many new sprinting, jumping, and throwing standards.) His U.S. teammate, John Carlos, claimed the bronze medal in 19.8, the same time accorded silver medalist Peter Norman of Australia. Both Smith and Carlos were black. When the band struck up "The Star-Spangled Banner" at the awards ceremony after the 200-meter final, Smith and Carlos each slipped on one black glove, raised their gloved hands, closed into fists, into the air (a gesture called a "black power" salute), and bowed their heads. For the first time in history, the athletes themselves had intertwined politics with the Olympics—and nobody was happy about it.

Some officials, in fact, were livid. The Marquis of Exeter was both the gold medalist in the intermediate hurdles at the 1938 Amsterdam Olympics and the president of the International Amateur Athletic Federation (IAAF). The Americans' protest completely contradicted His Lordship's ideas about amateur sport, as they contradicted everyone else's. The Marquis threatened to terminate all awards ceremonies. To smooth ruffled feathers, the USOC confiscated Smith's and Carlos's Olympic identity cards, essentially imprisoning them in the Olympic Village, tossed them off the team, and issued a statement categorizing their "untypical exhibition" as "discourteous" and an example of "immature behavior." Miffed, the two sprinters stalked back to the U.S., leaving behind them an American Olympic Team broken into two factions: athletes who—as was traditional—backed their peers against the actions of athletic officialdom, and athletes who felt the officials this time had acted justifiably.

Nationalistic politics have infused the Olympics ever since ancient Hellas. Hitler used the Berlin Games to aggrandize his Third Reich. During the Cold War, both the U.S. and the U.S.S.R. attempted to sway world opinion by parading successful Olympic teams. The athletes' protest during the 1968 Olympics stands as historically significant not merely because it was the first time athletes brought politics into the Games. Perhaps even more significant, it was the first political action taken in the Olympics for insular, monofocused reasons, a "one-issue" protest, as opposed to a coherent statement of national superiority. It would not be the last instance of one-issue politics in modern Olympic history, alas, alas.

Indestructible Ron Clarke nearly died in the Mexico City 10,000-meter final, held on the first day of competition. Running in his last Olympics, the great Australian ran out of air 1 mile from the end of the 6.2 mile race. Clarke ran with the other leaders for 21 of the 25 laps, but the other leaders were all from high altitude African nations: Kenya's Naftali Temu, Ethiopia's Mamo Wolde, and Tunisia's Mohammed Gammoudi. Four laps from home these three pulled decisively away from Clarke. Two laps from home, Temu locked up with Wolde for a fight right down to the wire, where Temu outsprinted Wolde by 2 meters to win in 29:27.4. Gammoudi took the bronze medal and Clarke's effort to finish in sixth place nearly took his life. He passed out on the infield lawn, doctors hovering over him with oxygen tanks. Most physicians and reporters expected Clarke to die later that night in the hospital to which he was removed, but the iron man recovered and competed in the 5 kilometers later in the Games. As testimony to the difficult conditions for long-distance runners at Mexico City, one needs only note Clarke's contemporary world record for 10 kilometers stood at 27:39.4, nearly 2 minutes faster than Temu's victorious time.

Redoubtable Ralph Doubell beat Kenya's Wilson Kiprugut in the 800-meter final, laying on a mighty pickup in the final straight to win the gold, break the Olympic record, and tie Peter Snell's world record in 1:44.3. America's Tom Farrell held on for the bronze medal.

Top miler Kipchoge Keino squared off against "pure" distance specialists in the Mexico City 5K final. Keino had tried the 10K run on the first competitive day but had passed out 3 laps from the tape, a fact rendering Ron Clarke's performance all the more remarkable. Keino clearly lacked the stamina of the 10,000-meter runners, but quite possibly enjoyed enough endurance to hang with a 5-kilometer field. Keino, in company with his countryman Temu and Gammoudi the Tunisian, dominated the race from the gun. Two laps from the medals, Gammoudi let out all his stops and took off. One lap from victory celebrations and defeat recriminations, the Kenyans let loose a surge that carried them to Gammoudi's shoulder. Summoning some personal demons, Gammoudi sprinted again and held the lead pulling out of the last turn and shooting for the tape. Keino whipped past Temu and drew a bead on Gammoudi. At 30 meters from the finish they ran stride for stride; then Gammoudi dug down and pulled away, snapping the thread 1 meter ahead of Keino in 14:05.0, while Temu gathered up the bronze medal. Ron Clarke finished fifth. In contrast to the 10,000-meter results, the winning time in the 5,000 was only 48.4 seconds slower than the then world mark of 13:16.6 for the event. There was one similarity between the two races. The world reference figure for the 5 kilometers was also set by Ronald William Clarke.

The distaff dashers at Mexico City had, collectively, an easier running time than did the men, simply because women were not yet permitted to run the distances. America's Wyomia Tyus successfully defended her 100 meters' crown by beating world record holder (and teammate) Barbara Farrell by a full meter in 11 seconds flat. Tyus took not only the gold, she also took Farrell's world record, bettering it by 1/10-second—on a wet track!

Colette Besson of France fell 1/10-second short of breaking Sin Kim Dan's world best for 400 meters, but greatly surprised Lillian Board of England, who never saw Besson until the flying Frenchwoman whipped by at the wire. Besson equalled Betty Cuthbert's Olympic record for the 400.

America's Madeline Manning conquered the field in the 800 meters, taking the gold in 2:00.9, 2/10-seconds under Ann Packer's Olympic record, although 4/10-seconds over the world record. America's Doris Brown finished fifth.

Pre-race favorite Irena Kirszenstein Szewinska of Poland cut her world record for 200 meters down from 22.7 seconds to 22.5 when she won the 200, totally unpressured by the rest of the field.

The American women's team took the gold and the world mark (43.6) from the Soviet team in claiming the 400-meter relay race with a 42.8 clocking.

Then it was time for the "Triple M" of the Games, traditionally held on the last day of track and field competition: the metric mile and the marathon. America had no hope for the marathon, but, in the metric mile, she had Jim Ryun.

Ryun had been training at altitude, at 6,907 feet in Flagstaff, Arizona, before heading down to Mexico City. Earlier in the year, he had competed for Kansas in the Big Eight meet at mile-high Boulder, Colorado. The 21-year-old Kansan felt poorly days before the Boulder meet. After racing, Ryun recalled: "When I finished the mile, I actually thought I was going to die." The problems proved to be mononucleosis. Five months before the

Madeline Manning (now Madeline Manning Mims), America's gold medalist in the 1968 Olympic 800-meter run, here runs to victory in the 1975 USA-Pan African-West Germany Meet held at Durham, North Carolina. Manning (wearing number 63) took this 800-meter final in 2:01.6; Gisela Klein (number 157) came second in 2:03.0, Angelika Travgott (number 168) was third in 2:03.3, 'and America's Kathy Weston was fourth in 2:03.7. (Photograph courtesy of Track & Field News.)

Olympics, Ryun had mono. As a consequence, he could not train as hard as an athlete in the final throes of Olympic tuning needs to train. On the other hand, he entered the Games as world-record holder for his event, but so did Ron Clarke.

The Kenyans apparently coveted the 1500 title. They set up a team effort evocative of the Finns' long-distance "trains." They sent Ben Jipcho out as a rabbit for Kip Keino. (To be charitable to Keino, one recalls he also ran in the 5-kilometer and 10-kilometer finals and attendant heats for the 5K and 1500, while Ryun focused exclusively on the 1500.) Jipcho rent asunder the already thin Mexico City air as he bombed out a 56-flat first 400-meter lap. Ryun intended to pace his first 3 laps in 60 seconds each, then kick like a maniac for the finish—a standard Ryun performance. The Kenyans obviously wanted none of it and intended to run the red blood out of Ryun's gams. Jipcho charged the second lap in 59.3, aggregating a midway split of 1:55.3. Keino, his arms characteristically rocking from side to side, ran relaxed in his teammate's slipstream. Keino was about 30 meters clear of Ryun and pulling away.

Keino took over from the fading Jipcho on the third lap, spent in 58-flat. He hit the three-quarters mark in 2:53.3; Ryun, in 2:59-zip. Then the Kansan put on the heat. West Germany's Bodo Tummler zinged Jipcho for the silver medal slot, but Ryun put him away as a nanny dispatches a nodding toddler. Jim was now 12 meters down on Kip. Ryun remembered his charge: "As I passed each of the other fellows, I could see their eyes rolled back in their heads, the agony on their faces. We had thought that 3:39 would win."

Jim Ryun moved from fifth place to second place in one-half lap. He had followed his race plan perfectly, refusing to be drawn into the Kenyan's oxygen-debt trap. Ryun said: "I could not be intimidated into going out too fast and going into oxygen debt too soon. There's no return from that point." Once in debt, man can move no faster. Ryun was now in debt, 15 meters behind Keino and unable to close it up. The pre-race predictions were wrong. 3:39 did not win the 1968 1500 final. Jim Ryun ran 3:37.89. He got the silver. Kipchoge Keino ran 3:34.91, and got the gold. Their performances honored both athletes. Ryun thought he would literally die after the race. "I was in tremendous oxygen debt," he said, "and the pain was the worst I had ever felt. I was struggling to breathe." It was Ryun's first loss at 1500 meters in three years.

Abebe Bikila suffered his first Olympic marathon loss in twelve years at Mexico City. He started the race on an injured ankle and was forced out. If it were any consolation to the great marathoner, the Mexico City gold was taken by his compatriot, Mamo Wolde in 2:20:26.4. Wolde let the hotshots in the field run for themselves for the first 25 kilometers. Gaston Roelants and Kenny Moore took the field out smartly, going through 10K in 33:54.8. Maybe it was a little too smart. They both faded badly toward the end. For the final 15K, Wolde calmly picked off the remaining leaders to finish well ahead of runner-up Kenji Kimihara of Japan (2:23:31) and bronze medalist Mike Ryan of New Zealand (2:23:45). Australian Derek Clayton, running with a cyst on his right knee's cartilage, took seventh in 2:27:23.8. (Questioned after the Games about the wisdom of running a marathon in such a condition, Clayton snapped: "Sure I needed an operation, but that would have meant giving the Games away. I told them I'd run even if it meant losing a leg.") Kenny Moore was the first Yank over the line, fourteenth, in 2:29:49.4; George Young, the next American, sixteenth, in 2:31:15, and Ron Daws, third Statesman home, twenty-second, in 2:33:53. Of all track and field events, the marathon is least suited for high altitudes.

A tragic postscript to the 1968 Olympic marathon occurred in 1969, when Abebe Bikila was permanently paralyzed in an automobile accident in Addis Ababa. Interviewed before his death in 1973, the superlative athlete revealed something of the stuff of which such people consist. He said: "Men of success meet with tragedy. It was the will of God that I won the Olympics, and it was the will of God that I met with my accident. I accepted those victories as I accept this tragedy. I have to accept both circumstances as facts of life and live happily." Like Zátopek and a few others, this toughest of athletes harbored one of the tenderest of spirits.

The Mexico City Olympics also received a happier postscript. In July of 1966, iron man Ron Clarke traveled to Prague, Czechoslovakia, to compete in a 3,000-meter track race, which he won. While visiting the city, Clarke met the incomparable Emil Zátopek. Clarke returned to Prague on his way back to Australia from Mexico. Again he visited Zátopek. At the end of their interview and just before Clarke was to fly back home, Zátopek presented the iron man with a wrapped parcel. Knowing Zátopek's sensitivity and humility, Clarke refrained from opening the package in front of him. Clarke felt Zátopek would be embarrassed at being thanked right then and there. The Australian ace therefore waited until flying home to open Zátopek's gift. Perhaps none other than those two athletes could imagine what Clarke felt on its unfolding. Inside lay Zátopek's gold medal, awarded for winning the 10,000-meter final at the 1952 Helsinki Olympics. It was inscribed "To Ron Clarke—Emil Zátopek, Prague, July 19, 1966." Zátopek had waited over two years to give Clarke the reward the Czech Locomotive knew he deserved. The iron man at last had his gold.

Steve Prefontaine represented another sort of toughness, a *macho* man out to humble his opponents. "Pre" entered the University of Oregon in 1969, coming off a string of twenty-seven straight track victories including a high school record run of 8:41.5 for 2 miles. Between his freshman year at Oregon and May, 1975, Pre would conquer 82 out of 102 outdoor races. The Oregon coaches, Bill Bowerman and Olympic 5K bronze medalist Bill Dellinger, believed their athlete would become the greatest distance runner in the world. Blessed with 3:54.6 miler's speed and endurance that Coach Bowerman claimed "had no breaking point," the hard-charging, hell-raising Prefontaine seemed fully equipped with all the artillery necessary to realize his coaches' predictions. Further, although occasionally cocky to the point of obnoxiousness, the young runner also had some of the sensitivity found in the greatest long-distance champions. Prefontaine once observed: "A race is a work of art that people can look at and be affected by in as many ways as they are capable of understanding." Yet none of this tenderness of insight found its way into Pre's race tactics. He preferred to grind his competition down right from the gun—a crude but effective strategy if, like Vladimir Kuts, one has the body and the will for it. In his four years at Oregon, Prefontaine was thrice NCAA cross-country champion, twice AAU

Steve Prefontaine was considered by some as running's "bad boy," but considered by all as a stellar distance runner. (Photograph courtesy of the University of Oregon.)

3-mile champion, gold medalist in the 5,000 meters (his favorite event) at the 1971 Pan-American Games, and the holder of fourteen American long-distance running records, most impressive of which was probably his 13:22.8 victory in the 1972 U.S. Olympic Trials 5-kilometer final. Had his career not been cut short, Steve Prefontaine may well have fulfilled his coaches' vision. He might well have become the premier distance man of his era.

Patriots' Day, 1969, saw the biggest and fastest field yet assembled for the Boston Marathon. A record 1,151 other runners chased Japan's Yoshiaki Unetani as he raced to a course record 2:13:39, quite some distance ahead of runner-up Pablo Garrido of Mexico's 2:17:30. Garrido's teammate, Alfredo Penaloza, came in third with 2:19:56, while America's Ron Daws proved the only native who could run with the foreigners, checking in fourth in 2:20:23. Just as historically significant, B.A.A. officials began contemplating placing restrictions on Boston Marathon entries after eyeing all those runners pouring into the Prudential Center.

Runner's World editor Joe Henderson was a contributor to the hordes pouring into the Pru basement, eating the post-race beef stew. In 1969 Henderson published a pamphlet, *The Long Run Solution*, that outlined a radical new approach to training: long, slow distance (LSD, an acronym likely inspired by the hallucinogenic drug known by the same letters and popularized at the time by former Harvard psychology professor, Dr. Timothy Leary). The LSD approach to training was summarized by the catch phrase, "train, don't strain." A victim of overly intensive interval workouts in high school and college, Henderson proselytized for his more humane way of achieving fitness. He noted an athlete could achieve outstanding aerobic

Joe Henderson, the man who invented "long, slow distance" and who, as editor, raised Runner's World *magazine to a level of popularity and excellence above its contemporaries. He is currently editor at* Running *magazine.* (Photograph courtesy of Joe Henderson.)

capacity without running mile after mile at a maniacal pace. What Henderson meant by the "slow" component of his LSD technique was that the athlete run workouts "at about a minute per mile slower than marathon race pace to two minutes below speed of the track distance." What many *thought* he meant was to go as slowly as one could for as long as one wanted. The LSD idea quickly developed its detractors, old-line competitors who sneered at the growing ranks of plump executives running with their shorts on the outside of their sweat pants (!); it also developed its passionate advocates. Both these camps misunderstood Henderson, who never argued serious run-

Amby Burfoot, 1968 Boston Marathon champion and currently East Coast Editor for Runner's World, *did not always have a beard, as this rare picture demonstrates. This is Amby winning the first Springbank International Road Race, in London, Ontario, in September, 1968.* (Photograph courtesy of Amby Burfoot.)

ning was without any pain. Henderson's idea differed little from the concepts of Coach "Billy" Hayes or Arthur Lydiard. The practical result of Henderson's LSD idea, however, was more sociological than athletic. The ranks of American runners grew more quickly now that it was considered acceptable to run slower and still think of oneself as a *runner*. (It was for the LSD advocates that the old-line runners coined the term-cum-epithet, "jogger.")

On June 21, 1969, Marty Liquori beat Jim Ryun in the NCAA mile championship race at Knoxville, Tennessee. It was the year Liquori was ranked Number One among the world's milers and the year that Ryun began to lose his preeminence. Three days later, Jayhawk Ryun pulled out of the NCAA 3-mile championship race with less than 1 mile run, explaining he was "stale from too much competition, too much pressure and too many races." Incontestably America's greatest miler to date, Jim Ryun in 1969 was becoming an object example of a problem facing almost every outstanding native American collegiate great. The college coach is not paid for what the athlete does after college; the coach is paid only for winning collegiate team titles. Jim Ryun got burned out long before his prime, as do many—sadly, perhaps most—potentially stellar American distance runners. As in many other areas of international sporting, economic, and political competition, the U.S. had yet to care about long-term planning; she would suffer because of her carelessness. Sadly, her athletes would suffer even more.

On May 30, 1969, Derek Clayton runs 2:08:33.6 for a marathon in Antwerp, Belgium, more than 1 minute faster than man has run before. Two hours later Clayton starts to vomit black bile and urinate blood.

Derek Clayton was to the marathon what Jim Ryun was to the mile in the late 1960s: simply the best in the world. It is therefore unfortunate that controversy has surrounded his world's best (not world record) marathon time. As more years passed with no other athlete even approaching the mark, mutterings surfaced to claim that the course must have been short. The Belgian Amateur Athletic Federation once again demonstrated the ineptitude of sports officials the world around by not remeasuring the course after Clayton's amazing run! One measurement would have laid all the controversy to rest, and the Belgian officials' failure to remeasure was particularly inexcusable in light of Clayton's having informed them *before the race* that he would be going for a world's best marathon time. (Clayton, coming off myriad 200-mile weeks, was aiming for 2:07!) Because the Antwerp course on which Clayton ran has never again hosted a marathon race, one has no means of comparing Clayton's race with any save those he ran against that day. Second place man Akio Usami ran 2:11:27.8, while third place Jim Adler clocked 2:16:34.4. Their times do not suggest a short course, and none has ever alleged Clayton took a shortcut somewhere en route. Indeed, Clayton could not conceivably be held accountable even were the course short. Like any other athlete in international competition, he could only go to the line assuming the officials had done their jobs properly. One fact remains: Clayton said of his Antwerp run: "I knew I could have run no faster." Unchallenged by any other marathoner of his day except Abebe Bikila, Clayton could reasonably assume his ultimate effort would result in his era's best time for the event. To those who reject Clayton's time because so long in the bettering, one reminds them Clayton's effort marked the end of the age of the marathon's obscurity. Very shortly thereafter, far more talent would fill marathon fields than ever before. Just as a field consisting of the top three milers of their own historical era resulted in the absurdly slow "typographical error" mile of 1936, just as Olympic finals almost never produce world records, neither did the infusion of more competition in the marathon event prove conducive to running faster times. In an evenly-matched field, athletes feel more pressure to win than to establish new world marks. Clayton was free to run with abandon because no other athlete could challenge him. Men such as Clayton, Nurmi, Zátopek, and Clarke are exceedingly rare athletes.

The rare Ron Clarke was 32 years old in 1969, his career winding down. There was a hint of grey at his temples, but there was still passion in his legs. He was ranked world Number One in the 5 kilometers and 10 kilometers and their English distance track equivalents, the 3 miles and the 6 miles. On January 24, 1969, Clarke set a world indoor 3-mile mark of 13:12.6 while running at Oakland, California. In July, 1969, he prevailed in the 10,000 meters in the U.S.-U.S.S.R.-Commonwealth meet at the Los Angeles Coliseum. His time was 28:35.4, over a minute slower than his current world record for the distance, but nearly 100 meters ahead of his nearest challenger that night. Running out of both youth and challenges, Clarke said the race was his hardest ever, and spoke of retirement on this final American sojourn: "I'm tired of traveling. I want to spend more time with my family. This will be my final trip."

The Trail's End Marathon in Seaside, Oregon, began in 1969 as a way to honor the Lewis and Clark Expedition. In its first year the race attracted 220 runners. In 1979, Trail's End's popularity forced the race directors to put a limit on the field: 2,500 runners.

It was a natural title to give an indoor track star, but only one man in history ever officially earned it. In 1970, middle-distance star of the Sports International Track Club Martin McGrady became "The Chairman of the Boards." On February 13, 1970, McGrady squared off against two Olympic champions: 800-meter gold medalist Ralph Doubell and 400-meter gold medalist Lee Evans. The event was the 600-yard run at the Los Angeles Times Indoor Meet. McGrady shot out of the hole like a randy deer, but Evans ran him down after 220 yards. The quarter-mile (440 yards) passed in 49.4 seconds. McGrady was 3 yards behind Evans, and Doubell was watching the race many more yards back. McGrady more than made up those 3 yards in the 160 yards remaining him. He flew out of the ultimate turn with his horns locked with Evans's. The two stags kicked hard for the goal, their chests thrust forward and their arms swept back more like high divers than middle-distance runners. Both McGrady and Evans hit in 1:08.7, but Mc-Grady got the nod and the world record. Doubell ran 1:09.8. Then the next night, at the Mason Dixon Games, the Chairman of the Boards casually lowered it to 1:08.5! It was only natural he receive *Track & Field News*'s World Indoor Athlete of 1970 trophy; he had earned it by "chairing" the fastest middle-distance races of the year.

The organizers had thought about it the previous year, and, in 1970, they acted. Time restrictions were first placed on Boston Marathon entries that year. A man had to have completed another marathon in under 4 hours to qualify for running the B.A.A. Marathon. England's Ron Hill smashed the Boston course record with a searing 2:10:30. He also took every course checkpoint record except for the very first one. Second man, and first American, Eamon O'Reilly also came in well under Unetani's former mark, recording 2:11:12. Kenny Moore was the next Yank home, coming sixth with 2:19:47. Women still could not run the Boston Marathon officially, although increasing numbers of them were doing it unofficially.

Women ran in the Yonkers Marathon for the first time in 1970, although their status there was also unofficial. Hampered by AAU and IAAF rules, no race director could allow women in his or her long-distance event and remain in the good graces of the sport's governing bodies. It must be understood that, in theory at least, any athlete competing in an unsanctioned event could be suspended from sanctioned competition for life. Race directors complied with international rules not only for the directors' interests, but also for the athletes'. Nevertheless, while New York's William Harvey was winning the "official" Yonkers Marathon in 2:31:10, Nina Kuscsik and Pat Tarwinsky were racing each other in a two-woman field. Kuscisik prevailed in 3:16, while Tarwinsky dropped out at 20 miles with a pulled muscle.

Jim Ryun evened the score with Marty Liquori, beating him by a good 2 or 3 inches in the NCAA indoor mile championship, both runners recording 4:02.6. It was Ryun's third NCAA indoor mile championship in a row. After the race, Liquori's father said, "My son will never lose to Jim Ryun again." Marty took the AAU and NCAA outdoor mile crowns from the Jayhawk and was ranked Number Seven in the world in the 1500/mile as a college junior.

Athletes such as Liquori or Prefontaine show their greatness while still in school, but it is not at all unusual for a long-distance runner to remain obscure until his post-collegiate career begins. In general, the longer the distance, the later an athlete reaches his or her peak for it. Sprinters are youngsters. Marathoners are the grey eminences of track. Frank Shorter won the New England prep school 2-mile championship in his senior year at Mt. Hermon School, but his track career at Yale was undistinguished, compared to what he would do later, except for his All-American ranking in cross-country as a senior and his NCAA 6-mile crown the same year. In the spring of 1970, the former medical student (he spent three months in the University of New Mexico's medical program) moved to Gainesville, Florida, where he joined the celebrated Florida Track Club and matriculated at the University of Florida in the law program. Shorter moved to Florida on the advice of Jack Bacheler, world-class distance runner and the motive force behind the Florida T.C. Stars ran for the FTC; in addition to Bacheler, there was Marty Liquori, Dick Buerkle, Jeff Galloway, and Barry Brown. What was Shorter's attitude on joining such an elite group? As he put it: "I remember when I first got there I was really cocky and I thought, I'm going to run all these miles, and get real good, and the times are going to plummet. Then I realized that I was going to have to take an attitude where I paced myself in training." Running with such peers, Shorter would probably have burned out had he not paced his training; but still remained something of a lone wolf, running by himself in the mornings rather than with the FTC "gang" on their long mileage roadwork. He ran the miles, and the times came down. Shorter emerged on the world scene in 1970, bringing the FTC along with him. He won the AAU outdoor 3-mile championship in 13:24.2 and tied with Bacheler in the AAU 6-mile champ race, both hitting the tape in 27:24.0. He won his first international title in the 10,000 meters in the U.S.-U.S.S.R. meet in 28:22.8 and claimed the AAU Cross-Country title (a 10K affair) in 30:15.8.

Versatility described the Florida T.C. runners. Although perhaps not as prominent a talent as a Shorter or a Liquori, teammate Barry Brown stood as one of the most "complete" runners to date. Brown ran everything from the mile to the marathon, although he achieved greatest eminence in the grueling steeplechase (with a personal record of 8:38.2). He ran on road, track, and cross-country. He started racing in 1958 at age 14 and was still going strong in 1981, claiming the national title at 30 kilometers in 1980. As the world of running became ever more populated with specialists, a journeyman runner such as Barry Brown bravely carried on the tradition of Ron Clarke.

The American southland got more than a grand track club in 1970. The south also got her first "megarace" (a road race with thousands of competitors). The Peachtree 10,000-Meter Classic emerged on July 4, 1970, the first "new" race to attract over 1,000 healthy runners. By 1981, the Peachtree, held each year on Independence Day, had over 18,000 runners coursing through its 6.2 miles—one of the highest population densities in all of running!

The New York Marathon also came off the starting line in 1970, but was not the race known to runners in the 1980s. Instead of roaming freely through all of New York, the course wound numbingly through lap after dull lap of Central Park. It was the first marathon hosted by the New York

Road Runners Club; the NYRRC would not take over the Yonkers Marathon until 1979. One-hundred-twenty-six men ran the first New York Marathon (no women were recorded as running it), and New York's own Gary Muhrcke hit the tape first in 2:31:38.

Iron man Ron Clarke ended his nearly incredible career at the British Commonwealth Games, held in Edinburgh, Scotland, in late July, 1970. This champion among champions finished fifth in the 5-kilometer final and second in the 10,000 meters in 28:13.4. The final chapter in the Ron Clarke running saga was not composed until 1973, however. Undergoing a routine physical examination pursuant to entering a new life insurance program, the iron man suddenly learned why he held seventeen world long-distance records but had never claimed an international title: he had a leaky heart valve. His attending physician, Dr. Garry Jennings, announced: "It's pure speculation, but Ron might have been able to compete very well at 85 percent of his huge capacity lap after lap, but if he was called on to sprint at the end, maybe he couldn't. Of course, it didn't stop him from breaking world records, provided he could go at his own pace." In the light of the new medical information, Clarke's heroism at the 1968 Mexico City Olympics, where physicians feared for his life after the 10K final, was raised to the second or third power. Ron Clarke had become the iron man in spite of his lack of heart.

As 1970 drew to a close, a Gallup Poll concluded approximately two million Americans were running, or "jogging," regularly (defined by the survey as three or more times weekly). The number of American runners had increased dramatically in less than five years.

X

Running for Sport
1971–1975

On the evening of February 19, 1971, a resurging Jim Ryun, who had opened the decade of the 1970s by running another world record mile, appeared before 11,781 track fans at the San Diego Sports Arena. The Kansas Jayhawk had been added to the program only two days before. When word got out, ticket sales skyrocketed. Some historians consider that meet to be the greatest indoor track gathering of all time. Before the milers stepped to the line, the crowd witnessed Lee Evans bomb the 600 in 1:08.7, the world's fifth fastest time. They saw Ralph Doubell nail the 1000-yarder in 2:06.3, the world's sixth best mark. A night of outstanding performances was in the making. In the last race of the meet, Australian Kerry O'Brien took on Yanks Frank Shorter and George Young, as well as fellow Aussie Kerry Pearce, in the 2-mile run, setting an absolute world best time of 8:19.2, 4/10 seconds under Ron Clarke's outdoor record and 8 seconds under the former indoor best, held jointly by Pearce and Young. (Frank Shorter set an American indoor 2-mile best of 8:26.2, good for third behind Pearce's personal best of 8:20.6.)

In between these races came the mile run, and it did not look like Jim Ryun's night. The Pacific Coast Club's Chuck LaBenz staked his claim to the lead from the gun, blasting the first quarter mile in 54.2. Ryun was 40 yards behind at that split, and 10 yards back of LaBenz's teammate, John

Mason. LaBenz kept the steam up, splitting the half mile in 1:54.6 and pulling out yet another 10 yards on the steady Kansan. Ryun's steadiness derived from experience. He knew LaBenz couldn't keep up such a hot pace, and indeed, the pace dipped by the three-quarter mark, passed in 2:57.7. Mason was right behind LaBenz; tough New Zealander Dick Quax moved past Ryun into third. It was actually a perfect Ryun race. He had paced sensibly and still had a lot left for his devastating, trademark kick in the final quarter—and a perfect rabbit to chase, in the form of Quax.

Ryun put Quax to sleep with 2 laps left. He lifted his knees and rocked his head from side to side and was *Jim Ryun*. He set after the leaders like a hungry hound after an old 'coon. Mason took the lead from LaBenz on the penultimate lap. Bang! The last lap—Ryun snatched the lead from Mason. In the last 160-yard lap, Ryun pulled out 12 yards on Mason, hit the tape in 3:56.4, and tied Tom O'Hara's hoary indoor mile mark, set on March 6, 1964. Jim Ryun was back, people said, but, in truth, he had never been away.

The early half of the 1970s saw a great deal of joy in the sport of running. Jim Ryun stood as an inspiration to American runners, and soon other American distance heroes would emerge. Perhaps the most historically significant aspect of the era, though, was the rise of the noncompetitive athlete, the man or woman who ran for running's sake and not for competition's. The popular media publicized the health factor in running, and, simultaneously, publicized how very unhealthy was the air Americans breathed, the food they ate, and the lifestyles they lived. The social and political turmoil of the 1960s had reduced Americans' traditional reverence for team sports and being a "team player." It was now more socially acceptable to pursue one's individual interests, to "do one's own thing." These factors combined to make the early part of the decade to be the American era of running for love of the sport, even if one never ran with, or against, another athlete.

Jim Ryun and Villanova senior Marty Liquori ran both with and against each other at Philadelphia's Martin Luther King Games in May, 1971. The press, with typical uncreativity, hailed it as the Dream Mile. (Ryun commented: "Gee, just once I'd like to see them call it "the mile," for a change. I think a lot of people are trying to see a lot of things in the race that aren't there.") Liquori peaked for the race, Ryun did not, preferring to plan for the long term: the 1972 Olympics at Munich. Ryun handled most of the pacemaking, going through the half in 2:03.3, a time Ryun felt indicated how badly out of condition he was. He dreaded the thought of having to kick hard in the last lap; he had not geared his training to speedwork at that point in his pre-Olympic training. He did, of course, kick hard on the last lap, but Liquori kicked harder. The Villanova super-runner won in 3:54.6, while Ryun clocked 3:54.8, a memorable contest between two evenly matched competitors.

In early spring of 1971, University of Minnesota senior Garry Bjorklund faced the problem confronted by most college graduates: what to do now?

Bjorklund had been racing since 1966. He set the Minnesota schoolboy mile record of 4:05.1 his senior year of high school. He set the American collegiate 6-mile mark the next year as a UM freshman. After that, improvement at the standard track distances came slowly to Bjorklund; his best college 10K time stood at 28:50.4, not good enough to warrant international aspirations. What Bjorklund did was move to the roads. Like many other good but not great college track runners, Bjorklund found road racing more rewarding, in all senses of the term, than track racing. In 1977 he moved up to the marathon, finishing fifth in his second marathon (New York) with an excellent 2:15:16.4, then winning his third long one (Baltimore) two months later in 2:13:46. A superb athlete in his own right, "BJ" symbolized the new American distance runner: the one who found his or her niche in front of the throngs on the roads, not among the elite in the arenas. The vistas of the sport had widened in 1970s America.

Women ran in the New York Marathon for the first time in 1971. Beth Bonner's "winning" time of 2:55:22 brought her home only 33 minutes be· hind Norman Higgins's victorious 2:22:54 on the Central Park course that September 19. Ubiquitous Nina Kuscsik finished less than 1 minute behind Bonner, joining her as the first two American women under 3 hours in the marathon.

Marty Liquori of Villanova University prevails over Jim Ryun, America's greatest miler to date, in the 1971 Martin Luther King Games' "Dream Mile." Liquori ran 3:54.6; Ryun, 3:54.8. (Photograph courtesy of The Boston Herald American.)

On December 5, 1971, Cheryl Bridges became the first American woman to break 2:50 for the 26.2 miles, running 2:49:40 in the Culver City (California) Marathon by chopping a huge 24 minutes off her course record. That same date, on the other side of the world, Frank Shorter won his first of four straight Fukuoka Marathons, claiming the laurels in 2:12:50.4. Fukuoka (Asahi) stands as the informal annual "world marathon championship." Shorter's four straight victories were completely unprecedented; however, Japan's own Toshihiko Seko promises eventually to challenge them, having won three straight Asahi races to date.

Oklahoma State alumnus Tom Von Ruden was normally a 1000-meter specialist on the boards. He set the American "1000" record in 1970 when he ran 2:21 flat for the distance. The next year he brought the record down to 2:20.4. On February 4, 1972, Von Ruden ran the third fastest indoor mile ever, clocking 3:57.9 in a meet at Fort Worth, moving up behind Tom O'Hara and Jim Ryun on the all-time mile list, demonstrating that versatility in an athlete does not necessarily mean extreme mediocrity in his or her different events.

If further demonstration of that point were needed, indoor track fans received it; in 1972 Kipchoge Keino came to run the American boards. Last seen under U.S. rafters in 1966, the 32-year-old Kenyan showed he ruled a track as strongly as ever, running 3:59.4 for the mile in his first race of the season, before finishing second to Jim Ryun in the mile run at Los Angeles's Sunkist Meet. An athlete who could race with the best from 800 to 10,000 meters, Keino always came through in his big races—perhaps because his versatility permitted him to have so many big ones.

Belgium's Emiel Puttemans paralleled orange-hatted Kip Keino in two ways. He came to run the American indoor circuit in 1972, and he was as versatile in the long distances as Keino in the middle distances. He broke both Ron Clarke's recognized (outdoor) 2-mile record and Kerry O'Brien's unsanctioned but absolute (indoor) mark when he ran 8:17.8 late in 1971. He lost to Steve Prefontaine in his first American indoor race, the 2-mile at the Los Angeles Times Meet, in which Pre clocked 8:26.6. Puttemans moved on to victory at the San Diego indoor meet, setting a European indoor 2-mile best of 8:30.4. Going back to run in Europe outdoors during the Olympic year, Puttemans copped world records at 3K (7:37.6), 3 miles (12:47.8), and 5,000 meters (13:13.0). Running indoors at Berlin in 1973, Puttemans, a professional landscaper, hit pay dirt. He ran 8:13.2 for 2 miles, a European indoor and world absolute record (if the IAAF recognized indoor marks, which, curiously, they do not). En route, Puttemans also set world indoor standards for 2 kilometers (5 minutes precisely) and 3 kilometers (7:39.2). In 1974, curly-haired Emiel took the indoor bests for 3 miles (12:59.0) and 5 kilometers (13:24.2). In 1976 he brought those marks down to 12:54.6 for 3 miles and 13:20.8 for 5K.

The track athletes always get hot in an Olympic year, but there was also big news at Boston in 1972. Women were officially accepted in the race. Thirty-three-year-old Nina Kuscsik took top honors in 3:10:26.4 only a month after a sub-3 marathon, while Elaine Pedersen came second in 3:29:05. Kate Switzer finished third in 3:39:50, again wearing a Boston Marathon number, but one different from that which she sported in 1967. This time, there was a big red *F* in front of the numerals, presumably to help nearsighted finishing chute workers. The qualifying time for men dropped to three and one-half hours. Finland's Olavi Suomalainen took the men's division in 2:15:39, leading from Colombia's Victor Mora (2:15:57).

America had well over one hundred marathon races annually by 1972, not all of them necessarily wonderful events. May, 1972, witnessed the introduction of a race since considered a classic, the Avenue of Giants Marathon in Weott, California. Excellent administration and a carefully measured 26.2-mile course attracted many of the entrants, but the site of the course probably appealed to even more—California's Humboldt State Park, home of a huge forest of even huger Redwood trees, which gave the race its name and unique character.

Jim Ryun won the 1500 meters easily in the U.S. Olympic Trials at Eugene, Oregon, in July, 1972. Marty Liquori, another prime American metric-mile hope, was out for the season with injuries. The longest distance races at the Trials proved beneficial for the Florida Track Club. Frank Shorter and Jeff Galloway both qualified for the 10,000 meter team at Munich while, in the marathon, Shorter and Kenny Moore, of the Oregon Track Club, deliberately tied in 2:15:57.8, and FTC teammates Bacheler and Jeff Galloway came in right behind them with another deliberate tie, 2:20:29.2. Because Galloway had already made the 10K team, USOC officials gave Bacheler the nod. The FTC's Barry Brown qualified for the Munich steeplechase. If Liquori had not been injured, the entire FTC team might have gone to Germany.

The 1972 Munich Olympics go down in history as the most tragic Games, either modern or classic, to date. Mishaps marred the competitions: an imposter ran into the Olympic Stadium ahead of rightful victor Frank Shorter in the marathon; Jim Ryun was fouled, felled, and finished from the 1500 meters in a preliminary heat. Overshadowing, indeed dwarfing, athletic problems was the politics of international terrorism. Madmen kidnapped and murdered sixteen Israeli Olympic athletes for reasons history finds no need to dignify in recounting. Suffice it to say that people the world over found it impossible to see the connection between the maniacs' goals and their means. The sad fact is that, in 1968, the athletes themselves brought radical politics onto the Olympic field and, in 1972, mindless, ultraradical "politics" came literally blasting through the Olympic walls to murder the athletes and to affect the Olympic institution itself.

Newly installed IOC president Lord Killian observed after the slayings: "The Games have become too big, too unmanageable. There are all sorts of proposals: to reduce the number of competitors, to reduce the number of events, or even to cut out some sports altogether; but it is very difficult. These things must not be rushed. They need a lot of thought." How sad that the officials of sport called for clear, unhurried thinking almost alone among the world's officials in the 1970s; for, by 1972, the politicians plainly regarded the Olympics as just another pawn in political chess. What an ironic fate for the Games, born of an enlightened desire to end hostilities and promote international understanding, by showcasing that which is finest and most artistic in the human being.

Out of tragedy, hope. Finland's Lasse Viren became the Sisyphus of the Olympics, rolling the rock of human aspirations again back toward the summit of the mountain. The 10,000-meter final was Munich's first distance running final, as traditional in the Games. The field was one of the most exciting in history, containing, among others, Emiel Puttemans, Mohammed Gammoudi, blindingly fast Englishman Davey Bedford, ageless Ethiopian Miruts Yifter, America's Frank Shorter, and the relatively obscure Lasse Viren of Finland. Bedford took the field out in a 4:15 first mile, but it was no longer a pace fast enough, in this age, to shake off the pack. The tightly bunched group of runners, spurred by the ardor of Olympic competition, finally produced the predictable effect. Somebody tripped and fell. Almost exactly halfway through the 25-lap race, 23-year-old Viren got his legs caught up in Puttemans's. Viren took a spill, and Gammoudi fell on top of him. The four fellows in the lead chugged off while the pile of bodies on the Munich backstretch impeded the balance of the field.

Viren sprang to his feet and charged headlong after the leaders! In a bit more than 1 lap he was at their heels. As Viren later recalled the moment: "I

Finland's Lasse Viren, shown here running a road race, claimed the 5K and 10K gold medals in both the 1972 and 1976 Olympic Games. (Photograph from the authors' collection.)

got up instinctively, but at no time did I think that I had lost the race." Every other runner in that pack must have felt the same, but about himself, not about Viren, for the lead changed constantly. Two laps from home the order was Spain's Mariano Haro, Yifter, Puttemans, Viren, and Frank Shorter. One lap from home the lead pack *was* Lasse Viren. The Finn was pulling away from the field with the authority of a Nurmi (to whom Viren's counselor-cum-coach, Rolf Haikkola, has compared his athlete in terms of personality). Olympic races rarely produce world records, but this was a rare Olympic race. Viren ran the final 800 meters of the 10,000 in 1:56.4. He broke the tape in 27:38.4, exactly 1 second under Ron Clarke's best. Puttemans finished in the silver with 27:39.6, and tiny Miruts Yifter won the bronze with 27:41.0. Spain's Haro claimed fourth in 27:48.6, and America's Shorter was fifth in 27:51.4—the fastest 10K field at that point in history, and dominated by "obscure" Lasse Viren. Gammoudi did not finish. Commenting on his time afterward, Viren said: "Everything was going fine because I could have gone on the basis of a 27:20 pace. Losing 5 or 6 seconds in the fall is a good indication that my record can be considerably improved. In my opinion, 27 minutes will be broken one day—not by me, but I'm sure I will live long enough to see it broken."

Viren had enjoyed little international success before Munich. He had claimed the Finnish Juniors' 3-kilometer championship in 1967 at age 17 and had won the 5,000 meters in the 1969 Finland-Sweden dual meet. Going into the Munich Games, his best distance times were 28:17.4 for 10K and 13:29.8 for 5K. Neither of these times would have placed him in the first four finishers of their respective Olympic finals. Viren had improved a lot by 1972.

He had improved so much that he became the first athlete since Vladimir Kuts to pull off the Woolworth Double, by winning the 5,000-meter final, too. Many of the leaders from the 10,000 entered the 5K also: Gammoudi, Puttemans, Bedford, and Haro. Mighty Miruts Yifter was slated to run, but got lost on his way from the men's room to the stadium entrance and missed the start. As an index of how punishing that 1972 10K was, Haro withdrew from the 5,000 final, Bedford finished next to last, and Puttemans ran fifth. America's great hope for a 5-kilometer medal was Steve Prefontaine, running his only Olympic event. Had Pre followed his normal strategy of "making the other guys hurt" right from the gun, he might have had a chance against Viren. Viren and the other seasoned international stars in the field preferred to run a slow first 2 miles, then sprint madly in the final 4 laps. Prefontaine did not burn the kickers off, à la Kuts, at the start, and he suffered for it. Four laps from the finish Pre tossed in a 62.5-second lap. His next lap was 61.2, bringing him almost up to leader Viren. Puttemans, Gammoudi, and England's Jan Stewart were all also in contention. The penultimate lap passed in 60.3 as Viren put on the steam for his victory sprint. Gammoudi, ever the veteran, also had saved himself for the last lap, and went with the

Filbert Bayi (number 11) comes up on the wire in a 1977 race in England. He was nipped before the finish by the runner to his right, wearing number 8—Sebastian Coe. (Photograph by Mike Street, coutresy of Track & Field News.)

Finn, moving up on Prefontaine's outside. As had other Olympians (Woodruff, Snell), Pre suddenly found himself boxed in in "his" race. Unlike the others, the Oregon runner did not get out of the box, but the trying left him spent. Not surprisingly, Gammoudi was not enthusiastic about letting Prefontaine by; it was not so much viciousness as the understandable desire on the part of the Tunisian to take the shortest line through the last 2 turns. Viren got his second Munich gold medal in the Olympic record time of 13:26.4. He had run his final mile in 4:01! Gammoudi claimed the silver medal in 13:27.4. Stewart won the bronze medal in 13:27.6, and Steve Prefontaine was fourth in 13:28.4, over 2 seconds ahead of next man Emiel Puttemans. Comparing the 5K final to the 10K final, Viren stated: "It was a much easier race. I saw that they were tired." The event seemed to take a great deal out of Steve Prefontaine, and he never raced quite so aggressively after it. When he returned to the U.S., Pre turned his aggressiveness toward the sport's governing bodies, denouncing the AAU, NCAA, and IAAF for constraining athletes from earning a living through their athletics. Had young Prefontaine won a medal at Munich, he might have seen more reason to compromise with the sport's controlling powers.

Viren was the outstanding male runner of the Munich Olympics, but he may not have been the outstanding runner. The Soviets' Lyudmila Bragina had strong claim to that accolade. For the first time in Olympic history, there was a women's 1500-meter footrace on the program at Munich, and, in her two qualifying rounds and final, Bragina produced three successive world records! Admittedly, any new Olympic event is "soft," meaning few athletes have made determined efforts to produce quality times in it; but as athletic standards in general improve over the years, so too does the term "soft" take on new meanings from one era to the next. The Munich women's 1500 was not anywhere as "soft" as the various events in which Babe Didrikson competed in 1932. As Bragina put it, however: "We are far from what a woman can do in the 1500. I am convinced that in the very near future our objective should be 3:56." She took the gold at Munich with her final world 1500 record of 4:01.4. East Germany's Gunhild Hoffmeister was second in the final with 4:02.8, and Italy's Paola Cacchi won the bronze with 4:02.9.

Eastern bloc women emerged strongly at Munich, completely ending American domination. Renate Stecher of East Germany equalled the world record in the 200 meters with her 22.4 gold-striking effort; Australia's Raelene Boyle came second in 22.5, and Poland's Irena Szewinska inherited some of the old Stella Walsh magic for third in 22.7. Nipped by Stecher 50 meters from home after having led all the way till that point, Boyle broke down and cried on the victory stand.

East Germany took the women's 400 meters as well, and on the same day as the 200. World record holder Monika Zehrt, age 19, set an Olympic best of 51.1 (1/10-second off her personal best) in her victory; Rita Wilden of the archrival West German squad took the silver medal in 51.2, and America's Kathy Hammond rounded off the medalist list with her 51.6.

The burly (150 pounds) Stecher doubled in the 100 meters, coming away from Munich with two gold medals. She did not break Wyomia Tyus's world and Olympic best of 11-flat, but she came close: 11.07 seconds. Australia's Raelene Boyle may have felt better after the 100 final, for she got the silver medal with her 11.2 effort. Cuba's Sylvia Chivas checked in with the same 11.2, but had to settle for the bronze.

The East German women defeated the U.S. women in the 1600-meter relay, thanks largely to Rita Kuhne's 50-second flat second "400 meter" leg. (The distance reads between quotation marks because virtually no relay runner runs a full one-quarter of the race's distance. Because of the 20 meter "passing zone" allowed for baton changes, the later the leg run, the shorter it tends to be. Consequently, although America's Kathy Hammond ran 50.2 seconds for the U.S. team's anchor leg, her time stands as considerably less impressive than Kuhne's.) The East Germans set a world best of 3:23.0, while the Americans came second with 3:52.2, nearly 20 seconds under the former world record and good enough only for silver! The West German women were third in 3:26.5.

Aside from the metric-mile event, if an East German woman did not win a final at Munich, a West German woman did. Until the 1972 Olympics, only one woman in history had run under 2:00 for the 800 meters, West Germany's Hildegard Falck, in 1:58.5. The first four finishers in the Munich final went under 2:00, Falck leading the mass charge with 1:58.55 to set an Olympic record. The Soviet Union's Niele Sabaite claimed second in 1:58.7, and East Germany's Gunhild Hoffmeister earned a bronze medal in 1:59.2 to go along with her silver medal from the 1500 meters. Bulgaria's Svetla Zlateva also broke the 2-minute barrier, running fourth in 1:59.7.

Running in front of the home crowd, the West German women upset the favored East Germans in the 400-meter relay. The West Germans' victorious time, 42.8 seconds, equalled the world record. The East German team ran 42.9; the third-place Cubans legged it in 43.4, and the formerly powerful American team came fourth with 43.4, just out of the medals.

The American men looked strong in the middle distances. Dave Wottle of the U.S.A. took home a gold medal from the 800-meters final after beating the Soviet Union's Yevgeniy Arzhanov. Arzhanov took off at the gun, an atypical Soviet runner in that he ran loosely and smoothly, lacking the wooden seriousness that characterized most Russian runners. Wottle's split was 26.6 for the first 200. He ran the first 400-meter lap in 53.4. At 600 meters, passed in 1:19.7, Wottle was closing on leader Arzhanov. Unfortunately, Wottle was also running in *seventh place* at this juncture. He sent a message down to the engine room and got an answer: Go for it! Twenty meters from the medals Wottle zinged Arzhanov and second-man Mike Boit of Kenya, claiming the gold in 1:45.90 by 3/100-second over Arzhanov, who ran 1:45.93, while Boit held on for the bronze, 1:46.0.

Wottle went into his event as world-record holder. American hopes stood even higher for the fortunes of the nation's other middle-distance world-record runner, Jim Ryun, but the hopes were dashed when Ryun crashed to the track in his first qualifying race. Running comfortably in qualifying position, about 550 meters from the wire, Ryun pulled out to pass another runner, who smacked the American hard in the chest with his elbow. A Pakistani runner, trying to get by Ryun, kicked Ryun in the foot. The already off-balance American fell crushingly to the track. Like Viren, he got back up, but, unlike Viren (who had not been deliberately and viciously fouled in the 10,000-meters tumble), he didn't make it. Ryun did not qualify.

Olympic rules allow for athletes who are fouled to receive another chance to qualify for their event, but, amazingly, the officials at Munich ruled Ryun had tripped over his own feet! Ryun had concrete evidence of foul play: a spike wound on the outside of his right heel, a ripped-up track shoe, and ABC-TV video tapes clearly showing the elbow in the chest and the spike in the foot. As Ryun put it: "It would have taken some pretty fancy footwork for me to spike myself on the *outside* of my right heel." None of it availed him. Ryun recalled: "Later I saw an Olympic official who told me, 'It's really unfortunate, but there's nothing we can do about it.' He suggested that I try again in 1976." Such official incompetence and callousness sadly belie the Olympic ideal and those athletes who uphold it through dedication and perfection.

No American qualified for the men's 1500-meter final at Munich. The Kenyans fielded the strongest contingent of qualifiers with Kip Keino and Mike Boit. (The exceptionally versatile Keino had already won the steeplechase in the Olympic record of 8:23.6, after using countryman Ben Jipcho as a stalking horse. Jipcho finished second in 8:24.6, burned off by Keino's amazing 57-second final lap. A runner must clear five barriers on each lap.) Only one of the Kenyans finished in the medals. Finland's Pekka Vasala upset orange-capped Keino, 3:36.3 to 3:36.8, while New Zealand's Rod Dixon carried on the Snell tradition, getting the bronze medal in 3:37.5. After the race, Vasala humbly commented: "Believe me when I tell you how much I regret that Ryun was not in the final. Had he been there, my tactics would have been quite different. I would have had two men to keep an eye on, but Jim wasn't there."

Frank Shorter, the son of an Army doctor, had been born in Munich in 1947, and, unlike the unfortunate Ryun, he *was* there, again, for the final long-distance event of the 1972 Olympics, the marathon. Perhaps Shorter's Teutonic nativity accounted for his chosen means of relaxing the night before his first Olympic competition; he chugged down about two liters of beer. Coaches advise distance runners to refrain from alcohol the night before a race in the heat, because alcohol inhibits both the body's cooling and oxygen-processing systems. Race day was in the low 70s and humid. Had Shorter not gotten "half looped" (as he put it), he might have run much faster. As it was, he had to settle for winning the marathon gold medal in 2:12:19.8, a mere 8.7 seconds over Bikila's 1964 Olympic best.

Because no other athlete felt like it, Shorter took the lead at the gun, running the first of 2 laps on the stadium track in 72 seconds. England's Ron Hill, running in what many described as his "space man's suit" (shorts and singlet made of shiny, heat-reflective material, shoes so light they had no tongues), took the lead shortly thereafter with tough guy Derek Clayton hanging on his shoulder. Hill hit 10K in 31:15 and then Shorter started to put on the pressure. The American increased his pace gradually between 10 and 15 kilometers and then fired from 15K to 20K. Shorter said after: "I didn't start running really fast until 15 kilometers. I may have been running 4:40 [per mile] pace or better for that 5 kilometers." At 20,000 meters Shorter had over a minute and a half on second-placed Karel Lismont of Belgium.

Shorter had more than that: he had the rapt attention of the American public (including a bartender at the Brothers Four bar in Falmouth, Massachusetts, named Tommy Leonard, who was inspired to start the Falmouth Road Race the next year by what he saw on his TV screen). ABC-TV was broadcasting the race live into millions of American homes. Moreover, ABC had Shorter's classics professor from Yale, writer Erich Segal, commentating on his former pupil's race. Segal was riding the crest of huge popularity as a result of his best-selling novel, *Love Story*. Americans who did not know the difference between a marathon and a steeplechase gave their attention nonetheless to the "celebrity commentator." Americans who had seen Billy Mills and Bob Schul clean up the long track distances in 1964 now saw American Frank Shorter whipping the world's best in the longest orthodox footrace of them all, especially inspiring in the light of Ryun's fall and the mindless terrorist murders. Americans who were "jogging" to stay healthy witnessed the easy grace with which the flowing Shorter ran and began to think of competition in terms of *fun* instead of pain, mentally comparing the boredom of exercising with the pleasure of *training as an athlete*.

Contrary to what popular historians have claimed, Frank Shorter in no way "invented distance running" by winning the Munich marathon, but he did serve as the focal point of the various social, political, medical, and athletic trends outlined in this and the preceding chapter. In winning the gold medal at Munich, Shorter became Point Zero for American distance running.

Shorter refrained from sprinting when he hit Munich Stadium and saw how close he was to Bikila's mark. He wrote later: "I had already decided early that I wasn't going to sprint in. . . . I've always maintained that anyone who's leading by any significant amount at the end of a marathon who sprints at the end is hot-dogging." Yet, when the composed Shorter broke the tape, he folded his hands over his head and said to himself, softly: "My God, what have I done?"

Silver medalist Karel Lismont came home in 2:14:31.8. Abebe Bikila's old teammate, Mamo Wolde, was the bronze medalist in 2:15:08.4. American Kenny Moore was the first man in out of the metal, finishing fourth in 2:15:39.8, while the third American, Jack Bacheler, got ninth with 2:17:38.2. It was an outstanding day for American marathoners, the U.S.A. winning the completely unofficial marathon team title. To celebrate, the team went out with author Segal that night and imbibed something a bit fancier than beer. Segal had recommended champagne.

It was after the Munich Olympics that big money started to flow into road racing in the U.S.A. The media exposure had awakened the public to a new form of fun. Many citizens already knew what it was to jog. Now they wanted to race—and to race against Olympic athletes. To attract such lofty stars to their road races, race directors became exceedingly generous in the "expense" money they offered. The sport of road running now had a sound commercial *raison d'être*. It would make all Americans physically healthier, and it would make some fiscally healthier, too.

The flow of cash into road running in America benefitted both the athletes and the companies that made athletic gear. Top racers served as role models to hobbyist runners, who in turn served as the prime consumers of running gear. By 1972 there were already far more hobbyist runners than there were world-class competitors in the U.S. Running-gear companies served their best interests in encouraging mass participation by simultaneously promoting and supporting the stars who put running before the public's eye. The more runners there were, the more consumers for running paraphernalia and, incidentally, the healthier the nation. To put money into road racing was only good business.

Why, then, did the money have to be disguised as "expense" payments and doled out under the table? Why not strike a straightforward business deal? The problem lay in rules governing international competition. Although standards defining "pure amateur" competitors were broadening and relaxing, they still existed. Further, Communist bloc nations belonging to such governing bodies as the IAAF and IOC lobbied vigorously against weakening the rules. Under a socialist socioeconomic system, an athlete could be supported by the state, devote his or her entire time to training, and still qualify as an amateur because he or she had not made a profit from athletics. Capitalist nations worked differently, with the state supporting only genuinely needy citizens. It was clearly in the best interests of the Eastern bloc to inhibit Western athletes' ability to train, so the Communists could win more gold medals in international competition. To comply with the spirit of these regulations, but avoid complying with the letter of them, athletes and track meet promoters had (since 800 B.C.!) embraced the idea of under-the-table payments. No one was happy with the system, but everyone participated. Such a system also enhanced the power of the race director; because all negotiations for cash were carried on secretly, it was difficult if not practically impossible for a runner to learn his or her true "market value." Not uncommonly, two athletes of comparable ability have received vastly different "expense" payments simply because one was a better negotiator than the other.

The "expense" system of payments to athletes enhanced the power of race directors, but also spread acrimony and distrust among the athletes. Although runners benefitted from the money flowing into road running after the Munich Olympics, they benefitted far less than did the shoe companies and some race directors. In fact, the huge injection of cash into the roads largely helped to create another unwanted, hindering, and totally unnecessary institution in the sport: the egocentric race director.

Some athletes possessed enough capital and personal contacts to benefit greatly from the post-Munich money flow. Marty Liquori was possibly chief among them. Liquori had already sidestepped rules governing "amateurism" by taking a college degree in broadcasting, which enabled him to appear *for a fee* as an expert commentator on the sport for television. The injured miler had served ABC-TV in such capacity at Munich and was exempt from discipline by the sport's governing bodies because he was, after all, a professional broadcaster. (Recall the USOC had expelled hammer-thrower Cliff Blair from the Olympic Team in 1956 because he was writing newspaper stories for pay; had Blair possessed a journalism degree, he would have been immune.)

Liquori saw another means of profitting from his sport. When he returned from Munich, he and Olympic Coach Jimmy Carnes opened a sporting goods store named The Athletic Attic. The idea took off like Liquori and Ryun on the last lap of a mile race, and the one store grew into a large chain. By 1975, Marty Liquori was a millionaire and able to devote himself to training full-time, if he chose. Because his name was not in the title of the enterprise, in contrast to Frank Shorter's or Bill Rodgers's later business endeavors, Liquori could franchise Athletic Attic stores. *He was not profiting from his name,* hence could retain his amateur status in the eyes of the IAAF. (If an athlete starts an athletically-related business and puts his or her name on it, he or she must own 51 percent of any business bearing that name, and must participate daily in the managerial process of the enterprise. Liquori was so famous and investing so early in the American running "boom" that he did not need to put his name on the enterprise in order to profit from it. "Everyone" knew Athletic Attic was Marty Liquori's store, just as he knew the Brooks "Villanova" shoe was the Marty Liquori running shoe.)

There were more runners, and running related businesses, than ever before in 1972 America. The country needed more races for the hobbyists to run, and at which to promote more new shoes and to create more paydays for top runners. The Charleston (West Virginia) Distance Run got its start in September, 1972, with Florida T.C. member Jeff Galloway leading the pack to the tape. A natural site for the road race, which has since become a classic, Charleston also houses the National Track and Field Hall of Fame.

The Nike/Oregon Track Club Marathon, popularly known as "the Nike/ OTC," also got its inaugural run in September, 1972, and stood as yet another example of corporate interest in the sport. The Nike Athletic Shoe Company, originally Blue Ribbon Sports, was one of the largest American running-shoe manufacturers by 1972. Nike grew even larger in succeeding years. Based in Beaverton, Oregon, Nike was one of the first running-gear makers to understand the commercial value of promoting road races open to large fields of hobbyist athletes as well as to elite racers. Moreover, Nike and a few similar organizations perceived the importance of "putting back into the sport," that is, of making investments that did not necessarily generate sales but created goodwill. The Nike/OTC course, although a full 26.2 miles, was designed to produce fast marathon times for competitors. The route is flat (meaning no hills) and rarely, if ever, suffers from hindering headwinds. Not surprisingly, the race became very popular and was used as the 1976 Olympic Trials marathon course. It was also used annually by athletes hoping to qualify to run the Boston Marathon.

The track world rocked hard on November 14, 1972, when Michael O'Hara announced the formation of the International Track Association. No stranger to sports, Mike O'Hara had previously founded the American Basketball Association and the World Hockey Association. The ITA represented professional track and field. Athletes were going to take money *over* the table. Payments would be contingent on performance in a given meet, not on negotiations beforehand.

O'Hara's sports credentials alone lent plausibility to the ITA, but O'Hara was by no means alone in the venture. Jim Ryun had signed to run the ITA circuit! Lee Evans, 400-meter gold medalist in the 1968 Olympics had signed; shotputter Randy Matson, another Mexico City gold medalist and the first man to break 69, 70, and 71 feet was on board; pole vaulter Bob Seagren, another Mexico City gold medalist and, like Ryun and Matson, a world-record holder, was on the ITA "team." Marty Liquori, replete with broad-casting school credentials, was going to be the announcer for every ITA meet. Later, international stars such as Gerry Lindgren, Jim Hines, and Kipchoge Keino joined. It certainly seemed like a winning proposition; the talent was there.

Yet, talent was not enough. ITA success depended on spectator interest to generate enough money for athletes to be willing to give up Olympic dreams. By 1972, it was getting obvious there was a lot of gold in an Olympic medal. A medal, "even" a silver or bronze, drastically increased the expense money an athlete could demand and expect to receive. An Olympic medal made its possessor "bankable." Leaving personal athletic pride aside, it would have been foolish for a runner to toss away a chance to enhance his or her income. If she or he were not going to the Olympics, the ITA circuit would have to take up the financial slack.

The ITA's first meet seemed to be an indication of success. Held on March 3, 1973, at Pocatello, Idaho, and costing fans double the normal ticket prices, the ITA indoor meet (almost all ITA meets were held indoors, it turned out) drew a near capacity crowd of 10,480, who witnessed three world records: Lee Evans's 1:16.7 600 meters (1 full second under the old mark); John Radetich's 7'4¾" high jump; Warren Edmonson's 10.2 100-meter dash. First prize for each event was $500, with a $500 bonus for establishing a world best; $100 went to the athlete who equalled a world record. The next ITA meet was held on March 24, 1973, at the Los Angeles Sports Arena, drawing a crowd of 12,280, by far the biggest audience that would ever watch an ITA meet. Sportswriters came down hard on the idea, and fans thereafter decided to spend their money on something else. Further, many athletes found they could earn more by taking money under the table as "amateurs" than they could on the pay-for-performances-rendered ITA circuit. ITA lingered, finally folding in 1976.

The results were predictable. The ITA idea was a direct descendant of the six-day pedestrian races of the turn of the century, which had also died after the novelty wore off. The rise of organized athletics, accompanied by govern-ing bodies soundly opposed to professionalism in running because it would weaken the bodies' power, combined with natural public fickleness to end the ITA. Perhaps if every major track star in the world had banded together and gone with the ITA, the circuit would have succeeded, but the major European standouts were also ITA holdouts. They were content with their current earn-ings. Why risk a certain income for the uncertainty of a new type of money sport? Lacking a coherent base of support among international athletes and vigorously opposed by the rulers of amateur sport, the ITA necessarily went belly up. This is a lesson from which modern athletes must learn if they would reform today's hypocritical "shamateur" system of international competition.

Filbert Bayi of Tanzania, a superlative athlete, stood as an example of the problems facing the ITA. Bayi would not have dreamed of running with the ITA. He emerged on the international scene in 1973 and soundly trounced one of the ITA stars, Kip Keino. Bayi was hot and young. He had a superb athletic career ahead of him, funded by an equally superb financial one of under-the-table payments on the amateur circuit. A runner who could beat Keino in the mile could obviously command more than $500 profit for appearing at a meet. In addition, Bayi offered meet promoters a talent that technology had made obsolete as far as ITA meets were concerned. Bayi was one of the first professional "rabbits" in the sport, a pacemaker par excellence for world-record attempts by other runners. The ITA tracks came complete with pacing lights built into them, beacons automatically setting a tempo for runners shooting for fast times. IAAF rules prohibited such technological tomfoolery for the amateurs. IAAF rules also barred the use of pacemaking athletes, but, like amateur purity, pacesetting is difficult to prove.

Track specialists such as Bayi could command especially large fees for their services. Less unique track athletes continued to receive the same fees as had always been offered them, but the dollars were going up on the roads. In 1973, a top-ranked road runner could command between $600 and $800 in appearance money for running a 10-kilometer road race. For a marathon, he could expect $2,000. Marathons offered larger paydays for athletes than did shorter races not only because the marathon took longer to run, but because it took far more time for the runner to prepare for it and to recover (and be paid again) after it. In contrast, an athlete who set a *best mark for the marathon* less than a decade previously received $500 from the race directors after his run and was flabbergasted to get it—it was the only money he had ever made above actual travel expenses in his many years of racing. By 1973, a top runner could expect to receive quadruple that figure regardless of how well he ran. (Of course, if he did not run consistently well, his price would go down.) The money going to the road runners in this new era took nothing away from the largess given the track; it simply made the track fees puny by comparison.

An athlete competing on the European track circuit in 1973 could expect between nothing and $1200 over actual expenses for appearing at a meet. A native who competed at home and who had not made a significant mark internationally could anticipate receiving real expenses—room and board—and nothing else. A runner with a good international reputation could expect a profit (that is, money in addition to true expenses) of $100 to $600 per appearance. An Olympic champion, or a then current (not former) European champion could demand up to $1,200 in profit.

One-hundred-twenty-nine runners lined up in Washington, D.C., in

March, 1973, for the first running of the Cherry Blossom 10-Miler, a race since hailed as a classic. Its first running was atypical: runners paid a $1 entry fee; every year since, there has been (amazingly) *no entry fee whatsoever!* The hosting DC Road Runners Club secured a huge sponsorship commitment for the era: $1,000, donated by an insurance company. The "outrageous" amount of sponsorship money indicated the transition under which American road running was going, in two ways: first, the fact that such a sum was suddenly available; second, that, by the standards of 1981, the sum was so ludicrously small. The first Cherry Blossom race typified the era in yet another way. It was claimed by miler Sam Bair, who joined the ITA pro circuit the next week.

Child wondermiler Mary Decker was a runner with no intentions of joining the ITA group. For one thing, she was too young at age 14 to run on the evening indoor circuit; for another, the future looked so bright she would have been imprudent to throw away the under-the-table gelt that European meet promoters would beg her to take. In 1972, little Decker ran the mile in 4:55. In 1973, 14-year-old Decker dropped her mile mark down to 4:37.4 and was able to compete in open races with adults. So apparent was her talent that the AAU asked her to join the U.S.A. Track and Field Team on their

Mary Decker (now Mary Decker Tabb) emerged on the international scene at the age of 15. In this June, 1974 race at Bakersfield, California, Decker ran 2:05.2 for 880 yards to defeat 15-year-old Robin Campbell. (Photograph courtesy of The Boston Herald American.)

international tour that summer. As a member of the U.S. Team, the young runner met a slightly older one, Steve Prefontaine, who recognized her talent and also recognized that her school coach was burning out an awesome runner. The volatile Prefontaine became a hero to Mary, and she and her family contemplated moving from their home in Boulder, Colorado, to Eugene, Oregon, to be closer to Prefontaine.

In February of 1974 she confirmed her status as one of America's top half-milers when she set the world indoor 880-yard record, 2:02.4, in the L.A. Times Meet in San Diego. She won her first national championship at the same distance outdoors, legging the 2 laps in 2:05.2. Then problems arose. The child prodigy became the child invalid. Growing as a talent, Decker was also literally growing as a person and therein lay the difficulty. In two years she had gained six inches of height and 25 pounds of weight. Although normal for a woman her age, the growth was stressful to her frame. Her legs hurt and finally refused to function. After a year of frustration, in which making the 1976 Montreal Olympics became plainly impossible, the formerly dashing Decker agreed to surgery. She would go under the knife, train, race, break down, and go back into the hospital. It would not be until the end of the decade that her condition and career would even begin to stabilize. Like other excellent American runners such as Wilma Rudolph and Glenn Cunningham, no-longer-little Mary Decker's debilitated legs would force her to come to terms with herself.

England's Dave Bedford came to terms with his disappointing 5-kilometer and 10-kilometer performances in the Munich Games when, on July 13, 1973, he broke Ron Clarke's world record for 10,000 meters by running the 25 interminable laps in 27:30.8.

On August 21, 1973, seven Boston long-distance runners undergoing that form of athletic crisis known as post-collegiate career anxiety decided to find themselves a good coach and form a good track club. The runners were Jack McDonald, Don Ricciato, Dave Elliot, Bob Sevene, Charles Diele, Kirt Pfrangle, and Dickie Mahoney. One night, while drinking beer, they started calling coaches they knew in an effort to find one who had the time to take on even more athletes . . . for no pay, of course. They finally convinced the track coach at Boston State College, Billy Squires, to cast his lot with theirs. McDonald came up with the name for the group: the Greater Boston Track Club. They would go on to become the first track club (and, to date, only track club) ever to win every American national distance championship; to place four men in the top ten at the 1979 Boston Marathon; to stand as arguably the greatest amateur distance track club in history.

At the first GBTC track workout, held August 28, 1973, on the Boston College track, Coach Squires surveyed his athletes. There were eighteen of them: six half-milers and seven 2-to-6 mile runners. It was not an auspicious beginning. Exactly two months later, October 28, 1973, GBTC claimed the AAU National 20-Kilometer Championship, a title the club has won every succeeding year to date. The club also took the individual title, as William Rodgers crossed the line first in 1:03:58.

The Greater Boston 2-mile relay team showed their stuff in the 1974 indoor track season. The GBTC relay team won at the New York Knights of Columbus Meet, took second at the Olympic Invitational Meet, and third at the AAU Nationals. GBTC as a unit won the team prize at the New England AAU Track and Field Championships. In the outdoor season, the Greater Bostonians finished third in the Penn Relays' Distance Medley, third overall among clubs at the National AAU Relays, and first club overall at the New England AAU Track and Field Championships. The performances were more than respectable; what rendered them astonishing was the fact the GBTC's total expenses for the 1974 season were $800! Shortly thereafter, New Balance Athletic Shoes, a Boston-based running-shoe company, started using the GBTC talent pool to test and develop new footwear. In return, New Balance helped defray the club's expenses. In the history of distance running, the Greater Boston Track Club stands as important because, along with the Florida T.C., it was one of the first eminent *postcollegiate* running clubs; because it would develop a staggering array of talent, and because its relationship with New Balance symbolized the developing union between commerce and athletics in American road running. GBTC concretely demonstrated that a distance runner's career does not *begin* to develop until he or she has been graduated from college; that a "hungry" athlete, one willing to (as Steve Prefontaine put it) "stand the pain and play the game" could beat a more gifted but less dedicated runner; and that the goals of top runners and commerce could be made mutually supportive.

The Falmouth Road Race had its inaugural running in August, 1973, the creation and pride of world-class bartender Tommy Leonard. Inspired by Frank Shorter's marathon victory at Munich, which he and his customers watched on the television of a Falmouth, Massachusetts, bar, Leonard conceived the notion of a road race between the Cap Cod towns of Woods Hole and Falmouth, a distance of 7.1 miles. The odd distance made for rejoicing among serious road runners. With the advent of the jogging boom, it seemed as though every new road race was 10,000 meters, so neophyte runners could compare their times to those of Olympic 10K performances— a completely invalid comparison, of course, for it is far harder to race on the track than on the roads. Seasoned competitors yearned for a variety of distances in their racing, and Falmouth represented that small voice against the homogenization of road running. A jovial personality, one of running's true "characters," Leonard also ensured the race would be surrounded fore and aft by many parties. The weather conditions for the inaugural Falmouth Road Race were described by one reporter as "a veritable monsoon" soaking the 98 original runners. The first man over the line was David Duba, in 39:16. The first woman, Jennie Taylor, ran 44:31.

Today, Falmouth stands as the world's most competitive and prestigious sub-marathon road race, an event in which dark horses challenge and often best Olympians. Perhaps not even at the Boston Marathon does such a significant disparity in talent between the frontrunners and the balance of the pack prevail as at Falmouth, where the course record averages a pace per mile under 4:30.

The Honolulu Marathon went to the line for the first time in December, 1973, and every year since has invited runners to attempt to break either of the course's records: the one for the fastest time or the one for the slowest. An idyllic end to the racing season, Honolulu attracts hordes intent on establishing a new record in either direction.

Running in the Culver City Marathon in California on December 2, 1973, 38-year-old Michiko (Miki) Gorman lowered the American women's marathon best to 2:46:36 in her second completed 26.2-mile run.

University of Chicago T.C. middle-distance man Rick Wohlhuter enjoyed perhaps his best year when 1974 rolled around. The mustachioed Wohlhuter set world records at 880 yards (1:44.1) and 1000 meters (2:13.9) in addition to an American 800 meters best (1:43.9). Wohlhuter got off to a sprightly start in the indoor season, taking the AAU indoor kilometer championship in 2:06.8, winning the coveted Sullivan Award for stellar indoor track performance and the *Track & Field News* Athlete of the Year prize for equally lofty outdoor running.

Big, handsome, long-haired miler John Walker of Aukland, New Zealand, hit the American boards for the first time in 1974, beating Steve Prefontaine in the mile run at the L.A. Times Invitational Meet; Walker clocked 3:58.9 in his 11-lap debut, while Pre crossed the line in 3:59.5. A feat quite respectable in itself, it was made more so by the fact that Walker had raced a 3:56.0 mile in New Zealand the day before, then spent fifteen hours on a plane to reach Los Angeles.

Walker decided the mile was the right distance for him in 1971, at age 19, after years of soccer, tennis and rugby. He had raced only sporadically as a youth. In 1966, at age 14, he won a cross-country race and set a course record that stands unbroken to date; at that point he decided to devote more time to running. Time would tell it was a choice well made.

Marty Liquori's decision to be a runner came to full fruition in the 1974 track season, the second best season of his career. He ran 3:56.6 for the mile, 8:25.4 for 2 miles, and 13:40.6 for 5 kilometers.

Tony Waldrop of the University of North Carolina released one of the most surprising indoor miling seasons in history in 1974. On February 12, 1974, Waldrop removed Jim Ryun's and Tom O'Hara's joint indoor mile mark from the record books, hoofing the 11 wooden laps in 3:55.0 to lower the standard by 1.4 seconds. More amazingly, Waldrop went on to run eight more sub-4 miles that undercover season, many of them paced by his North Carolina teammate, Reggie Macaffee, who had the distinction of being the best American indoor mile rabbit of the era. (Filbert Bayi, to whom Waldrop would finish second in Bayi's world outdoor mile record, stood as the preeminent rabbit of the day, period.) Macaffee and Waldrop trained and raced together, the former getting his outdoor mile time down to 3:57.2, the latter, to 3:53.2. Waldrop never again had so grand a season as his one in 1974, but no athlete needed a grander season.

Opportunities for road racing grew around the globe in 1974. The year marked the first West Berlin Marathon.

One of the best organized and most festive of major American road races got started in September, 1974: the Virginia 10-Miler, held in Lynchburg, won by John Vitale. In contrast to a growing national trend, the race directors laid out a particularly *difficult* route, figuring the personal satisfaction of overcoming hills appealed to at least as many runners as the satisfaction of running a personal best for a given distance. They figured correctly; today, the race is a classic.

While Derek Clayton's maniac run in 1969 at Antwerp left the best men's marathon mark static, the best women's marathon time continued to tumble. In October, 1974, France's Chantal Langlace ran the marathon in 2:46:24. In December, 1974, America's Jacqueline Hansen ran the quick Culver City Marathon in 2:43:54.6. On December 8, 1974, Frank Shorter claimed his fourth straight, and final, Fukuoka Marathon in 2:11:31.2.

Road running was booming, but the boom occasionally blew up in runners' faces. On December 1, 1974, Greater Boston Track Club member Bill Rodgers won the AAU-sanctioned Philadelphia Marathon, in 2:21:57. The entry blanks and attendant promotional materials promised the first-place finisher an expense-paid trip to the Pan-Am Games Trials Marathon, "but that turned out to be a lie," Rodgers recalled. The prize he received "was the most junky, clunky watch I ever saw in my life" with an estimated value of $5. The watch came with "the works," that is, no money inside.

Things picked up for the GBTC in 1975. The 2-mile relay team again won at the Olympic Invitational Relays and the New England AAU Track and Field Championships indoors. Moving outside in the spring, GBTC won the AAU National 30 Kilometer Championship and successfully defended their 20K national title. Two club members had particularly good seasons. High school sophomore Al Salazar, so talented that Coach Squires permitted the schoolboy to run with the adult "horses," set national age-group records at 3 miles and 5,000 meters as a member of the U.S. International Juniors Team. Bill Rodgers finished third overall in the International Cross-Country Championships in Rabat, Morocco, in March, covering the 12,000 meters in 34:20. The GBTC covered its 1975 expenses with $1062 total.

He is skinny, blond, and apparently poor: he runs in cheap painter's gloves to keep his hands warm on the 50-degree day, and his t-shirt, on which he has hand-lettered "Boston/GBTC," substitutes for a spiffy singlet. Billy

Rodgers of Jamaica Plain, Massachusetts, is running stride for stride with top Canadian marathoner Jerome Drayton, fighting for the lead 9 miles into the 1975 Boston Marathon.

"Go, Jerome!" the crowd lining the route shouts. They recognize the Canadian in the impenetrable sunglasses, a 2:11 world-ranked runner. Inscrutable behind his eyes' walls, Drayton responds and surges ahead. The unknown American throws off his white gloves and surges harder than Drayton. The Boston crowd is about to learn something: do not get Bill Rodgers ANGRY in a race.

The lanky Yank puts Drayton away for good just outside Natick, running 30 yards clear of the Canadian. Not knowing how to drink while running, Rodgers comes to a dead stop five times: four of them to drink, once to tie a flopping shoelace. Each time he halts, the crowd screams in consternation; but Rodgers has an insurmountable lead and enjoys the infinitesimal respites from his running wrath. He runs calmly, apparently serene, his clean Yankee looks hiding the rage inside him more effectively than Drayton's mirrored shades. It's not until he crosses the finish line at the Prudential Center that the facade fades. He has run 2:09:55, nearly 10 minutes faster than he has before, and set a new American men's marathon mark. He spies the clock. "It can't be true," he says. "I can't run that fast."

Surprises abounded at the 1975 Boston Marathon. Bill Rodgers, almost literally unknown, set a new course and American men's best, while West Germany's Liane Winter lowered the women's world best to 2:42:24. (Finishing second to Winter was Kate Switzer, running an excellent 2:51:37 and smiling broadly in yet another official number.) With his victory at Boston and subsequent rise to Olympian heights, Rodgers demarked the start of yet another road racing era: the rise of the pure road runner. Rodgers competed in track and cross-country in high school and college, but drifted away from running during his graduate school sojourn. Even while an undergraduate, Rodgers's main influence was his roommate at Wesleyan University, 1968 Boston Marathon champion Amby Burfoot, who preached the gospel of long runs through woods and on the roads instead of hard intervals on the track. In the 1933 Boston Marathon, track star Les Pawson brought speed to the marathon, overwhelming the pure road runners. At the Munich Games, track standout Frank Shorter added the final note to the American distance symphony begun by Billy Mills and Bob Schul in winning the long-distance track events. All these fellows had powerful track backgrounds; Rodgers did not. His best time for the mile, set in 1968, was 4:18.8. He would go on to set a world record at 25,000 meters on the track (1:14:12) in 1979, and an American record for 30,000 meters (1:31:50) in the same effort. He would set American track records at 15 kilometers (43:39.8), 20K (58:15), and 10 miles (46:40) in 1977, as well as the U.S. mark for a 1-hour run (12 miles, 1,351 yards). He would run the 10K on a track in 28:04.4 while finishing fourth, one place out of the running, in the

1976 U.S. Olympic Trials in that event; but Rodgers justifiably thought of himself as a road runner and marathoner. He would eventually run more marathons under 2:12 than anyone else in history (10 as of 1981); he would compete against and beat ace track runners such as Shorter and Japan's Toshihiko Seko on the roads. Most importantly, perhaps, his humble and disarming personality would help to motivate thousands more to start to run.

Bill Rodgers became the first modern American road racing hero, a designation he himself never accepted. He once commented: "In running, it's different [from 'professional' sports]. The spectators are becoming the runners, and then we're all out there on the starting line together, so there's this huge merging—all the barriers are broken down! So how can you have a hero? That's why I say it's more than a sport; it's very different." Rodgers would go on to win the Boston Marathon three more times, and the New York Marathon four times in a row, the Falmouth Road Race three times straight, and innumerable road races at other distances, and many other marathons; yet he was proudest not of his running achievements as such, but of the charitable programs in which he could participate as a result of them: the Boston Marathon Multiple Sclerosis Drive and the U.S. Special Olympics program. As had Nurmi, Zátopek, and Clarke, Bill Rodgers personified his era in running history. A man with gentle but iron will, he was of the people, for the people, but in his prime, always two steps ahead of them. Although his performances in elite races earned him the appellation "The King of the Roads," Rodgers had the common touch of the good person.

On May 30, 1975, Mary Decker lost her friendly coach, and the rest of the track world lost a champion, when Steve Prefontaine died in an automobile accident in Eugene, Oregon. Twenty-four-years old, Pre had just reached his prime as a distance runner.

Filbert Bayi went undefeated on the American indoor track circuit in 1975, winning the Wanamaker Mile at the Millrose Games in 3:59.3, the mile at the L.A. Times Invitational in 3:59.6 (where he beat John Walker), the mile at the San Diego Meet in 3:56.4, and the AAU indoor championship mile in a sluggish 4:02.1. Bayi had set the world record at 1500 meters, 3:32.2, the previous European outdoor track season, so none was surprised at his 1975 displays of 4-lap speed. Americans hardly cheered, though, when, on May 17, 1975, the torrid Tanzanian took away Jim Ryun's 8-year-old mile world record with a 3:51.0 effort at Kingston, Jamaica, prevailing over Marty Liquori, Rick Wohlhuter, indoor mile record-holder Tony Waldrop, and Eamonn Coghlan.

Liquori ran his fastest mile ever, 3:52.2, in finishing second to Bayi. During the indoor season, the loquacious Liquori lowered his indoor mile best from 4:00.8 to 3:55.8. The young businessman perceived some handwriting on his wall, though, and decided he should move up in distance and let the new generation of fleet milers go by. His adjusted training resulted in an

American 2-mile record of 8:17.1. By the end of 1975, Liquori ranked fifth in the world as a miler, but third in the world at 5,000 meters.

Bayi's performance wrought a profound influence on another miler, Kiwi John Walker. He decided he wanted not only the mile record, but a particular mark. John Walker intended to be the first miler under 3:50.

Walker became the mile's answer to Derek Clayton. He recalled: "Nobody in New Zealand would train with me. I was pushing myself like an animal for 15 weeks, and the only thing that kept me sane was the goal at the end of the rainbow: the world's record for the mile." In August, 1975, after a fourteen-race buildup, Walker ran 1500 meters on the famed Bislett track in Oslo, Norway, in 3:32.4, almost tying Bayi's world record. He felt he was ready, so requested the meet promoter for his next race to delete the scheduled 1500 from her program and add instead a mile race. To get her to agree, Walker had to concede to publicizing his world-record attempt beforehand. The pressure was on.

Apparently Walker thrived on it. Nine thousand fans crammed into the stadium at Goteberg, Sweden, the night of August 12, 1975. Walker, the image of a Greek god, took the track behind an 800-meter specialist "rabbit." Apparently the rabbit did not thrive on the moment's pressure. He died after a lap. Walker, pacing himself, ran the first 2 laps in 1:55. The crowd began to chant his name. Miler Ken Hall moved up in Walker's draft, giving some welcome pressure to the New Zealander's drive. The big miler ran the next lap in 58.5. The gun! The effort! Hall fell back. Walker ran away, hitting 1500 meters in 3:34.3, running with the strength of a lion, his mane flowing in his wake, hitting the mile in 3:49.4, running the ultimate lap in 55.9 seconds, realizing his dream. "My God," he said.

The Montreal Olympics were nigh, and Walker was determined to take Olympic gold in the 1500. As part of his preparations and to test his speed, Walker set a new world record for 2,000 meters: 4:51.4. He had two world records that pre-Olympic year: one for a mile in 3:49.4 and one for 2 kilometers run at a *3:54-per-mile* pace.

Jon Anderson won the Nike/OTC Marathon, held on October 12, 1975, in 2:16:08, followed by the very tall and equally witty Don Kardong in 2:19:14. The big story of the race was found in the women's division. Jacki Hansen, coming off three months of 100-mile weeks, checked in with 2:38:14 to lower both the American and world women's marathon bests. Thus the first part of the decade ended. It had begun with joggers who ran for health and for sport and closed with athletes who trained with the intensity of brutes.

XI

Running for Money
1976–1979

The latter half of the 1970s was characterized by the intimate relationship between running and money. The San Diego Indoor Meet of 1976 exemplified that bond, costing meet directors $2,500 to get both John Walker and Rod Dixon on the same track for one race. Walker, in his first race of the American indoor season, lost to his fellow New Zealander; Olympic medalist Dixon clocked 3:56.8, while world-record holder Walker ran 3:57.5.

Politics, as well as money, influenced the 1976 Montreal Olympics. In 1968, athletes had protested on the field. In 1972, they had been murdered by terrorists. In 1976, national governments got into the act directly, not propagandistically. The African nations boycotted Montreal, casting a pall over the victories of many of the runners in the Games. A New Zealand rugby team had toured and competed in South Africa early in 1976. South Africa, a nation with a white-minority ruling class and a black majority subjected to a state policy of racial discrimination called apartheid, had long been barred from Olympic competition due to her racist policies; yet the Organization of African Unity also wanted a ban on New Zealand participation in international competition. The IOC reasonably declared the matter beyond their jurisdiction. Miffed, the African nations boycotted.

As a result, neither Miruts Yifter nor evergreen Mohammed Gammoudi ran the 10,000 meters at Montreal. To speculate on how their presence would have affected the final's outcome, if at all, is misleading. Just as it is futile to compare athletes of different eras, so too is it hopeless (and, in fact, vain) to second-guess a race's results "if only so-and-so had run it." The heat and passion of Olympic competition obviates predictions or conclusions based solely on comparing runners' times in previous similar races. Finland's Lasse Viren, who competed at Montreal, exemplified that point. Viren had performed with consistent mediocrity in the races he had run since his Munich long-distance "double" four years previously. To count him out of contention at Montreal because of that record would have been foolish. The outstanding distance runner at Montreal as at Munich, Viren again won the 10K final, besting a field in which apparently all contestants had shot their athletic bolts in qualifying rounds, Viren included.

The weather at Montreal was humid (68 percent relative humidity on the day of the 10,000-meter final) but mild (temperature in the low 70s); still, it was not climatically conducive to fast, long-distance legging. The seasoned runners in the field—Viren, Belgium's Karel Lismont and Emiel Puttemans, England's Brendan Foster—held back in the early going. The field split the first 1,000 meters in 2:53.0. Portugal's Carlos Lopes paced the pack through 5K in 14:08.9, picking up the pace, running the sixth kilometer in 2:43.4. Viren and Foster went with him. The balance of the field started to keel over. At 8K, faster Foster started going slower (perhaps tired by his altercation, *the minute* before the race, with stadium guards who did not want to let him on the track—many athletes complained of overly tight security). Viren remained on loping Lopes's shoulder until just before the start of the last lap, when the bearded Finn assumed his rightful role of front-runner. He pulled out 30 meters on Lopes in 1 lap. He ran his final kilometer in 2:38.4, his final 800 meters in 2:05.4, his final lap in 61.3, and his 10,000-meter final in 27:40.4 to take his second straight 10K gold. Viren's second 5,000 meters passed in 13:31.5, showing that strategy in long-distance track running had reverted from Kuts's approach of a fast start and dying finish back to Zátopek's technique of burning the second half of the race away. Lopes claimed the silver in 27:45.2, and Foster bravely finished with the bronze medal in 27:54.9.

Viren's victory brewed controversy for two reasons. One was his behavior on his victory lap. The thin Finn pulled off his track spikes and held them aloft for all to see—and photograph. A police officer by profession, Viran also worked as a sales representative for the company that made his shoes. With the running-gear market having grown so lucrative by 1976, the publicity attached to a champion wearing a given brand of shoes was invaluable. At the Montreal Olympics, shoe companies paid runners who won a gold medal in a specific brand of shoes a $10,000 bonus. None knows if Lasse Viren accepted any bonus or if his feet were really hot and sore, but many felt his display excessively commercial for the Games.

Similar ambiguity surrounded the second reason for controversy about Viren's win. Why did he run so well in the Olympics and so relatively poorly the other three years of an Olympiad? Rumors circulated that Viren received transfusions of blood before competing in order to boost his maximal levels of oxygen processing. The technique theoretically worked as follows. An athlete permits his trainer to draw out and store a quantity of the athlete's blood some time before racing. The runner's body then generates new blood to compensate for the loss, as happens to any healthy blood doner. By transfusing the athlete with more blood than his body normally carries, the trainer raises the absolute number of red, oxygen-carrying, blood cells in the runner's body, theoretically giving him significantly more endurance. Called blood packing, the process does not depend on drugs to enhance performance. Viren denied relying on blood packing, and none ever demonstrated he had used it. Further, there are other great athletes who produce stellar performances only in the duress of the ultimate competition, the Games. The fact that Viren was accused of athletic irregularities, though, suggests how suspicious the Olympic world was becoming and how far the Games had moved from the premises of trust and international understanding on which they had been founded, first by the Delphic oracle and second by Baron de Coubertin.

Viren's 5,000-meter victory paralleled his 10K tactics. The field included two Kiwi milers, Rod Dixon and Dick Quax, who decided to move up in distance, but the pace was still to Viren's liking—slow. The first 1000 meters went by in 2:41.5, quicker than the first kilometer in the 10K final, but pedestrian by world 5,000-meter standards. Brendan Foster led.

The second kilometer passed in 2:45. Then Viren took the lead and slowed the pace down, running the next lap in 68.8 seconds. It seemed a stupid tactic. The milers in the race had far stronger finishing kicks than the Finn's. Why let them stay with him and blast past on the last lap?

After 2 laps at Viren's sluggish pace, Brendan Foster dropped down to a lower gear and charged ahead, but then died. Quax winged to the fore, but the pack went right with him, West Germany's Klaus-Peter Hildenbrand taking over as pacemaker in another lap. Attrition whittled away the lead group over the next 3 laps, but it was still a considerable herd at the bell lap, with Quax, Dixon, and Hildenbrand hanging on Viren's tail, perhaps not seeing the stress lines on the Finn's face, not sensing his vulnerability. The expected kicks emerged 300 meters from home. Dixon, bronze medalist in the Munich metric mile, pulled up on Viren's shoulder—and Viren ran away from him! He ran away from everybody. Hildenbrand and Quax futilely chased the fleeing Finn. Viren hit the wire in 13:24.8, miler Quax in 13:25.2, Hildenbrand in 13:25.4, and miler Dixon in 13:25.5. Viren sped the last kilometer in 2:26.5, the last lap in 55.4! He said after: "I was afraid with 200 meters to go, because there were so many good milers in this race." Then he made an announcement that perhaps explained why he had truly wanted a slow 5,000-meter pace and accepted the risk of getting out-gunned in the last lap: he intended to run the Olympic marathon, his first, to be held the very next day.

Viren stood as indisputably the preeminent *long*-distance man at Montreal, but not necessarily the most astonishing distance ace. That accolade went to a middle-distance specialist known in his native Cuba as *El Caballo*, meaning "the horse": Alberto Juantorena, the man who brought brutal sprint speed to middle-distance running. After watching the meaty Cuban run, John Walker observed: "He's the prototype of the athlete of tomorrow."

The popular press persisted in comparing the muscular Juantorena (6'2-¾", 185 pounds) to a football running back, but he actually got his athletic start as a basketball player for the Cuban national team. One day in 1971, after deciding big Alberto had gone as far as he could on the courts, his coaches had him run a 400-meter lap to see if he might have track potential. Juantorena ran in basketball sneakers. He ran 51 flat. He had track potential. He competed at the Munich Olympics after training only seven months for running, and got as far as the semi-finals in the 400 where he finished, by his own estimation, "only 5 centimeters" out of the running for the final.

Few doubted the bull-like Juantorena would make the Montreal finals in the 400, but many questioned his 2-lap ability. The great Mal Whitfield had been one of only a handful of runners even to attempt the 400/800 double, and he never succeeded. No one else had, either. Although the 10K is twice as long as the 5K, many athletes excel at both; both are incontestably long-distance events. Just as incontestably, the 800-meter run is a middle-distance race, but the killer 400 meters fall in the grey zone between the outright sprints and the paced middle distances—two highly disparate events. The Cuban's chances at the 800 improved with the African boycott, which eliminated world-record holder Mike Boit and several other able Africans. Juantorena's chances got even better when John Walker, running in the footsteps of Peter Snell and attempting to double in the 800 and 1500, got bounced from the former during a preliminary heat. Still, ace American Rick Wohlhuter made the final and, true to form, gave Juantorena trouble right from the gun. Wohlhuter took the lead, hitting 200 meters in 25.5. Juantorena was 2/10-second back. Going through the first 400 meters, the Cuban pulled even with the American, and Sri Ram Singh of India came from nowhere to run with them. Juantorena ran the first lap in 50.9, 1/10-second faster than he had in basketball shoes in 1971. The many Americans in the crowd watched expectantly. They knew Wohlhuter liked to wait till the final half-lap, then turn on the speed and devastate his tired rivals; yet it was Juantorena who edged ahead at 600 meters. Belgium's Ivo Van Damme started to move up, albeit probably too late. Wohlhuter responded, straining—and lost it. Juantorena pulled away like a late mail train, and Van Damme whipped past the Yank 30 meters from home. Juantorena broke the worsted in 1:43.5, a world record, running the final lap in 52.6, the final 100 meters in 11.9. Van Damme ran 1:43.9 for the silver, and a tied-up Wohlhuter grasped the bronze with his 1:44.1. (Few noted the young Briton who finished fifth, in 1:45.4. His name was Steve Ovett.)

After his 800 victory, it seemed folly to bet against Juantorena in the 400, but the Americans there gave it their best shot. Before the race, America's Maxie Parks boasted: "I'm not chasing after him. He's chasing after me." It was Americans Fred Newhouse and Herman Frazier who tried to bind El Caballo's legs, though; Parks, although in the final, was, in a manner of speaking, out of it. Newhouse roared off at the gun, hitting 200 meters in 21.5 seconds, 1 meter up on Frazier and 3 meters up on Juantorena. The careening Cuban nailed Frazier 100 meters later and galloped after Newhouse, still 2 meters in front. He caught him. They ran as twins for possibly 20 meters, then Juantorena called on his 800-meter endurance and walked away, winning in 44.26 to Newhouse's 44.4. Frazier collected a bronze medal in 44.95. After the race, Juantorena stated: "I saved some for the last 50 meters. I always try to save a little strength for the finish." Newhouse commented: "I was thinking to myself, 'Hey, I got the gold medal'; then, with about 20 meters left, I realized he was right there with me. I guess I was a little more tired than he was."

Alberto Juantorena did more than bring 400-meter speed to the 800. He also brought 800-meter strength to the 400. Neither event would ever be the same. In one Olympics, Juantorena revolutionized two distinct events, and must therefore be recognized as one of the most important athletes in

Cuban Alberto Juantorena, nicknamed El Caballo ("the horse") because of his power and speed, performed the unprecedented (and to date unduplicated) feat of conquering both the 400m and 800m finals in the 1976 Olympics. The scene shows him winning an 800m race in England in 1977. (Photograph by Mike Street, courtesy of Track & Field News.)

running history. "I respect no runner," he said after Montreal, and perhaps none respected him, but many, many feared him.

Juantorena went on to run the anchor leg of the men's 1600-meter relay in 44.7 seconds, the second-fastest lap run in the race. (Jamaica's Seymour Newman, far better rested than the kingly Cuban, ran 43.8.) El Caballo's fatigued but excellent effort lent credence to a statement he made in later years: "Under any condition I can run 400 easy. I can go without training for three months and run a good 400. It's hard for me to think about the 800, about running 2 laps."

Mac Wilkins, America's gold medalist in the discus, announced after his victory that he had won the medal for himself, not for the United States. Wilkins later explained: "My intention was to shake up people back home, to get them to realize things here in Montreal didn't run smoothly and that the athletes were caught up in a bureaucracy at a time their minds should have been free to concentrate on athletics, not USOC bungling." The internal and external politics of international athletics, combined with totally state-supported athletic programs in Eastern bloc nations and a relatively poor American showing, brought U.S. athletes' tempers out into the open at Montreal.

The third running doublist at Montreal was the Soviet Union's Tatyana Kazankina, who swept both the 800 meters and metric mile. In the 800, she bided her time for a lap and a half, running sixth at that point and allowing East Germany's Anita Weiss to take the pace. Coming out of the last turn she turned it on, crossing the line with both a gold medal and world record, 1:54.9. Bulgaria's Nikolina Shtereva came second in 1:55.4, and East Germany's Elfi Zinn finished third in 1:55.6, 1/10-second ahead of the wilted Weiss.

In the 1500, another rabbit emerged in the person of Finland's Nina Holman, who took the field out in a 68.7-second lap and a 2:18.9 first 800 meters. The East German team, represented in this race by Gunhild Hoffmeister and Ulrike Klapezynski, stormed past as Italian Gabriella Dorio tried to hold the lead, succeeding for 300 meters. Then, again from out of the ruck, Kazankina came on, passing first Klapezynski and, 50 meters from the tape, Hoffmeister, winning in 4:05.5 to Hoffmeister's 4:06 flat. Klapezynski nabbed the bronze, ½-second in front of 800-meter silver medalist Shtereva. Kazankina's last lap took 56.9 seconds, and the world-record holder in the event (in 3:56.0) said after: "I think I could have gone under 4 minutes if necessary." It wasn't.

The only woman to challenge Kazankina's glory at Montreal was one competing in her final Olympics, Poland's ageless Irena Szewinska, who set a world record in winning the 400 meters in 49.29. Christana Brehmer of East Germany finished second, in 50.51, and her teammate, Ellen Streidt, finished third, in 50.55. Juantorena had a 0.14-second margin of safety in his 400-meter victory; Szewinska's 1.22-seconds breathing space was nearly incredible. Even more remarkable was the record she was leaving behind her. Running under her maiden name of Kirszenstein in the 1964 Tokyo Games, she had won the silver medal in the 200 meters, been a member of the gold-medal-winning 400-meter relay team, and taken another silver medal in the long jump. In the 1968 Olympics, Mrs. Szewinska, now married to her coach, hit bronze in the 100 meters and gold in the 200. In 1972, she won a bronze in the 200. At the time of her Olympic retirement, Irena Szewinska's total of seven medals accounted for one-third of all Poland's women's track and field medals. She was arguably the most versatile woman athlete ever seen in the Olympics.

Annegret Richter of West Germany beat favored Renate Stecher in Stecher's unfruitful defense of her 100-meter crown. The West German ran 11-flat; the East German, 11.13. West Germany's Inge Helten finished third in 11.17.

The national order was the exact reverse in the women's 200-meter final. The East Germans took gold with Baerbel Eckert's victorious 22.37, an Olympic record, while the West Germans picked up a silver, courtesy of Annegret Richter's 22.39. Husky Renate Stecher, described by some journalists as "built more like a thrower than a runner," added a bronze medal to her collection with her 22.47 effort.

The East German juggernaut rolled through the women's 400-meter and 600-meter relays. In the 400, the East Germans took the gold with an Olympic record of 42.55. West Germany came second, in 42.59, and the Soviets third, in 43.09. (The U.S. team finished seventh, in 43.35.) In the 4-lapper, the East Germans set a world record with their triumphant 3:19.2, besting the Americans' 3:22.8 silver-medal effort and the Soviets' 3:24.2 drive for the bronze.

John Walker's drive for the 1500 meters' gold almost cost him his goal. He ran his qualifying heat in 3:36.9, breaking the unofficial Olympic record for metric mile qualifying heats set in the heat just preceding his. The short-lived record was 3:37.9; the fellow who set it was Steve Ovett. The other milers at Montreal also went too fast in their prelims; many, such as Ovett, squandered too much stuff and failed to make it through the semifinals into the main event. To add to the burden on the milers' sore muscles, it rained on the day of the final, drenching the track.

Walker had been busy since bombing out in the 800. He said later: "Being beaten in the 800 heats was a blessing in disguise. When that happened I went and sat down with my coach and talked about it. I decided I needed to work on my speed." The large miler's natural speed was inhibited by a case of Achilles tendinitis; one presumes he ran his sharpening exercises in extreme pain. John Walker was a man under intense pressure at Montreal. After, he commented: "I *had* to win that [1500 meter] gold medal, healthy or not; otherwise, my world record would have meant nothing. People would have criticized me for setting it. They'd have said I peaked too early."

Few, if any, knew of Walker's tendinitis, but many wondered at the way he ran the final. Cordner Nelson wrote in *Track & Field News* that Walker "ran like a novice." The pace for the 1500 was exceedingly slow: a first lap of 62.5, a second of 60.7, and a third of 58, aggregating a 3-lap split of 3:01.2. Ireland's Eamonn Coghlan (who virtually lived in the United States), started pushing the tempo after the first lap and a half, because he and Walker were in the same boat: "pure" milers (as attested by Walker's failure in the 800) up against a field of half-mile specialists. The endurance men had to run the speed out of the sprinters' legs. Heads nodded when Coghlan went out front to make the other runners hurt, but heads were also scratched when Walker did not do the same. Years later, Walker admitted: "I could have gone to the front and made it hard and fast all the way. That would have put a strain on those half-mile kickers, but it also would have been tough on me, so I decided to gamble."

At 100 meters into the last lap, it was time to call in Walker's gamble. Who held good cards, and who had been bluffing? Amazingly, it turned out Walker held good cards . . . and had Lady Luck on his shoulder, too. Taking over from Coghlan crossing the line for the third time, Walker had a 2-meter lead on the fast men in the field. Rick Wohlhuter and Ivo Van Damme both seemed in excellent medalist positions, owning more fast-twitch muscle than Walker. They proved it. Van Damme sprinted the final 200 meters in 25.3, Walker in 25.4; but the quick Kiwi ran the last lap in 52.7 seconds, and the ultimate 300 meters in 37.9! (Peter Snell had run the same final 300 in 38.6 to take his Tokyo gold. Snell was hardly slow.) Walker hit the tape in 3:39.2, the slowest Olympic metric mile champ in 20 years. Belgian Van Damme got a 1500 silver to go with his 800 meters', clocking 3:39.3. West Germany's Paul-Heinze Wellmann received the same time as Van Damme, but settled for the bronze, as he jumped headfirst through the air to nose out a tiring Coghlan.

The final Montreal running event, the marathon, proved nearly a great one for the U.S. team. Bill Rodgers took the field out at a smart pace, clipping 5 kilometers off in 15:19. Nine other runners paced just behind him; among them Frank Shorter, Jerome Drayton, Karel Lismont, Lasse Viren, and Waldemar Cierpinski, a former steeplechaser who had run his first marathon two years previously in 2:20 and had elected to change events (or, more likely, was told he had elected to change events by East German sports officials). Rodgers pulled the pack through 10K in 30:48, nursing an injured foot and starting to feel the strain of it. By 20,000 meters Rodgers had fallen back slightly and Shorter had taken over the nominal lead. By 25K fast Frank had pulled out 30 meters on the field, but by 30K Cierpinski had caught him and surged away! He ran 13 seconds clear of the American by 35,000 meters. It was raining; Cierpinski liked running in the rain. He pulled away even more. America's Don Kardong charged ahead of Lismont, moving into bronze medal territory. Lasse Viren held on in fifth. The race was ending, and Kardong got a cramp. Cierpinski hit the stadium and heard his national anthem playing, not in anticipation of his victory, but to celebrate the East German women's 1600-meter relay world record. Cierpinski crossed the line about the time Lismont passed Kardong to secure the final medal; Cierpinski crossed in 2:09:55, 2:16.2 under Bikila's Olympic best, then kept on trucking for another lap, seeing the "one more lap" sign hanging out for second man Shorter and thinking it for himself. Shorter took the silver in 2:10:45.8; Lismont, the bronze, in 2:11:12.6; and the unfortunate Kardong came forth in fourth, 2:11:15.8. Nearly 2 minutes behind the American came the fifth finisher, in 2:13:10.8—Lasse Viren.

A rumor circulated after Montreal that Cierpinski's win had been worth a bonus of 10,000 Deutsche marks. A fact also circulated after the Games. The ITA track circuit had offered John Walker more than $280,000 to turn pro for the next four years. ITA made similarly lucrative offers to Rod Dixon and Dick Quax. All the New Zealand Olympians turned the ITA down, possibly an indication of how much more they expected to make on the amateur circuit, receiving payments under the table. The refusal spelled doom for the ITA idea. The balance of ITA meets for 1976 were cancelled after the Olympics. Founder Mike O'Hara, pretending only to "curtail" his circuit, commented: "The relevant gold medal winners [from Montreal] and many amateur track athletes seemingly enjoy the best of two worlds— that of receiving high per-meet expenses and remuneration and retaining their amateur status as well."

John Walker's future was not rosy after the 1976 Olympics, appearances notwithstanding. First, the Organization of African Unity pressured European meet directors not to accept New Zealand athletes. Bad political feelings die hard in the wonderful world of amateur sport. As leverage, the OAU could either offer meet directors outstanding Africans in virtually all events in exchange for cooperation, or they could withhold top black stars in punishment. Walker lost a chance to race at Zurich as a result of such pressure.

Second, Walker was badly injured, nearly crippled; not tendinitis, but swelling in his mighty calves restricted blood flow in his legs after 30 minutes of running (one of the rare cases on record). Turning from one surgeon to another, Walker would not regain his form until the end of the decade.

The New York Marathon gained a new form in 1976. It left the confines of Central Park and ran through all five city boroughs. The new route made the course far more interesting and popular, but obviously invalidated comparisons between times set on the new venue and those established on the former course. Recovered from his Montreal injuries, Bill Rodgers ran 2:10:09 on what most observers felt was a "slow" course (due to its many turns and the deteriorating condition of New York street surfaces), received a converted bowling trophy as his award, and found the police had towed away his Volkswagen Beetle while he was racing. Miki Gorman won the women's race, clocking 2:39:11 at age 41, leading 57 other women across the line. A total of 2,090 runners took the gun in the 1976 New York Marathon, testifying to the sport's blossoming popularity. In the 1975 New York Marathon, 535 had started.

Rodgers was super hot on the roads in 1977, but not hot enough in the Boston Marathon. Locked in a duel with Jerome Drayton, but drained by the 72-degree heat, he withdrew at the top of Heartbreak Hill, while Drayton cruised home in 2:14:46. Miki Gorman continued winning the big ones, claiming Beantown in 2:48:33. She was now 42 years old! The qualifying restrictions tightened that year in the Boston Marathon. To run in 1977, a man younger than 40 must have completed another full marathon in less than 3 hours. Women and men over 40 ("masters") were required to tender sub-3:30 credentials to B.A.A. officials before stepping to the line.

France's Chantal Langlace took the women's world's best marathon time down to 2:35:15.4 in a marathon at Oyarzun on May 1, 1977.

Billy Rodgers won the Falmouth Road Race for the second time in August of that year, taking over a minute off Frank Shorter's course record of 33:36 by hitting the wire in 32:23. Defending champion Shorter came fifth in 33:34.

The Falmouth Road Race typified the direction of the running boom in the decade. In 1976, 2,090 runners started at Falmouth (the same number of runners ran the 1976 New York Marathon, but had 20 more miles of room); in 1977, the figure was 2,850—for a 7.1 mile race, quite a population density. Falmouth race officials do not start accepting entries until mid-April. In 1977, the entries were closed by May 1. (In 1981, they closed 2 days after opening.) The quality of the Falmouth field counted just as much as the quantity in terms of pointing running's historical direction in 1977. International level competitors abounded on the front line, but none drew more attention than Rodgers or Shorter. Rodgers had captured the public's eye with his 1975 Boston Marathon victory and modest manner. Shorter had done the same, but with his Munich gold-medal effort and aggressive running-gear marketing. The representatives of the popular press, casting about for superficially interesting story "angles," began ballyhooing a Shorter/Rodgers rivalry, simplifying matters by painting Rodgers as the humble road runner and Shorter as the sophisticated trackster. To add to the essentially contrived issue (both Rodgers and Shorter denied ever feeling a rivalry toward each other beyond what world-class athletes commonly feel in competition), Shorter injured a foot early in 1977, allowing some journalists to play down any Rodgers victories as besmirched because against an unfit opponent. The Rodgers/Shorter head-to-heads between 1976 and 1978 were neither more nor less than any of the other great match-ups in running history: Gehrmann/Wilt, Ryun/Liquori, or Anderson/Haegg. As with the other great match-ups, they produced superb athletic efforts by both runners, and the sport in general benefited. One decries oversimplification, especially when visited by sportswriters who know not the difference between a spike and a sprint, but the fact remains that the "confrontations" between Frank Shorter and Bill Rodgers focused a lot of attention on running, creating interest in a wide audience. It was an important point in the development of public participation in contemporary American road running.

The Greater Boston Track Club baptized its Freedom Trail Road Race in September, 1977, an 8-mile run through the scenic and historical wonders of both Boston and Cambridge conceived by running "guru" Tommy Leonard. Not astonishingly, GBTC member Bill Rodgers won the inaugural running. Very astonishingly, the members of the GBTC had, through their personal contacts, assembled a field that would normally have cost a race director an estimated $120,000 in under-the-table payments. GBTC paid a total of $10,000 to the entire field. Some of the athletes running the inaugural Freedom Trail, in addition to Rodgers, were GBTC members Randy Thomas, Vin Fleming, Danny Dillon, and Mique Roche; Gary Bjorklund and Mike Slack (the two of them collectively known as "the Minnesota Twins"); 1976 Boston Marathon champion Jack Fultz, and perennial Boston Marathon standout Tom Fleming; Jerome Drayton, who won the 1977 Boston Marathon; Olympians Frank Shorter and Don Kardong; 1976 Boston Marathon winner Kim Merritt and schoolgirl Lynn Jennings, who would become Bonne Bell National Champion later in 1977. The Boston College marching band also showed up . . . to play music, not to run. As a sign of the running boom, the GBTC exploded from 37 to 400 members during the Freedom Trail festivities. Someone had decided to print a GBTC membership application on the back of the Freedom Trail entry blank, and—to Coach Squires's horror—hundreds of hobbyist runners accepted the apparent invitation. Other elite American running clubs were experiencing similar growing pains at the time.

Forced to sit out the previous Olympic year by injuries, Marty Liquori was back on the 5,000 meters' track in 1977. He was crowned AAU 5K king at the organization's outdoor championship meet, then went to Europe and ran 3:38.6 in a metric mile "sharpening" race, demonstrating he hadn't lost his miler's speed or killer's instincts. The speedy businessman next conquered Henry Rono, Dick Quax, Miruts Yifter, and Samson Kimombwa in Zurich's World Class Night 5,000-meter run, where Liquori not only surprised alleged pundits but also set a new American 5K record of 13:16. Liquori lowered the mark to 13:15.1 eleven days later at the inaugural World Cup meet, but also lost to the blazing Yifter. Nonetheless, *Track & Field News* ranked him Number One in the world at the 5K for 1977.

Liquori slipped to world Number Two in 1978, but claimed both the AAU 3-mile indoor title and the AAU outdoor 5K top prize. In 1979, the 30-year-old former miler decided to prepare seriously for his final Olympics, the 1980 Moscow Games. World politics intervened, almost unquestionably taking motivation out of Liquori's buildup. He competed in the U.S. "Olympic Trials" at Eugene, Oregon, in 1980, and finished last in the 5,000 final. In a gesture of retirement, America's first successful running businessman pulled off his track spikes and threw them into the jammed, hollering stands. Perhaps he would have rather heaved them at the USOC instead.

On September 10, 1977, West Germany's Christa Vahlensiek staged a raging battle with her countrywoman, Manuela Angenvoorth, in the West German marathon championship held in Berlin. Vahlensiek dropped the women's world marathon best down to 2:34:47.5, pulling away from Angenvoorth at 33K after a shoulder-to-shoulder race till that point. Angenvoorth finished second in 2:38:09.4, but may have been consoled by her husband's finish in the simultaneously run men's race. Paul Angenvoorth claimed third spot in 2:15:42. The women's marathon best time had tumbled precipitously in but a few years. Experts predicted no more than 4 minutes could be cut from Vahlensiek's mark. One would have thought experts would have abandoned such predictions with the advent of Roger Bannister.

Shortly after Vahlensiek startled the world, American author James F. Fixx published his *Complete Book of Running*, his own svelte legs gracing the jacket and his catchy prose caressing the reader's eye. Ostensibly a methods book, Fixx's *Complete Book of Running* in fact proved more effective as inspiration. An author who truly understood running *and* the demands of popular writing had finally come on the scene, and the entire sport profited. *The Complete Book of Running*, filled with anecdotes, humor, and sound advice, appeared just as the public began looking for such a comprehensive, popular, work. Jim Fixx probably added some several million new runners to America's athletic population, as had Dr. Ken Cooper and Frank Shorter, at similar critical junctures in the sport's development, before him.

Bill Rodgers called the Fukuoka race "the Holy Grail, the Super Bowl of marathoning," and he won it in 1977, bouncing back strongly from his fast run in the 1977 New York Marathon, which he won for the second straight time in 2:11:28. Miki Gorman took her second straight New York title as well, running 2:43:10. Four-thousand-twenty-three people had run the New York Marathon. Considerably fewer (about 80) competed in the elite Fukuoka race. Rodgers battled with Soviet ace Leonid Moiseyev and outstanding Japanese athlete Shigeru So for the first half of the event, then pulled away strongly by the 30-kilometer mark, winning in 2:10:55.3, the world's fastest marathon time for that year. Rodger's New York clocking was the world's second-fastest marathon time for 1977!

With interest in marathons growing like mushrooms in a rain forest, it was heartening to long-time American road runners to see the initiation of a road race at a shorter, but still standard, distance. In February, 1978, the Gasparilla Distance Classic went to the starting line; 15 kilometers of road racing on the flat streets in and around Tampa, Florida. It was won by Bill

Atlanta's Gayle Barron is on her way to victory in the 1978 Boston Marathon, where she ran 2:44:52. Her husband Ben currently coordinates the Bonne Bell 10K National Series for Women. (Photograph courtesy of *The Boston Herald American*.)

Rodgers in 44:29. As an index of running's burgeoning popularity, the field at Gasparilla grew from 1,000 to 2,000 to 9,000 in the first three years of its running.

Bill Rodgers became the first man in history to win marathoning's "Triple Crown" when he claimed the 1978 Boston Marathon in 2:10:13, the first of three Boston wins in a row for the GBTC flash. Boston Billy did not breeze to victory, however. Finishing second, in 2:10:15, was Texas seminary student Jeff Wells, who had dedicated his race to the Lord and run the second half of the course in history's fastest time to date. Atlanta's Gayle Barron led all other women over the line in her personal best clocking of 2:44:52.

Bill Rodgers patently stood as the most capable marathon runner of his era, but his conquest of the "Triple Crown" was a feat that could not possibly have been accomplished before 1976. The three races in the informal championship are the marathons at Boston, New York, and Fukuoka. Bill Rodgers was the first, and to date sole, man to claim all three in a row. The New York Marathon did not emerge as a world-class race until it left Central Park in 1976, and it was at least partly due to the public interest generated by celebrities such as Rodgers that inspired the growth of the New York Marathon's horizons. It is not unfair to conclude Rodgers won the title he had helped create.

He came from Kenya and he ran like a god. He was Henry Rono, a man whose interest in running derived from the demands of his native culture, not from the spotlight of American media attention. During a period of 80 days in 1978, he set four world records at four different distances: 3,000 meters (7:32.1), the steeplechase (8:08.4), 5,000 meters (13:08.4), and 10,000 meters (27:22.4). None had ever approached such a concentratedly awesome performance any time before, not Ron Clarke, not Nurmi.

Henry Rono was born Kipwambok Rono to the Nandi tribe of Kenya's Great Rift Valley in 1953. Kipchoge Keino hailed from the region, as did Samson Kimombwa, the man whose 10K world record Rono broke. Running was part of the Nandi tribe culture, necessary for getting to and from school, tending crops, and herding cattle. Rono was moved to consider competitive running by the example of Kip Keino, who lived in a neighboring village. He heard Keino give an address in 1971, and that is when he decided to be a runner. Rono did little with his motivation, however. When he was graduated from high school in 1975, he laced up army boots instead of racing spikes. In contrast to Nurmi and Zátopek who flourished as distance runners due to their military careers, Rono quickly decided he hated the service. The Kenyan Army, however, gave him his first taste of competition. He learned he liked the steeplechase, much as he disliked the military. His best army steeple time was 8:29. His military running resulted in a berth on the Kenyan Olympic team, an opportunity squelched by the OAU-led boycott of Montreal. The Olympic disappointment counted as but a minor problem for Rono; he had already decided his future lay not in the army but at Washington State University in America, about whose track and field program he had heard from the brother of a Kenyan hurdler then competing for the school.

WSU coach John Chaplin's policy was to win track meets for his employer, and he and several other American coaches had taken the controversial approach of recruiting the best possible talent, regardless of age or national origin. Henry Rono of Kenya, 25 years old, became a WSU freshman in the fall of 1976. Almost immediately he won the NCAA cross-country championship, and Coach Chaplin, with several world-record holders already on his team, predicted big things for the WSU frosh.

Rono was injured for much of 1977, but managed to eke out times of 13:22 for 5,000 meters and 27:37 for 10,000 meters. He also repeated as NCAA cross-country champ. He started off 1978 by beating Bill Rodgers in the San Blas (Puerto Rico) Half Marathon on February 5, running to victory in 1:04:46. Turning to the track season, Rono warmed up with a 13:31 effort for 5K, then ran 13:21.8 *in a blizzard!* The Kenyan prized the 5K event above all others. He observed: "It's a meeting of a short- and long-distance race. It requires the most effort for me. I also think it is the most beautiful of races. For my 5,000-meter record, I had a secret plan. I felt that day I just wanted to go out smoothly and easily and only then would I run faster and faster."

A certain poetry infused both Rono's running and his thinking. On April 8, one week after racing through the blinding snow in his last 5K run, Rono took 4.5 seconds off Dick Quax's 5-kilometer world record at Berkeley, Cali-

Henry Rono of Kenya, one of the most awesome long-distance runners of the present era, set four world records in 80 days in 1978. He plans eventually to run under 27 minutes for 10K. (Photograph courtesy of the Washington State University.)

fornia, running 13:08.4. On May 13, 1978, Rono went to the Northwest Relays held at Seattle, Washington. Just before he ran the steeplechase, he told Coach Chaplin he was going to break the world record—somewhat of a surprise announcement to the coach. Rono took 2.6 seconds off Anders Garderud's world mark in the event, clocking 8:05.4. On June 11, 1978, Henry Rono raced the 10,000 meters in a meet at Vienna, Austria, taking 5 seconds off Samson Kimombwa's world record as he ran 27:22.5. On June 27, 1978, Rono ran the 3-kilometer event held at Oslo, Norway, in 7:32.1, removing 3.1 seconds from Brendan Foster's world standard. Then he rested.

Chaplin, rather stunned by Rono's drives, commented: "Henry is the most intense runner I've ever coached." Intensity seemed the key to Rono's performances. Some of it must have come naturally to him. After setting his world records, the great Kenyan said: "As far as I know there aren't any other runners who run like me. Maybe one will show up. If I see him, if I can listen to the way he talks, I'll know if he's better than me. I don't have to see him train. All I need is to hear him talk. Then I'll know how he feels, how intense he is. If he's more intense than me, then he'll beat me." Yet it clearly required some physical gift to run as Rono ran, running the second 1500 meters of his world record 3K in 3:42.6, for example. While some might classify Rono's approach to running with Percy Cerutty's—that is, an emphasis on psychological attitude over scientific training schedules— some evidence suggests Rono may have demarked a new age in racing and training. Although Coach Chaplin carefully gave Rono (and his other standout WSU runners) full credit for victory, Chaplin's interval training gave Rono the opportunity to meld his mind and body. Rono made this important statement: "Before I came to America, I knew nothing about interval training. I learned it is more mental than physiological. The muscles do not change when you do interval work, but the mind changes very drastically to accept pain. If you train to absorb the pain, you are never going to be good, but if you train to *break* the pain, then you go into a new level. I learned the pain; so, in 1978, I worked hard and got the records."

No body could stand such intense effort constantly, and, in 1979, Rono essentially disappeared from the track world, resting and pursuing his college degree in industrial psychology. He would return, perhaps the closest heir yet to Paavo Nurmi; for, although Rono put his faith in his mind instead of in the beautiful machine that was his body, his attitude came straight from Peerless Paavo: "Many runners worry about who is in the race, or they think about the time they must run to win. I only try to run as fast as I am capable—nothing less."

Runners in the late 1970s came in all levels of ability and attitude, and those less elite than Henry Rono needed places to race. In August, 1978, another excellent megarace emerged: America's Finest City Half-Marathon. It took athletes on a scenic tour from Cabrillo National Monument to Balboa Park in San Diego, California, and offered among its amenities physicians and podiatrists at each of the four aid stations en route.

Another outstanding American 15 kilometer race was founded in June of 1978 in the form of the Cascade Run-Off in Portland, Oregon, won by Gary Bjorklund in 44:06. Although its three aid stations boasted no podiatrists, each was staffed by at least one doctor and one nurse, and there was a ready ambulance on the course for the severely distressed.

At least one athlete needed considerable medical aid in the 1978 Falmouth Road Race, held on August 20 that year. The race had grown in quantity: 3,400 runners. It had also bloomed in quality: 9 Olympians, 11 sub-4 milers, and 16 AAU national champions. Many predicted the first mile would pass in 4:10 or less, with the final one in about the same time. Runners with great endurance but relatively little leg speed, such as Rodgers or Salazer, would have no prayer in the face of the milers' kicks . . . which is precisely why, when the speed men rested after the first mile burst, the King and the Rookie both kept running feverishly. In Salazar's case, he hung on rather too feverishly. Refusing to lose contact with Rodgers, the gutty Salazar fell victim to heat prostration in the final mile. Running 2 steps behind Rodgers until then, the Rookie faded to tenth by the finish. Alberto did not recall crossing the finish line. He was delirious, his brain temperature well over 100 degrees. Contrary to Falmouth legend, Salazar did not receive premature last rites, but he did exclaim, as medical personnel packed his wracked body in one hundred pounds of ice: "I don't want a doctor! I want a priest!" He recovered quickly, fortunately. Many observers noted Salazar's Falmouth effort as an indication of his inexperience, but the most sagacious among them also noted it as a demonstration of his miraculous courage and will to prevail. Zátopek and Snell were similar.

The 1978 New York Marathon deserved a special place in running history for three reasons, only two of them apparent to the press at the time. First, Norway's Grete Waitz, running in her first marathon, lowered the world women's best for the distance to 2:32:30. Second, Bill Rodgers claimed his third straight New York runathon. Kept hidden from the press, for understandable reasons, was a new facet to the New York Marathon, one suggested to race director Fred Lebow by a top international distance coach: predetermined under-the-table payments to athletes on the basis of finishing position.

Even the casual observer of road racing in 1978 knew top competitors were profiting from so-called expense payments, but not even the athletes knew exactly what anyone (other than themselves) was receiving. The deliberately obscure system of under-the-table payoffs gave race directors enormous bargaining latitude, almost always to what the athletes felt was their detriment. In most major races where such payments were made, the dollar figures were negotiated before race day, leaving runners who soundly trounced others who received more money than they feeling used by and resentful of the system. The promoters of the "new" New York Marathon sincerely wanted to elevate their race to the level of an international classic, and quickly. The new route and other amenities moved it far in the desired direction. By establishing a definite schedule of clandestine payments reckoned on the basis of finishing position, the New York organizers removed a lot of athlete anxiety, making the race extremely attractive to highly ranked runners. The payment schedule inaugurated in 1978 awarded $10,000 to the first-place man, going down a sliding scale to the eighth-place man, who was offered $800. (It must be emphasized that the athletes were not forced to accept the money. History does not record who besmirched his or her amateur status in the New York Marathon.) In 1978, the first-place woman was offered $5,000, with another sliding scale going down to the fifth-place female, who could collect $500. Less money was offered women runners because they competed in a smaller, presumably less demanding, field than did the men. History also notes that some shoe companies and other running-connected enterprises offered bonuses to "their" runner who performed well at New York and elsewhere. One athlete who did not win at New York in a later year, but who placed well up in the field and also set a national record for his/her sex collected a total of $12,000 for that one race, including bonus payments.

Information about running and money would not emerge until long after the 1978 New York Marathon, but data on wonderwoman Grete Waitz was instantly forthcoming—and demanded. The 25-year-old schoolteacher had been competing on the international track scene since 1972, when she ran the Olympic metric mile. Her personal best at the distance, 4:04, was good enough for a Norwegian national record, but too slow to compete with runners from Eastern bloc countries. The standard track distance at which Waitz's endurance made her more competitive, 3,000 meters, was not an

Olympic event, and she probably lacked the speed to win a medal even if it were. After being shut out of the medals at the Montreal Olympics, Waitz temporarily quit running, but started training hard again in 1977. (Her defeat was especially bitter in the light of her being ranked Number One in the world at 1500 meters going into the 1976 Games.) She struck gold in the 1977 World Cup 3,000, running 8:43.5, then drove the mark down to 8:36.8 for the year's fastest clocking, resulting in her world Number One ranking among women at that distance. Then, on March 25, 1977, Grete Waitz entered and won her first World Cross-Country Championship, a title she has since defended successfully three times to date. Although Waitz arrived in New York a marathon and road-racing novice, track experts predicted she had "found" her event. Christa Vahlensiek's coach predicted, in front of Vahlensiek, that "If Grete Waitz finishes, she will win." Waitz's extraordinary endurance, combined with her years of training for international *track* competition, brought a new level of talent and expertise to women's road racing. Patti Catalano, the preeminent American woman road racer of the era, said of Waitz: "She's making girls realize they can't work out like girls. They have to work out like athletes."

Working out hard as a track athlete often worked out well for runners' finances in 1978. European meet promoters offered middle- and long-distance Olympic or European champions as much as $2,000 to appear at a meet and run one race. Internationally ranked non-champion runners commanded between $400 and $800 to run a distance track race on the same circuit. Unfortunately, only the male athletes received such stipends. Spectators seemed to regard the faster times set by men as of a higher athletic order than the women's equally severe but less speedy efforts. Meet officials saw no sense in offering money to athletes who did not draw the fans. The

Jan Merrill, one of the greatest milers in American history is here shown on her way to victory and a world record for 10,000 meters run on the road in the 1981 Bonne Bell Championship Race at Boston. Merrill races no more than two road events annually, and has yet to lose a 10K contest. (Photograph courtesy of Harry Werlin.)

most a top woman distance runner could expect in 1978 was to have her real expenses covered. The situation was even worse for American women track stars. By 1978, only three Americans could convince European meet directors to cover travel and lodging costs, and they were the country's top three milers: Francie Larrieu, Jan Merrill, and Mary Decker. The only thing a woman runner could expect to receive under the table when competing in a track meet was a game of footsie.

It was cool and drizzly in Boston on Patriots' Day, 1979, so Bill Rodgers wore his trademark white gloves to keep his hands warm and his non-trademark wool cap to keep his head warm; the hat perfectly reflected Rodgers' characteristic sense of whimsy (in which respect he paralleled Emil Zátopek)—sewn onto it was the figure of cartoonist Charles Schultz's beloved creation, Snoopy the Dog. Another Rodgers characteristic manifested itself during the race proper: cool courage. Japan, hoping to restore the glory of the Rising Sun in Boston Marathon history, had sent to Boston a runner Rodgers himself called the "wunderkind of marathoning": 22-year-old Toshihiko Seko. As had Zátopek in the 1952 Olympic marathon, Seko carefully stalked the pre-race favorite, Rodgers, during the competition. Rodgers, Seko, and Gary Bjorklund ran together for some 15 miles, then Bjorklund fell back, calling out: "2:08! Go for it!" to the departing duo. Bjorklund sensed that if Clayton's marathon world best were to be bettered, a matchup between the men who were probably the two greatest marathoners of their age would produce it. Then came the Newton hills, which none had ever run as fast as Rodgers. Agonizingly, Billy White Gloves inched away from the Japanese track standout. At 20 miles, cresting Heartbreak Hill, Rodgers finally broke contact and pulled decidedly ahead. Seko, who had run implacably till that point, indulged himself in one human gesture: he puckishly stuck out his tongue at Rodgers's disappearing back. Boston Billy hit the Pru Center tape in 2:09:27, lowering both his personal and the American best for the marathon. Seko came second in 2:10:12, the fastest runner-up time in Boston history, and the third fastest ever clocked on the course. In third place came Rodgers's Greater Boston teammate, Bob Hodge; in sixth came Rodgers's and Hodge's teammate, Randy Thomas; in tenth came Rodgers's, Hodge's and Thomas's teammate, Dickie Mahoney: a great day for the Greater Boston Track Club. Another track-trained athlete, Joan Benoit of Cape Elizabeth, Maine, came first among the women in the new female Boston best of 2:35:15. She wore a Red Sox cap and not merely as protection from the weather. She said later she had worn it to remind herself not to get overconfident and blow the race, as the Red Sox annually do in pursuit of the baseball championship. (One of the more colorful women road runners in the late 1970s, Benoit had a favorite prank of biting people on the rump when least expected. As Julie Shea observed at the 1980 World Cross-Country Championships in Paris: "It's time to leave a party quick when Joanie starts biting people on the bottom.")

Joan Benoit won the 1979 Boston Marathon. This photo shows her after winning a 3K road race (in 9:50) at Syracuse, New York, on April 26, 1980. It was her first race after an appendectomy and having a cyst removed from her knee. (Photograph courtesy of Joan Benoit.)

New qualifying regulations at Boston in 1979 meant many runners' hopes for competing in the marathon had been blown. Men under age 40 had to run another marathon under 2:50 to be able to run Boston officially that year. Women, and masters men, had to have run another marathon under 3:20 to qualify. Many were unhappy, but experts agree that the qualifying restrictions on the Boston Marathon did far more than keep the B.A.A. field of manageable size. The restrictions directly contributed to the rising overall quality of American marathon running, because "average" runners now had concrete incentive to improve. Running history owes a large debt to race director Will Cloney for remaining firm in the face of often vituperative arguments that he eliminate qualifying standards. America is a healthier and faster nation as a result.

On April 26, 1979, Gerard Nijboer of Holland ran the Amsterdam Marathon in 2:09:01, giving the 24-year-old public relations agent history's second fastest marathon time. Nijboer had not heard his split times along the way, a result of logistical problems, and was astonished when told his finishing time. He said after: "My first thought was, 'I'll bet the course was short,' but I talked to the race organizers and they got me a letter of certification. The course was remeasured three times after the race, and reporters were invited so they could see it done. There's not 1 meter wrong; it just couldn't be more precise." Unlike Derek Clayton's Antwerp Marathon, no doubt surrounded the validity of the course Nijboer had completed. Further, Nijboer's uncontroversial clocking lent plausibility to Clayton's best, for it was no longer so nearly incredibly faster than anyone else's.

In July, 1979, English 800-meter specialist Sebastian Coe produced a time for the mile run that *was* nearly incredibly faster than anyone else's—3:48.95 (officially recognized as 3:49.0, according to IAAF regulations). Coe held the world record for 800 meters, 1:42.4, but few reckoned him as a miler . . . other than mile record holder John Walker. Before the race, held at the fabulous Bislett track in Oslo, Norway, and known as the Golden Mile, Walker observed: "Most fast 800-meter men are like Juantorena: quarter-milers moving up; but Coe has all the attributes of a pure miler. He ran that record 800 [also on the Bislett track] on strength, not speed. He is the only man in the field capable of the record, so I bloody well hope something happens to slow him down."

Nothing did, and none could reasonably have expected a slow pace in a race including not only Coe and Walker but also Eamonn Coghlan (world indoor mile record holder, in 3:52.6), Steve Scott (the American who bid fair to surpass Jim Ryun), Dr. Thomas Wessinghage (Germany's European 1500-meter champion), and Dave Moorcroft (England's gold medalist in the 1979 Commonwealth Games metric mile). Other athletes of similar fleetness filled out the field and, with no championship resting on the line, there was no incentive to run tactically, every motive to race brilliantly.

Coe raced, taking the lead for the first 100 meters to avoid being shunted in the first turn, then pulled aside to let designated pacemaker Steve Lacy, of the University of Wisconsin, charge through the first lap faster than 57 seconds. Scott raced, hanging on Lacy's tail, going through the 800 meters in tandem with him at 1:54.0. Coe was ½-second astern. Five hundred meters from home Coe pulled even with Scott, then took the lead, striking 1200 meters in 2:52.0. John Walker, running in fifth place, heard Coe's split and began mentally to prepare himself to lose his world record. Coe ran on, alone, parting the tape in 3:48.95. Steve Scott came second, just missing Jim Ryun's American record with his 3:51.11. John Walker finished sixth, in 3:52.9. Perhaps the most startling statistic of all was the time for tenth man Ken Hall of Australia—3:55.3. It was the deepest, fastest field in the history of the mile. (John Walker was still recovering from surgery on his legs. Although he had begun to train normally late in 1978, he could not be considered back on normal form by the time of the Golden Mile; but Walker's complete return to form in no way necessarily guaranteed him victory over Coe.)

None run with him. The front runner runs alone.

Craig Virgin runs into the wind in the AAU 10,000 meter championship, grateful for its challenge, excelling as he accelerates. He asked the others before the start to mount an assault on the American record. They refused, noting the wind, and now he runs 67-second laps alone, far ahead of them, perhaps far above them. "You have to shoot for the stars if you want to hit the moon," he says.

Two pushed at his heels for six laps. One has dropped out, the other will finish unplaced. Virgin has only himself for company, and the wind. 3,000 meters pass in 8:11.4, 5,000 in 13:44.9. Pictures of success pass through Virgin's imagination. He and the other men seem in two separate races, which, in fact, they are. Excellence is lonely. The announcer screams his time; the experienced Virgin runs his 25th lap in 61.3, a wolf who keeps the sheep from closing. He takes the tape savagely, a thousand-dollar smile, flecked with saliva, beaming. He has run 27:39.4, breaking the former record, setting a new American standard. Later he will say: "What makes a champion? Consistency, as far as being there race after race; competitiveness, a fighter, he didn't give up until the race was over; sportsmanship; resiliency; courage." He is the American champion. He is the front runner who runs alone.

Craig Virgin was not the only athlete to set an American 10K record at the 1979 AAU outdoor championship meet in Walnut, California, but the other broken record made the St. Louis T.C. speedster's solo effort even more impressive. High-school senior Mary Shea went bare knuckles with Joan Benoit in the women's 10-kilometer race, trading—and sharing—the lead, both turning in 32:52.5 performances with the nod going to the schoolgirl from Raleigh, North Carolina. While many runners prefer to run relaxed and free from a competitor's pressure, it is not the kind of situation conducive to the intensive effort required to break records. Shea and Benoit had each other as incentive. Virgin had no one but the ghost of Steve Prefontaine.

Virgin had set his first national record six years previously when, at age 17, he pushed the American high school 2-mile record down to 8:40.9. Few had thought he would get even that far, not in terms of athletic performance, but in terms of aging. A victim of congenital kidney malfunction, young Virgin's prognosis was that he would not live through high school. Advances in medical technology and the concrete evidence of the boy's continued

Craig Virgin is America's greatest male long-distance runner to date and president of his own public relations/marketing firm, Front Runner, Inc. (Photograph by T. L. Simmons, courtesy of Front Runner, Inc.)

existence forced revision of the prognosis, but he was forbidden all contact sports. In running, the contact between competitors is only psychological, but no less vicious than in boxing. Craig Virgin, given his life back, decided to run. His father had.

He set the American 15-year-olds' 2-mile record as a sophomore, the first ever under 9 minutes, in 8:57.4. The next year, leading up to his absolute schoolboy 8:40.9 2-mile record, Virgin ran the mile in 4:05.5 and, at a juniors meet in the Soviet Union, 13:52.8 for 5,000 meters, defeating all the adolescent Russians and other Americans there. His body struck at him again when he entered the University of Illinois in 1973. He injured an ankle and came down with pericarditis, but still managed to claim fourth place, in 13:35.2, in the 1975 AAU 5K outdoor championship race. In 1976 Virgin won the AAU cross-country championship, a form of the sport particularly beloved by this man who spent much of his youth "herding" (in fact, chasing) cows around the family farm in Lebanon, Illinois. He would go on to manifest his cross-country ability by becoming the first American to claim the IAAF World Cross-Country Championship on March 9, 1980, in Paris, the only international competition in that politically befouled year that was attended by all major running nations. (He would defend the title successfully in Madrid in March, 1981, against the rest of the world in general and against an awesome team of Ethiopians crowding the first five places until the last lap, in particular.)

In 1976, the leggy Lebanonian made the U.S. Olympic Team, finishing second to Frank Shorter in the 10,000 meters' trials held at Eugene, Oregon. He became ill at Montreal and did not make the 10K final. He became the fastest U.S. 10,000-meter runner in 1978, clocking 27:57.2. Until then, Virgin competed only on the track and in cross-country. Then he noticed road racing. Later he would say: "To me, that's the essence of running: a runner is a runner. I don't believe in all this *specialist* b.s., that you have to either specialize on the track or on the road." Virgin took to the roads. There was, among other things, money on the roads.

He ran his first marathon on January 14, 1979, at San Diego, and won it in 2:14:40, the fastest first marathon ever. He claimed victory over Bill Rodgers, the week after Boston Bill won the B.A.A. Marathon, in the Trevira Ten-Mile Twosome road race in New York. (Virgin's female partner for the event, Ellison Goodall, won the women's division, giving the couple not only the individual titles but also the overall combined-time grand prize.) He started a string of three victories in a row at the 1979 Peachtree Road Race, running 10,000 meters of road in 28:30. To complete his signal year, Virgin beat the universe-class field competing in the Falmouth Road Race that August, breaking Bill Rodgers's course record by running 32:19.7 and demonstrating his supremacy on the roads as well as the track and the muddy, rolling fields. A former college rival of Virgin's, Michigan State alumnus Herb Lindsay, finished second, marking Falmouth as *the* race for an ambitious, emerging road runner to showcase himself or herself. Ellison Goodall also set a new route best of 38:15.7 in claiming the women's race. Bill Rodgers finished third, to a huge ovation.

Virgin's pre-Falmouth statements annoyed many road runners. He announced he had come to Falmouth to beat Bill Rodgers in Rodgers's own backyard, to demonstrate Midwesterners could run the roads as well as New Englanders. Moreover, commitments to compete in Europe forced Virgin to leave Falmouth before the race's awards ceremony, leaving many muttering about his arrogance and lack of consideration. Craig Virgin later said: "My goal is to try to tell the rest of the world—especially the general sports public—that a runner is as good an athlete as a football player or basketball player, or hockey player or baseball player. A lot of the things that I do are not directed toward hard-core runners—they're going to be interested anyway." Carrying this philosophy over into his professional life, Virgin founded his public relations and marketing firm in 1979, calling it, significantly, Front Runner, Inc. In light of his American records, athletic longevity, and remarkable versatility, history recognizes Craig Virgin as the greatest American male distance runner to date.

One of the greatest American female distance runners made a comeback in the 1979 AAU meet where Virgin made his 10K record. Francie Larrieu, at age 27 the grande dame of American track, doubled in the 1500 and 3,000 meters at the AAUs, winning both. The previous year she had stepped off the track 3 laps into the metric mile; observers considered her washed up. 1978 had been a tough year for Larrieu, the American mile record holder (4:28.2). She was going through a divorce, and the AAU was going through with its threat to suspend her if she accepted money competing on a television sports show, "ABC's Superstars," which she did. Reassessing her personal and athletic goals, Larrieu decided she was as determined as she'd been at age 12 to compete on the international level. (Her brother Ron ran on the U.S. 10-kilometer team at the Tokyo Olympics.) Back on track at the 1979 AAUs, Larrieu beat a rebounding Mary Decker in the 1500 by over a meter, breaking the wire in 4:06.6. Two hours later, fast Francie became AAU 3-kilometer queen by besting young standouts Julie Brown and Jan Merrill (who had broken Larrieu's American metric mile mark in the 1976 Olympics while a cold-ridden Larrieu watched from the sidelines) in 8:53.8. "I'm back," Francie Larrieu said.

The Stockholm, Sweden, Marathon got under way the same year Francie Larrieu refound her way. The August, 1979, inauguration of the race instantly marked it as an international classic, drawing thousands from around the globe.

Nearly as many reporters covered a 10,000-meter road race in Maryland on September 15, 1979, as athletes ran in the Stockholm Marathon. The race, the Cacotin Mountain Park Run, was taken by an increasingly famous Herb Lindsay, but the media mavens were there to watch the thirty-ninth president

Francie Larrieu, former American record holder for the mile, wins the mile run at the 1979 U.S.A. Indoor Track and Field Championships at Madison Square Garden. Her time was 4:39.2. (Photograph courtesy of The Boston Herald American.)

of the United States, Jimmy Carter, run his first race. Carter had become well known for his love of "jogging," running 5 miles or so daily. He had telephoned Bill Rodgers after Rodgers's 1979 Boston Marathon triumph and invited Billy and co-victor Joan Benoit to a state dinner at the White House. He became increasingly enthusiastic about athletics, apparently, and announced he would attempt his first 10K road race in 46 minutes, a highly respectable time for a hobbyist executive runner Carter's age and condition. What, in fact, transpired was that he dropped out at around 4 miles, a physical wreck, after having averaged around 8:20 per mile till then—hardly an arduous pace for one intending to average 7:25. Carter later told Herb Lindsay, who received almost no media coverage: "I never thought you'd beat me. They had to drag me off [referring to his accompanying Secret Service agents, who had carried him when he had collapsed]. I didn't want to stop." Four months later, President Jimmy Carter would initiate a U.S. boycott of the 1980 Moscow Olympics, exercising arguably illegal pressure on the USOC, depriving athletes of four years' labor and seriously undermining the idealistic pinnacle of the athletics he allegedly enjoyed. History would show Carter's Olympic policy as sadly misguided. History does not know if President Carter's attitude toward athletics was changed by his unfortunate race in the Cacotin Mountain Park Run, but history notes the president's behavior (not performance, which is an irrelevant criterion for such things) at the race showed he was not an athlete. He was a politician.

Politics of a different sort played a role in the 1979 National Cross-Country Championships, but few knew it at the time. Before the race, Alberto Salazar of the GBTC proclaimed of his team: "We're going to pound until we can't pound any longer, just like the NCAAs." It was the final jewel in the GBTC distance championship crown, the only team title the club had not taken. They had finished third in 1977 and 1978. GBTC wanted the title badly; unknown to most, many of the club's members had received offers from running shoe companies to join the track teams the companies were then forming—for a fee, of course. In a negotiated settlement, the GBTC runners who received such offers agreed to stay with the club until they buckled down and won the cross-country title. Little hard bargaining was needed. The athletes really wanted the collective crown. Years later, Greg Meyer, who had left GBTC to run for a shoe company team, commented: "You can't replace the closeness that we had when we were on Greater Boston. I mean, we just kicked everybody's butt! And it was every . . . I mean, it was *friends* of yours!"

The friends on the GBTC burst away at the gun. At 2 miles, they were running 1-2-3-4-5, Salazar leading. By the finish, Herb Lindsay had intervened; he came in second. Alberto Salazar finished first, claiming the individual title; Bob Hodge finished third; Danny Dillon finished fourth; defending champion Greg Meyer finished fifth; Randy Thomas finished twelfth. The team with the lowest number, after adding up the finishing places of its members, wins in cross-country racing. The GBTC total was 25. The runner-up team, a running-gear company effort backed by commercial funding, boasted a total of 179. The GBTC crown sparkled, completed.

Rookie Salazar went on to win the 1979 Freedom Trail Road Race that September, although a course deviation by the press truck nearly cost him his victory. Misled by a course worker's directions 2 miles from the finish, the truck started to go the wrong direction, and Salazar chased right after it. His route deviation allowed second-man Bill Rodgers to catch up to the intense Salazar. Heading into the final mile of the 8-miler and running leg-by-leg with each other, the Rookie turned to the King and said: "Do what you have to do to win, 'cause I'm *not* going to tie!" He did not tie. Salazar won, a remarkable effort that went largely unnoticed by so-called long-distance running experts.

An effort long-distance experts could not help noticing was Alan Kirik's signal win in the historic London-to-Brighton ultramarathon on September 30, 1979, making him the first American in the 28-year history of the event to vanquish all comers over the 55-plus miles.

The London-to-Brighton race, which varies between 55 and 56 miles depending on road conditions, was first held in 1897. It did not become a reliable annual event, however, until 1951. Not only does the course deter athletes with its almost inconceivable length, it also boasts three exceptionally hilly sections, the first between 10 and 18 miles, the second between 30 and 34 miles, and the third a whopping hill from 45 to 46 miles. An extremely demanding course, London-to-Brighton's rigors help explain why, when one of Kirik's handlers called out to him at 36 miles, "Do you need anything?", Kirik replied tartly, "Yeah, a psychiatrist!"

The 35-year-old Kirik began running long distances in 1968, when he returned home from the Vietnam war. Several months before the London-to-Brighton ultramarathon, he established an American 50-mile record of 5:00:30 in the classic 50 mile/100 kilometer race held annually around Lake Waramaug near New Preston, Connecticut. It had been only the second time Kirik had raced 50 miles; his inaugural 50-mile effort had been a 5:15 run in Central Park, taking 13 minutes off the course record. Because the London-to-Brighton route varies so much from race to race, it is meaningless to keep track of course "records," but Alan Kirik won the 1979 London-to-Brighton in 5:32:37, an average mile pace of 6:02. His reward was the traditional Arthur Newton Cup, named after the excellent pedestrian who competed in C. C. Pyles's "Bunion Derbies" and other ultramarathon races in the 1920s and 1930s, and the Ernest and Winifred Neville gold medal. Kirik's booty for winning the prestigious London-to-Brighton ultra-distance run reflected the historical tradition of ultramarathoning as an outgrowth of the pedestrianism movement at the turn of the century.

One of the athletes Kirik defeated was pre-race favorite Don Ritchie of Scotland, who had won the event in the two previous runnings. On June 15, 1979, Ritchie had set the world record for running 100 miles on the roads. Racing in New York's Central Park, Ritchie covered the first 26.2 miles in 2:40:50 and the next "marathon" in 3 hours flat, ultimately culminating in an 11:51:11.6 clocking for 100 miles. Ritchie's world record on the track for the same distance stood at 11:30:51.

Europeans generally enjoy an advantage over their American cousins in ultra-distance races simply because Europe has more interest in the sport than currently prevails in the U.S. America offers only a few annual ultramarathon races to her approximately 2,500 ultra-distance athletes. Probably the most famous, because most difficult, American ultramarathon is the Western States 100, a 100-mile race run on a footpath over the Sierra Nevada Mountains in California between Squaw Valley and Auburn. The trail first climbs 17,040 feet, then drops 21,970 feet. The fauna also present problems. One of the notes handed runners before the start of the 1978 race stated: "We have made several attempts to mark the trail, but the bears keep destroying the markings." Further, until 1978, the footraces had been held concurrently with a horse race called the Travis Cup over the same path! Runners and horses had to fight each other for a grip, with the humans understandably coming out second best to the beasts.

On October 5, 1979, 29-year-old Barney Klecker of Minneapolis, Minnesota, showed that Kirik's triumph over an international ultramarathon field was no fluke. Racing in the Athletics Congress 50-Mile National Championship (on the roads) in Chicago, Klecker broke both Alan Kirik's American 50-mile road record and Don Ritchie's 50-mile world track record (4:53:28) with his 4:51:25 effort—an average pace of 5:49.7 per mile! A 4:11 miler and 2:16 marathoner, Barney Klecker promised to bring speed to the ultra-distances, just as track men before him had successfully moved up to the standard marathon event.

Grete Waitz, a track woman who moved up to the marathon, made history in the 1979 New York Marathon. Running her second marathon ever, she established her second world's best time for women and broke another of the sport's "impossible" barriers. She ran 2:27:33 for New York's 26.2 miles, the first female under 2:30. Bill Rodgers made it four in a row at New York, coming home in 2:11:42, leading 11,404 other athletes to the Tavern-on-the-Green finish line. Grete Waitz finished sixty-ninth overall, an index of how far women had come in the world of endurance athletics since the 1928 Olympics when officials concluded 800 meters was too far for women to run. (Frank Shorter finished seventh, in 2:16:15, indicating he was successfully recovering from corrective surgery performed on his injured foot in April, 1978.)

Athletes such as Waitz and Rodgers helped move running into the truly modern era; fittingly, the greatest runner of the postwar era was at the 1979 New York Marathon to observe them: Emil Zátopek. The Czech Locomotive was visiting the U.S. for the first time (his visa granted at the request of *Runner* magazine's publisher, George A. Hirsch, one of the major sponsors of the New York Marathon), and was highly impressed with what he saw. "It was like a miracle for me," he exclaimed. "All those people jogging!" He struck up a friendship with Bill Rodgers but, before seeing the King of the Roads in competition, the good Czech wondered how "this gentle boy" could "ever have the fighting spirit" to compete at the ultimate international levels. Although claiming that "I am not in good condition," Zátopek nonetheless offered significant observations about the development of running in the late 1970s. He said: "The modern world is much troubled and in stress. Also, the world is increasingly more technical; and many do not want to lose contact with natural movement and nature. Running is the simplest and most natural movement, like swimming for fish and flying for birds. It is possible to jog till the last day of life."

Zátopek surprised all who met him with his physical and intellectual vigor. Ever the man of integrity, Zátopek admitted revising his opinion after seeing Boston Bill claim his fourth New York Marathon triumph: "I was wrong about Bill Rodgers. He is more than a gentle boy—although he is that, too. He is also a fighter. He could make a very fine Olympic champion." Late in 1981, Zátopek also revised his estimate of his own running future, announcing he would run in the Frankfurt, West Germany, Marathon on May 23, 1982.

Possibly the influence of Bill Rodgers helped the Beast of Prague change his mind. Shortly before leaving the United States, Emil looked at a photograph of him together with Rodgers, and remarked, "Two generations of runners!" Bill smiled and replied, "Yes—young and younger!"

XII

Modern Running
1980–1981

The growth in track club memberships, road races, and marathon entries suggested the datum, but a Gallup Poll in 1980 confirmed it. There were 30 million runners in the United States.

The man whose personal example probably influenced some of those millions to become athletes won his third straight, and fourth total, Boston Marathon in 1980. Bill Rodgers had gained a reputation as a runner who wilted on a hot day, and many attributed his disappointing Montreal Olympics marathon showing to the heat and humidity then prevailing. The temperature at Boston on April 21 was well into the 80s, and it was sunny, rendering the temperature on the unshaded pavement well into the 90s. By 17 miles, Bill Rodgers was running all alone in what he afterward called his toughest Boston race by far. By 20 miles he was experiencing "a psychological ordeal. I can't describe what crowd support meant to me. I was pretty close to exhaustion." The Boston crowd adored Bill Rodgers, smiles sprinting to their faces as the King of the Roads passed by, carried on the crest of their loving enthusiasm. He hit the Pru Center in 2:12:11. Policemen held him by each arm to support him in his walk to the victory stand. Veteran Rodgers observers had never before seen the King appear so totally depleted. Jerry Nason, covering his forty-seventh Boston Marathon, wrote: "He finished bushed, with a capital B. It was a guts run, with a capital G.

252

He proved he COULD run on a hot day. . . . Rodgers yesterday unloaded by far the swiftest hot-day (70 degrees, plus) race ever achieved between Hopkinton and Boston." Rodgers also became only the second man ever to win three Boston Marathons in a row; the first was Clarence DeMar. Rodgers's total of four B.A.A. victories tied him with Gerard Cote, who was there to congratulate him, as the second greatest total number of Boston Marathon wins; DeMar's mark of seven will not be approached in the balance of human history.

Montreal's Jacqueline Gareau came first among the women at Boston in 2:34:26, leading local favorite Patti Catalano (2:35:08) across the line. Catalano had finished second the previous year as well, and all knew how she yearned for triumph in her hometown. Gareau's triumph went uncertified for about a week, the result of an incident created by an imposter "athlete" who jumped into the race less than a mile from the finish line. Such incidents were becoming more common.

The 1980 Olympics typified the perversions being visited on the idealistic world of sport. In December, 1979, the Soviet Union intervened militarily in Afghanistan, a nation the U.S.S.R. considered in her sphere of influence. The Eastern bloc nations termed the Soviet action a necessary defense of the legitimate, troubled, Afghan government, beset by a rebellion among Afghan citizens. The Western bloc nations, led by the United States, termed it an invasion and demanded immediate withdrawal of Soviet troops. President Carter announced it would be improper for the U.S.A. to participate in the "Soviet" Olympics as long as Soviet troops were in Afghanistan. The United States, with total lack of understanding of international sports protocol, tried to convince the IAAF and IOC to change the Games' site from Moscow to somewhere else. That did not work. The U.S. Government tried

Bill Rodgers receives water and encouragement from Coach Bill Squires during the 1980 Boston Marathon. The King of the Roads went on to claim his fourth Boston Marathon title in 2:12:11 on the 90-degree day. (Photograph from the authors' collection.)

to convince other nations to boycott the Olympics. That *partly* worked. Many North Atlantic Treaty Organization members pressured their respective Olympic Committees to agree to a boycott, although some OCs (such as England's) resisted the pressure and sent teams anyway. The Americans did not go, nor did the Japanese, the French, the West Germans, the Canadians, the Belgians, the Australians, and the New Zealanders. Every other major track power went to Moscow.

IAAF regulations clearly state a nation's Olympic Committee must operate autonomously; it cannot be an agency of the national government. The same principle of separation of sport and state manifests itself in the IOC awarding the Olympic Games to a city and not to a country. The 1980 Games were the *Moscow* Olympics, not the *Soviet* Olympics. History has shown that even when a state strives to pervert the Games for propaganda purposes, it fails. The world has yet to produce a propagandist equal, let alone superior, to Josef Goebbels of the Third Reich; yet those Olympics have gone into history as the "Owens Olympics," not the Nazi Games. While decrying the Soviet Union for sundering the trust on which international diplomacy operates, the Carter administration resorted to extremely questionable pressure tactics to force the USOC to withhold an American team from the 1980 Games. USOC President Bob Kane and Executive Director F. Don Miller later revealed that Joe Onek, assistant to Presidential Counsel Lloyd Cutler, claimed to be speaking for Carter himself when he told the USOC heads: "Go along with the boycott and do it now or we will destroy the USOC. We'll take away your tax exemption. We'll take away your passports." Many sports are represented on the USOC that, curiously, are not Olympic sports by any stretch of human imagination, such as roller skating. The American Boy Scouts also have representatives sitting on the USOC. When it came time for a vote, the non-Olympic majority voted, "Boycott." President Carter had won. Perhaps the Delphic oracle wept.

The British, the Soviets, the Ethiopians, and the East Germans celebrated wildly after the 1980 Olympics, because these four nations claimed every distance-running event at the Games. In the women's races, the Soviets and East Germans claimed every medal save two, the bronze medal in the 200 meters and the silver medal in the 400. The women's 100-meter final was an Eastern bloc benefit. The Soviets' Lyudmila Kondratyeva took a squeaker over Marlies Gohr of the fierce East Germans, 11.06 to 11.07. The German Democratic Republic's Ingrid Auerswald came home "far" behind for the bronze medal in 11.14 seconds. A fight just as tight prevailed in the 200-meter final, won by East German Barbel Wockel in 22.03. The hairsplit here was between the silver and bronze medalists: Russian Natalia Bochina ran 22.19 to Jamacian Merlene Ottey's 22.20.

World-record holder Marita Koch, one of the longest athletically lived of the normally "nickle rocket" East Germans, simply walked away with the

400 gold medal, setting a new Olympic standard in the process. Koch's victorious 48.88 put her in a different universe from second woman Jarmila Kratochvilova's 49.46. Czech Kratochvilova crossed the line 2/10-second ahead of East German Christine Lathan. (Poland's great Irena Szewinska came out of retirement to run the Moscow 400, but failed to make the final.)

Nadyezhda Olizaryenko of the U.S.S.R. won the women's 800 meters in 1:53.5, and right behind came two of her teammates to make a clean Soviet sweep: Olga Mineyeva (1:54.9) and Tatyana Providokhina (1:55.4).

Two-lap champion Olizaryenko settled for a bronze medal in the 1500 meters. Thirty-year-old Tatyana Kazankina successfully defended her metric mile Olympic crown in 3:56.6, comfortably ahead of East Germany's Christine Wartenberg (3:57.8) and well in front of speedster Olizaryenko (3:59.6). Kazankina had finally shown she *could* go under 4 minutes in the Olympics "if necessary." In 1976, it hadn't been. In 1980, it was.

Kazankina's performance stood as particularly impressive in light of her retirement after the 1976 Olympics. She was going to become a mother, and she feared she was also going to become too old to compete internationally. A mommy she was; too old she was not. She began training seriously again a year before the Moscow Games. In July, 1980, she announced her return with a world 1500-meter record: 3:55 flat. Kazankina passed the Moscow 800 meters by, believing herself too old and slow to compete in the event whose gold medal she possessed from Montreal; yet she ran the first lap of the 1500 final in 65 seconds. Will determines speed nearly as much as does youth, or age.

Ethiopia's Miruts Yifter reckoned he was around 37 years old by the time the Moscow 10,000-meter final rolled around. None, including Yifter himself, knew exactly how old the tiny (5'6¼", 132 pounds) but mighty distance ace was, only that he was well over 30, no younger than 33, probably no older than 39. People of Yifter's culture were less painstaking in keeping such records than those in the West. Yifter himself preferred to win medals than to keep records, judging by his performance at the 1980 Olympics.

The 10,000-meter final pitted Yifter and his Ethiopian teammates, Mohammed Kedir and Tolosa Kotu, against fabled defending champion Lasse Viren. Viren's prospects did not shine this time. He had qualified for the 10,000-meter final on a fluke: running fifth on the last lap of his preliminary heat, 75 meters behind the fourth man and last qualifier, Viren enjoyed the good fortune of his immediate adversary suddenly dropping out. Even had he finished fifth, Viren's heat time would have made him one of the final qualifiers for the final, but Lasse Viren had not before slid into Olympic finals on technicalities and good luck. Neither did he claim a medal this time around. The three Ethiopians took and shared the lead. Yifter, nicknamed "the Shifter" due to his penchant for suddenly changing a race's pace either up or down, waved to his fans in the stands, clearly relaxed. The

Ethiopian Miruts Yifter, 5K and 10K gold medalist in the 1980 Olympics, races through the streets of San Blas, Puerto Rico, in the famed annual half-marathon footrace. (Photograph from the authors' collection.)

first 5 kilometers passed in a very slow 14:03, and the crowd hooted derision. The pace picked up at the halfway point. Viren surged into the lead. Yifter took it back. Viren took the lead again. Kedir then tossed the Finn aside. Viren forged into the lead again, thrice in the same lap. Yifter shoved him down this time. The Finn would not win. Two laps from home Viren, desperate, tried to burn the impossible speed out of Yifter's short legs. Viren sprinted. Yifter, almost yawning, casually stayed right with him, allowing him 1 lap of minor glory in the lead. The last lap: Kedir serenely passed Viren and led for 50 meters; then Yifter started to run a little harder, gaining 10 meters in two strides. Viren's teammate, Kaario Maaninka, who had to plead with Finnish track officials to be a member of the Olympic team, rushed in, passed Kedir . . . but not even a rampaging gazelle could have tagged Yifter. Yifter's last lap, not all of it run hard, took 54 seconds; his final 5,000 meters, 13:39.7; his 10K final, 27:42.7, an Olympic record, stunning for its lack of apparent effort. Lasse Viren came fifth, behind Yifter, Maaninka, Kedir, Kotu.

The 5,000-meter final virtually repeated the 10,000's scene. The three Ethiopians toyed with the pace and the balance of the field, running the first kilometer in 2:38, the second in 2:45. Lasse Viren was not there. He was out running the marathon, held simultaneously, and dropped out of it after running with the lead pack for 20 kilometers, possibly ending his excellent Olympic career. Eamonn Coghlan and Tanzania's Suleiman Nyambui were there, hanging right with Yifter and Company. Going into the bell lap, 3:52 miler Coghlan moved out past nominal leader Kedir. The Irish rover led for a good 100 meters, then two whirlwinds in the forms of Yifter and Nyambui shot past. Yifter let Nyambui dream of winning for several seconds, then shifted up into, oh, third gear or so and just ran away from everyone. Yifter broke the tape in 13:21.0. Nyambui won the silver in

13:21.6, and a resurging Kaario Maaninka struck bronze in 13:22.0, winning more long-distance medals at Moscow than any other Finn.

The long distances were Ethiopia's at Moscow; the middle distance's were England's. Sebastian Coe went into the 800-meter final holding the world record at the distance, 1:42.4, then he drew lane 8 which, in the staggered start, sent him off "last" behind all other competitors. More important, it forced Coe to run tightest through the turns.

Coe and Steve Ovett had become archrivals, in the public's perception at least, since Coe's mile world record eclipsed Ovett's status as England's pre-eminent miler. With Ovett in lane 2, orthodox strategy would have been for Coe to use his enormous strength to wear away Ovett before the last lap, for Ovett had truthfully stated in 1979: "To beat me, you must be prepared to run 49 seconds for the last lap, and the last 200 meters in 23 seconds." Ovett boasted killer speed.

He also boasted killer tactics. As representatives of the "decadent capitalist nations," the English were not popular at Moscow. Coe seemed happy to run in last place on the first lap, but Ovett was trading blows with a couple East Germans who took strong physical—and unsporting—exception to letting the Englishman by. Elbows, hands, and wrists clashed on that first lap, paced slowly by England's David Warren in 54.3. Coe moved to the outside and started pulling up. Ovett bulled his way out of the East German box, charging pellmell after new leader Nikolai Kirov of the U.S.S.R. Coe, seeing these two breaking away 300 meters from the medals, froze for a nanosecond, then summoned every cell of fast-twitch muscle at his call. At 200 meters from the tape, Coe ran sixth. Ovett broke the wire

Steve Ovett of Britain, 1980 Olympic 800m gold medalist and former world record holder for the mile, is shown after a 1980 mile victory at England's Crystal Palace. His time was 3:52.9. Note the Soviet singlet Ovett wears—it is his favorite. (Photograph courtesy of *The Boston Herald American*.)

in a plodding 1:45.4. Sebastian Coe, silver medalist, ran 1:45.9, while Kirov settled for bronze in 1:46.0. Coe's charge was astonishing both for its speed and for its ineptitude. He had frozen.

It might have been Peter Snell speaking instead of Ovett when the new 2-lap king commented after his victory: "Now I must motivate myself for three more races over 1500 meters, which, after you've won a gold medal, is very difficult."

Coe led the first lap of the metric mile showdown, taking the field out in 61.8 for the first 400-meter lap. It was slow. East German Jurgen Straub muscled the dawdling Coe aside on the start of the third lap, and Ovett moved up to his teammate's shoulder. The third lap went down in 54.2; the Englishmen went down after Straub, biding their time, implacable in their superiority, holding position until the right moment. It came in the final turn; Coe swung wide to pass, and so Ovett. Coe's feet clutched into the artificial track, his head swung to the right in fear of Ovett's passing. It did not come; Ovett could not close and manifestly gave up the chase to let Straub take the silver medal. Coe ran 53.3 for the last, partly strolled, lap, winning in 3:38.4, then fell to his knees and kowtowed to the Moscow track, the top of his head bussing its surface. Relief infused his features. Straub came next, in 3:38.8, while Ovett walked into the bronze medal with 3:39.0.

Waldemar Cierpinski ran past Gerard Nijboer 2 kilometers from Lenin Stadium and went on to win his second straight Olympic marathon in 2:11:03, a feat not quite ranked with Abebe Bikila's because achieved against a depleted field. Nijboer was the silver medalist, in 2:11:20, and took a postrace lap with Cierpinski. Russian Satymkul Dzumanazrov was the bronze man with his 2:11:35. The German Democratic Republic, yielding either to inflation or to Cierpinski's inflated status, this time gave the "amateur" 15,000 marks for his golden effort.

Until Coe won the Moscow gold medal for 1500 meters, Steve Ovett had not lost a metric or English mile since May, 1977. Perhaps significantly, the Olympics 1500 was the first time the two outstanding milers had consented to face each other, and, at Moscow, they had no choice in the matter. Labeled a "bad boy" by the sporting press, Ovett never hesitated to speak his mind; yet he had said some things before both Coe's mile record and the Moscow Games that seemed, in retrospect, curious: "I don't get wrapped up in records. I respect Rono not because of his records, but because he is a great racer who wins lots of races when he's not breaking records. . . . Everyone thinks that anyone who gets an Olympic gold medal is someone different, something mystical, which is not true. I know a lot of complete idiots who are Olympic champions and I know a lot of great athletes who never were. I think as long as you enjoy your running and enjoy life, then Olympic gold and things like this are immaterial." Ovett had beaten Rono in a 2-mile race during Rono's supreme year, 1978, the Briton dashing past the Kenyan to record 8:13.5, a world record. Possibly the victorious Ovett felt he could be charitable to Rono. None knows certainly if, or how, Ovett chaffed over his loss to Coe in the Moscow mile, but he apparently had fumed over Coe's mile world record. Ovett had wanted to go to Moscow as the record holder. On July 1, 1980, he succeeded. He ran at Oslo's Bislett Stadium, scene of Coe's record, and paced behind rabbit David Warren, running the mile in 3:48.8, the third man under 3:50, and the fastest one of them. Appraised of the time, the track world sighed. If only Ovett would get serious! He could run everything from the 800 (1:44.1) to the half-marathon (1:01:38), but toyed with his sport. An amateur international runner should be more serious, complained spectating devotees; but Ovett reiterated: "Lasting fame is not important to me, as long as I've enjoyed myself while I've been here. I'm quite happy with my life."

Mary Decker had been happy for a while in 1980. Earlier in the year she had become the first woman ever invited to join the prestigious Athletics West track club, a shoe-company effort bankrolled by Nike. In 1977 and 1978, she had had the sheaths that enswarthed her aching Achilles tendons surgically sliced open. The procedure worked. She could again run and had spent 1979 building up her endurance and speed. Running at the Mount Smart Stadium in Aukland, New Zealand, in August, 1979, Decker claimed the women's world record for the mile in 4:21.7. She ran the 1980 Millrose Games 1500 meters in 4:00.8, breaking Francie Larrieu's former 4:03 standard to bits. Moving to the Astrodome Invitational the next week, Decker ran the fastest women's mile—undercover or otherwise—in history: 4:17.55. On February 22, 1980, she took two American records in one race at San Diego's Jack-in-the-Box meeting: 800 meters in 1:58.9, 880 yards in 1:59.7. She then went to run in Europe and, in a brave but ill-advised head-to-head with Tatyana Kazankina in the Zurich 1500, Decker finished second (3:59.43, her first sub-4 metric mile) to the eternal Soviet (3:52.47) and tore her tendons all over again. Nike would see she received the best possible medical care. She, if tempered by temperance, would probably be back.

In August, 1980, many of the internationally ranked runners in the Greater Boston Track Club left to join teams backed by shoe-company money. The situation was symptomatic of the direction top-level road running had taken. New Balance, the company to whose track team most of the former GBTC aces gravitated, had been paying these same runners consultants' fees for several years. In return, the athletes had tested prototype shoes for New Balance. Now the company's marketing department wanted to see more direct return on investment and was also willing to pay world-class runners as much as $14,000 annually simply to run. It was an offer difficult to refuse, and one no different from those tendered by Nike, adidas, Athletic Attic or Sub-4. Most members of truly amateur clubs such as GBTC felt their teams the subject of "raids" by the shoe companies. The economic realities of running could no longer be considered less important than the camaraderie of training. Money was now there on the roads, and money spoke very loudly.

Running for the Athletic Attic track team, Olympian Rod Dixon won the 1980 Falmouth Road Race, but missed breaking Craig Virgin's course record because he slowed in the final mile to wave to the raging crowd looking on. The Olympic medalist had replaced the silver feather of his native New Zealand on his chest with the corporate logo of Marty Liquori's and Jimmy Carnes's chain of athletic gear stores. Dixon's Falmouth victory symbolized the changes in road running being wrought in that era in two other ways. First, none of the popular press had even considered him a dark horse at Falmouth; he was, after all, "only" the bronze medalist at 1500 meters! That meant two other guys had beat him—clearly, a loser. The press's oversight of Dixon indicated the insularity suffusing road running. Any athlete not a "real" road runner could not win Falmouth. (The press by then thought Frank Shorter and Craig Virgin "pure" roadies!) Second, and related, Dixon showed that distance track athletes had the legs of the "pure" road runners, and a whole lot more. The insular attitude among road racers probably sprang at least partly from feelings of inferiority. The roads lacked both the elitism and the intensity of the track, until the track runners came to the roads. Rod Dixon's Falmouth triumph signaled a melding of the two worlds, track and road, or at least a serious blurring of their boundaries.

The divisions between road and track athletes cleared slightly in the 1980 Montreal International Marathon held in September. Patti Catalano, as pure a road runner as anyone could imagine, consoled herself for her second straight bridesmaid's finish at the Boston Marathon by winning the Montreal women's division in the new American best of 2:30:57. It was also the second fastest woman's time in the world, behind only Grete Waitz's. Jacqueline Gareau, 1980 Boston Marathon champion, came second in 2:31:41. At the finish line, they embraced.

It was his first marathon, and in the space on the entry application where the New York Road Runners request the athlete estimate his or her finishing time to aid in seeding the field, Oregon senior Alberto Salazar wrote "2:09." The Rookie then went out and ran to victory in 2:09:41, the fastest first marathon in history by some 4 minutes, the second fastest marathon time for an American man ever. In the same 1980 New York Marathon, Grete Waitz made it three for three: three marathon victories in three marathons (her only three), and three world women's best times. In 1980, the Norwegian speed queen ran 2:25:41, precisely 16 minutes behind Salazar, who commented he had run harder 10,000-meter track races than the effort required of him at New York. With that statement, the boundaries between road and track cleared somewhat. The road runners were, to put it mildly, unflattered, but could hardly deny the concrete fact of Salazar's blazing conquest of a marathon course considered until that day "slow."

An organization was founded at the end of 1980 that surprised and confused the running world as much as Salazar's nonchalant marathon debut. The Association of Road Running Athletes (ARRA), (who numbered among their ranks Bill Rodgers, Patti Catalano, Greg Meyer, Don Kardong, Herb Lindsay, and virtually every other American [and several foreign] road runner of any stature save for Frank Shorter, Craig Virgin, and Joan Benoit) stood for nothing less than open road racing. ARRA announced a series of races for cash, the money paid openly, "over-the-table," to athletes on the basis of their finishing positions. IAAF reaction was unambiguous: any runner accepting money openly risked losing his of her amateur status, hence, ability to compete in international events. In short terms, run in ARRA and forget the Olympics. Many ARRA athletes, regardless of their success in road racing, stood only a slim chance of making an Olympic distance final, however. Further, the boycott of the Moscow Games spread cynicism among athletes throughout the world about the value of staying an "amateur" for Olympics that might never again transpire. Finally, distance runners late in 1980 felt it was time they were recognized as athletes every bit as competent as those the public knew were professionals: the football, baseball, hockey, and basketball stars, and the golfers and tennis players. Bill Rodgers had achieved notoriety years earlier for proclaiming: "It sickens

Patti Lyons-Catalano sets a world road record for 10K while winning the 1980 Bonne Bell National Championship. (Photograph courtesy of The Boston Herald American.)

me that an 'athlete' like Joe Namath is held up to youngsters as a good example. I'll be running over Joe Namath's grave!" Athletes less volatile than Rodgers simply wanted to be able to see the same advisor as Broadway Joe at the Morgan Guaranty Bank.

Defenders of the "shamateur" system, where everyone took money underhandedly and everybody knew about it but no one admitted he did it, pointed out that the purses offered by initial ARRA events actually represented a cut in income for most top performers. By early 1981, the very best men road racers could expect appearance fees around $3,000 for a 10,000-meter race; the very top women could expect about $2,000. An excellent, but not Olympic level, male road runner could command an average of $1,000 per race, plus his real expenses; a woman at the commensurate level would receive a bit more than half that. (The longer the race, the more money a runner could command. Typical marathon fees stood nearly twice typical 10K stipends. One Olympic marathoner received $20,000 plus his real expenses for running one international marathon in 1981, and at least one woman received over $10,000, albeit in a different race.) Again, one notes that women's fields were still considerably smaller than men's, hence the disparity in appearance fees. Bluntly, it was easier to be a top-ranked woman than it was to be a top-ranked man on 1981's roads; there was less competition. Only rarely were the women even able truly to *race* each other. Obscured from one another's view in "mixed" megaraces such as the Peachtree Road Race, women road runners could only chug along as fast as prudently possible and hope it was fast enough to get home first. The emotional stimulus of going head-to-head was still lacking in most women's races.

The leading men have raced by; now the crowd gapes in awe at the women, particularly the blonde. She runs free, relaxed, well, because she is elated. She is elated because she runs so well.

Cool, muscular, fair Allison Roe of New Zealand runs the eighteenth mile of the 1981 Boston Marathon in the wisps of intense, wiry, dark Patti Catalano's long flowing hair. Patti, running her third Boston and seeking her first victory, said before the race, "If I'm ahead at 18, no one can catch me."

At that moment, America's Greg Meyer charges up the Newton hills ahead of his countrymen, Bill Rodgers and Craig Virgin. Japan's Toshihiko Seko runs just behind. Virgin turns to Rodgers, points to Meyer, and asks, "Is he catchable?" Rodgers, thinking of Emil Zátopek's question to Jim Peters at Helsinki, hedges, saying, "I dunno."

Virgin sprints away from the King of the Roads for good. Seko scoots right with him, the two quickly rendering Meyer ancient history. Seko stares straight ahead, breathing like a baby. Wildness haunts Virgin's eyes; his mouth foams slightly. The two men share water with each other, but cannot share each other's language.

Behind them all runs Old Johnny Kelley in his fiftieth Boston Marathon, carried on the crest of the loudest adoring clamor in Boston history, a man surfing the wave of myth.

Roe bears down at 20 miles, hammering, hammering. She floats extravagantly high over the road, her track muscles taking the pace in stride. Catalano clings low to the tarmac, knowing only the roads, only that this is HER Boston Marathon, seething with dark passion. Her eyes, normally coals, compress into black diamonds of rage and pain.

At nearly the same time, Virgin wonders how long he can keep Seko's pace. Seko answers. Turning onto Beacon Street at mile 23, the Japanese champion suddenly accelerates, runs 80 meters clear of Virgin. Seko runs on, winning in 2:09:26. Virgin comes second in 2:10:26. Bill Rodgers is third in 2:10:34. Finishing, he says, "When I saw I couldn't win, I wanted to do what the Japanese do: run honorably."

Twenty-three miles from the Pru, Roe springs. The two women race together several steps. Catalano's muscles bulge with power and anxiety. Lean men race along behind them, slower. For the first time in Boston history, the women in the crowd see a real women's race. They scream hysterically in a rapture of sisterhood, urging on not Allison Roe but Everywoman Runner.

Roe passes. She and Catalano do not speak. Their running is their language.

Roe runs 2:26:45, a Boston record, the second swiftest woman ever. For the third year, Catalano comes second, 2:27:51, beating her old best by 2 minutes. As she finishes, Toshihiko Seko is telling the press, "In Japan,

New Zealander Allison Roe emerged as a star long-distance runner when she won the 1981 Boston Marathon in the course record time of 2:26:45. She went on to set a women's world best time of 2:25:29 in the 1981 New York Marathon. (Photograph courtesy of The Boston Herald American.)

when you respect somebody you show your respect by going beyond his achievements."

Allison Roe spies her finishing time and says, "I really didn't think I could run that fast." Patti Catalano says, "I didn't do anything wrong. The only thing I did wrong was get second, and that's not bad."

Old John Kelley finishes in 4:01:25 to a tumult never before heard in the B.A.A. Marathon. The crowd loves every legend. Old John himself finished third at Boston, once. He finished second, seven times. He won the Boston Marathon twice.

Two weeks before the Boston Marathon, Craig Virgin had run what was then the fastest time ever for a 10-kilometer road race, 28:06, breaking Greg Meyer's two-year-old 28:11 mark. On July 4, 1981, Virgin would lower the time to 28:03.4 at the Peachtree Road Race. An injured knee would reduce his performance level for the rest of the year, reduce him to jogging 4 miles daily just to keep fit. He was back in training by December, 1981.

Bill Rodgers's Boston Marathon effort stood at his tenth marathon race run under 2:12, his sixth under 2:11, a record unapproached by any other athlete in history. If any currently had a chance to surpass Rodgers, 1981 Boston-champion Toshihiko Seko would be he.

To date, Seko claimed three consecutive Fukuoka Marathons, running 2:09:45 in the 1980 version. As had Virgin, Seko showed his prowess while a schoolboy, emerging as Japan's champion 800-meter and metric mile high school runner. In 1977 he met Kiyoshi Nakamura. The 62-year-old coach saw promise in the 19-year-old athlete, and said: "God gave Seko to me and I want to thank God by making Seko the best." Nakamura, who held

Toshihiko Seko (wearing number 9) prevailed in the 1981 Boston Marathon with a course record of 2:09:26. He is shown here leading Shigeru Sou at the 36K mark in the 1979 Fukuoka (Japan) Marathon, which Seko won. (Photograph by Asahi Shimbun, courtesy of Track & Field News.)

Japan's 1500-meter record (3:56.8) for 16 years, put Seko on the same regimen as other Nakamura athletes, a program redolent of the thinking of Percy Cerruty. Nakamura called his system "Zensoho." "The idea is to clear your mind of everything and to let your body function naturally, undisturbed by thoughts. We must study the Bible, Scriptures and all famous works. We must study nature: mountains, rivers, the stars, sun and moon. All of them are our teachers; and, more specifically, we must study the other top runners. That way he's still Seko, but he has a part of all his competitors in him, which will enable him to beat them." Toshihiko Seko, physically gifted and coached with compassion, stands as potentially the most eminent male marathoner to date.

The running world's focus on the marathon event intensified in 1981. The Frankfurt (West Germany) Marathon had its first running in May, 1981, making the sport wider in international scope. More important, the IOC announced almost simultaneously that they had designated a women's marathon for the 1984 Olympics at Los Angeles. With the marathon now an Olympic event, one expects women's 26.2-mile times to tumble amazingly. The same pattern has prevailed in every other event suddenly elevated to Olympic status. One suspects that, by the time of the Los Angeles Games, women will run very close to 2:20, or under it.

Some of the brightest Olympic hopefuls potentially endangered their future in the Games on June 29, 1981, at the Cascade Run-Off, the first event on the ARRA's race calendar. Claimed by Greg Meyer in 43:18.9, the Nike-sponsored 15-kilometer race paid Meyer $10,000 openly, and gave the same amount to women's division winner, Anne Audain (50:32.8) of New Zealand. In fact, New Zealand women took the first three places at Cascade. Lorraine Moller came second, winning $6,000, and Allison Roe suddenly turned "pro" to claim third. Patti Catalano finished an uncharacteristic fourth, winning $1,500. ARRA president Don Kardong announced that the race "marked the first time in the history of our sport that the athletes, in conjunction with race directors and sponsors, willingly participated in a race, free of under-the-table payments, with a prize money structure available for those who wished to accept it. While in direct opposition to the national governing body and international amateur rules, the world class athletes that participated have put their eligibility on the line to defend an unrestricted form of competition, rather than exist in the current system of under-the-table payments and selectively enforced rules."

Some runners at Cascade hedged. Frank Shorter had committed himself to run, but was unhappy with certain procedures. He and some others wanting to protect their amateur status wanted two separate finish-line chutes, one for "professionals" and one for "amateurs." When ARRA offered only one chute, Shorter solved his problem of commitment to run but desire to remain untainted by running the race on the sidewalk! Bill Rodgers, although an outspoken ARRA member, did not accept over-the-table money at Cascade and denied receiving under-the-table gelt.

Fears proved justified. Within a month of the Cascade Run-Off, the New Zealand Amateur federation suspended the three Kiwi women who took money. Anne Audain exploded: "What the hell are they going to do? They just lost their three top women distance runners!" Audain's American counterparts, such as Greg Meyer and Herb Lindsay, vowed never to return a dime of their winnings, but took the precaution of placing the loot in special bank accounts they would not draw on until the legal air cleared.

While ARRA battled for the athletes' right to run the roads for manifest pay, the European track circuit in 1981 witnessed arguably the greatest series of mile runs in history, led by at least two athletes earning $20,000 apiece *per race*—all under-the-table, of course.

Bunnyrabbit Bob Benn draws the field through the first lap in 56.7 this July 11th Oslo night. Steve Ovett strokes along in his wake, nearly dreaming in this "Dream Mile." The rest of the field runs behind, alert, pulsating. The next lap is 58.5, then Benn drops out, exhausted. America's Tom Byers, who beat everybody in the field in a mile two weeks previous because mistaken for a rabbit who would die, and did not, cruises into the lead past Ovett, is pushed right back down by countryman Steve Scott, running tonight to break from the pack, to win. Scott's lap, the third, takes 58.1.

Ovett sprints past 220 yards from home. In his wake teems the most bunched and swiftest miling team in history. Sensing the determined group-mind behind, the enigmatic Englishman tonight looks over his shoulder once, twice, four times, anxious, while running for the win. He is suddenly home in 3:49.25, the width of a synapse ahead of the rest. Spain's Jose-Luis Gonzalez runs the last hundred meters in 14.8 seconds; Scott, in 15.1—one cell oozing past another in a hemorrhage of shared haste. Gonzalez grabs second in 3:49.67. Scott, at last!, breaks Jim Ryun's American record with his 3:49.68, the third man in the body under 3:50. Big, brutal John Walker strides in fourth, in 3:50.26, pulled by Scott and pushed along by America's Todd Harbour, who also elbows Jim Ryun aside with his 3:50.34. Englishman Steve Cram carries on the shared onslaught, coming sixth in 3:50.38, his pulse hovering around 200 and pursued by the West German physician, Dr. Thomas Wessinghage, seventh in the winning group, 3:50.91.

Surveying the speed, depth, and shared determination of the pack, which surpass the 1979 Golden Mile's, John Walker growls: "That has to be the greatest mile race of all. At my age, I should know. I seem to have run in most of them." Like every other athlete of his class, he seems to have run WITH most of them, too. Ladas is dead. Modern runners compete by cooperating.

The depth of the Oslo "Dream Mile" assured the race's place in history all by itself but, in the near-miraculous miling summer of 1981, the race also stood out precisely because it *was* a race. Running at Zurich, Switzerland, on August 19, 1981, Seb Coe broke Steve Ovett's world record for the mile with a 3:48.53 effort; Coe was deliberately paced in the "race" by, first, Tom Byers, then by Kenyan Mike Boit. On August 26, 1981, running in his favorite singlet (a Soviet jersey) and behind his favorite rabbit, Bob Benn, Ovett took the record back at Koblenz, West Germany, with his 3:48.40. On August 28, 1981, Coe again ran behind Athletics West's Byers and again took the world record for the mile: 3:47.33. (On July 11, 1981, Coe had lowered his world record for the kilometer to a stupendous 2:12:18 at the Bislett Track.) These were all fabulous running efforts, but they were not true competitions. They were set-up races for superstar athletes. They were *not* "fixed" races, as some of the pedestrian combats of the turn of the century had been, but the athletic red carpet had been rolled out for one athlete alone in each field. As a *race*, the Oslo Dream Mile loomed above any of them.

As if to show the difference between a race and a rabbit-run, Sydney Maree raced Steve Ovett in a meet at Rieti, Italy, on September 9, 1981. Reliable Bob Benn took Ovett, and everyone else, out at 56.6, then ran the

Alberto Salazar closes in on the finish line in the 1981 New York Marathon, where he ran the world's fastest marathon time to date—2:08:13. Notice the balloons starting to soar from the crowd (upper right of the photo), a signal that the race has been won. Notice also the police officer restraining exuberant race director Fred Lebow from rushing out prematurely to hug the Rookie. (Photograph from the authors' collection.)

next lap in 57.7. James Robinson towed the Englishman from 1,000 meters to 1,320 meters. Maree, a South African living in the U.S. and seeking American citizenship, hauled Ovett through almost all of the last lap. At 80 meters from the wire, Ovett swung wide and went into his patented killer's sprint—and Maree ran away from him, tearing the worsted in 3:48.83! Ovett finished in 3:50.23, not necessarily the inferior athlete but, that night at least, the inferior racer.

Also racing at Rieti that September 9 was an athlete from whom little substantial had been heard in three years: Henry Rono. Running in his favorite event, the 5,000 meters, Rono led until the 4K mark, on world-record pace, then began to fade. East Germany's Hans-Jorge Kunze finished first, in 13:10.40, a European record, while Soviet Valeriy Abramov also moved by the Kenyan to take second, in 13:11.99. Rono finished third in 13:12.47. Two days later, racing in London, Rono won the 5K, getting down to 13:12.34. Then, on September 13, 1981, Rono ran the 5,000 meters at Knarvik, Norway. He ran the race in 13:06.20, 2.4 seconds under his own world record. Rono was back; the heir to Nurmi, Zátopek, and Clarke again ran well! The man whose stated goal was "to be in the history books as the greatest" had added great credibility to any argument in that direction. Rono normally trained 80 miles per week, normally took four weeks (never more than six) to prepare for any very special race he wanted. When the intensity of Rono's training matched that of his personality, an argument placing him with Nurmi, Zátopek and Clarke could not be dismissed.

Alberto Salazar predicted the winning time at the 1981 Falmouth Road Race would be "under 32" minutes; the thought was dismissed as unrealistic. The pundits might have learned from Salazar's New York Marathon. Alberto ran 31:56, obliterating Craig Virgin's 32:20 course record, to average 4:29.8 per mile and become the new Falmouth champion. "I wanted to make sure it was a hard pace," Salazar modestly said later. Second-man Rod Dixon, who before the race declared, "This is my Olympics," ran 32:16. Joan Benoit, newly installed at Boston University as women's distance-running coach, beat Vermonter Judi St. Hilaire, 38:16 to 38:39. It was Benoit's third Falmouth title, having won also in 1976 and 1978.

More fallout from the ARRA Cascade Run-Off came in September, 1981, when The Athletics Congress (formerly the AAU) suspended from further amateur competition Greg Meyer, Patti Catalano, Ric Rojas, Benji Durden, Cindy Dalyrmple, Ed Mendoza, John Glidewell, and Peter Pfitzinger. Herb Lindsay, wanting to compete in the World Cross-Country Championship, had struck a deal with TAC, so was not suspended. Lindsay's bargain, which would become the prototype for other athletes seeking to save both face and competitive status, entailed placing his Cascade earnings in a TAC escrow account, on which Lindsay could then draw to pay training and living expenses. New Zealander Allison Roe struck a similar agreement with the NZAA. Lorraine Moller, winner of the all-women Avon International Marathon in 1980, refused compromise when Avon officials asked her to do the same so she could defend her title. To date, both Greg Meyer and Patti Catalano have followed Lindsay's lead. It seems fair to assume others will as well, and that the usefulness of the ARRA will prove historically short but piquent. Had ARRA not forced the issue, the national and international governing bodies of the sport would have no concrete incentive to revise the accepted methods of "shamateurism." ARRA, considered imprudent by some, nevertheless forced a breath of reality's air into the politics of international "amateur" competition, and the entire sport profited thereby.

On September 26, 1981, an event billed as the Fifth Avenue Mile heralded another major rapprochement in the world of distance running. The ARRA/TAC confrontation helped close the gap between professional and amateur athletes. The Fifth Avenue Mile, creation of New York Road Runners president Fred Lebow and opposed by outgoing IAAF head Adriaan Paulen as "blatantly professional," was a mile-long road race featuring some of the best milers in the world. Steve Ovett withdrew at the last minute, pleading illness but very possibly fearing disciplinary action from the quix-

. . . all of them runners. (Photograph courtesy of *The Boston Herald American.*)

otic men who governed the sport. Sydney Maree shot through the straight, slightly downhill mile in 3:47.52, ahead of Mike Boit (3:49.59) and Thomas Wessinghage (3:50.48). Heavily sponsored and televised nationally, the Fifth Avenue Mile may have created a confused impression in the minds of casual running fans. Many wondered why it "wouldn't count" if someone ran a faster time than Coe's 3:47.33 in the event. Such misunderstandings can be corrected, one fervently hopes. The Fifth Avenue Mile brought pure track to the roads. Just as fervently as one hopes for fans' enlightenment, one wants to see an end to the rift in the sport between road-oriented athletes and track-oriented ones. As Craig Virgin said: "A runner is a runner."

What a runner was Alberto Salazar! He predicted he would complete the 1981 New York Marathon in 2:08. Now some took him seriously, but in utter amazement. Salazar ran 2:08:13, 21 seconds under Derek Clayton's best time and 48 seconds under Gerard Nijboer's. He ran his sixteenth mile in 4:33! (After the race, Alberto fell into his mother's arms.) The wonderful aspect to Salazar's new world marathon best was that it was established on a course not only still used annually, but used by upwards of 14,000 runners. Alberto Salazar had emerged as the new American road-running expert. He was no longer the Rookie. Further, the New York Marathon emerged as the world's referential course for marathon times. Other courses ran the full 26 miles, 385 yards, but none other held the world's fastest effort.

New York held it for women as well as for men. Allison Roe, newly returned to amateur purity, surpassed Grete Waitz on the road that October 27 morn. The quick Kiwi bid farewell to the Norwegian ace at 12 miles, when Waitz was forced to slow, then withdraw, with strained lower legs ("shin splints"). Roe set sail after early leader Julie Brown nailed her at mile 14 and ran home free, crossing the line in 2:25:29, 12 seconds under Waitz's best. Young, strong, fiercely motivated, trained for both track and road, Salazar and Roe point to running's future, while behind them run tens of thousands, some in competitive pursuit, some in combat with themselves, some for health, some for company, but all for sport, all in their own good form, all of them runners.

Boston, Massachusetts
December 5, 1981

Further
Suggested Reading

The following list is particularly for those who know little or nothing about distance running and its history. It is not exhaustive. We have made a strong effort to include recent sources so they may be located easily. Not all items listed pertain directly to distance running as a sport; some of them enhance one's appreciation of distance running as an integral part of life. Where titles are not self-explanatory, annotation is provided.

Anderson, Bob. "*Runner's World* Exclusive: Two Champions—Past and Present—Discuss the Art and Science of Marathoning," *Runner's World* 17 (January 1982): 22–27. Derek Clayton and Alberto Salazar talk after Salazar had run 2:08:13 at the New York Marathon.

Anonymous. "The Invasion of Falmouth," *Runner's World* 15 (November 1980): 58–59. Falmouth becomes the most important sub-marathon road race on earth.

Anonymous. "National Collegiate A.A.-Meet Won by Illinois University," *The New York Times*, June 19, 1921, 4:1.

Anonymous. "Steve Ovett Pushes Mile Record to 3:48.8," *Runner's World* 15 (September 1980): 70–72.

Bannister, Roger. *The Four-Minute Mile.* New York: Dodd, Mead, 1955.

———, et. al. "The Magic of the Mile," *Runner's World* 14 (June 1979): 52–71.

Benyo, Richard. "Derek Clayton: The World's Fastest Marathoner," *Runner's World* 14 (May 1979): 66–73.

————. "The Heat is On for 1980," *Runner's World* 14 (October 1979): 76–81. A profile of Bill Rodgers.

————. "*Runner's World* Midnight Invitational," *Runner's World* 14 (March 1979): 42–46. Alberto Salazar holds off Craig Virgin to win his first *RW* 5-miler.

Berenyi, Ivan. "Meet the World's Best Marathoner," *The Runner* 3 (January 1981): 64–67. Profile of East Germany's Waldemar Cierpinski.

Bloom, Marc. "Jesse Owens: The Legacy of an American Hero," *The Runner* 2 (June 1980): 30–39.

————. "Made in Japan," *The Runner* 3 (July 1981): 36–43. Toshihiko Seko's 1981 Boston Marathon victory.

————. "Viren's Road to Moscow," *The Runner* 2 (August 1980): 26–31.

Burfoot, Amby. "Craig Virgin: Running in the Fast Lane," *Runner's World* 15 (March 1980): 54–65.

————. "The Day the Women's Running Movement Came Into Its Own," *Runner's World* 13 (August 1978): 58–61. Martha White wins L'Eggs 10K road race.

————. "Evolution of Training Systems, Part I," *Runner's World* 16 (September 1981): 34–38.

————. "Evolution of Training Systems, Part II," *Runner's World* 16 (October 1981): 81–86.

————. "Evolution of Training Systems, Part III," *Runner's World* 16 (December 1981): 60–63.

————. "The First Woman of Running," *Runner's World* 17 (February 1982): 62–66. The story of Julia Chase.

————. "Grete," *Runner's World* 16 (March 1981): 39–51.

————. "New York City Hosts the Ultimate Mega-Marathon," *Runner's World* 15 (January 1980): 50–57.

————. "The New York City Marathon," *Runner's World* 13 (October 1978): 70–77. A report on Grete Waitz's first marathon.

————. "1978 Boston Marathon," *Runner's World* 13 (June 1978): 46–59. Amby reports on his old college roommate, Bill Rodgers.

————. "The Race to Decide 'King of the Road,' " *Runner's World* 13 (November 1978): 42–49. The 1978 Falmouth Road Race, claimed by Bill Rodgers.

————. "Sebastian Coe," *Runner's World* 14 (September 1979): 70–74.

————, with Wischnia, Bob and Kissin, Roy. "The Year of the Olympics," *Runner's World* 15 (September 1980): 46–65.

————. "Year of the Raging Rookie," *Runner's World* 16 (March 1981): 32–34. Alberto Salazar takes his second *RW* 5-mile race.

Carlson, Peter. "That Championship Season," *The Runner* 3 (November 1980): 58–62. Patti Catalano's 1980 season in retrospect.

Chacour, Michael. "What One Can Do Well, Two Can Do Better," *Runner's World* 14 (July 1979): 30–31. Ellison Goodall and Craig Virgin win the inaugural Trevira 10-Mile Twosome race for couples in New York.

Chapman, Brian. "Waldemar Cierpinski," *Runner's World* 13 (March 1978): 68–70. Interview with Cierpinski back when he had only one Olympic gold medal for the marathon.

Clayton, Derek with Perry, Paul. *Running to the Top*. Mountain View, CA: Anderson World, 1980.

Cooper, Kenneth H. *Aerobics*. New York: Bantam Books, 1968.

————. *The New Aerobics*. New York: Bantam Books, 1970.

Costill, David L. "Hitting the Gender Wall," *The Runner* 1 (October 1979): 60–65. America's foremost exercise physiologist explains why men will always run faster than women.

Darling, Ernest Franklin. "Boy Wonder of the Bunion Derby," *The Runner* 1 (March 1979): 44–51.

Decker, Mary. "Women All in a Roe," *The Runner* 3 (July 1981): 44–53. Decker interviews Allison Roe after the 1981 Boston Marathon.

DeMar, Clarence. *Marathon*. Shelburne, VT: New England Press, 1981.

Dodd, Ed and Osler, Tom. "The Distance Was No Object," *Runner's World* 13 (August 1978): 66–69. Ultramarathoning in the 1920s and 1930s in America.

Donovan, Wally. *A History of Indoor Track and Field*. El Cajon, CA: Edward Jules, 1976.

Dubowitz, B. and Pearse, A. G. E. "A Comparative Histochemical Study of the Oxidative Enzymes and Phosphorlase Activity in Skeletal Muscle," *Histochemie* 2 (1960): 105.

Editors of *Runner's World*. "A Decade of Running," *Runner's World* 14 (December 1979): 50–71.

Editors of *Track & Field News*. *Olympic Track & Field*. Los Altos, CA: *Track & Field News*, 1977.

Edstrom, L. and Nystrom, B. "Histochemical Types and Sizes of Fibers of Normal Human Muscle," *Acta Neurologica Scandanavia* 45 (1969): 257.

Falls, Joe. *The Boston Marathon*. New York: Macmillan Publishing, 1977.

Fixx, James F. *The Complete Book of Running*. New York: Random House, 1977.

Furlong, William Barry. "Craig Virgin: A Heartland Saga," *The Runner* 1 (September 1979): 32–41.

Gambetta, Vern. *How Women Runners Train*. Los Altos, CA: *Track & Field News*, 1980.

Gibb, Bobbi. *To Boston With Love*, 2nd ed. Rockport, MA: Gibb Art Works, 1966. The first woman to run the Boston Marathon tells, and illustrates, her story.

Glanville, Brian. *The Olympian* (novel). Boston: Houghton Mifflin, 1980.

————. "Roger Bannister and the 25th Anniversary of the Four-Minute Mile," *The Runner* 1 (May 1979): 24–35.

Goldberg, Leslie. "Grete Waitz: Northern Lightning," *The Runner* 1 (April 1979): 44–51.

Gollnick, P. D., et al. "Enzyme Activity and Fiber Composition in Skeletal Muscle of Trained and Untrained Men," *Journal of Applied Physiology* 33 (1972): 312.

Goodman, Cary. "Alberto Juantorena: Man of the People," *The Runner* 2 (January 1980): 44–51.

Gubernick, Lisa. "L'Eggs: Northern Lightning Strikes Again," *The Runner* 1

(September 1979): 78–81. Grete Waitz wins yet another L'Eggs 10K championship.

Gynn, Roger and Martin, David. *The Marathon Footrace*. Springfield: Charles C. Thomas, Publisher, 1979.

Hansen, Jacqueline. "Bells Ring in Boston," *Runner's World* 14 (January 1979): 60–61. Joan Benoit's victory in the 1978 Bonne Bell championship race.

Harriman, Peter. "One Race That Fits All," *Runner's World* 14 (July 1979): 74–79. Profile of Don Kardong's Lilac Bloomsday Race.

Harris, H. A. *Sport in Britain: Its Origins and Development*. London: Stanley Paul, 1975.

Henderson, Joe. *Jog, Run, Race*. Mountain View, CA: World Publications, 1977.

———. *The Long Run Solution*. Mountain View, CA: World Publications, 1976.

———. *Long Slow Distance: The Humane Way to Train*. Mountain View, CA: World Publications, 1969.

———. *Run Gently, Run Long*. Mountain View, CA: World Publications, 1974.

———. "The Year Running Became the Sport of the '70s," *Runner's World* 14 (January 1979): 82–89.

Higdon, Hal. "Cinderella Story," *The Runner* 3 (October 1980): 62–67. Lorraine Moller wins the 1980 Avon International Marathon in a pair of borrowed racing flats.

———. "Special Report—The AAU: Kingdom in Crisis," *The Runner* 1 (September 1979): 54–65.

James, William. *The Varieties of Religious Experience: A Study in Human Nature*. New York: New American Library, 1958.

Johnson, Rich. "Greg Meyer Nips Alberto Salazar in AAU Cross-Country Championship," *Runner's World* 14 (February 1979): 90–91.

Jordan, Tom. "T & F N Interview: Craig Virgin," *Track & Field News* 33 (May 1980): 50–53.

Kaumans, Jacobus. "The World's Second-Fastest Marathoner," *Runner's World* 15 (September 1980): 66–67. Gerard Nijboer runs 2:09:01 in the 1980 Amsterdam Marathon.

Kenny, Joe. "Fifty on the Fly," *Runner's World* 15 (December 1980): 66–67. Barney Klecker runs a 50-mile world record on the roads.

Kesey, Ken. "Moments of Madness and Clarity," *Running* 5 (September/October 1980): 22–34. The 1980 U.S.A. Olympic Trials.

Kieran, John and Daley, Arthur. *The Story of the Olympic Games, 776 B.C. to 1968*. Philadelphia: J. B. Lippincott, 1969.

Kirik, Allan. "Good Show, Yank," *The Runner* 2 (January 1980): 52–55. A first-person account of the first American victory in the London-to-Brighton ultramarathon.

Kornbluth, Jesse. "The Disappearance of Gerry Lindgren," *The Runner* 3 (May 1981): 72–81, 83.

———. "Pre: A Race to the Finish," *The Runner* 1 (October 1979): 38–49. Steve Prefontaine remembered.

Laney, Ruth. "Francie Larrieu," *Runner's World* 15 (February 1980): 34–37.

Liquori, Marty. "Jumbo: Legacy of a Great Coach," *The Runner* 3 (June 1981): 68–71. The great miler recalls his coach, "Jumbo" Elliot.

Lovesey, Peter. *Five Kings of Distance*. New York: St Martin's Press, 1981. Outstanding.

Lydiard, Arthur and Gilmour, Garth. *Run to the Top*. London: Herbert Jenkins, 1962.

Maier, Hanns. "Conversation With . . . Toshihiko Seko," *Running* 8 (May/June 1982): 73–78.

———. "Seko," *Runner's World* 16 (June 1981): 45–47.

Martz, Ron. "Hot Time in Old Beantown," *Runner's World* 15 (July 1980): 44–48. Bill Rodgers's "hot" 1980 B.A.A. victory.

——— and Post, Marty. "The Mile Resurfaced as the Magic Distance," *Runner's World* 15 (January 1980): 68–74.

Masback, Craig. "The Glory of the Golden Mile," *The Runner* 1 (October 1979): 58–59.

Maule, Tex. "Jim Ryun: Starting Over," *The Runner* 3 (July 1981): 24–33.

———. "Liquori: The Last Hurrah," *The Runner* 2 (April 1980): 24–33.

McCarthy, Colman. "John A. Kelley: An Intimate Interview," *The Runner* 3 (April 1981): 32–39.

Merrill, Sam. "James F. Fixx," *The Runner* 3 (November 1980): 24–30.

———. "John Walker's Fight to Stay On Top," *The Runner* 1 (August 1979): 32–37.

———. "The Man Who Runs New York," *The Runner* 4 (November 1981): 52–61. Interview with Fred Lebow.

———. "Zátopek—Then and Now," *The Runner* 2 (December 1979): 42–49.

Meyer, Greg and Regan, Vince. "Goodall Leads the American Women to Gold," *Runner's World* 14 (July 1979): 134–136. U.S.A. women's team wins 1979 International Cross-Country title.

Moore, Kenny. *Best Efforts*. New York: Doubleday, 1982.

———. "A Glittering Run in a Golden Mile," *Sports Illustrated* 51 (July 30, 1979): 16–19.

———. "The Parisian Whirl," *Sports Illustrated* 52 (March 24, 1980): 32–37. Craig Virgin wins his first International Cross-Country championship.

Morgan, Warren. "Cinque Mulini," *Running* 6 (January/February 1981): 46–51. A look at an obscure but world-class Italian road/cross-country race.

Morris, C. J. "Human Muscle Fiber Type Grouping and Collateral Re-inervation," *Journal of Neurology and Neurosurgical Psychiatry* 32 (1968): 440.

Munroe, Wayne. "The Saga of Allison Roe," *Runner's World* 17 (March 1982): 28–31.

Nabokov, Peter. *Indian Running*. Santa Barbara: Capra Press, 1981.

Nason, Jerry. "The Legend of Clarence DeMar," *The Runner* 1 (May 1979): 64–69.

———. *The Story of the Boston Marathon*. Boston: The Boston Globe, 1965.

Nelson, Cordner and Quercetani, R. L. *Runners and Races: 1500m/Mile*. Los Altos, CA: Track & Field News, 1973.

Nideffer, Robert M. *The Inner Athlete: Mind Plus Muscle for Winning*. New York: Thomas Y. Crowell, 1976.

Noyes, Russel, Jr. and Kletti, Roy. "Depersonalization in the Face of Life-Threatening Danger: A Description," *Psychiatry* 39 (1972): 19–27.

Olsen, Eric. "A Cascading Conflict," *The Runner* 3 (September 1981): 36–41. A report on the first modern "pro" race.

———. "Alberto Salazar: Body and Soul," *The Runner* 3 (February 1981): 24–31.

———. "Frank Shorter's Comeback—Still a Question," *The Runner* 1 (August 1979): 38–45.

———. "Henry Rono: Around the World Records in 80 Days," *The Runner* 1 (April 1979): 32–42.

———. "In TAC We Trust," *The Runner* 4 (March 1982): 54–59. An examination of the TAC athletes' trust-fund idea.

———. "Mary Decker: At the Crossroads," *The Runner* 2 (January 1980): 24–29.

———. "Shorter and Rodgers: The Beat Goes On," *The Runner* 4 (November 1981): 24–33. The history of the Shorter/Rodgers "rivalry."

———. "Slow Down, You Move Too Fast," *The Runner* 3 (April 1981): 24–31. Another Eric Olsen profile of Mary Decker.

Osler, Tom and Dodd, Ed. *Ultramarathoning: The Next Challenge.* Mountain View, CA: World Publications, 1979.

Osmun, Mark. *The Honolulu Marathon.* New York: J. B. Lippincott, 1979.

Parfit, Michael. "Kenny Moore: Parallel Lives," *The Runner* 2 (November 1979): 26–31.

Pickering, Ron and Harris, Norman. *The Sunday Times Book of the Olympics.* London: Times Newspapers, 1972. Excellent.

Reavis, Toni. "The Race for the Dollars," *Runner's World* 15 (October 1980): 89–92.

Reese, Paul. "Toughest of the Tough," *Runner's World* 13 (May 1978): 44–47. The Western States 100-mile race.

Riley, Rick. "Henry Rono," *Runner's World* 14 (February 1979): 68–73.

Rodgers, Bill with Concannon, Joe. *Marathoning.* New York: Simon and Schuster, 1980. BR's biography.

Schaap, Richard. *An Illustrated History of the Olympics,* 2nd ed. New York: Alfred A. Knopf, 1967.

Schneider, Howard. "Steve Ovett," *Runner's World* 14 (August 1979): 84–89.

Semple, Jock with Kelley, John J. and Murphy, Tom. *Just Call Me Jock.* Waterford, CN: Waterford Publishing, 1982.

Shapiro, Jim. *On the Road: The Marathon.* New York: Crown, 1978.

Sheehan, George A. *Dr. Sheehan on Running.* Mountain View, CA: World Publications, 1975.

———. *This Running Life.* New York: Simon and Schuster, 1980.

Shorter, Frank. "Breaking Away," *The Runner* 4 (January 1982): 28–33. Interview with Alberto Salazar after the 1981 New York Marathon.

Sillitoe, Alan. *The Loneliness of the Long-Distance Runner* (novella). New York: Alfred A. Knopf, 1959.

Spear, Mike. "Emil Zátopek Gives Modern-Day Runners the Truth Behind the Myth," *Runner's World 1982 Annual* 16 (1982): 8–11, 89.

———. "The Last Marathon," *Runner's World* 13 (May 1978): 68–73. A brief history of Jim Peters.

Squires, Bill with Krise, Raymond. *Improving Your Running*. Brattleboro, VT: Stephen Greene Press, 1982.

Stampfl, Franz. *Franz Stampfl on Running*. London: Herbert Jenkins, 1955.

Straus, Hal. "Mind Over Muscle," *Running* 6 (September/October 1981): 24–29.

Temple, Cliff. "The Running Boom Comes to Europe," *The Runner* 3 (September 1981): 78–83.

———. "Sebastian Coe: Raw Speed," *The Runner* 2 (May 1980): 26–33.

———. "Virgin in Madrid: Olé, Olé," *The Runner* 3 (June 1981): 26–31.

Texas, James. "Take the Money and Run," *The Runner* 1 (January 1979): 16–21.

Thomas, James H. *The Bunion Derby: Andy Payne and the Great Transcontinental Footrace*. Oklahoma City: Southwestern Heritage Books, 1980.

Ullyot, Joan. *Women's Running*. Mountain View, CA: World Publications, 1976.

United States Olympic Committee. *The Olympic Games*. Colorado Springs: Olympic House, 1979.

Vermel, E. M. (Ed.). *Vitamin B_{15} (Pangamic Acid): Properties, Functions and Use*. Moscow: Science Publishing House, 1965.

Virgin, Craig. "The American Cross-Country Experience," *Runner's World* 14 (September 1979): 62–65.

Wallach, Len. *The Human Race (Bay to Breakers: Largest Run for Fun in the World)*. San Francisco: The San Francisco Examiner, 1978.

Welch, Jack, "T & F N Interview: Bill Rodgers," *Track & Field News* 34 (November 1981): 16–20.

Willcott, Paul. "Ken Cooper: Aerobics Crusader," *The Runner* 2 (September 1980): 56–61.

———. "Manning's Back on the Track," *The Runner* 2 (June 1980): 64–71. Profile of Madeline Manning Mims.

Wilt, Fred. *How They Train* (three volumes). Los Altos, CA: *Track & Field News*, 1969.

Wischnia, Bob. "Mary Decker," *Runner's World* 14 (November 1979): 48–52.

———. "The Resurrection of Al Salazar," *Runner's World* 15 (October 1980): 78–83.

Yalouris, Nicolaos (Ed.). *The Eternal Olympics: The Art and History of Sport*. New Rochelle, NY: Caratzas Brothers, 1979.

Yao, Margaret. "Loneliness, Sure, But Have You Tried The Beta-endorphin?" *The Wall Street Journal*, December 1, 1981, 1:1, 21.

Index